Finding Home and Homeland

Finding Home and Homeland

Jewish Youth and Zionism in the Aftermath of the Holocaust

AVINOAM J. PATT

Wayne State University Press

Detroit

13 12 11 10 09   5 4 3 2 1

Library of Congress Cataloging-in-Publication Data

Patt, Avinoam J.
    Finding home and homeland : Jewish youth and Zionism in the aftermath of the Holocaust / Avinoam Patt.
        p.   cm.
    Includes bibliographical references and index.
    ISBN 978-0-8143-3426-3 (cloth : alk. paper)
    1. Jewish youth—Germany—Politics and government—20th century.
2. Holocaust survivors—Germany—Politics and government—20th century.
3. Zionism—Germany—History—20th century.   4. Holocaust, Jewish
(1939–1945)—Influence.   5. Israel—Emigration and immigration.
6. Germany—Emigration and immigration.   I. Title.
    DS134.26.P38   2008
    320.540956940835'0943—dc22   2008035495

∞

Designed and typeset by BookComp, Inc.
Composed in Adobe Jensen Pro

To my wife, Ivy, and our beautiful children, Maya and Alexander,
for their love and support

To my parents, Yehuda and Nurit Patt,
who instilled in me a passion for history

And to my grandparents, Alexander and Elfriede Hale,
who never ceased in their lifelong pursuit of knowledge

Contents

Acknowledgments

This book would not have been possible without the support and assistance of numerous people. The idea for the dissertation originated in a graduate seminar at New York University taught by David Engel on Jewish Displaced Persons in postwar Europe. I would like to acknowledge the efforts of my advisors, David Engel and Molly Nolan, for their dedicated reading and thoughtful commentary on various drafts of this manuscript, and my committee members Atina Grossmann, Marion Kaplan, and Ron Zweig for their helpful suggestions. I would also like to thank Tony Judt and Jair Kessler for their support during my work as a graduate assistant at the Remarque Institute. Many colleagues read various sections of this book, but I would like to express my appreciation in particular to Jessica Cooperman, Noam Pianko, and Lila Corwin Berman for reading and commenting on various sections of this text when it was still in dissertation form. Thank you also to my undergraduate professors at Emory University, including Michael Berger, David Blumenthal, Deborah Lipstadt, and Kenneth Stein, who first introduced me to the field of Jewish history.

Financial assistance was provided by the Center for Jewish History fellowship and a dissertation grant from the National Foundation for Jewish Culture. Further support for the project has been provided by the Cahnman Publication Subvention Grant, awarded by the Association for Jewish Studies. At the YIVO Institute for Jewish Research, the library and archives staff provided invaluable assistance. In particular, Herbert Lazarus, Yeshaya Metal, Aron Taub, and Fruma Mohrer made my time conducting research at YIVO a pleasure. I am particularly grateful to my colleagues on the Educational Program for Yiddish Culture at YIVO, Adina Cimet and Jesse Cohen, who were always eager to discuss my research and its wider implications within the framework of European Jewish history and culture. In Israel, the archival

staffs at the Haganah Archives, the Central Zionist Archives, and Yad Vashem
Archives were also of tremendous assistance. My former colleagues at the
United States Holocaust Memorial Museum in Washington, DC, including
Jürgen Matthaus, Lisa Yavnai, Suzanne Brown-Fleming, and Daniel Greene,
as well as countless others who either read or commented on various aspects
of this project deserve special acknowledgment. My appreciation as well goes
to the participants in the 2005 USHMM Summer Research Workshop on
Jewish Displaced Persons—some of the ideas from those discussions have
made their way into these pages. A warm thanks to Judith Cohen, Caroline
Waddell, and Michlean Amir for research assistance in the archives and
photo archives. I am grateful to the staff at Wayne State University Press,
including Kathy Wildfong, Carrie Downes Teefey, and Yvonne Ramsey, for
their assistance and patience. And of course, to my friends and colleagues at
the University of Hartford and at the Maurice Greenberg Center for Judaic
Studies—including Richard Freund, Susan Gottlieb, and Maha Darawsha—
my most sincere appreciation.

A number of individuals who personally experienced the events described
in this work generously shared memories of their time in Kibbutz Lochamei
Ha-Getaot al shem Tosia Atman after the Holocaust. Monish Einhorn,
Zelig Litwak, Shmuel Leitner, Eliyahu Raziel, Haim Shorrer, and Miriam
Yechieli helped to add context and color to the descriptions of their life in
the kibbutz. Along with the other kibbutz youth described here, their
resilience and dedication in reconstructing their lives in the wake of tragedy
is truly a testament to the strength of the human spirit. I owe a debt of gratitude to Galia Soroka and the late Dov Soroka for their assistance in con-
tacting the members of Kibbutz Tosia Altman living on Kibbutz Gazit and
elsewhere.

Thank you to my parents, Yehuda and Nurit Patt, and my siblings, Iddo,
Hanoch, Suzie, and their families, who share in my passion for history and
instilled in me an appreciation for the good question. Finally, my unending
gratitude goes to my beloved wife, Ivy, whose love and support enabled me
to accomplish this task, and to Maya Rose and Alexander Simon, who serve
as a constant reminder of the importance of the future.

Introduction

Jewish Youths and the Zionist Choice in the Postwar World

One month after Allied forces defeated the Third Reich, M. Winogrodzki, a Jewish Holocaust survivor freshly liberated from Dachau, composed a report on conditions for Jews like himself in the newly created U.S. zone of occupation as the group eventually to become known as displaced persons (DPs) was beginning to form. Concern for the large number of young people that he found among the liberated Jews in Bavaria was a prominent feature of his report. "Here in the Munich region," he wrote, "there are both large and small concentration camps with a Jewish population of ca. 50,000, of which a great number are young, for the most part without parents and therefore without existing supervision."[1] His observation was borne out by a series of reports and surveys presented by various agencies representing a broad spectrum of interests from the earliest weeks following liberation and for years thereafter in which the proportion of Jewish DPs between the ages of fifteen and thirty was consistently estimated at more than half and often above 80 percent of the total Jewish population.[2]

For those at the time who were familiar with the broadest outlines of the experience of European Jewry under Nazi rule, these statistics should not have been surprising. Every Jew within the Germans' reach had been marked for death. Avoiding the death sentence demanded quickness of foot and wit, audacity, adaptability, physical stamina, and the ability to blend inconspicuously into often hostile surroundings in addition to no small measure of luck. Those qualities generally tend to be present in greater measure among the young than among their elders. Chances for survival were also often enhanced by absence of concern for dependent children, also more common among teenagers and young adults than among those beyond the customary age of marriage. It is no wonder, then, that Jewish survivors numbered disproportionately in those age ranges. Similarly, it stands to reason that a relatively large number of Jewish DPs should have been orphans; parents whose children were teenagers during the early 1940s were already of an age where the physical and mental demands of survival were increasingly likely to prove too much to bear. Nor is it surprising that many who observed these young, largely orphaned Jews during the first weeks following liberation commented prominently on their seeming lack of direction, perhaps even their paralytic confusion, concerning how they might begin to resume normal lives. Winogrodzki summed up the situation succinctly when he wrote, "These children, who no longer have parents, do not know when and where they should go."[3]

Within a matter of months, however, observers from the U.S. Army, international aid organizations, Palestine, and elsewhere witnessed much of this aimless, amorphous body of youngsters transform itself into a highly organized society displaying a clear sense of purpose and direction for the future. That sense of purpose was not only manifest in the highly visible displays of support for the Zionist program in Palestine that were to become a prominent feature of Jewish DP life among the She'erit Hapletah (Surviving Remnant).[4] It was also evidenced in the decision of between one-third and one-half of Jewish DPs between the ages of fifteen and twenty-four to remove themselves from the network of assembly centers and DP camps maintained by the occupying powers and international relief agencies and to actively prepare for migration to Palestine. These young people gravitated toward alternative social frameworks, generally called by the Hebrew names kibbutzim (collective settlements) and hakhsharot (training farms). Such institutions quickly became a focus of attention, particularly among the leadership of the Zionist movement and the various youth movements associated with it. They acquired widespread visibility among the DP population as a whole to the point where military and civilian officials and workers often represented the kibbutz and hakhsharah populations as encompassing the overwhelming majority of Jewish youths.[5] This rapid transformation was surprising, as was the powerful influence it exercised on the consciousness of observers.

Both phenomena require explanation. Why did so many Jewish youths choose such a course so quickly, and why did the course they chose come to characterize the conduct of young Jewish Holocaust survivors as a whole? These are not idle questions; their answer bears heavily upon the history of the establishment of the State of Israel in 1948. Following World War II, the seemingly overwhelming Zionist enthusiasm of the Jewish DPs, witnessed in part by the gravitation of a significant portion of Jewish DP youths to kibbutzim and hakhsharot (which in turn formed the backbone of the clandestine Bricha movement of Jewish departure from Eastern Europe), was vital in informing the diplomatic decisions that led to the creation of the State of Israel as international observers representing the United States, Britain, and the United Nations weighed the desires of the large Jewish refugee population in Europe.[6] Likewise, the founders of the newly created State of Israel pointed to a clear relationship between the Holocaust and Israel, with survivors actively participating in the founding of the state. Israel's Declaration of Independence, read by David Ben-Gurion on May 14, 1948, asserted that the remnant that survived the Holocaust continued to migrate to Palestine, undaunted by difficulties and dangers, and "never ceased to assert their right to a life of dignity, freedom and honest toil in their national homeland."[7] Some framed the two seminal events in twentieth-century Jewish history as inextricably linked, as a "fateful historical reaction" that led the DPs to claim their place in a Jewish state. In fact, even in the middle of World War II, as the Nazi annihilation of the Jewish community of Europe reached its height, Benzion Dinur concluded that "the only path of escape from the fate of destruction is the return to the Jewish homeland."[8] For this reason it seems essential to understand the sources of that enthusiasm especially among young people, who bore a significant portion of the burden in the battles for Israel's independence.[9]

Until now explanations have developed along three distinct lines, all of which present the Zionist conclusion for the DPs as a result of factors largely beyond their control. Most scholars have accepted the dominant Zionist representation offered at the time, namely that the active steps Jewish DP youths took to prepare themselves for migration to Palestine by joining kib- butzim and hakhsharot were a natural outgrowth of their experience under Nazi rule. One of the earliest articulations of this argument was offered by Koppel S. Pinson, a sociologist who had been sent to the DP camps in the American zone of Germany by the American Jewish Joint Distribution Committee (JDC) to assist in the formation of an education policy for the Jewish DPs:

> The events of 1939–1945 seemed to discredit completely those philosophies of Jewish life prevailing before the war which were not centered around Pales- tine. The Zionists were the only ones that had a program that seemed to make sense after this catastrophe. . . . Without Palestine there seemed to be no future for them. Anti-Zionism or even a neutral attitude toward Zion- ism came to mean for them a threat to the most fundamental stakes in their future.[10]

This thesis of an "intuitive Zionism" born directly from the war was affirmed in 2002 in a comprehensive study of Jewish DPs in postwar Germany. As Ze'ev Mankowitz has argued, "from the outset the dream of a Jewish home in Palestine permeated the public life of the She'erit Hapletah." In the wake of the Holocaust, he suggested, survivors understood that "the creation of a Jewish state in the Land of Israel was taken to be the last will and testament bequeathed by the dead to the living. . . . For many, their almost intuitive Zionism stood for the warmth, unquestioning acceptance and security of home; for the more politically minded it signified the only real hope for the rescue and rehabilitation of the little that remained of European Jewry and, in the longer term, the promise of the Jewish future."[11]

In this regard, the DPs were actors on their own behalf (motivated by ideological conclusions) who, having come to the Zionist realization after the war, did all they could to reach their homeland. Fifty years later, however, a group of Israeli scholars threw this chain of historical inevitability into question. In fact, some suggested that the Holocaust almost prevented the creation of the State of Israel by depriving the Yishuv (the prestate Jewish settlement in Palestine) of the European manpower reserve it so needed, mak- ing the DPs the last hope of the Yishuv to establish a state.[12] Others argued that the creation of the state was not an obvious conclusion to the Holocaust assisted by the survivors who "continued to migrate to the Land of Israel, undaunted by difficulties." Idith Zertal questioned the nature of the relationship between the Yishuv and the survivors and the clandestine immigration movement at its center:

> Was it a narrative of love and redemption, of "great mercies will I gather thee"? Was it indeed a "central experience" in the life of the embryonic Israel? Or was it mostly an ingenious political endeavor effectively implemented against the backdrop of the chaos in post-war Europe, aimed at achieving, through the unique power of the helpless Holocaust survivors, the higher goal of the Zionist leadership—the establishment of a sovereign Jewish state in Palestine?[13]

Zertal concluded that the Zionists in the Yishuv had cynically manipulated the dispirited and demoralized survivors for their own political ends. Whereas before the war the Zionist movement sought out the strongest and most active Zionists as candidates for aliyah, or immigration to Palestine, Yosef Grodzinsky similarly suggested that after the war the "the Zionist activists turned to the weakest. They selected from the 'human dust' good human material for the state on the way—to take the survivors from the furnaces to the smelter."[14] According to Grodzinsky, "the leadership of Palestinian Jewry and its emissaries invested considerable thought and planning in the DP camps and carried on intensive, coordinated activity in order to bring all of the refugees from the Holocaust to Palestine."[15] Without such activity, Grodzinsky suggested, relatively few DPs would likely have gravitated toward Zionist frameworks. Characterizing Jewish DPs as "stateless, homeless people, recently persecuted, whose current circumstances were also unstable," he noted that whereas 80–97 percent of Jewish DP camp residents routinely responded to investigators' questions about where they wished to rebuild their lives with ringing declarations that Palestine was their only hope, only 40 percent of them eventually made their way to the Jewish state after 1948.[16] Moreover, he asserted, many of those who did ultimately act on their Zionist declarations did so only because their arms were twisted, sometimes quite crudely, by Zionist operatives, who cared little for the DPs' own needs and much more for those of their movement.[17]

Proponents of this second thesis view the postwar experience of Holocaust survivors as more important than the war years in shaping their decisions following liberation. A third group of scholars has similarly emphasized the importance of the postwar context but has identified features other than the activities of Zionist organizations as crucial. These scholars have pointed to the role of diplomatic and political developments in the mid-1940s in shaping a collective, national identity among Jewish DPs. Dan Diner, among others, has noted that at the end of the war U.S. and British occupation officials refused to categorize Jews as a distinct people among the DPs; instead, Jews were identified as belonging to the dominant nationality of their countries of residence. The Allies only changed their approach under the impact of a series of events that occurred during 1945–46 (including most notably the publication of the Harrison Report), coming to construct Jews as a separate national group with its own particular needs and interests. According to Diner, this "subjectification" of the Jews as a national entity played into Zionist hands. If Jews were indeed a nation, then they were, as Zionists had long claimed, entitled to national independence and territorial sovereignty. Thus Zionism came to appear to Jewish DPs as the ideology most in tune with contemporary international political thinking.[18]

Unfortunately, none of the proponents of any of these theses has yet adduced truly compelling evidence in their support. Although they have brought to light much important information, their analysis of that information has been inadequate for two reasons. First, they have drawn conclusions mainly from statements about DP attitudes and behavior made by outside observers, not from sources produced by the Jewish DPs themselves. The tendency to approach the topic in this manner is unsurprising, for the volume of material produced by foreign observers and administrators such as the United Nations Relief and Rehabilitation Administration (UNRRA), the JDC, the U.S. Army, or Zionist emissaries from Palestine active in the DP camps far outweighs the amount of source material created by the DPs themselves. Such a methodological approach, however, perpetuates the perspective of outsiders writing about the DPs, making it more difficult to understand the DP situation through DP eyes. The significance of postwar Zionism among the DPs is hence measured against the barometer of its impact on developments in Palestine and party divisions in the Yishuv. This historiographic focus is as much a function of much of the material on Jewish DPs being written by emissaries from Israel as it is part of a tendency to assume Zionists from Palestine as the primary agents in postwar Europe.

Nevertheless, it turns out that a considerable amount of material in a number of forms produced by the DPs themselves does exist. The social, cultural, and political organizations created by the DPs, including the Central Committee of Liberated Jews and its local and regional committees as well as the various political parties and youth movements created and constituted by DPs, all kept detailed records of their activities. However, even beyond these institutional records, the flourishing DP camp press provides valuable insight into the daily concerns facing the DPs as well as the considerable political and cultural activity taking place within all of the Jewish DP camps. On the individual level, diaries, letters, and testimonies collected by the Central Historical Commission, parties, and youth movements, including the diary of the Hashomer Hatzair kibbutz, *Kibbutz Lochamei HaGettaot 'al shem Tosia Altman*, provide the individual perspective lacking in so much of what has been written on the DPs. Such material is sufficient to permit the DPs to speak about their postwar experiences in their own voices and to infer conclusions about the reasons for their actions on the basis of what they themselves had to say about them.

Second, virtually all of the previous historical literature has regarded the Jewish DPs as an undifferentiated mass. In particular, it has uniformly failed to take note of the overwhelming youth of the Jewish DP population. Yet it seems especially important to place the age of the Jewish DPs in the foreground in understanding what moved them to take the various courses they did, because a large number of them made fundamental decisions about their futures at a stage of life marked in the best of circumstances by confusion, emotional turmoil, and an often contentious relationship with agencies of socialization. The decisions made by young Jewish DPs have to be understood in relation to both their particular background as Jews and their universal background as young people struggling to move on with their lives in the aftermath of the Holocaust.[19] For those youths who had survived the Holocaust in concentration camps, this was especially true. They were forced to confront adult decisions both during and after the war but were left without parents or family to help make such decisions. Many of these young survivors chose to join the kibbutz groups created by the Zionist youth movements in Germany, Poland, and elsewhere, accepting the promise of departure from Europe that they offered. Beyond being defined by the choices made by young survivors, however, youth was also externally classified according to categories created by the UNRRA, other aid organizations, political groups, or yeshivot and universities created for young survivors. As will be discussed in the first chapter, the Jewish DP leadership invested a considerable degree of responsibility in what they referred to as the *jidisze jugnt*, the Jewish youth whom they saw and identified as the future of the She'erit Hapletah. In contrast, it should be noted, some DPs the same age as members of the youth movement or kibbutz residents were living different lives focused on other goals, such as marrying, having babies, or even attending university. Indeed, a growing literature on the postwar rebirth of the Jewish survivor population has highlighted the often remarkably active and productive DP population, which gave rise to a flourishing press, historical commissions, religious institutions, educational frameworks, a vibrant political life, and various cultural outlets. The myriad activities of the Jewish DP population reflected both a highly talented population responding to the previous six years of oppression, persecution, and murder and a dynamic, temporary civilization being created in the transitional space that was the DP camp in postwar Germany. DPs were called upon to fulfill multiple roles out of an obligation to the past, either as new parents creating the future of a destroyed European Jewry, as "historians" testifying to Nazi persecution, or as *halutzim* building for the Zionist future.

Thus, the term "youth" in this context came to be in many ways a political and ideological chosen identity and not merely a matter of age. DP society accorded an esteemed position for those who made the choice to affiliate as youths and thus as part of the Zionist future, as will be demonstrated in the pages that follow. While it is difficult to define an age range for this group, those who could care for themselves after the war and had not yet created their own families generally fell between the ages of fifteen and thirty. Those under the age of fifteen were often placed in orphanages and children's homes and defined as children. For the purposes of this study, youths will be understood as being those who perceived themselves to be in this transitional stage of life, not having fully embraced the responsibilities of adulthood (family, full-time employment) but old enough to seemingly care for themselves and be prepared for membership in a new society. Many chose to affiliate with youth movements and in many cases were identified by the DP leadership and outside observers as the organized and nonorganized youths. For the most part, the youths who constituted the kibbutz groups ranged in age from fifteen to thirty. Furthermore, "youth" often came to be constructed as a seemingly male category, both as a function of the demographic dominance of young men and of projections of appropriate pioneering behavior by the DP and Zionist youth movement leadership.

This study analyzes the behavior of young Jewish DPs against their dual background as both Jews and young people adjusting to life after calamity. It focuses on the large youthful segment of the Jewish DP population in order to determine what Zionism meant to its members, how deeply the Zionist idea struck root among them, and why it did so as evidenced by the materials produced by young Jewish Holocaust survivors themselves. As will be seen, this Zionism was central in the formation of a new DP identity after the war, especially for the survivor population in postwar Germany, a group that was disproportionately composed of young people under the age of thirty. The perceived Zionist enthusiasm of the DP population, and this younger segment in particular, played no small part in the diplomatic steps that led to the creation of the State of Israel. Zionism, however, was not merely an obvious conclusion to the Holocaust or a means to the creation of the Jewish state. It was a functional Zionism that could operate therapeutically, redemptively, and productively whose appeal was broadened by the many roles it could seemingly fill.

I
Germany and Poland
after Liberation

1

Jewish Survivors in Postwar Germany, 1945

Now, gradually after liberation, the inmates of Buchenwald began to live again. Once apathetic and hopeless, they now nearly went mad with joy. Freedom! Freedom! We lived to see it! Their faces were ablaze. They began to talk about going home. To their own countries, to father, mother, wife, and child. And the Jews? Well—the Jews . . .

The Jews suddenly faced themselves. Where now? Where to? They saw that they were different from all the other inmates of the camp. For them things were not so simple. To go back to Poland? To Hungary? To streets empty of Jews, towns empty of Jews, a world without Jews. To wander in those lands, lonely, homeless, always with the tragedy before one's eyes . . . and to meet, again, a former Gentile neighbor who would open his eyes wide and smile, remarking with double meaning, "What! Yankel! You're still alive!" Yes, the Jews faced themselves. Was our tragedy only beginning?

Hayim-Meir Gottlieb in Leo Schwarz, *The Root and the Bough*

The final Allied push into Germany signaled the end of the war for many of the Jews who had managed to survive the long years in Nazi concentration camps and ghettos. Yet it did not necessarily signal the end of their suffering. The Buchenwald concentration camp was one of the first camps to be

13

Three young Buchenwald survivors pose shortly after liberation, April 11, 1945.
(USHMM, courtesy of Joe Yablon)

liberated by American forces of the 4th Armored Division on April 11,
1945. Although there had been fifty thousand prisoners in the camp at the
beginning of April, many died in the first days and weeks following liberation. Most of the Jewish prisoners were found in the Little Camp, where
conditions were at their worst. The American soldiers who arrived in the
camp were horrified by what they saw: stacks of dead bodies and survivors
who were "just skin and bones." Twenty to twenty-five prisoners per day died
in each cellblock in the days following liberation as the years of starvation
and disease took their toll.[1]

The concentration camp of Dachau was liberated almost three weeks
later on April 29 by American soldiers of the 157th and 222nd Infantry
Divisions of the U.S. Army tasked with the conquest of Munich. While
30,000 prisoners were liberated at Dachau, some 2,466 died in the following month and a half.[2] Marcus Smith, an American GI who liberated
Dachau and later wrote about his experiences, estimates that some 2,700

Jews were found alive in Dachau at the time of liberation; Jews thus consti-tuted 9 percent of the surviving inmate population.[3]

In the first days and weeks following the liberation of Germany by the Allied forces, the country was inundated with the liberated captives of the Nazi regime who sought to make sense of the new situation for which they had long hoped. Most of the liberations of the camps took place in April and early May 1945 (e.g., Buchenwald, April 11–12; Bergen-Belsen, April 15; Dachau, April 29; Mauthausen, May 3; Theresienstadt, May 9). With the conclusion of the war on May 8, up to 10 million forced laborers, POWs, and other displaced persons (DPs) flooded the roads of Germany in the desire to return home. While millions of DPs were successfully returned to their home countries by the U.S. Army, close to 1.5 million refugees avoided repatriation for fear of being branded collaborators upon their return home.[4] According to statistics prepared by the United Nations Relief and Rehabil-itation Administration (UNRRA), there were 1,488,007 DPs in Germany, Austria, and Italy of which 53,322, or 3.6 percent, were Jews. There were also 900,000 Poles, 140,000 Balts, 121,000 Hungarians, and a variety of other European nationalities as well.[5] Singled out for extermination by the Nazis, Jews were least likely to have survived the war and thus constituted a small minority of the total number of refugees in Germany upon liberation. In this initial period, however, with the categorization of DPs according to national origin from enemy and Allied countries, those Jews who did survive were frequently placed with former collaborators from their countries of origin in DP camps. This was in keeping with Allied policy, which defined a DP "as any civilian who because of the war was living outside the borders of his or her country and who wanted to but could not return home or find a new home without assistance."[6]

The creation of a unified policy toward the Jewish DPs developed fitfully, with the Jewish refugees tossed between postwar diplomatic considerations that had to weigh the competing interests of the postwar reconstruction of Germany, the developing Cold War with the Soviet Union, Anglo-American relations, and British policies in Palestine in addition to the best interests of the DPs. The Jewish DPs in the American zone were cared for by a number of bodies on several levels. The preparations for dealing with the DP problem had already begun during the war; in November 1943, representatives from forty-four countries met at the White House to establish the UNRRA. The

UNRRA was established on November 29, 1943, to work as an administrative and subordinate branch of the military to administer camps and provide supplemental supplies, such as food, clothing, medical supplies, and other forms of assistance, to those awaiting repatriation (shelter and medicine were army responsibility). Former New York governor Herbert Lehman was appointed its director general. According to an agreement between the Supreme Headquarters Allied Expeditionary Force (SHAEF) and the UNRRA on November 25, 1944, the UNRRA agreed to work under direct command of SHAEF, while SHAEF acknowledged the UNRRA's postwar responsibilities.

The SHAEF guidelines on DPs and refugees from December 28, 1944, as outlined in Administrative Memorandum 39 identified a DP as any civilian who because of the war was living outside the borders of his or her country and who wanted to but could not return home or find a new home without assistance. DPs were divided into categories by place of origin into those from enemy and Allied countries. In addition to the newly defined DPs, stateless persons were defined as "persons who have been denationalized, whose country of nationality cannot, after investigation, be determined, who cannot establish their right to the nationality claimed, or who lack the protection of any government." Such persons were entitled to receive the same treatment as DPs from Allied nations; enemy and ex-enemy nationals persecuted because of race or religion were entitled to the same treatment. SHAEF ceased functioning in mid-July 1945, when responsibility for the care of DPs was transferred to the victorious three major powers in occupation zones. As agreed upon in the conference at Yalta, Germany was divided into American, British, and Soviet zones of occupation, with a small area in the southwest of Germany made into the French zone of occupation. The majority of the Jewish population, perhaps some thirty-five thousand out of fifty thousand liberated, was in the American zone of occupation, many of them around Munich.

While most DPs after the war made the decision to return home with ease, the Jewish DPs did not face such a clear decision. Members of prewar and wartime Zionist groups began to advocate for immigration to Palestine, while members of the Jewish socialist Bundist Party argued for a return to Poland, where Jewish workers could assist in the struggle to rebuild Poland. Most survivors, however, were less concerned with political debates so soon after liberation. Many Jewish survivors did in fact choose to return to Poland (and elsewhere) to seek family first and foremost, Bundist and Zionist arguments notwithstanding.[7]

Unsure of what awaited them at home and often fairly certain that their families had been destroyed during the war, those who decided to stay in a DP camp also had to face the fact that this meant continuing to live with collaborators who also refused to return home. In general, Polish and Baltic Jews were the least likely to return to their home countries, while Jews from countries such as Hungary, Romania, France, and to a lesser extent Greece (where the destruction of the Jewish community had been far more extensive) were far more likely to return to their countries following liberation.[8] Surveys of the Jewish DP population in the American zone of Germany from October 1945 corroborated this information, indicating that the vast majority (as much as 75 percent) of Jews who remained in Germany were in fact from Poland.[9]

While such decisions were deeply personal, many among the Jews were aware of the political impact of such decisions. As Chaim Rosenfeld, an eighteen-year-old Czech Jew liberated at Dachau, described, liberation brought with it new choices and new questions of belonging for Jewish survivors:

> Here my second tragedy began. I didn't know who was alive and who was not. I spoke with people from my own town, they told me they were going to America, I said that I was going to Eretz Israel but that first I was going to my hometown. . . . In the registry office I said I was from Carpatho-Russia. The Russians didn't want me, the Hungarians didn't want me: "Ibrei, zhid (kike)." I went to the Czechs and said I was Czech, not Jewish. Here I saw something that is engraved in my memory to this day. Every nation had a flag. I had no flag. Everyone had one except me. Everyone walked with his beautiful flag, but I had no flag.[10]

Even before they could think about finding family or seeing what was left of "home," many among the She'erit Hapletah felt that they had an obligation to those who had not survived. Jewish survivors sought out the assistance of American Jewish chaplains in order to bury the dead and create burial plots wherever possible. Survivors also utilized the services of chaplains in order to communicate directly with the outside world. Robert Marcus, a chaplain who arrived in Buchenwald at the end of April 1945, assisted survivors by mailing letters on their behalf or facilitating contact with world Jewish organizations. Survivors often sent their first letters to non-Jewish friends and neighbors, believing that no Jews had survived the war to receive their letters.[11] Many of the letters handled by the chaplains could not be delivered to their hometowns because of misspellings and insufficient information and thus ended up in the hands of the World Jewish Congress (WJC). Other survivors turned to the WJC because they had nowhere else to turn. The letters conveyed the desperation of the survivors, who felt completely isolated. Chaim Finkelstein described his predicament to the WJC now that he was alone in the world: "All of my relatives have been killed by the Nazis. I wonder how and why I have survived. I do not know what to do with myself. I would be very grateful to you if you were to facilitate my immigration to Palestine or to the United States."[12]

While the first days and weeks were occupied with continuing the struggle to survive, liberation also brought a realization of all that had been lost during the war. Survivors were now without homes, family, food, or shelter. Orphaned, alone, often weak and traumatized, survivors were immediately forced to encounter different questions of existence: not whether they would continue to live but where, how, and with whom.

The Choice to Remain in Germany

Jewish DPs who had made the decision to remain in Germany thus faced a choice: they could stay in the DP camp (generally German military barracks, former POW and slave labor camps, tent cities, industrial housing, apartments, hotels, sanatoriums, etc.), at times continuing to be housed with wartime collaborators, or they could leave. One way to leave the DP camp was to settle in Germany permanently. Indeed, some of the liberated chose to reconstitute prewar German Jewish *kehillot* (communities), although this was a choice that was more likely to be embraced by the fifteen thousand or so German Jews (many of whom had been in "privileged" marriages) who had survived the war. Those who did choose to live in German cities faced an uncertain status and constant housing shortages.[13] In conducting a survey of conditions faced by Jewish DPs in Germany, Chaplain Abraham

Klausner, who had arrived in Dachau in the third week of May 1945, visited approximately fourteen thousand Jews living in seventeen DP camps following liberation. He found deplorable conditions, poor accommodations, no plumbing, no clothing, rampant disease, continuing malnourishment, and a lack of any plan on the part of the American military for the "stateless Jews." As Klausner summarized in a June 24, 1945, report to Philip Bernstein, executive director of the committee on army-navy religious activities:

> There seems to be no policy, no responsibility, no plan for these . . . stateless Jews. . . . Twelve hours a day I tell my lies. "They will come," I say. "When will they come?" they ask me. UNRRA, JDC, Red Cross—can it be that they are not aware of the problem? It is impossible. . . . Of what use is all my complaining; I cannot stop their tears. America was their hope and all America has given them is a new camp with guards in khaki. Freedom, hell no! They are behind walls without hope.[14]

"Liberated but not free, that is the paradox of the Jew," Klausner concluded in his report detailing the condition of the Jewish survivors.[15]

Portrait of U.S. Army Chaplain Rabbi Abraham Klausner. (USHMM, courtesy of Herbert Friedman)

In the first few months following liberation, conditions among the Jews in the DP camps were indeed far from ideal, making the resolution of the most basic needs a pressing concern. For example, members of the Jewish committee organized in Feldafing voiced concern over insufficient food for the Jews in the camp and intolerable living conditions in the wooden barracks, with no walls, no washrooms, and the constant danger of an outbreak of typhus.[16] And in fact, of the approximately fifty thousand to sixty thousand Jewish survivors among the millions of other DPs at the time of liberation, within the first week following liberation, some twenty thousand Jews perished from complications arising from disease, starvation, and the camp experience.[17] There were reports of poor treatment of Jewish DPs at the hands of their liberators, with Jewish DPs being denied rations, housed in camps with former collaborators, and denied freedom of movement from camps. Jewish DPs pleaded for assistance from the U.S. military, the U.S. government, and the UNRRA. Noting that many Ukrainians who had collaborated with the SS continued to be well fed, the Jewish prisoners, who had always received the worst nourishment, continued to be malnourished:

> We apply to you in the matter of food. The jewish [sic] political ex-prisoners at various DP camps in Bavaria get an insufficient ration of food, as most of the liberated from the KZ till now erceive [sic] the consequences of underfeeding and hard work, a great number of them was sick with typhus. This caused, that the jewish ex-prisoners in the DP camps are hungry. . . . We beg to allot an additional ration of food for the Jewish political ex-prisoners.[18]

Disease and insufficient food were not the only concerns troubling Jewish DPs. The fact that Jewish ex-prisoners continued to be clothed in the shreds of striped prisoner garb was also troubling to the Jewish survivors, who had begun to organize in order to represent their needs before the military authorities. "We were liberated in striped prisoners' clothes, and we are sorry to state that till now the thousands of jewish ex-prisoners have no proper clothing, underwear or shoes."[19]

For those Jewish DPs who chose the temporary existence of the DP camps, liberation was far from all they had hoped for. Beyond the wish for food, clothing, shelter, and security, Jewish DPs expected some validation of their survival, a sign that the outside world had not completely forsaken them. Expecting to be welcomed by the world with open arms, Jewish DPs found liberation to be a rude awakening, as they still struggled to obtain bearable living conditions and yearned for contact from the rest of the Jewish world, which had still largely been denied access to the DP camps. As Chaplain Klausner had noted, the American military seemed to lack any plan for the Jewish refugees who had chosen not to return to their home countries.

Self-Help and the Jewish DPs

In the first two months following liberation, it became apparent to the young survivors who made the choice to remain in Germany that apart from the thirty or so chaplains in the American occupation zone and the occasional Jewish brigade soldier canvassing Germany for Jewish survivors (a Jewish military formation comprised of Jews from Palestine attached to the British Army), world Jewry would be unable to provide the aid desperately needed by the survivors. Many among the She'erit Hapletah thus resolved that they would have to help themselves.

The survivors who had chosen to remain in Germany shared several characteristics (beyond the decision not to return to their prewar homes), which aided in their early organization and helped them to form a unified political identity so soon after liberation. Paramount among these was the demographic nature of the population. The group of Jewish survivors who formed the first core unit of the She'erit Hapletah was to a large extent a self-selected group of young adults. The hardships of the war and the process of Nazi selection meant that they were much more likely to be from the younger segments of the population, between the ages of fifteen and thirty and overwhelmingly male (often more than 60 percent). It would seem that the survivors themselves and the first to encounter them perceived the young nature of the surviving population. While the American Jewish Joint Distribution Committee (JDC) did not gain access to the survivors until the beginning of August 1945, its first demographic studies of the Jewish DP population in the American zone of Germany bore out the observations of others. A statistical survey of the 4,976 Jewish residents of Landsberg taken on October 1, 1945, estimated that 65 percent of the population were males over the age of fourteen, 30 percent were females over the age of four-teen, and only 5 percent were children between ages six and fourteen. Of the nearly 5,000 residents, only 20 were children less than six years of age. Young adults composed the vast majority of the population of Jewish DPs, with surveys pointing to individuals between the ages of eighteen and forty-four constituting 85.8 percent of DPs in November 1945 and 80.1 percent in February 1946. A survey of Jewish DPs in Bavaria taken in February 1946, when the first groups had arrived from Poland but before the sizable infil-tration later that year, reported that some 25,164 out of 30,269 counted (or 83.1 percent) of men and women were between the ages of fifteen and forty. Of the total population, 61.3 percent were between the ages of nineteen and thirty-four, and more than 40 percent of the 30,000 Jews surveyed in Bavaria were between the ages of fifteen and twenty-four. It was thus clear that youths represented a special category in the population of Jewish survivors.[20]

The experience of survival in a concentration camp also left a decisive impression on survivors, often leaving them more prone to embrace collec-tive forms of identification when family ties were no longer available.[21] The fact that they had decided not to return to their home countries (generally Poland or Lithuania) meant that they were largely alone in the world, with few remaining attachments, no prewar roots to return to, and limited respon-sibilities to anyone but themselves. They had failed to be persuaded to return to Poland by Bundists who had soon left the DP camps and rejected the possibility of establishing a permanent life in Germany, instead choosing the temporary one of the DP camp. While prewar and wartime experiences could be significant in influencing the choices they made, ultimately the choice of what to do next would be dictated by the postwar reality.

In many cases it was the surviving members of Zionist youth movements and political parties who undertook the self-help work and in turn became most active among those seeking to convince survivors to avoid a return to Eastern Europe. Many youth movement members were in fact instrumental in preparing for liberation before the end of the war.[22] These were generally youth movement leaders who had experience leading and organizing Jewish youths before and, in some cases, during the war. This experience made them well suited to lead the younger Jewish population that had survived life in German concentration camps. For the young Jewish survivors in the DP camps (primarily under the age of thirty-five) regardless of whether they had experience in a Zionist youth group before the war, such groups emerged as attractive options, providing them with the camaraderie, support and replacement family they so desperately craved.

The experience of the Holocaust effected a radical change in Zionist youth movement leaders' views of the Jewish public and the Jewish future. Whereas before the war these leaders and activists in Zionist youth organizations focused their efforts on training the elite among Jewish youths for a future life in Palestine, the Holocaust led them to the conclusion that the only possible future for European Jewry as a whole had to be in the Land of Israel.[23] During the war, these youth movement activists had shifted their efforts away from only Jewish youths and had sought to lead the Jewish public in the ghettos of Poland and, to the extent possible, within the concentration camps as well. Jewish youths would constitute the vanguard of such efforts to influence the eventual departure of Jewish survivors from Europe. In the period before and after liberation, they stood ready to employ their skills in organizing and training Jewish youths. In the first weeks and months following liberation, this organization took place on an ad hoc basis, with local groups coming together in various places in postwar Germany, generally still living in the camps from which they had been liberated.

Kibbutz Buchenwald

Among the liberated young Jews in Buchenwald were three former He-Halutz members who had remained active during the war in organizing groups of Zionist youth in Buchenwald and Auschwitz. (He-Halutz was an umbrella organization for a number of pioneering Zionist youth movements in interwar Europe.)[24] Arthur Posnansky and Yechezkel Tydor, who marched in the death march from Auschwitz to Buchenwald in January 1945, joined Eliyahu Gruenbaum in Buchenwald and in the tumultuous last few months before liberation began to plan for the postwar period.[25] Tydor, before his transfer from Buchenwald to Auschwitz in the autumn of 1942, had organized the youths in Buchenwald and formed an aid committee to assist them in the camp. Already in his early forties, Tydor had taken on the role of mentor and father figure to the youths in the concentration camps in which he lived.[26] Posnansky, in his twenties, was active in He-Halutz both before and during the war years, serving as the leader of hakhsharot

Members of the Kibbutz Buchenwald hakhsharah are gathered outside their barracks beneath a banner bearing their name in Hebrew. (USHMM, courtesy of Eva Tuchsznajder Lang)

in Germany (Haffenberg and Neuendorf) in the early 1940s.[27] The three would be central in the organization of Kibbutz Buchenwald, the first kibbutz hakhsharah, or Zionist training farm, in postwar Germany.

The diary of the collective group that began to come together in Buchenwald following liberation reveals the early considerations that entered the minds of the young survivors already faced with the question of where to go next. Since liberation, Arthur Posnansky had sought assistance from Nathan Schwalb at the He-Halutz office in Geneva in organizing "the hundreds of Jews, parentless, homeless, without any relatives" in Buchenwald who desired to go to hakhsharah but were frustrated at the lack of contact from Jewish organizations.[28] Once they had made the realization that the world had no plans for the Jews, however, Posnansky, Tydor, and the Buchenwald group proposed an option that could remove from the squalor of the DP camp the survivors who had begun to recover from the war.

Perhaps for the thousandth time the Jewish committee in Buchenwald was holding a meeting on the question: Where to? A Polish Jew, a German, a Czech, a Hungarian—each faced the same burning problem: Where should the few surviving Jews of Buchenwald go? How could we ever have believed that at the end of the war the surviving Jews would have no more worries, that everything would be fine! The world, we had thought, would welcome our few survivors with open arms! We, the first victims of the Nazis. They would love us! Quickly enough, we saw that the world had other things on its mind than Jewish suffering. So where to? Comrade Posnansky put forth an idea: into our own kibbutz. To build a group of Buchenwald's youth, and find a farm where we could prepare for Palestine. A wonderful idea. There would be no lack of candidates for the kibbutz, for energy was reawakening in the survivors and seeking an outlet. From that idea sprang Kibbutz Buchenwald.²⁹

The early leaders of this small group thus resolved to create a Jewish farm organized around the ethic of collective living and approached Chaplain Herschel Schacter for assistance in creating a kibbutz hakhsharah to train young Zionists for aliyah to Palestine. With the assistance of Schacter and an American colonel, the kibbutz secured a former Nazi estate near Eggendorf, making their Kibbutz Buchenwald the first kibbutz hakhsharah to be formed in the DP camps of the U.S. zone of Germany on June 3, 1945. According to Judith Baumel in her monograph on Kibbutz Buchenwald, the founders organized the kibbutz out of a desire to avoid the temptations of black market activity and in order to resist the desire to exact revenge on the German populace.³⁰ Arthur Posnansky also pointed to the double function of the farm, which could help to remove DP youths from the potentially demoralizing surroundings of the DP camps and train them for the pioneering lifestyle through *shituf* (sharing), socialization, and vocational training.³¹ The model of Kibbutz Buchenwald would emerge as a highly popular one for Jewish youths eager to escape the demoralizing atmosphere of the DP camp or simply seeking the camaraderie that the kibbutz could provide.

Irgun Brit Zion and the Survivors of the Kovno Ghetto in Dachau

As was the case in Buchenwald, Jewish youths and former youth movement leaders living in the concentration camp of Dachau before the end of the war also began planning for what they hoped to be the continuation of Jewish

A member of Kibbutz Buchenwald plows the fields with a team of horses. (USHMM, courtesy of Fred Diament)

life once the Germans had been defeated. A group of Zionist activists from Kovno, gathered together in Kaufering (a Dachau satellite camp), published the underground handwritten newspaper *Nitzotz* (the Spark) while still under German rule. Echoing the Zionist anthem Hatikvah, the newspaper proclaimed on its masthead "Od Lo Avda Tikvatenu" [We Have Still Not Lost Our Hope], evidence of its authors' continuing faith in their ability to survive and in the belief that the Jewish state would eventually be created.[32] Its publishers were former members of Irgun Brit Zion, a mainstream Zionist youth movement in the Kovno ghetto who had been deported to Germany at the end of 1944.[33] Seven issues of *Nitzotz*, written by Shlomo Frankel, appeared prior to liberation. In its pages, the members of the Hitachdut HaNoar HaLeumi (Union of National Youth) youth movement debated the future of Zionism in the wake of European Jewry's annihilation and described the activities that their underground group was engaged in within the Kaufering camp. A number of the early leaders of the Jewish DPs in Germany, including Samuel Gringauz, Zalman Grinberg, and Leib

Garfunkel (head of the organization of Holocaust Survivors in Italy) as well as the founders of the early DP Zionist youth group Nocham (No'ar Chalutzi Meuchad, or United Pioneer Youth), emerged from this early group in Dachau.³⁴ In the pages of *Nitzotz* both before and after liberation, the members of Irgun Brit Zion (and the editor, Shlomo Frankel) lobbied for the importance of Zionist unity, a characteristic that would be central to the early organization of the She'erit Hapletah in Germany. Gringauz, Grinberg, and Frankel were later among the most active in creating the official institutions that would represent the Jewish DPs in Germany, helping to organize the Central Committee of Liberated Jews and the United Zionist Organization (UZO).³⁵

As liberation approached, in the chaotic situation shortly before the end of the war Dr. Zalman Grinberg managed to secure the use of a hospital for the survivors at St. Ottilien (near Schwabenhausen in Bavaria), which was to become one of the early centers for survivor organization. With the knowledge that American forces were nearby, Grinberg took control of the military hospital at the monastery in St. Ottilien and was appointed director of the hospital upon the arrival of American troops the next day.³⁶ Four hundred Jews soon found refuge in the monastery, and on May 27, 1945, a few weeks after the end of the war, a Liberation Concert was held there. The She'erit Hapletah of the Kovno Ghetto Orchestra gave a concert following a speech by Grinberg and the recitation of Kaddish, the Jewish prayer for the dead.³⁷ While demonstrating striking resourcefulness in the wake of tragedy, the survivors in Dachau and the surrounding area were also disenchanted with the slow arrival of Jewish relief organizations, leading to a sense of abandonment that would remain a central feature in the constant striving for independence on the part of the She'erit Hapletah. In a letter to the WJC written by Grinberg at the end of May 1945, this disappointment was evident because four weeks had passed since liberation and "no representative from any Jewish organization has come to be with us after the worst tragedy of all time." As he concluded, "we must, ourselves, with our own diminished strength, help ourselves."³⁸

Despite feeling deserted, young Jewish DPs did seek to establish contact with world Jewish organizations. In a number of locations in the American zone of Germany, Jewish youths and young adults came together in Zionist groups, organizing collectively in the place of lost family and friends. In their letters, they questioned why the refugees of every other country had already received assistance, but the Jews still had to fend for themselves. The Zionist groups who organized themselves in Buchenwald, Dachau, and elsewhere in Germany sought to perform the service that foreign aid groups were performing for the survivors of other national groups. They could come up with temporary solutions to alleviate poor conditions in the DP camps; however, a more long-term solution, namely departure from Germany, was most desired.

Many of the small Zionist groups reached out to Nathan Schwalb in Geneva, where he directed European operations for the He-Halutz pioneering movement. During the war Schwalb, from his post in Switzerland, had been at the center of He-Halutz efforts to provide assistance to Zionist youth movements throughout Europe. In the Buchenwald camp soon after liberation, the Va'adat Ha-No'ar Ha-Halutzi (Committee of Pioneering Youth) sent a letter to Schwalb asking for immediate immigration to Palestine, fearing that otherwise youths would want to return to Poland. The Zionist youths felt the pressure of communists and Bundists who sought to convince survivors to return to Poland:

> And as the repatriation of Polish citizens to their land has become a reality, this fact has placed us, the Zionist youth, into a very difficult situation: the fact that no Zionist institution and not even the Joint [JDC] has reached us, no sign of life, awakened in us a sad feeling that we are alone in the world and there is no one who will take an interest in us. A small gang of "*yevseksim*" is taking advantage of this situation to convince a lot of Jews that it is better to return to Poland and in their activity they convince the Jews that no country in the world will accept the Polish Jews and that we have no choice but to either stay in a camp in Germany or to travel to Poland. And because life in a camp is already so ugly to us and no one has any desire to stay in a camp, this leads to travel from here to our distress . . . to Poland.[39]

For this reason, the Committee of Pioneering Youth in Buchenwald, led by Jochanan Goldkranz, Aron Feldberg, and Tuwiah Kaminsky, sought assistance from He-Halutz in sending a representative to the camp to organize immigration to Palestine ("the only correct path") for the seventeen hundred Jews in Buchenwald, especially the five hundred youths among them. The group was committed to preventing repatriation to Poland and stressed that such a move was urgent in order to convince the youths that a return to Israel could actually happen soon and thus dampen the desire of the youths to return to Poland.⁴⁰

Still, while some did indeed choose to return to Poland, this meant that those who did stay behind and were committed to active political organization were more likely to be from, or at least receptive to, the Zionist camp. This group in Buchenwald, surely influenced by the leaders of Kibbutz Buchenwald, had already made the choice to inform the many youths who remained in Buchenwald that their only possible future could be in the Land of Israel.

Groups of youths and young adults in other locations in Germany also sought out the assistance of He-Halutz. M. Winogrodzki, who had described the large numbers of youths in Bavaria in a letter to Schwalb, was also of the firm belief that the young orphaned survivors there had to go to Palestine: "It is my belief that these children must absolutely be brought to Palestine. This task must absolutely be undertaken by He-Halutz .... We do not have the appropriate political representation like other countries. ... We live here in Dachau as god-forsaken and still do not know when we can leave this world renowned hell. . . . Many Jews in Dachau have died recently from Typhus, TB, etc. . . . Send us help as fast as possible."⁴¹ As was the case in Buchenwald, there was a sense in Dachau and in Bavaria in general that the great number of youths out of the fifty thousand or so Jewish survivors lacked adequate political representation. Many of the Jewish DPs with Zionist leanings believed that Zionist youth groups could best fill this gap and that the international leadership of Zionist youth organizations was best equipped to understand their situation. Such was the case for a group of Zionist youths who organized themselves in the French zone of Germany as well. While assistance they had received from a French Jewish chaplain was beneficial, they told Schwalb that "only you as a member of He-Halutz and member of the Zionist party can truly understand us. ... In the last time one always hears the question, 'Where are our friends from Eretz, where is the Zionist organization? Have we been forgotten as orphans?'"⁴²

In Buchberg by Toelz in the American zone, a group of a few hundred Jews had separated themselves from a large number of Russians awaiting repatriation following liberation. Among the leaders of the group was Levi Schalitan, a young journalist and former underground activist in the Siauliai ghetto in Lithuania. The group advocated a move to Bad Toelz, where they joined up with other veteran Zionist leaders in late May 1945. In Bad Toelz, Schalitan met Yitzhak Ratner, a Zionist veteran from Kovno, and Yosef Leibowitz, another survivor of Siauliai and a former member of Irgun Brit Zion in Kovno. The three resolved to work together to organize the surviving Jewish Zionists in a united group that could rise above prewar party politics and advocate for immigration to Palestine and the creation of the Jewish state.[43]

Approximately one month after liberation, Ratner reported to the Zionist Executive in Jerusalem on the early efforts at creating a local Zionist committee at the DP camp in Freiman-Flakkasserne near Munich.[44] Zionist groups were operating in all the camps in the vicinity of Munich, Ratner reported, and a central committee was being established in Munich despite the lack of contact from any official Zionist body and continuing American and Russian pressure for repatriation. In order to prevent the repatriation of Jews to Poland and their subsequent dispersal, he advocated the concentration of Jews in one area, a move that could greatly facilitate aliyah to Palestine.[45] Despite appeals for outside assistance, the Zionist groups could not waste time in organizing themselves; they removed themselves from non-Jewish DPs and former collaborators and began to band together to advocate for their own needs.

Shortly thereafter, the first official delegation of the Jewish Brigade to the She'erit Hapletah, under the command of Aharon Hoter-Yishai, happened to visit Freiman-Flakkasserne on June 20, 1945. Following a meeting with Hoter-Yishai, the representatives of the Zionist center in the camp decided to hold a festive gathering in order to welcome the Palestinian soldiers. On June 24 representatives from Zionist groups in Feldafing, Buchberg, St. Ottilien, Landsberg, and Munich met there in the first conference of the Zionists in Bavaria. The conference called upon the survivors to embrace the lesson taught by the war: "to liquidate the European Galut and to go on aliyah to Eretz-Israel."[46]

One of the first priorities of the early Zionist leaders, undertaken in the first month following the Zionists' organization, was the formation of a youth movement to assist in the organization of the youths in the Jewish DP camps. Zionist youths had come together in a number of different places throughout Germany; it was thought that to be most effective they must be concentrated under the umbrella of one organization. First, however, the young leaders of the She'erit Hapletah sought to represent the political needs of the Jewish DPs as a whole before the American occupation forces and the world.

Young survivors in Germany encountered the world of freedom, but it seemed as if the outside world had little idea of what to do with them. American soldiers were poorly equipped to handle the scenes they encountered in the concentration camps, Jewish aid groups such as the JDC had an extremely difficult time gaining access to occupied Germany (the U.S. Army would not grant access to nongovernmental organizations), other national groups began to organize themselves or return home, and young Jewish survivors were pulled in a number of different directions, unsure of where their future would lie.[47] The first priority for young Jewish survivors would be to address their most pressing material needs in the wake of the Holocaust. This was a community that had decided to help itself for as long as the stay in Germany would last. It was in this context that a social framework such as Kibbutz Buchenwald could emerge as an attractive option.

The Popularity of Kibbutz Buchenwald

The Jewish DP youths and the DP population as a whole who had remained in the DP camps of Germany first and foremost sought to have their basic needs met. This meant obtaining food, security, shelter, and health care in the first weeks following liberation. Beyond this, however, they sought to make up for the years they had lost during the war. Many had received no schooling or vocational training for the adult world during the previous six years. Orphaned and alone, they also desperately sought camaraderie and companionship. The early political leadership of the She'erit Hapletah, composed of many former members of Zionist youth groups, was overwhelmingly attuned to the needs of the youths in the DP camps. And because young people under the age of thirty comprised the primary constituency in the DP camps, it was also crucial that the DP leadership meet their needs. The emerging popularity of the alternative living experiment near Buchenwald demonstrated the value of this option to DP youths and the Jewish DP leadership.

The group that formed Kibbutz Buchenwald chose to continue working following liberation, foregoing the so-called idleness of DP camp life for the hard work of creating a training farm. "Everyone knew that since liberation one could live a life of comparative ease in Buchenwald. Plenty of food, and nothing to do. And yet here we were, and there were many who wanted to join us."[48] In the first few weeks of Kibbutz Buchenwald's existence, the group of sixteen Jewish survivors who had moved to the farm in Eggendorf expanded daily, attracting young survivors from Buchenwald and other nearby camps who preferred the alternative presented by the farm to the idleness of the camps.[49] On the first Sabbath after the move to the farm, the group hosted a group of American Jewish guests, including Chaplain Herschel Schacter and Jewish soldiers of the U.S. Army: "We ate, sang, made humorous speeches, and had a good time. Before the end, Chaplain Schacter spoke, underlining the historic importance of what we are doing." The kibbutz counted thirty comrades (including four women) and began to organize cultural work, a chorus, and regular discussions and study groups.[50]

The move to a farm on German soil gave rise to a number of ethical and moral dilemmas that were debated by the members of the kibbutz: Was it appropriate for them to cultivate German soil, even on a temporary basis? Should they, as young pioneers, be allowed to have intimate relations with German women? To what extent should they observe Jewish religious law in order to accommodate religious members who sought to maintain kashruth (Jewish dietary laws) or observe the Sabbath?

The founders of the kibbutz decided that they would not remain on German soil one day longer than they had to, thereby resolving the dilemma of working "diese verfluchte deutsche Erde" (this accursed German soil).[51] They could reconcile this with the knowledge that they were working toward a higher goal, that of settlement in Palestine. The question of relations with German women was representative of the larger question of the Jewish relationship to their recently defeated oppressors. Within Kibbutz Buchenwald, which had been founded partly out of a desire to avoid Jewish revenge against Germans, the question was debated in accord with the principles of collectivism that the kibbutz tried to maintain in making decisions for the group as a whole. Hayim-Meir Gotlieb, citing the horrors that had only recently been endured at the hands of the Germans, had no doubts as to the correct course of action:

> Now, concretely, as to whether as halutzim we can permit ourselves to have relations, I mean intimate relations, with German women. The answer is clear: No. Comrades, don't misunderstand me. I don't call for blood revenge on German civilians. I am only saying that simple human self-respect must prevent us from having relations with German women. Yes, it is true that we were shut up for years in camp, without the sight of a woman, and now, coming out of prison into glowing freedom, our blood is warmed and we want to live a bit. This is quite natural. But friends, I ask you to remember one thing: When our beloved Jewish girls burned in the crematoria, their clothes were brought to Germany, and these very girls might be wearing their dresses, their rings . . . after all, comrades, we are people who can, when necessary, control our instincts.[52]

The kibbutz decided that any comrade guilty of intimate relations with a German woman would automatically be expelled from the group. In this regard, the duty to the kibbutz collective and the Jewish people as a whole outweighed the necessity of any individual human urges, regardless of whether other Jewish survivors made such choices. The question of relations between German men and Jewish women does not seem to have been discussed, reflecting both the gender imbalance in the surviving population and on the kibbutz (twenty-six men to four women in early June 1945) and the unthinkable nature of such a relationship after the war to the surviving Jewish men. In fact, among the male survivors engaged in this discussion, Jewish women seemed to symbolize first and foremost their sense of obligation to the dead. In the sphere of religious observance, on the other hand, it was decided that no single member would be able to impose his or her will on another. Members would not be discriminated against on the basis of religious observance, and if some chose to maintain dietary laws, this would be allowed.

On June 23, 1945, Kibbutz Buchenwald was forced to move from its initial location in Eggendorf, which had fallen under the Soviet zone of occupation, to a new farm in Geringshof.[53] With assistance of UNRRA personnel and equipment, the by now fifty-three male and female comrades successfully took over a former religious-Zionist hakhsharah that had been

appropriated by a German farmer during the war. The members of the kibbutz began to organize cultural activities on the new farm, including educational courses, intellectual discussions, singing, and dancing.[54] Although the
Geringshof farm was in poorer condition than the estate at Eggendorf, the
members took pride in their labor, cutting grass, turning over hay, harvesting barley, and driving, cleaning, and feeding the horses. In a July 1945 letter
to the Jewish Agency, the kibbutz appealed for aliyah certificates to Palestine,
hoping that their efforts would demonstrate their Zionist credentials.

> Through our physical labor in this kibbutz, we have meant to demonstrate
> that we are not yet destroyed, but that we still have a will to live and to build.
> We have meant to demonstrate our dislike of continuing to live in the camp,
> even as liberated people, and our dislike of philanthropy and dependence on
> others. . . . We comrades of Buchenwald come to you with only one request:
> we want to go, and shall go, to Palestine, and we ask you to help us so that we
> may go there without delay.[55]

Still, the desire to obtain aliyah certificates became a further point of fric-
tion dividing the kibbutz, as members with more Zionist experience sought
to argue for their merit over previously non-Zionist members in obtaining
certificates.[56]

On July 21, 1945, the kibbutz received its first visits from representatives
of the Yishuv in Palestine. An army car drove into the yard of the kibbutz,
but "instead of the usual American insignia, was a yellow Star of David on a
blue-white field." Chaim Ben-Asher and Arieh Simon of the Jewish Brigade
informed the kibbutz of the coming conference of Jewish survivors in
Munich and encouraged the members to enlist other survivors in the struggle for a Jewish state.[57] On the same day, Rabbi Marcus of the U.S. Army
brought the kibbutz a most distinguished guest, Eliyahu Dobkin, head of
the Jewish Agency's Immigration Department. The members of the kibbutz
were greatly excited by his visit, eager to hear about the possibility of their
departure for Palestine. Dobkin, visibly moved by their effort in forming the
kibbutz, nonetheless disappointed them in response to their request regarding aliyah certificates. In effect, this amounted to their first encounter with
the Yishuv's effort to instrumentalize the Jewish survivors in the fight for a
Jewish state. As was noted in the kibbutz journal, "Now we asked what news

U.S. Army Chaplain Mayer Abramowitz officiates at a wedding ceremony for displaced persons at Kibbutz Buchenwald in Geringshof. (USHMM, courtesy of Mayer and Rachel Abramowitz)

he had for us. His reply disturbed us greatly. For he suggested that we should remain here as a kibbutz for the time being, since our existence made us a symbol of vital political importance to the Jewish cause."[58] Furthermore, the Jewish Agency still did not have enough aliyah certificates, and Dobkin argued that those certificates that were available should be given to those in more dire circumstances than they. Needless to say, this did not please the kibbutz members, who argued that their departure need not mean the end of the kibbutz and its political value. "Even if we were given the means to proceed to Palestine, there were plenty of others who would come into the kibbutz and maintain it in Germany as the next immigrant group."[59] It was precisely this point that the five representatives of Kibbutz Buchenwald sought to argue at the first conference of Liberated Jews in Bavaria on July 25, 1945.

Jewish Youths and the Central Committee of Liberated Jews: The Political Organization of the She'erit Hapletah

While the members of Kibbutz Buchenwald had been busy developing their farm and preparing themselves for what they hoped would be their eventual aliyah, the difficulties that accompanied securing land for Zionist training farms from occupation authorities and German district administrators meant that for the vast majority of Jewish DP youths, life for the time being would continue within a DP camp. In order to better represent their own interests before the U.S. Army and UNRRA as other national groups of DPs did, the Jewish DPs organized the Central Committee of Liberated Jews in Bavaria in June and July 1945 with the assistance of U.S. Army chaplain Abraham J. Klausner and representatives from the Jewish Brigade.[60] The political organization of the She'erit Hapletah and the priorities of its largely Zionist leadership would greatly influence the options available to the younger segment of the Jewish DP population.

The Central Committee leadership was encouraged by the model of the kibbutz as a sign that this could be the most productive way to organize youths. For those who were nonorganized and thus most at risk of demoralization, black market activity, and idleness, the leadership worked to create constructive alternatives for them. Witnessing the success of the Buchenwald model, these alternatives would come to revolve around the kibbutz (and the informal educational opportunities it provided) and vocational training (again, often within the framework of the kibbutz).

The early organization of the She'erit Hapletah was therefore marked by two parallel concerns, both aimed at addressing the basic needs of the Jewish DPs: (1) a focus on the present material needs of the survivors for food, shelter, medicine, and security, and (2) the question of immigration, with debates over return to Poland (and elsewhere) or departure for Palestine. The two issues were linked: by providing services for those DPs in Germany, the leadership could prevent a return to Poland and maintain the size of the pool for aliyah in Germany. Realizing that DP youths would be most likely to embrace a future life in Palestine, the Central Committee of Liberated Jews focused its efforts in the area of aliyah on DP youths. It is important to note that in the discussions of the Central Committee and the Zionist organizations formed in the DP camps, the younger segment of the DP population was almost always referred to as *di jugnt* (the youth) or *jidisze jugnt* (Jewish youth). The age group to which this term referred to was not specified, although it did seem to indicate a broad definition of those among the younger segment of the DP population who were either already affiliated with Zionist groups or could potentially be affiliated in such a way.[61]

The discussions and resolutions taken at the first meeting to organize the Central Committee of Liberated Jews in Bavaria on July 1, 1945, at Feldafing made it evident that the early leadership of the She'erit Hapletah viewed Palestine as the most desirable solution to the lingering Jewish question for the estimated fifty thousand survivors in Germany. While the leadership was aware of the need to address the concerns of those who did not desire to make aliyah, as one representative from Lithuania named Garfunkel suggested, the lack of contact from world Jewry indicated that "aliyah is the only way to solve the Jewish question."[62] The Jews had only one possible destination: Palestine.[63] In its resolutions, the committee called for unity among the Jews in an effort to build the Jewish state while demanding that the British open the gates of Palestine to create the Jewish state. The conference included eight Lithuanian Jews as well as five Jews from Poland, four from Hungary, three from Romania, and one from Greece. Rabbi Abraham Klausner was appointed honorary president, and Dr. Grinberg was elected chairman of the Executive.

At the same time, the DP leadership worked to ameliorate conditions in the DP camps and prevent Jewish DPs from being housed with former collaborators. The reports of continuing deprivation in the liberated camps and poor organization of recovery issued by the survivors and the Jewish chaplains serving there did eventually succeed in prompting American officials to take a greater interest in the problem of the DPs. Treasury secretary Henry Morgenthau Jr., responding to a request from American Jewish leaders, proposed to Joseph Grew, the undersecretary of State, that Earl Harrison, dean of the University of Pennsylvania Law School, be sent to Germany to investigate conditions there. In response to complaints emanating from the DP camps and reports of mistreatment of survivors at the hands of troops, President Harry S. Truman sent a letter to Harrison on June 22, 1945, endorsing the mission and requested that Harrison send him a report regarding the "needs of stateless and non-repatriable refugees among the displaced persons in Germany and to determine the extent to which those needs are

Earl Harrison, sent by President Truman to tour DP camps in summer 1945. (USHMM, courtesy of J. Barton Harrison)

being met by military, governmental and private organizations."[64] Once Harrison arrived in the camps in Germany, the Jewish DPs, along with Abraham Klausner and soldiers from the Jewish Brigade, worked to make sure that he was aware of the miserable conditions facing the Jews.[65]

The groundwork that was laid at the first conference in Feldafing on July 1, 1945, and the Executive Committee conference held on July 14 crystallized in the July 25, 1945, Founding Conference of Liberated Jewish Political Prisoners in Germany.[66] With ninety-four delegates representing the approximately fifty thousand surviving Jews in Germany and Austria, the conference was an opportunity for the Jewish DPs to state their concerns and come together as a cohesive, political group. The survivors also demonstrated an impressive awareness of public relations, inviting reporters and officials of the American occupation authorities to the conference and holding its closing and highly symbolic ceremony in the infamous Munich beer hall where Hitler initiated his failed putsch in November 1923. A number of issues became evident from the testimony of the delegates. Conditions were highly variable in the various DP centers; in Feldafing, for example, which had six thousand Jews, conditions were exceptionally bad with a lack of clothing and shelter, while other locations had fewer than one hundred Jews. Still, the Jewish DPs expressed their commitment to ameliorating the situation of the Jewish survivors by themselves, welcoming any outside assistance that might eventually arrive. Eliyahu Dobkin, the highest-ranking Jewish official to reach the DPs as head of the Jewish Agency's Immigration Department, assured the conference that the technical means for aliyah were already available (notwithstanding his earlier statements to the members of Kibbutz Buchenwald); all that stood in the way of mass Jewish immigration to Palestine were the restrictions of the British. The representatives supported a general call for an independent Jewish state and equality of Jewish rights worldwide.[67] Immigration to Palestine, especially of the youths in the DP camps, was the desired goal of the Zionist leadership on the Central Committee. However, as long as departure was not imminent, planning would have to be done to make the youths a productive element of both the DP population and of their future home in Palestine.

Yechezkel Tydor and four others came to the conference as the representatives of Kibbutz Buchenwald. In a sense, they came as the representatives of those young adults who had made the choice to break away from the DP camp and solve the problems of liberation on their own. What the representatives heard was a newly formed Central Committee that sought to appropriate not only the position as voice of the She'erit Hapletah but also as arbiter of questions related to the future of the younger segment of the She'erit Hapletah. The representatives at the first meeting of the Central Committee were highly concerned with demoralization, depression, and idleness among the DPs. In discussing the situation of "the youth," many of the representatives on the committee, particularly among the Zionists, reiterated their belief in the value of productive physical and educational work so as to remove them from the potentially damaging effects of the DP camps.[68] This could best keep the youths occupied during their time in Germany while helping them to prepare for a new life in Palestine and lead DP society as a whole in a spiritual rebirth. The belief that it was necessary to plan for the future of the youths meant that the younger segment of the population would continue to be viewed as an object by the leadership. Still, this would open a number of options for those youths who made the choice to remain in Germany to use their time productively, almost always within the framework of the larger Zionist project of aliyah.

While there was a general consensus that the future of the She'erit Hapletah (and therefore of the youths) was of paramount concern, a number of competing suggestions emerged over how best to occupy surviving Jewish youths. As it was becoming increasingly clear that international help would be slow to arrive, all were in agreement as to where the initiative would have to come from. Dr. Nabriski, from the camp in Landsberg, called for a simultaneous effort to broaden and deepen efforts for a mass immigration to Palestine (Eretz Israel) among the DPs while working to improve the current situation in the DP camps. He argued that cultural work (to improve morale) was just as, if not more important than, economic efforts. "Although the economic situation is very important, the cultural and spiritual work is even more important. All those who have emerged from the concentration camps, *above all the youth*, must organize and prepare for a new, free life. Because we are still waiting for help from the outside world, we must do everything with our own strength."[69] Jacob Olejski, also from Landsberg and a survivor from Kovno, noted the absence of any help from Jewish world organizations and concluded that the Jewish DPs would be forced to "do it ourselves." He called for the Jewish masses to be organized in central points and for work to begin in the DP camps aimed at instilling the spirit of free life and avoiding demoralization. "First and foremost," he argued, "the *youth* must be trained for productive work to prepare for life in Eretz Yisrael."[70]

While Nabriski and Olejski spoke more generally about making Jewish youths productive, the representatives of Kibbutz Buchenwald were convinced that their collective group could serve as a model for the rest of Jewish DP youths. Tydor called for further kibbutz hakhsharot for agriculture and artisanry to be formed in other places in Germany. Other members of Kibbutz Buchenwald were also present, including Elik Greunbaum, Simcha Dimant, Paltiel Rosenfrucht, and Leib Gruenfeld.[71] Tydor, in his address to the conference as head of Kibbutz Buchenwald, recalled that "each group spoke of its problems and maladies. Then it was my turn to represent a group that had taken the initiative to leave the camp, to live in a healthy environment in preparation for aliyah. In light of our success I suggested that others take advantage of the fluid situation to 'appropriate' confiscated estates while it was still feasible."[72] According to Tydor, the idea was initially not embraced enthusiastically; many among the Zionists feared establishing a program that could encourage Jewish youths to settle roots too deeply in Germany.[73]

Ironically enough, within a few days following the conclusion of the conference, the members of Kibbutz Buchenwald received notice on August 5 from Rabbi Robert Marcus that they had been granted eighty aliyah certificates, a number that exceeded their total kibbutz membership. Two members were sent to the Bergen-Belsen DP camp in the British zone to select new members from among the halutzim already organized there. In recruiting more members to fill the immigration quota and ensure the continued functioning of the kibbutz on the Geringshof farm, the leaders of the group encountered the difficult question of which members merited aliyah most or whether they should accept the offer of immigration at all rather than remain in Germany as a fighting vanguard in the Jewish struggle. Their internal discussions also reflected the degree to which they understood their outsized symbolic significance regarding diplomatic negotiations over Palestine, for the more militant halutzim from Bergen-Belsen believed that they should reject the certificates in protest against the restrictive British immigration policy.

> Our comrades returned on August 10, from Bergen-Belsen, where they had met with the halutz group in connection with our move to Palestine. What they had to present to us was unexpected and unbelievable; the message they brought created a crisis. These people of Bergen-Belsen, they said, are true halutzim, prepared to sacrifice themselves and to set aside their individual desires, placing the needs of the Jewish people first. They believe that there is something more important than their own migration to Palestine. First, they believe, they must struggle for Palestine to be opened to all the Jews of Europe. They are convinced that we should not accept the eighty certificates offered to us, but should return them, since the Jews of Europe cannot be saved by eighty certificates, and through our acceptance England will be able to claim that she is helping Jews.[74]

Nonetheless, after some discussion the decision was made to accept the certificates; some of the halutzim from Bergen-Belsen came to fill the quota for Palestine. On August 27, 1945, the group of eighty left Fulda and boarded the *Mataroah* in Toulon on September 2, 1945.[75]

After the departure of the first leaders among the aliyah group, the early unity that had reigned at Kibbutz Buchenwald gradually dissolved. Religiously observant members from the Poalei Agudat Israel movement who had come to replenish the ranks of the kibbutz found that they were limited in their degree of observance and thus decided to form their own kibbutz, Chafetz Chaim, formed in Gersfeld in September 1945. In fact, the prevalence of kibbutzim among Poalei Agudat Israel would also demonstrate the transideological popularity of the kibbutz idea, as religious youths with next to no prewar Zionist experience joined this outwardly Zionist social group.[76] Following the departure of the first wave from Kibbutz Buchenwald, later members continued to populate the farm, arriving primarily from the Landsberg DP camp under the auspices of the united Zionist pioneering organization Nocham.[77]

The Central Committee Focus on Youths in the DP Camps

Subsequent meetings of the Central Committee of Liberated Jews in Bavaria showed a continuing focus on the question of organizing the Jewish youths and caring for their physical rehabilitation and cultural education within the framework of the DP camp.[78] Consistent with its political position, the Central Committee decided to form a special department to handle the question of youths and cultural education in the DP camps, the cultural department. At the August 8 meeting, Levi Schalitan, the young editor of *Undzer Weg*, part of the early group in Buchberg and a survivor from Siauliai, Lithuania, active in the underground movement there, emphasized the importance of "culture above all. We must educate the Jewish youth and the Jewish people anew . . . we must struggle to organize and send the people to Eretz Yisrael."[79] Similarly, Avraham Melamed (Landsberg) suggested that: "One of the problems is youth education. Youth have suffered and lost hope, become demoralized. We seek to educate the youth anew. The youth have lost their ambition. We must support a radical effort in the education of our youth. I call for the creation of a special department in the ZK [Zentral Komitet, or Central Committee] to care for the youth in order to return them to constructive life."[80] And indeed, the cultural department undertook the responsibility to look after the spiritual (Zionist) education of the Jewish DP youths.

Developments in the Landsberg DP camp demonstrated the options available to DP youths and the choices that many were making. While the DP leadership sought to occupy youths in the DP camps and prevent demoralization, groups of youths were already organizing on their own. In fact, the Central Committee seemed to be responding to developments already taking place in the DP camps. At the same August 8 meeting, Samuel Gringauz reported that Zionist youth movements had already begun to function actively in the Landsberg camp. Many Jewish youths who had decided to remain in the Landsberg DP camp were making the choice to occupy themselves actively in Zionist youth groups. The thirty-five hundred Jews in the camp would soon be living in a purely Jewish camp, as the number of non-Jews was dwindling rapidly. Cultural institutions such as drama and music groups and Hebrew courses were already available in the camp. A vocational school offering courses in shoemaking, automobile mechanics, and electronics was at the disposal of any Jewish youth who wanted to come to the camp. As Gringauz noted, the Zionist youth groups in Landsberg were already engaged in serious activity, and the large number of intelligent, active people in the camp gave him reason to be optimistic about the cultural life and moral situation at Landsberg.[81] Gringauz, who would be elected president of the Landsberg camp in October, came from the same background as many of the other early leaders of the youth cause. Decidedly older (forty-four years old at liberation), he had been deported from Kovno at the end of 1944 and was active in the Zionist underground of the Kaufering camp outside Dachau before liberation.

The younger Jewish survivors, who had initially joined more informal Zionist groups that came together in the DP camps, thus gradually faced a more organized network of Zionist institutions, as the Central Committee worked to provide them with a more formal educational framework through the opening of vocational schools and later the People's University. This would parallel the informal education provided by the kibbutzim of the Zionist groups organized in the DP camps.[82]

Central Committee support for a Zionist position facilitated the development of a Zionist framework for youths. As a technically nonpartisan group, however, the Central Committee left authority over the official formation of Zionist institutions to the political parties that were in the process of formation. Thus, at the end of July the Central Committee gave its official approval to the newly formed United Zionist Organization (UZO) to be the representative of the Zionists in the DP camps. Whereas Jewish DP youths had once appealed abroad for assistance from Jewish organizations, the formal political organization would now be taking place within the DP camps of Germany. The UZO, in turn, would communicate with Schwalb of the He-Halutz office in Geneva and with the Jewish Agency executive in Palestine on behalf of Zionists in the DP camps.

The Central Committee and the UZO reached a decision that the UZO would be responsible for all activity related to culture, Zionist education, hakhsharah, aliyah, and Zionist activity in general.[83] The early leadership of the UZO, in its communications with the Jewish Agency, affirmed the need to have one organization to represent all of the Zionists in the DP camps of Germany.[84] The early impetus toward a unity that would supercede interwar party divisions among the She'erit Hapletah in the Central Committee and the Zionist organizations was a distinctive aspect of the early Zionist organization in the DP camps in Germany. This aim of the UZO seems to have emerged out of the earlier goals of the Irgun Brit Zion group from Kovno in Dachau, which stressed the need for Zionist unity in the wake of the Holocaust. While division between Zionist political groups would emerge strongly by the end of 1945, the early unity among Zionist organizations and within Zionist groups may have assisted in the creation of an educational and vocational system focused on youths in the DP camps. For previously nonorganized Jewish youths in the DP camps, this alliance between the political leadership and the Zionist organization provided one unified framework, Zionist in nature, with which to affiliate.

Responding to the move of Jewish youths into the Zionist groups, at the second meeting of the Zionist organization in Bavaria on August 20 in Landsberg the Zionist leadership decided that in addition to the official formation of the UZO, they would authorize the creation of Nocham. Such an official youth movement could systematize the loose clusters of youths who had already congregated in the various DP centers and guarantee greater membership for the UZO and Nocham, also facilitating the process of aliyah to Palestine from the DP camps.[85] In this initial period, the various Zionist youth movements agreed to participate within the Nocham framework. The nature of Zionist education would be pioneering and would include cultural, professional, and self-defense hakhsharah (all geared to train *chalutzim,* or pioneers, for life in Palestine).[86] This would aid in the ultimate aim of the Zionist movement in Germany: to capture hearts and create a new Jew through educational and informational work.[87] Three weeks later during the September 11–12, 1945, preparatory meeting in Landsberg for the upcoming Zionist conference at Frankfurt, the founding principles of Nocham and the UZO were laid out: the creation of a Jewish state; construction of the country on socialist principles; elevation of labor, agriculture, hakhsharah, and Hebrew language and culture; and aliyah by all means. The new group also took upon itself shekel collection (the membership dues of the World Zionist Organization) and called for activity on behalf of the Labor Federation (Histadrut) in Palestine; in keeping with its complete identification with the Zionist Executive in Palestine, the UZO also excluded the Revisionist youth movement Betar from the united camp.[88]

These initiatives followed closely on Earl Harrison's August 24 bombshell in which he issued his scathing indictment of the inhumane American treatment of the Jewish DPs, charging that the only difference between American and Nazi treatment of the Jews is "that we do not exterminate them."[89] He recommended that the Jewish DPs be classified as a special group within their own separate camps and be granted the immediate transfer of one hundred thousand Jewish refugee certificates to Palestine. These policies (excluding the transfer of refugees to Palestine) were implemented almost immediately by General Dwight D. Eisenhower, who was assisted in his work by Rabbi Judah Nadich, the newly appointed adviser on Jewish Affairs.[90] New authority over their own Jewish camps and the hopefulness with which immigration to Palestine was now viewed bolstered the Jewish leadership's redoubled efforts to prepare youths for aliyah.

Jewish DP Camps and the "Productivization" of Jewish Youths

The creation of separate camps for Jewish DPs meant that Jewish youths would be presented with the option of participating in kibbutzim and vocational training courses that would be established in the newly Jewish DP camps. Jacob Olejski, former director of the Jewish vocational training organization ORT in Lithuania, was the driving force behind the creation of vocational courses for youths in the DP camps, which were first organized in Landsberg, Föhrenwald, and Feldafing.[91] The courses offered at the schools would be central to the program to provide a productive outlet for the youths during their time in the DP camps.

In its first efforts in the DP camps, the cultural department linked formal education with the vocational and spiritual education necessary for rebirth. Youths were an object of focus because they came to be seen as representing the future of the She'erit Hapletah as a whole. At a speech made at the opening of the school year on October 1, Olejski reiterated the importance of productive work: "unemployment is the mother of all sin . . . we can heal the soul of our people through work." For Olejski, the building of the Jewish settlement in Palestine would require people healthy both in body and mind who could use their muscle power in useful and constructive work. Thus, he issued a call to those enrolled in the school to put themselves to work.[92]

A sewing class in an ORT (Organization for Rehabilitation through Training) training workshop in the Landsberg DP camp. On the wall is a large portrait of Theodor Herzl within a Star of David, as well as portraits of other Zionist leaders. (USHMM, courtesy of George Kadish/Zvi Kadushin)

Above all, the creation of the vocational schools was aimed at both the organized and nonorganized youths (or kibbutz and nonkibbutz youths) in the camps, who were called upon to enroll in the schools. In a "Call to the Jewish Youth in Bavaria" published in the camp newspaper the *Landsberger Lager Cajtung*, the cultural office of the Landsberg DP camp called upon the youths to engage themselves in productive work through the vocational schools that had been established:

> We call on the organized youth, who are preparing themselves for life in Eretz Israel, to make use of their time here and learn a trade.... Because Israel is a land under construction.... We also call on the unorganized youth to not just pass the time but to use the winter months to learn a trade and to enroll in the vocational schools.... *Let us not leave the time unproductive, as it was as we sat in the ghettos and the camps.* ... Learn a trade; be a productive, useful human being for yourself, for your people, and for your land.[93]

This call was coordinated with the opening of vocational schools and the People's University in the DP camp on October 9, 1945.[94] Those youths not affiliated with kibbutzim were also invited to join the classes.

The productivization of the youths was not only esteemed as a method of assisting in the struggle to create a Jewish state in Palestine but was also linked to the idea of revenge against Germany and the redemption of the Jewish people after years of oppression. Samuel Gringauz, head of the Landsberg DP camp, suggested that the tragedy of the Jews and the idea of revenge needed to be turned to constructive ends, as he indicated in his memorial address in the Landsberg camp synagogue on Yom Kippur, September 17, 1945:

> But you, the youth, cannot and should not live in a situation of memory and sorrow. You must live and build, work and liberate yourselves. Remember the words of our great poet: "Nikmat dam jeled hakatan od loh barah hasatan" [Satan has not yet created a fitting revenge for the blood of a small child].... For you, our young people, are the agents of our revenge which ought to be a proud assertion to continue life. You must readily show the world and all our enemies that despite everything we are here to stay. Your revenge must be in working and toiling for your own land. You must create and build, dance and sing, open yourselves to life, to living and labor.[95]

If the youths could find the energy to make themselves productive, then perhaps too the Jewish people could be reborn. As Olejski suggested, "Only you, Jewish youth, in the difficult struggle . . . awaken in me energy, in order to further build the foundation, in order for you to give the rest of my strength to fulfill my social duties to the Jews." And the best way for Jewish youths to awaken energy in the rest of the people was to "learn a trade, for your spirit, for your soul—become good and useful people, as our people expects this from you."[96] Jewish youths thus had a duty to be the revitalizing force in the rebirth of the Jewish people after the catastrophe. As Jewish youths emerged as the most vocal and desirable element of the Jewish DP population, such a focus could also serve to empower youths who until now had only been the victims of persecution and dehumanization.

The activities available for Jewish youths in the DP camps thus increasingly came to focus on two parallel, yet interconnected, tracks: (1) kibbutzim to provide organization, structure, and informal education for the DP youths, and (2) more formalized education and vocational training designed largely to occupy those youths living in the kibbutzim within the DP camps. Jewish youths in the DP camps could thus either choose to remain among the nonorganized Jewish public in the DP camps or could join kibbutzim that provided structure, informal education, camaraderie, and access to more formalized education in schools and vocational training. Whereas the first kibbutz group formed in postwar Germany, Kibbutz Buchenwald, represented the model of a kibbutz that moved out of a DP camp to a training farm, the collective groups of youths organized by the youth movement were also referred to as kibbutzim. Many of these kibbutz groups would remain in the independent Jewish DP camps that were created in late 1945. The late creation of separate DP camps and the delayed access of international Jewish organizations meant that Jewish schools and an educational system were not up and running until 1946. For this reason, through the end of 1945 the kibbutzim in the various camps and the vocational schools that had been opened in Landsberg, Föhrenwald and Feldafing, remained nearly the only organizational framework for Jewish youths. The Jewish youths who joined these groups would be engaged in holy work that elevated their status among the rest of the DP population. The younger segment of the Jewish DP population was entrusted with the burden of the future of European

Jewry; this task made the creation of options for youths and the choices made by youths all the more significant.

The UZO, Nocham, and Debates over the Place of Jewish Youths in DP Society

The First Conference of the UZO took place in Frankfurt am Main during October 23–24, 1945.[97] The discussions of the first conference of the UZO reveal the degree to which youths dominated the program of the Zionist organization and the amount of productive and cultural work that had already been done by late October 1945. Perhaps most attractive to many among the Jewish youths, and central to discussions at the conference, was the question of leaving DP camps for hakhsharot (agricultural training farms) in the German countryside. For Jewish youths in the DP camps, the more formal organization of kibbutzim in the larger youth movement framework would mean access to more educational materials and a wider network of movement resources and, hopefully, immigration certificates.

As was noted at the UZO conference, the Zionist organizing in Germany had proceeded apace since liberation in early May. Shlomo Frankel, editor of *Nitzotz* and a former member of Irgun Brit Zion who had "visited all the places of settlement, camps, and kibbutzim from Bavaria to Bergen-Belsen," reported on the overall state of Zionist activity in the DP camps. According to Frankel, hakhsharah continued to occupy a central place in Zionist activity, and thus far twelve hundred members had been organized in kibbutzim.[98] One agricultural farm was in existence in Bavaria, but Frankel recommended increasing the number of farms so that all the kibbutzim could be moved out to productive work. Despite contact with Schwalb of He-Halutz in Switzerland, "who has promised us many things," nothing had yet been received.[99] Still, in an effort to expand the cultural work in the DP camps, the UZO and Nocham would endeavor to have a seminar for *madrichim* (group leaders; literally guides or instructors) once the promised educational materials and manpower arrived from Israel.

Members of kibbutzim in attendance also testified to the robust activity taking place within the kibbutzim, including workshops, cultural work, and language classes for instruction in Hebrew. In all these cases, members argued for the need to create agricultural centers in order to prepare youths for "the hard life that lies before them [in Palestine]." The representative from Landsberg (Cohen) also testified to the fact that it was only the members of kibbutzim who participated in the vocational schools set up by Olejski in the DP camp.[100]

While the responsibility of the UZO and Nocham to organize and provide for the youths in the DP camps was clear, there was disagreement as to what the place of the youths and the Zionist youth movement should be in the Jewish DP community. How much were Jewish youths in kibbutzim to be involved in the general life of the DP camps? Would it be preferable for youths to move away from the camps so as to enable concentration in kibbutzim in order to prepare for aliyah? In a sense, such debates were a continuation of prewar arguments over the responsibility of the elite Zionist youths to the broader Jewish society. Gad Beck, a member of Nocham and a representative of the hakhsharah and aliyah department, argued that in order for Jewish youths to be able to lead independent, collective, and productive lives, they should be able to remove themselves from general Jewish life and be concentrated in kibbutzim.[101] On the other hand, some argued that the movement to farms too quickly could deteriorate the cultural life within the DP camps and leave newly arriving kibbutz groups without a model for future behavior. Others suggested a compromise, requesting that when kibbutz groups departed for hakhsharah some of their members be left behind in order to lay the groundwork and serve as role models for future arrivals. The decisions made by Jewish youths, who had emerged as a vital element to rebuilding the Jewish community, began to take on more importance than merely addressing their own personal futures. Zionist leaders projected goals and aspirations onto the youths and in doing so tended to speak for them. The youths in the DP camps both in and out of the kibbutzim on the other hand would clearly have different understandings of what was best for them as individuals. Some had chosen to join groups such as Kibbutz Buchenwald for any number of reasons, whether social, political, or simply pragmatic. Now, with so much significance bestowed upon the place of youths (literally and figuratively), young Jewish survivors could no longer be construed as making decisions only for themselves.

The debate over integrating Zionist youths into the DP community also reflected a broader question over the degree to which the Zionist organization was responsible for wider leadership of all the Jews in the DP camps, Zionist and non-Zionist. Dov Sheinzon summarized the position of those seeking a broader appeal, arguing that the kibbutz could not focus only on the elite and had a responsibility to the broader DP population. As he suggested, "we have complete faith in our chalutz, but he must pull behind him the masses and not remain isolated behind his four walls; we need to engage the public."[102] In this sense, the young halutzim in the kibbutzim could not only be focused on preparation for life in Palestine but would also have to represent the DP community as a whole, providing spiritual and moral support to the wider public. According to Sheinzon, the young chalutz could not just march ahead of the rest of the DP camp, blazing a trail for others to follow; the pioneers also had the responsibility to work with the broader DP community and to do some heavy lifting themselves.

The Nocham youth movement thus focused its efforts on two fronts in an effort to address the needs of the young constituency in the DP camps: moving youths organized in kibbutzim out of the DP camps and onto hakhsharot and expanding the scope of the movement to include the non-organized youths. Implicit in debates over how soon and what quantities of youths to send out of the DP camps was a shared belief in the centrality of hakhsharah to the preparation of the Zionist youths for life in Palestine. For the fifteen hundred youths who were already members of the movement, this meant continuing vocational, agricultural, and Zionist education within the framework of the kibbutz. Establishing a solid educational foundation would become even more significant as Nocham grew to include nearly five thousand members in Bavaria by the middle of November 1945 with the arrival of more youths from Poland, Hungary and elsewhere.[103]

In accord with its role as a leader of the Jewish DP community as a whole, in addition to organizing the groups of Zionist youths already living together in the DP camps, Nocham worked through the newspapers in the DP camps to reach those youths not affiliated with the movement. Through the DP press the movement's branch in Landsberg boasted of its many accomplishments, including its activity in the schools and in cultural endeavors, and called upon the nonorganized youths to heed their responsibility to the dead in order to ensure the future of the Jewish people in the wake of destruction:

> After almost half a year we can say that although we were few at the begin-
> ning, the youth has heeded our call—today our youth movement sets the
> tone for the whole social, cultural, and productive life in the camp. . . . How-
> ever, our pride is not complete—there is another youth besides ours which is
> unoccupied—we say: *"Youth awake, open your eyes, where are you going? Is this
> the way? Are you the porter of the holy will of the 6 million martyrs? The people
> calls to you, the martyrs call to you! . . . Secure your future, the future of coming
> generations, the future of the entire Jewish people."*[104]

Shortly after the conclusion of the Frankfurt conference, the UZO and Nocham received official recognition from Schwalb in the He-Halutz office in Geneva, solidifying the position they had already assigned themselves in the period following liberation. Nocham was designated as having the respon-sibility for preparing all those arriving in the Bricha (the semiorganized movement of Jewish departure) from Poland for the task of hakhsharah and aliyah.[105] Those eighteen through twenty-four years of age would be thought of as senior members (*bogrim*) in the movement and were the responsibility of the department on hakhsharah and aliyah. All children under age twelve would be sent straight to general children's homes, children from the ages of twelve to seventeen were to be organized in youth groups of Nocham, and those ages seventeen and over would be organized in the kibbutzim and kibbutz hakhsharah of He-Halutz Ha-Meukhad (United Hehalutz).[106] This arrangement guaranteed that those youths organized in kibbutzim by Nocham would then be integrated into mainstream Zionist movement upon arrival in Palestine. Akiba Lewinsky of the youth aliyah division of the Jew-ish Agency also designated Gad Beck (of Nocham) responsible for the task of coordinating youth aliyah from Germany.[107]

In accord with the agreement reached between the Central Committee and the UZO, the Zionist organization and its youth movement, Nocham, would be responsible for moving youths out of the DP camps and onto agri-cultural farms to train for immigration to Palestine. For Jewish youths in the DP camps, this could be one of the most appealing aspects of joining a kib-butz, providing the alternative to depart the demoralizing atmosphere of the

DP camp for the clean air, good food, and better accommodations of a farm. As the Zionist youth organization began to focus its efforts on moving DP youths already organized in kibbutzim out to training farms to facilitate the move to aliyah, land for such farms needed to be acquired. Planning for such a move assumed that farming was a viable option; however, as of the end of August 1945, there was only one Zionist farm in the American zone of Germany, Kibbutz Buchenwald in Geringshof. By the end of October, the number of farms had increased to five and would reach nine by the end of the year and thirty-five by May 1946.[108] How did the Zionist plan for the creation of farms succeed in such a short time?

The Expansion of the Farming Project in Postwar Germany: Plans to Occupy Youths

The members of Kibbutz Buchenwald and Chafetz Chaim were able to secure land for their farms through the assistance of American Jewish chaplains and military officials who viewed their cause favorably. The development of a larger agricultural plan would require more formal approval and active collaboration from the administrative bodies in the U.S. occupied zone of Germany—Office of Military Government, United States (OMGUS); the UNRRA; and the JDC—in addition to the efforts of the Central Committee and the first Jewish Agency *shlichim* (emissaries sent from Palestine to assist in the organization of Zionist activity) to arrive in the zone. Although UNRRA support for the project was not based on an administrative policy of Zionist activism, it did share the Zionist belief in the functional value of agricultural training. The UNRRA was ultimately most concerned with creating a policy, together with the U.S. Army, that could effectively deal with the Jews in the DP camps and those arriving from Poland in increasing numbers in the fall of 1945. The model of the kibbutz hakhsharah functioned as a practical solution to the problems of overcrowding, black marketeering, and idleness feared by administration authorities. Following the publication of the Harrison Report and the visit of David Ben-Gurion to the American zone, young Jewish DPs interested in moving to agricultural training farms encountered administration officials increasingly receptive to the idea of agricultural training. Even more so, they encountered supportive administration authorities who believed that this was the option most desired by the young Jewish DP population.

The JDC, the UNRRA, and the Zionist Solution to the Problem of Overcrowding

Within the first few months after liberation, officials in the American zone were aware that large numbers of Jews would be arriving from the East. Many Jews had returned to Poland from Germany after liberation in order to search for family, but it seemed that many more were arriving with the increasing number of Bricha groups, never to return to Poland. The Bricha (literally "flight") was the semiorganized movement of Jewish departure from Poland that took shape shortly after the liberation of eastern Poland (for more on its organization and development in Poland, see chapter 2). Large numbers of Jews began to arrive in the American zone of Germany in groups organized by the Bricha toward the end of 1945. As Joseph Levine of the JDC reported to Eli Rock, field supervisor of the JDC, in late October 1945 the daily arrival of Jews from Poland would constitute a growing problem: "Jews are arriving daily from Poland who were never here but who somehow managed to survive elsewhere. On the other hand, many Jews are arriving who went to Poland immediately after liberation and who are returning either alone or with relatives."[109]

In his report to JDC staff on October 25, 1945, Rock reported that during the six weeks since Eisenhower implemented Harrison's suggestions "the situation of the Jews had improved considerably," with physical, housing, clothing, and food needs gradually being met.[110] Still, he argued, many problems remained that became "more important as the improvement in the physical needs of the people takes place." For the JDC, once the physical needs of the DPs had been tended to, the priority was to occupy them in activities that could turn DPs away from the counterproductive activities of black marketeering and brooding on the past, thereby helping them to avoid charges of laziness and uncleanliness.[111] Furthermore, Rock noted that in the six weeks since mid-September, some ten thousand Polish Jews had entered Bavaria following anti-Jewish outbreaks in Poland (including incidents in Krakow, Rzeszow, Kielce, Lublin, and Warsaw). Many of them were completely lacking in food and clothing, and the vast majority of them demanded immediate medical attention. The fact that without the legal status of DPs they were denied the requisite care and attention only served to exacerbate the situation. Rock suggested that once their legal status was rectified, "more facilities must be found at once in the area, where they can be placed. . . . In addition to a [new Jewish camp], farm and vocational projects must be found."[112]

Conditions in the DP camps did begin to deteriorate with the arrival of large numbers of Jews from Eastern Europe in the fall of 1945, meaning that the prospect of leaving Jewish DP camps for farms would continue to be an appealing one for Jewish youths arriving in groups from Poland. Reports from the JDC testified to problems created by the arrival of large numbers of Jews, indicating such difficulties as a lack of camps in the eastern U.S. zone to accommodate arrivals from Poland, many Jewish refugees wandering the streets of Munich without food, and an intense need for clothing and medicine for the new arrivals.[113] The American military authorities sought to create new camps to reduce overcrowding and improve sanitary conditions, as was the case in the creation of Föhrenwald as an alternative to Landsberg and Feldafing at the end of October. Nonetheless, as was often the case, as soon as one group was moved out of the camp, a new kibbutz from Poland appeared to fill its place, frequently refusing orders to move until it had secured permission from its own youth movement leadership.[114]

The American military government in Germany was therefore quite aware of the large numbers of Jews arriving in their occupation zone from the East. General Joseph T. McNarney (U.S. zone commander, Germany) was very sensitive to the criticism levied at his predecessor Eisenhower over treatment of Jewish refugees in the Harrison Report. Thus, in October 1945 McNarney proposed an interim plan for dealing with Jewish infiltrees to provide them with reasonable care until a decision was made regarding their treatment.[115] Still, U.S. Army authorities did not want to turn the American zone of occupation into a refuge for East European Jews. The American authorities were primarily concerned with avoiding the creation of a large unassimilable minority that would impose a heavy financial burden on the military government.[116] Such concerns notwithstanding, for the time being McNarney would allow the almost uninhibited entry of Jewish DPs into the American zone, potentially exacerbating the situation in the existing camps.

Members of the Nocham Kibbutz Hatkhiya hakhsharah dance a hora in the Föhrenwald DP camp, August 1945. (USHMM, courtesy of Alex Knobler)

Aid workers and officials of the military government took note of the
early success of hakhsharot by DPs liberated from concentration camps in
Germany. As Saul Elgart of the JDC noted after a visit to Kibbutz Buchenwald in October 1945, "This group, I believe, is a fine example of what occupational therapy and sound planning can do for our ex-concentration camp
inmates."[117] American Jewish chaplains such as Herman Dicker and Abraham Spiro sought to assist the Jewish DPs in acquiring property for farms.
Dicker reported in September 1945 on his as yet unsuccessful effort to
obtain the use of former Jewish property in Bamberg, "This [agricultural
training] could also serve as a preparation and education for all those who
are desirous of going to Palestine and who want to acquire skills needed in
that country."[118] Spiro had more success in securing farming land for Jewish
DPs despite initial opposition from American military officers. After failing
to obtain farmland through Colonel C. J. Reilly in September 1945, Spiro
secured a farm with the aid of the Bayreuth District Administration, and
in the middle of November Kibbutz Geulim (The Redeemed) opened at a

ceremony attended by Reilly and General Frank Keating (commanding general, 102nd division).[119]

David Ben-Gurion and the Jewish Agency in Germany

In addition to the support of the aid agencies and the military, the visit of David Ben-Gurion to the U.S. zone of Germany seems to have influenced the development of a unified agricultural policy for the Jewish DPs, as the Jewish Agency began to see the value of using the Jewish DPs as an instrument in the struggle to create the Jewish state. In October 1945 Ben-Gurion, in his capacity as head of the Jewish Agency, visited the DP camps in Germany, where the Jewish DPs welcomed him as "the personal embodiment of all their hopes for the future."[120] Major Irving Heymont, responsible for the administration of the Landsberg DP camp, described Ben-Gurion's visit to Landsberg on October 22, 1945, and the excitement that the visit engendered among the camp population. The camp was already abuzz because the day before the first election of the camp committee had occurred, with the Ichud Zionist slate of Samuel Gringauz emerging victorious. As Heymont related: "To add to the excitement of election day, the camp was visited by Mr. David Ben-Gurion—the head of the Zionist organization in Palestine. *To the people of the camp, he is God. It seems that he represents all of their hopes of getting to Palestine.* . . . I don't think that a visit by President Truman could cause as much excitement."[121]

In his visit to the DP camps, Ben-Gurion became convinced of the Zionist enthusiasm of the She'erit Hapletah, strongly influenced by its early organization and initiative in the creation of training farms. On the visit he also formed crucial connections with the American leadership of the U.S. zone. Ben-Gurion conveyed to Eisenhower the immense gratitude of the Jewish people "for the colossal work of rescue and rehabilitation performed on behalf of the Jewish survivors."[122] According to Judah Nadich, Eisenhower was rather impressed by his meeting with Ben-Gurion: "Later General Smith told me that, although the meeting between General Eisenhower and Ben-Gurion had been a brief one, General Eisenhower was very much taken by the Jewish leader and told General Smith that Ben Gurion had impressed him as a top notch statesman and a man of brilliant intellect."[123]

Mayor Irving Heymont, director of the Landsberg DP camp, converses with David Ben-Gurion during his visit to Landsberg. Also pictured is U.S. Army Chaplain Rabbi Abraham Klausner (left) and UNRRA Camp Director Abraham Glassgold (far right). (USHMM, courtesy of Sarah Huberfeld)

Through his meetings with Eisenhower and General Walter Bedell Smith, Ben-Gurion learned that U.S. Army authorities did not intend to stop Jewish infiltrees from Eastern Europe from entering the American zone; sensing an opportunity, he outlined a plan that would mobilize Jewish Agency resources in order to assist in the process of bringing as many Jews as possible into the occupation zones that were under U.S. command.[124] Furthermore, Ben-Gurion submitted a number of suggestions to Eisenhower and Bedell-Smith on how to improve the morale of the Jewish DPs: to concentrate the Jews in a separate region, either urban or rural; to allow the Jewish DPs to govern themselves, subject to the ultimate authority of the U.S. Army; to provide agricultural training through instructors who would come from Palestine; to confiscate Nazi farms; to provide vocational and paramilitary training to the DPs; and to establish weekly flights between the camps and

Palestine to bring in instructors and books.[125] Eisenhower was quite receptive to all of Ben-Gurion's suggestions except for his proposal to concentrate Jews in a separate region.[126]

Irving Heymont, in his capacity as American head of the largest DP camp, also discussed the overcrowding situation at Landsberg with Ben-Gurion "without glossing over anything," detailing his struggles to move DPs to Föhrenwald. Ben-Gurion conveyed to Heymont his abiding concern with securing agricultural work for the DPs. As described by Heymont,

> He [Ben-Gurion] was very much interested in hearing whether we had taken over any farms for people. I explained that we were powerless to do so unless we were given direct authority. He told me that Gen. Walter Bedell Smith [chief of staff to General Eisenhower] was keenly interested in that phase and that it probably will not be long before we do get the orders to take over some farms. *I hope he is right. Many of the people, particularly those in the kibbutzim, are anxious to get out on farms. It would also help to relieve the overcrowding and enable more people to lead a normal life.* There are plenty of farmers around here who were active Nazis.[127]

Like Ben-Gurion, Heymont also seemed to find the idea of transferring the farms of Nazis over to Jewish youths from the DP camps quite appealing. Not only could such a plan help to restore normality for the survivors, but seizing farms could also serve the double purpose of working as a form of punishment for former Nazis.

American officials also liked the idea of hakhsharot as a method of mental and physical therapy for wartime ills. As Nadich commented on the agricultural settlement at Geringshof, the survivors' involvement in physical labor lessened problems with discipline and morale. Furthermore, "not only was their work helping to fill their present requirements, particularly with regard to fresh vegetables, fruits, and grains, but they were successfully preparing for their future, the kind of future they greatly desired, life in a cooperative colony in Palestine."[128]

At the time of Ben-Gurion's visit to the DP camps in late October 1945, two hakhsharot had been created (as of the end of September), and three more farms were established in October. Thus, five agricultural training settlements were already in existence, with the early success and popularity of Kibbutz Buchenwald demonstrating to Ben-Gurion and his American hosts

the viability of an agricultural plan on a larger scale. The interaction between
Zionist youths and the authorities facilitated the expansion of the project,
while the increasing involvement of Zionist emissaries from Palestine in
Jewish DP affairs only served to confirm this course of action.

The views of Nadich, Heymont, Eisenhower, and others also reflected a
belief that agricultural training was what Jewish DP youths most desired.
Establishing training farms thus had numerous benefits: they were practical,
therapeutic, and in the best interests of the military authorities. Importantly,
the support for farms also demonstrated a view that such a program reflected
the will of the Jewish DP youths who would populate the hakhsharot.

The Acquisition of Land for Zionist Farms

By early October 1945 the UNRRA and the JDC had already been actively
involved in the acquisition of German property for farms.[129] In order to
obtain land on behalf of the DPs, the UNRRA had to go through the U.S.
Army, the occupying power and chief arbiter over usage of recently occupied
land. Despite support for the farms in principle, a number of factors complicated the acquisition of land, including army needs and usage for the
German population, especially orphans and the elderly. DPs did occasion-
ally secure land on their own, without going through official channels. Many
of these farms were the property of Germans, some having been the estates
of the Nazi Party elite (including the farms of Hermann Göring and Julius
Streicher). At times the Germans who had lived on the farms before occupation remained there after a kibbutz had moved in, perhaps as much as 20
percent of the time.[130] But the UNRRA's difficulties in gaining farmland
for Jewish DPs also reveal the balancing act which the U.S. Army as occupying power was forced to perform. In certain cases, property that seemed
like an ideal location for a hakhsharah was deemed inappropriate by American authorities because it could be better used for German invalids and
refugees or was reserved for use by the Army in order to house troops.[131]

In addition to coordinating between the UNRRA and the U.S. Army,
JDC officials acting on behalf of DPs also sought to secure the assistance
of Bavarian ministry officials.[132] This was because at times, ownership of
farms was held by the Bavarian Ministry of Agriculture, as in the case of

the 240-acre farm at Schönbrunn, near Landshut (seventy kilometers north of Munich), that had been a farm school up until May 1945 under state ownership.[133]

For the UNRRA to acquire land for the DP farms, it was necessary to convince the U.S. Army of the desirability of such projects. Not only did the UNRRA have to demonstrate that land was appropriate for young Jewish farmers, it also had to convince the army that farms would not have a disruptive impact on the German economy. Jack Whiting, UNRRA zone director, in effect became a spokesperson for the merit of these hakhsharot, arguing to military officials that "it is, in my opinion, a fact that the use of the properties by the Jewish displaced persons would increase the productivity and actually contribute more to the local German economy than present usage does."[134] Furthermore, Whiting tried to convince American officials to use farms in response to the unimpeded Jewish infiltration from the East. As in the confidential request that he submitted to the U.S. 3rd Army, Whiting argued that the farm school at Schönbrunn, to be used as a "farm training school for young Jewish DPs," could be helpful to "relieve overcrowding at Feldafing, Landsberg, and Wolfratshausen."[135]

In many cases, officers in the U.S. Army occupation force shared this positive view of agricultural training. It seems that those who were most directly responsible for administration of the Jewish DPs consistently advocated such positions, while their superiors in the American military had to be concerned with balancing more pressing issues, namely the reconstruction of the German economy.[136] In his capacity as head of the Landsberg DP camp, Heymont constantly strove to reduce the overcrowding that plagued the camp, also seeing the training farms as a useful tool at his disposal. In his October 23, 1945, letter written the day after Ben-Gurion's visit to the camp and their discussion on the possibility of securing farms for DPs, he reported on his visit to a former Nazi school for girls at Greifenberg with the assistant division commander, General Onslow S. Rolfe. As Heymont suggested, the school could become a "model community" for kibbutz youth, a use preferable to serving the needs of the German population. Although the local military government wanted to use it for German refugees from Austria, Heymont related, "when he saw the place, Gen. Rolfe agreed that it is too good to use for German refugees. . . . It is a wonderful place and should give the kibbutz people a good opportunity to live their collective life. I hope we get it, even though it will bring up problems of supply and administration of a camp annex."[137]

The agricultural training farms were not intended to be self-sufficient communities; their value would be primarily in training young charges for life in Israel and removing them from the demoralizing atmosphere of the DP camps. The hakhsharot were thus dependent on support from the JDC, the UNRRA, and the Central Committee to remain viable. In the case of Kibbutz Buchenwald at Geringshof, the JDC gave them help in the form of money and counsel and represented them in various dealings which they had to have with the UNRRA and the military government. The late date in the agricultural year with which the kibbutz was founded made it impossible for the kibbutz to perform a full harvest, so the JDC provided them with a supplementary ration of food, which could carry them over for the year. Likewise, the JDC was asked to subsidize the budgetary needs of the kibbutz at Gersfeld (advancing it three thousand marks), which it would do following receipt of a budget. The case was similar at Greifenberg.[138]

The creation of agricultural training farms by the Jewish DPs could also be presented as one of the success stories of the Jewish survivors liberated from concentration camps only six months earlier. American authorities were correct in interpreting such projects as acts of punishment and symbolic revenge, for this was how the DPs populating the farms also interpreted their presence there. Jewish DP youths on Kibbutz Nili, once Julius Streicher's farm, described with pride the accomplishments that farming in Germany represented:

> Not long ago, Pleikhershof was the estate and seat of one of Hitler's highest associates, the editor of the sadly famous "Stürmer," Julius Streicher. In the office where for many years the great Jew-hater sat and wrote his bloodthirsty anti-Jewish articles . . . , where Streicher wrote to the German people, "The Jews are our misfortune," can be found today the secretariat of an agricultural pioneering school, of Jewish boys and girls, coming from all corners of Europe, learning to work the land, agriculture, cattle-herding, etc.—that which is in the first line necessary in the building up of "Erec-Jisroel." This is one of the greatest Jewish satisfactions, which we can have . . . in Streicher's writing room, and in the whole palace, is to be able to see Hebrew writings and slogans, like "Am Jsroel chaj" [*the people of Israel lives*], "Necach Jsroel loj

jeszaker" [*the strength of Israel will not lie; in initials NILI*], so have we named our new kibbutz, the first agricultural school in Bavaria.[139]

Baruch Cheta, the first leader of the kibbutz, thus reported with satisfaction in the pages of Landsberg's wide circulation newspaper that members of the new kibbutz were making use of Streicher by using the "modern Jewish Haman's" own personal land to prepare themselves for life in the Jewish state. Kibbutz Nili had been appropriated for Jewish DPs by the American army, which ordered the evacuation of Russian and Ukrainian DPs living on the farm in October and November 1945.[140] Work began each day at 4:00 a.m. with the milking of the cows, and guards patrolled the farm "preparing for the reality of Erec Jsroel." In addition, "cultural work" had already begun with Hebrew lessons; Cheta also reported that members had learned by heart the Hebrew words for "cow" and "horse" as well as those for agricultural tools and other essential items of farm labor. The work was difficult, but it was done with humor, energy, and the singing of Hebrew "songs of building and struggle."[141] Readers of the *Landsberger Lager Cajtung* could read that with the creation of Kibbutz Nili in Pleikhershof, "the white and blue flag flies over Streicher's farm." There could be no mistaking the symbolic value of this gesture by a kibbutz named Nili, based on the acronym of the initial letters of the Hebrew verse "Netzach Yisrael Lo Yeshakker" ("the Strength of Israel will not lie"; I Samuel 15:29). The young farmers symbolically exacted their revenge on the "great Jew-hater," affirming the eternal presence of the Jewish people on the appropriated Nazi land.

The kibbutz acquired at Greifenberg as an annex of Landsberg also enjoyed increasing success.[142] The kibbutz was established on a former SS rest camp approximately fifteen kilometers from Landsberg and occupied a large building with the capacity for 250 residents. In a JDC report on the kibbutz from January 1946, M. J. Joslow suggested that the kibbutz had ideal conditions to make it a model kibbutz. "Because the group is newly organized, opportunity is afforded to inaugurate a program without first having to undo previous errors. The age group lends itself to specific training." Classes in Hebrew and lectures in Zionism were conducted at the kibbutz, and as an annex of Landsberg, its educational program was under the supervision of Jacob Olejski. Joslow was enthusiastic about using the setting for educational purposes "to make up for time lost in the concentration camps," vocational

Carrying rakes and hoes, members of Kibbutz Nili pass through the entrance arch
on their way to the fields. Painted on the arch are the Hebrew words for "welcome."
(USHMM, courtesy of Ruchana Medine White)

instruction, and even physical education in the large gymnasium at the
camp. As Heymont had suggested, Greifenberg represented an ideal place to
allow Jewish youths to live a collective life away from the large DP camps.

Agricultural instruction would also be vital to making the farms viable,
and UNRRA and JDC officials were quite aware in late October 1945 that
"there [is] only a small number of agricultural trainers and teachers at disposal so that instructors have to be sent by the Jewish Agency."[143] The arrival
of Jewish Agency agronomists in early 1946 would be a direct outgrowth of
this need. The period between late September and January 1946 was crucial
in expanding the number of farms in the American zone (thirteen farms with
1,345 residents by January 1946).[144]

Still, farming was not necessarily the immediate goal in the creation of
kibbutzim away from the DP camps. More so, such sites afforded young
DPs the opportunity to make productive use of their time by engaging in

informal Zionist education, language instruction, socialization, and vocational training. The farms were also used by the growing Zionist youth movement Nocham as centers for education and instruction of youths organized in kibbutzim within the DP camps who could visit the farms from time to time.

Nocham continued to build on its early success in attracting youth movement members and held its first two-week seminar at the kibbutz in Greifenberg on January 21, 1946. There fifty-eight young leaders attended lectures on the history of Zionism, the geography of Palestine, the problems of Zionist diplomacy, and other topics offered by Jewish Brigade soldiers and members of the UZO.[145] The participants who attended the first seminar heard Yitzhak Ratner of the UZO explain what he believed was the rationale for the creation of Nocham. Nocham had to exist to honor those who had died at the hands of the Nazis. "This movement was created on a bloody backdrop. The idea of Nocham was created in the underground, in the ghettos, and in the concentration camps. . . . The movement makes its way by the bonfires of Treblinka and in accord with the needs for the building of the people and of the land."[146]

The leadership of the UZO and those on the Central Committee who were active in creating a framework for the successful functioning of Nocham as the United Zionist youth movement in the DP camps understood the imperative to organize youths in a Zionist manner as a product of two complementary drives. One was to honor the deaths of the Jewish victims of the Holocaust by ensuring the future of the Jewish people through the building of a Jewish state in Palestine. The second imperative of productivization, however, supported the development of kibbutzim in the DP camps and proved to be most appealing to Jewish youths after the war.

At its first seminar for madrichim in January 1946 Yitzhak Ratner, who had undertaken the more formal organization of Zionist youths beginning in June 1945, could declare with satisfaction that although "Nocham was the fruit of a terrible situation . . . that which passed on these people united them and forged their path" in a united youth movement.[147] While unity among the surviving Zionists in Germany was highly esteemed, the arrival of increasing numbers of youths already organized in the kibbutzim of various other Zionist youth movements would change the situation in Germany dramatically.

Conclusion

The situation in the Jewish DP camps had improved significantly by the end of 1945. Still, outside observers noted continuing concern over DP morale, overcrowding, and disillusionment with the lack of aid from the outside world.[148] Such concerns notwithstanding, leaders of the She'erit Hapletah had reason to be enthusiastic about the prospect of preparing young immigrants for life in Palestine, particularly after Harrison's positive recommendations to President Truman.

In the early period following liberation, Zionist youths and prewar activists in Zionist movements had undertaken the organization of the sizable cohort of youths that had survived the war and remained in the DP camps of Germany.[149] While the first organization among the DPs took place on a local ad hoc level, the groups of Jewish youths and former youth movement leaders came together with survivors in other camps. The position adopted by Zionist youth movement leaders who struggled against Bundists and communists, the subsequent departure of these political opponents for Poland, and the demographic preponderance of youths among the surviving Jews placed these leaders in an ideal position to fill the power vacuum that existed among the Jewish DPs after liberation. The process of self-selection that occurred among those who remained in Germany meant that much of the young Jewish DP population would be favorably inclined to the social framework of the kibbutz. In the creation of the Central Committee of Liberated Jews and the UZO, these survivors were uniquely positioned to take advantage of the demographic situation that existed in postwar Germany, utilizing their prewar and wartime experience in political organization. They succeeded in monopolizing the question of youth, turning the future of young survivors into a political issue whose resolution would define the future of the She'erit Hapletah as a whole. Of equal importance, the early leaders of the Jewish DPs and the models presented by Zionist youths in Kibbutz Buchenwald convinced outside agencies and the DP population as well that the Central Committee, the UZO, Nocham, and the other Zionist youth movements had a viable plan for occupying the young survivors productively in a manner that could facilitate their eventual departure from Germany. The support of administration authorities and aid agencies would also be crucial in demonstrating the ability of the Central Committee and the UZO to provide for the needs of their constituents. Likewise, the American administrators came to believe that the Zionist option was the choice most desired by the younger segment of the Jewish DP population. The options available to young survivors to occupy their time while living in the DP camps thus increasingly took on a Zionist character. The choice to join kibbutzim or to participate in vocational courses did not necessarily indicate a predisposition to Zionism per se on the part of the youths; however, the availability of such a productive use of time at all could be highly desirable.

What then was the appeal of the Zionist option for those youths who chose to join these groups? The fact that Zionist leaders were well positioned to provide for the sizable contingent of Jewish youths did not mean that youths joined kibbutzim by default. The nature of life in the kibbutz itself, the productive options that it provided for Jewish youths after the war, and the future that it represented seemed to play a large role in the decision to join. However, this was a choice made by the youths who would compose the kibbutzim, not the movement leaders who organized them, and to truly answer this question it is necessary to approach the problem from the perspective of the kibbutz members themselves.

2
"The Way of All Jewish Youth"?
Young Survivors and Kibbutzim
in Postwar Poland

On November 12, 1945, 110 Jewish young people from Poland organized in two groups arrived in the Landsberg camp of displaced persons (DPs) outside Munich. After two weeks in transit from Poland, traveling by train using forged documents that disguised them as Greeks, the youths managed to sneak into Landsberg. Only four months earlier, most of the young survivors in the two groups were orphans living alone in Poland, uncertain of what their future would hold. Now they had taken their first step on the journey that they hoped would end in their ultimate arrival in Palestine.

By the time these young people entered Landsberg, two types of kibbutzim had developed in the DP camps. The first groups were created by survivors of concentration camps in Germany who had formed kibbutzim such as Kibbutz Buchenwald, Kibbutz Hafetz Hayyim, and Kibbutz Nili in the first weeks and months following liberation. The second were from kibbutzim that had been established earlier in Poland and then were transplanted to the DP camps. These youths had joined groups established by the Zionist youth movements in liberated Poland, which had set up kibbutzim in order to provide for the needs of Polish Jewish survivor youths. These kibbutzim were transported clandestinely at intervals to DP camps as part of an operation called the Bricha, a Zionist-operated movement aimed at bringing Jewish Holocaust survivors out of Eastern Europe and into Palestine. Over the course of 1945 and even more so in 1946, a sizable proportion of the DP population was made up of youths arriving in kibbutzim of the Bricha from Poland.[1] In the first six months after liberation, the general and Zionist leadership of the DPs began to formulate a plan to accommodate the large number of youths who had survived in Germany and the increasing number of youths who began to arrive in the Bricha kibbutzim from Poland. Unlike their counterparts in Germany, many of these Polish youths had already had their first encounters with the Zionist framework of the kibbutz in Poland and were thus, to a greater extent, part of a cohesive group upon their arrival in Germany. Nonetheless, their experience of Zionism was also a work in progress that had begun to be shaped first in Poland.

The unified framework that characterized Nocham in late 1945 fell apart with the arrival of kibbutz groups from Poland that were already identified with such groups as Hashomer Hatzair, Dror, and Hanoar Hatzioni. Only those kibbutzim affiliated with Gordoniah continued to function under Nocham's umbrella.[2] Although the framework created in the immediate postwar period by the Central Committee and the United Zionist Organization would be vital to the continued successful functioning of the kibbutzim in Germany, the Polish youths represented a distinct category in DP society, independent from the other survivors from the moment of their arrival in Germany. Most works that have discussed youths and kibbutzim in postwar Germany have failed to account for the crucial distinctions that existed between those groups that were composed of former concentration camp inmates in Germany and those kibbutzim formed by Zionist youth movements in Poland, which were joined by youths who had survived from camps, forests, hiding places, the Soviet Union, and elsewhere. In order to understand the dissolution of the unified framework created in Germany in 1945 and the origins and appeal of Zionism for many of the youths who joined kibbutzim after the war, however, it is essential to study the organization of these kibbutzim in Poland before the youths arrived in Germany. Far from joining for ideological reasons, most youths chose to become part of kibbutz groups for their practical and material benefits.

For the most part, descriptions of the Bricha and the postwar organization of the Zionist youth movements in Poland have either been written by former participants in the Bricha movement or based on sources that convey the perspective of the organizers or emissaries from Palestine.[3] While these works have detailed the efforts of those survivors who organized the Bricha or the Zionist emissaries who helped to facilitate their departure from Europe, there has been little effort to tell this story from the perspective of the youths who joined the kibbutzim. This focus also helps to explain how the Bricha movement did in fact succeed in recruiting so many young survivors to join their networks of departure from Poland.

The two Hashomer Hatzair kibbutzim described above united after their arrival in Landsberg and came to take the name Kibbutz Lochamei HeGetaot al shem Tosia Altman (Ghetto Fighters Kibbutz, named after Tosia Altman; hereafter Kibbutz Tosia Altman). The kibbutz members wrote a collective diary detailing the history of the kibbutz, providing an excellent opportunity to study its experience from within. Forty years after the completion of the diary, it was translated from the original Yiddish into Hebrew by surviving members of the kibbutz.[4] The two madrichim of the kibbutz, Miriam and Baruch Wind (Yechieli) who served as the guides, teachers, and spiritual leaders of the kibbutz, had returned to Poland after spending the war in the Soviet Union. In Poland they organized separate kibbutzim in Sosnowiec and Bytom before departing for Germany. After spending fourteen months in the American zone, eight of which they spent farming the soil of Germany, the kibbutz left for Palestine in early 1947. They arrived there only in the spring of 1948 following a year-long internment in Cyprus.

For the Jewish youths who joined kibbutzim in Poland such as Kibbutz Tosia Altman, liberation brought not only freedom but also the need to face the future. Many young survivors desperately sought companionship and a way to make up for the six years they had lost during the war. Still, those who joined kibbutzim after the war were generally not typical of the prewar Zionist elite among Jewish youths who before the war had made their way through the ranks of the movement to the final stages before aliyah to Palestine.[5] After the war, these kibbutzim came to be populated by young Jewish survivors who chose to join the kibbutz for other reasons. Why did these survivors end up in the kibbutz of a Zionist youth movement after the war dedicated to collectivism, communal living, and a socialist-Zionist ethic? What was the appeal of Zionism for them and how might this experience have changed over the course of their time in the kibbutz? To answer these questions, it is necessary to understand what options were available to Jewish youths after the war in Poland.

The Postwar Organization of Polish Jewry

Starting in the summer of 1944, the Red Army began to liberate eastern portions of Poland and the Baltic States from Nazi occupation; Warsaw would not be liberated until January 1945. As individual Jews began to emerge from their hiding places or from the Nazi camps, they tried to organize the remnants of the destroyed Jewish community. The city of Lublin in southeastern Poland became one of the first centers for Jewish political reorganization following its liberation on July 23, 1944.[6] As recounted in *Dos Bukh fun Lublin* (The Lublin Memorial Book), Jewish survivors, only recently liberated from Nazi camps, came to Lublin searching for both physical and moral support:

> Each day a liberated Jew in a terrible condition would come to Lublin: physically and morally broken through the painful years. . . . The former "Peretzhoyz" on Czwartek St. slowly became filled with the wretched. These were Jews from all the dispersed communities (*tfutzes*) of Europe: from Hungary, Romania, Czechoslovakia, and other countries, where the German hangmen went savagely mad. . . . Among these Jews were also former residents of Lublin. These were only individuals, a small number. All in all there were only in Lublin a few hundred souls of the 43,000 Jews who lived in the Lublin before the war.[7]

Liberated Jews first searched for family and friends looking for news of who had survived and how most had perished. From the beginning, it was altogether unclear what sort of Jewish population existed in the wake of the war in Poland.[8] Reports emerging from Lublin by January 1945 did not paint a promising portrait of the Jewish situation. It was estimated that in the five to six months since the liberation of the eastern sections of Poland, some seven thousand Jews had been registered in the liberated territories, two-thirds of them freed by Russian troops who liberated death and concentration camps. Twenty-five hundred survivors had been found in the Lublin area. The surviving population was overwhelmingly male (75 percent), and the majority of men and women were between the ages of eighteen and forty-five. A report sent to the Jewish Agency described the "new ghettos" that were being created for the Jews in Lublin and Bialystok. Reports described hundreds of Jews—dirty, sleeping on the floor, and crammed thirty to forty to a room—living in "inhuman conditions" in shelters such as the Peretz-hoyz in Lublin. The Jewish populations continued to be ravaged by disease and malnutrition, and the public kitchens could not provide sufficient food to satisfy the minimum needs of the hungry and the needy. Jews had considerable difficulties regaining possession of lost property, both individually and communally. While many Jewish orphans were wandering the streets of Lublin, the Jewish orphanage there continued to be occupied by Polish institutions. The surviving Jewish population faced continuing violence and hostility on the part of the local population, with Jews facing both physical and verbal attacks as well as vandalism to their homes and shops.[9]

While a number of the survivors were young orphans who had survived the war only to emerge alone, it is unclear what percentage of the Jewish public after the war was under the age of twenty. Many of the statistics kept by local Jewish committees organized after the war listed those between the ages of eighteen and forty-five as adults; anyone under the age of eighteen was listed as a child. Still, based on a number of sources, the historian David Engel estimates that some 10–12 percent of the Jewish population in Poland in 1945 was between the ages of fifteen and twenty.[10]

The first recourse for many Jewish youths in Poland after the war was to turn to the local Jewish committees that had been formed seeking answers to their most pressing needs, including food, shelter, health, and security, before they could turn to the larger questions of how and where to continue their lives. Beginning in the summer of 1944 in eastern Poland, Jewish survivors rapidly organized a system of communal and political organizations.[11] The new communist-dominated government allowed a number of Jewish political parties and organizations to operate freely. Almost all prewar parties were reconstructed and legally recognized by the Polish government, including the Bund (and its youth organization, Tsukunft); Marxist Zionist parties such as Left Poalei Zion (youth group: Borochov Youth) and youth movements such as Hashomer Hatzair; non-Marxist socialist and bourgeois Zionist groups such as Poalei Zion Right (also known as Poalei Zion

Zionist Socialists), Dror, Ichud, and Hitachdut; and the religious Zionist Mizrachi. Of the major prewar parties, only the ultraorthodox Agudos Yisroel and right-wing Revisionist Zionists were not officially recognized.[12] As many of the liberated Jews began to turn to the Jewish committees for assistance, the ability of vying political groups to provide for survivors would go a long way toward securing a crucial base for political support and success. Bundist, communist, and Zionist groups jostled for control of the Jewish committees in liberated cities, struggling to secure access to resources provided for the Jewish community of survivors.[13] From an early point in time, there was a great deal of competition among the Jewish political groups for control of the "Jewish street."[14]

The first convention of the Central Committee of Polish Jews (CKZP), headed by Emil Sommerstein, a prewar Zionist activist and Zionist deputy to the Sejm, was held on November 29, 1944, in Lublin.[15] From the outset, although dominated by a Zionist majority, the CKZP leadership consisted of people belonging to prewar political parties or underground organizations set up during the war, including communists and Bundists, as well as members of the Jewish Fighting Organization and former partisans.[16]

The Jewish political leaders who struggled for predominance on the local committees recognized the importance of addressing the constituency of youths in liberated Poland, presenting alternative visions for the future. While the Zionists rejected any potential for a viable future in Poland and emphasized emigration, the Bund charged the Zionists with being indifferent to the needs of the Jewish community, alleging that the Zionists manipulated the desperation of the Jewish refugees for their own ends.[17] The Bund was committed to fighting together with the Polish working class in Poland's postwar redevelopment and accused Zionist leaders of attempting to create a state of panic in order to encourage emigration. The Bund also tried to appeal to Jews in DP camps in Germany to return to Poland in order to help in rebuilding the country. For Jewish youths in Poland, the Bund attempted to work within the framework of the Jewish committees, children's homes, and schools, although their influence and identification with such social service institutions was less than that of the other political parties.[18] In 1945 the CKZP established children's homes, although less than 20 percent of the total number of Jewish children were housed in them; most of the Jewish children who survived did so with their families.[19]

Among Zionists, closer contact with the younger Jewish public was also facilitated through the work of youth movement activists on local committees, in children's homes, and in soup kitchens.[20] The Bundists and communists were quite conscious of the so-called Zionist offensive and feared the influence of the Zionist groups in the children's homes, alleging a Zionist campaign of removing children from the homes for movement in the Bricha.[21] And indeed, Bundist charges of an organized Zionist campaign to redeem Jewish youths were not without basis. One of the primary forces in the Zionist effort to redeem Jewish children was the Koordinacja HaTzionit Legeulat Yeladim (Zionist Coordination for Redemption of Children), which was established at the beginning of 1946.[22]

For the political parties vying for control of the committees, Jewish youths formed a vital constituency not only because of the number of youths who had survived but also because of their future potential to these political movements. For the Jewish youths who turned to the committees, the ideological debates over the Jewish future were largely insignificant in garnering political support. Support would be determined by the ability of political groups to provide for the basic needs of survivors. Nonetheless, the Zionist youth movements seemed to emerge from the war in a better position than other Jewish parties to meet the needs of Jewish youths in Poland.

The kibbutzim of the Zionist youth movements became a viable option for many among the Jewish youths for two reasons: Zionist youth movements became interested in organizing the greater Jewish public, and Jewish youths saw them as most capable of satisfying their needs from among the choices available to them in postwar Poland.

The Wartime Transition of Zionist Youth Movements into Leaders of the Jewish Public

Whereas in many cities immediately prior to the war Zionist groups occupied at best a secondary status behind the Bund and Agudos Yisroel (the political party organized to represent the interests of Polish Jewry's sizable religious community), almost immediately following liberation Zionist youth movements emerged as a central pillar of the surviving Jewish community.[23] This was not a sudden postwar development; throughout the course of the war, members of Zionist youth movements had embraced leadership positions in ghetto resistance and partisan fighting organizations.[24] The performance of political groups during the war years would play a crucial role in their positioning immediately following liberation.

At the beginning of the war most of the official Polish Jewish leadership either fled Warsaw and the other major cities of Poland for the Soviet Union or abroad or were captured, imprisoned, and executed. Many prominent political leaders from across the Jewish political spectrum left Poland with the initiation of German hostilities.[25] Some of those leaders who did stay behind during the war were forced to participate in the Judenrat (Jewish Council) of their cities and towns during the war. After the start of the war, however, a number of Zionist youth leaders who had managed to flee to the east made the decision to return to occupied Poland. This was the case among the youth movement leadership of Warsaw, many of whom had fled to Vilna in order to escape the Nazi invasion in September 1939. Once the youth movements managed to reorganize in Vilna, leaders of Hashomer Hatzair, Dror, and He-Halutz such as Mordechai Anilewicz, Zivia Lubetkin, Yitzhak Zuckerman, Yosef Kaplan, Frumka Plotnicka, Tosia Altman, and Samuel Breslaw elected to return to Poland voluntarily after several months spent in Russia and Lithuania.[26] The youth movement leaders who returned to Warsaw were motivated by a sense of responsibility as local leaders, not only to their young *chanichim* (movement members) but also to the Jewish community as a whole.[27]

This is not to suggest that the success of the Zionist youth movements in securing leadership roles was by default, simply through filling the leadership vacuum. Other leaders remained behind, and yet the youth movements succeeded in rising to prominence on the "Jewish street" during and after the war.[28] Under the occupation, organized Zionist youths worked to understand better the needs of a wider Jewish public. Whereas before the war their activities had been focused on the elite among Jewish youths training for aliyah to Palestine (hagshamah and hakhsharah), during the war their sense of responsibility began to expand. Strikingly, youth movements increased educational activity during the occupation and established kibbutzim in the ghettos.[29] The expansion of youth movement activities during the war was also accompanied by the ability of the youth movements to communicate between ghettos and thus maintain better organization of the movements than other political groups while also publishing an underground press.[30] Tosia Altman, for example, spent the first half of 1940 traveling to the various Hashomer Hatzair branches in the Generalgouvernement and Galicia to assist in organizing the movement.[31]

These youth movement leaders in turn became the leaders of the ghetto resistance.[32] The war also forced the Zionist youth movements to take the initiative in determining political and social action underground. Before the war, the youth movements were largely dependent on shlichim from Palestine in determining policy formation. During the war, however, largely cut off from the outside world and far more independent and autonomous than before, the youth movements maintained their organizations while the Jewish political parties collapsed, and the youth movements functioned as a source of information from the outside world, emerging as an alternative leadership organization to the Judenrat.[33] The youth movement leaders, because they were indeed younger than the other political leaders, were not confronted with the impossibly difficult task of serving on the Judenrat. Nonetheless, the youth movements quickly became highly critical of the Judenrat and the Jewish police, often making them the first targets of both their political and physical attacks in the ghetto underground.[34] In many cases, the youth movements were often the first to assess the early Jewish massacres as part of a comprehensive program and were thus instrumental in the early organization of armed resistance.[35] The mobility of the youth movement leadership also enabled them to publicize the first news of atrocities in Lithuania, as was the case in Tosia Altman's return from Vilna to Warsaw in late 1941. Even so, after the war many in the youth movements were highly critical of themselves for neither recognizing the danger nor organizing resistance earlier. Notwithstanding such self-criticism, this wartime leadership placed the youth movements in an excellent position to assume a leadership position following the war, both in their own eyes and in the eyes of other survivors.[36]

The Postwar Organization of the Youth Movement and Bricha

During the war, some youth movement leaders discussed their visions for the postwar Jewish world. Upon liberation in the Rudnicki forests of Lithuania,

Abba Kovner, Vitka Kempner, and Ruzhka Korczak (wartime leaders of the Vilna resistance) began to envision collecting the remaining survivors and "pav[ing] a way to Palestine as soon as possible."[37] As Kovner relates, the members of the youth movements were not only interested in effecting their own departure from Europe but also saw it as their responsibility to forge a path that would allow all of the She'erit Hapletah to leave the land of the catastrophe and depart for Palestine.[38]

Lublin developed as an early center of postwar Jewish organization, and youth movement members who had spent the war in partisan groups, ghettos, and in hiding as well as those so-called Asiatics returning from Central Asia and the Soviet Union met there in January 1945 to discuss the future.[39] There was a general consensus on the need for the Zionist solution by this budding leadership, and agreement was reached on the official formation of a Bricha movement, with a coordinating committee led by Mordechai Rosman, Nisan Resnik, and Stefan Grajek.[40] While the members of this initial group in Lublin were split over the need for immediate or gradual departure, those who remained in Lublin and later in Warsaw focused their efforts on the organization of the Jewish public for departure from Poland. Kovner argued for immediate departure, suggesting that any effort to reestablish Jewish institutions on the accursed European soil would be a betrayal of the Jewish dead: "It strikes us as inappropriate that while this whole cemetery is still new and fresh, institutions are being set up as though nothing had happened. . . . The group I head is gripped by two ideas that are inherently different. Flight and revenge—not flight for ourselves, but as a path for She'erit Hapletah, not to leave Jews in the European graveyard."[41] Zuckerman agreed with Kovner over the need for departure from Poland but rejected immediate departure and Kovner's ideas for revenge. Instead, Zuckerman argued that youth movement activists could not desert the Jewish public and needed to remain behind in order to assist in organization. Kovner left with a group in March 1945; Zuckerman and Lubetkin stayed behind to begin organizing what was left of the Jewish public.

Youth movement leaders pointed to their roles as wartime leaders of Polish Jewry as justification for the role in leading the Jewish community after the war.[42] As Zuckerman suggested, the leadership role of He-Halutz in the resistance left them in the best position to lead Jewish youths in Poland following the war: "In sum, did He-Halutz disappoint? Absolutely not! And

Abba Kovner, leader of the United Partisans' Organization, FPO (*Fareynegte Partizaner Oranizatsye*), in wartime Vilna and one of the early organizers of the postwar *Bricha* movement. (USHMM, courtesy of Vika Kempner Kovner)

the conclusion is that no other force has the power to exalt and raise the youth except He-Halutz. Instead of fading, we should reinforce its strength. The way of He-Halutz is the way of all Jewish youth. We want a working nation and a working youth; that is our lesson and our ambition." For Zuckerman, He-Halutz was no longer the province of only the "elite" youths in the Jewish community; now, "the way of He-Halutz [was] the way of all Jewish youth."[43]

Zuckerman realized the need to work on the ground, organize kibbutzim, and provide aid, thus tending to the needs of the Jewish population on an immediate level and not just on an ideological basis. This choice to focus on the majority of Jewish youths and not just the elite would entail a significant shift in the approach of Zionist youth movements after the war, not only in the numbers who joined the movement but also in the perceived ideological quality of the new membership.

Wartime experience was not the only factor, or necessarily the primary one, ensuring the leadership of the Zionist youth movements after the war, especially since the Zionists were not the only ones to participate in the resistance. The youth movement leadership may have believed itself to be in the ideal position to organize the Jewish remnants in Poland, but the appeal of the Zionist option would be based on the postwar needs of the survivors. During the course of the war the youth movements transformed themselves from elitist movements focused on a small slice of the population into community leaders enlisted in the task of tending to communal destiny and attending to the needs of the larger community. Instead of merely responding to the needs of the community, however, the youth movements would also work to shape the direction of communal behavior in the future.[44] Nonetheless, the first few months of 1945 did not see a mass enlisting in the Bricha among the Jewish public; for the most part, survivors were far more concerned with rebuilding their daily lives.[45] Thus, the appeal of the youth movements would have to lie not only in the promise of departure but also in the ability to address daily needs on the most basic level. This they managed to do through participation on Jewish committees, thereby securing access to vital resources and through the creation and support of kibbutzim. Jewish youths and the Zionist youth movements would enter into a mutually beneficial relationship, the youths providing the movement with a critical manpower reserve and the movement providing an alternative living situation for the youths in the form of the kibbutz. In the process, the elitist nature of the Zionist youth movements would be transformed through the membership of the survivor youths who would constitute the core of the postwar movement in Europe.

The Organization of the First Kibbutzim in Postwar Poland

The first group of Jewish youths to officially form a kibbutz in postwar Poland did so in Warsaw in March 1945. A group of young survivors of the Hasag concentration camp joined together in the city of Częstochowa where they were attending a Polish school. Zuckerman stumbled upon the group and suggested to them that they form a kibbutz in Warsaw. As he recalled the initial encounter in his memoirs:

The first children were discovered by chance. . . . The same thing happened to me in Częstochowa. In the place I entered, I saw two adjoining rooms with a

very small transom between them. I asked who was there and was told it was
Jewish children, a group of Jewish sixteen-year-olds. I was curious, I went in,
and asked where they were from. They told me they had been in hiding for a
long time. The children had been in Camp Hasag and were now going to a
Polish school. "What do you live on?" I asked them. And they said: "We steal!"
They stole coal and bread. . . . They were all orphans. Their tale made a great
impression on me. . . . We started talking. I told them about Eretz Israel, about
the youths. I said they didn't have a future here as Jews, since they were going
to Polish school. I told them we were a Halutz movement, forming kibbutzim; and if they wanted we would gladly take them. I gave them my address
in Warsaw: Poznanska 39. Later, I found other Jewish youths and got in
touch with the older fighters I found in Częstochowa. They could easily find
me in Warsaw through the Central Committee of the Jews in Poland. . . . I
returned to Warsaw. One day a delegation of those young people showed up.
They decided to form a kibbutz. That was a great joy for us. That group was
the basis for the first kibbutz formed in the courtyard.[46]

The youths living in the apartment had thus already made the choice to
band together in order to make it in postwar Poland. Zuckerman presented
them with an option that would allow them to remain together as a communal group and perhaps provide a more promising future (outside of
Poland). In March 1945, the sixteen survivors from the Częstochowa group
formed a He-Halutz *maon* (hostel) in Warsaw.[47]

In accordance with the effort to organize willing segments of the Jewish
public for departure, the Hashomer Hatzair youth movement, in unison
with Dror, began to organize kibbutzim in a number of cities in Poland in
the spring and summer of 1945, including Warsaw, Łódź, Sosnowiec, Bytom,
and Kraków.[48] During the summer of 1945, the movement also opened
kibbutzim in Będzin, Częstochowa, Gliwice, and Katowice. The political
debate among the various Zionist movements did not eliminate the potential for cooperation among various movements, with Left Poalei Zion, Poalei
Zion Right, Dror, and Hashomer Hatzair joining together in June 1945 to
form the League for Labor Palestine.[49] In addition to the movements joined
together in the league were the General Zionists and Mizrachi, who initially
combined with Gordoniah, Akiva, and Noar Zioni to form Ichud. Ichud, like
the United Zionist Organization and Nocham in Germany, was intended as
a political group to represent the unity of the She'erit Hapletah but from

an early point in time was involved in a great deal of competition with the pioneering youth movements.[50] Ichud and the Gordoniah movement also focused their efforts on creating kibbutzim, stating in June 1945 that the "hakhsharah points in Poland . . . [are] the first step in the education of the youth and its guidance in the light of the pioneering ideals."[51]

These kibbutzim were not only composed of the youths who joined them; as part of the movement, they were led by madrichim who were sent to organize kibbutzim and then instruct the youths in the ways of the youth movement. One such leader, Miriam Wind (nee Richter), arrived in Lublin in March 1945. A member of the Hashomer Hatzair youth movement before the war, she first escaped from her hometown of Rowno to Vilna in 1939 (at the age of eighteen); after her capture in Romania in 1941, she escaped and spent the years from 1942 to 1945 in Tashkent, where she met her husband, Baruch.[52] Once in Lublin after the war, she met with the leaders of Dror (Zuckerman and Lubetkin) and Hashomer Hatzair (Israel Glazer and Shlomo Mann), who instructed her to organize and lead the third kibbutz in Sosnowiec.[53] She parted from her husband, who was sent to lead the fourth kibbutz group in Bytom, and began to organize the kibbutz there in the beginning of April. The movement focused on organizing kibbutzim in Silesia, where many youths were to be found after repatriation by the Polish government. The Bricha also took advantage of the close access to Germany in formulating routes of departure from Poland. Miriam looked for the first members of the kibbutz at the Jewish committee in Sosnowiec, where they had gone to look for family. She also wandered in the city looking for children to join the kibbutz. Youths arrived on trains, resettled by the new Polish government in Silesia, and were redeemed from monasteries and Polish families where they had hidden during the war. The first groups were organized in Bytom and Sosnowiec at the end of April 1945 and departed for Germany three months later in the beginning of August.[54]

The madrichim such as Baruch and Miriam were uncertain of what they would find among these traumatized children and young adults. In the encounter with the survivor youths, it became clear that there would have to be a process of negotiation between the goals of the movement and the needs of the survivors. An educational program written by Shaike Weinberg (later to become the director of the Diaspora Museum in Tel Aviv and the U.S. Holocaust Memorial Museum) for Hashomer Hatzair activists working

with kibbutzim identified what he understood to be the central characteristics of this "new human material." He characterized the youths by their
lack of education, absence of a normal childhood, stunted mental development, and general demoralization and distrust in man.[55] In addition, these
youths displayed a "hatred of physical labor and physical activity in general"
as well as "strong resentment and anger toward the collective lifestyle . . . and
a cynical relation to ideals in any form." With this in mind, he urged the
madrichim to deepen loyalty to the movement while not arousing in the
youths the renewed feeling of being placed in a framework of coercion. Prewar age divisions were now less important: "Division into different age
groups has also lost its significance: a youth aged 15 may be thought of as
a graduate [boger] in most cases, and he can be included in the bogrim group
with those aged 18–20." The ideal activity was agricultural work in kibbutzim when possible or at the minimum a few hours a day of service work.
In the cultural sphere, holiday ceremonies (both Jewish and Zionist for
social life), socialist education, general education to make up for lost time,
and the teaching of Hebrew, Jewish history, the history of Zionism, and the
Hashomer Hatzair movement were of central importance. And indeed,
such educational techniques were put into place by Baruch and Miriam in
the kibbutzim in Bytom and Sosnowiec. From the perspective of the youth
movement, the leadership believed that Zionism, specifically Hashomer
Hatzair Zionism, had the power to heal these broken youths by turning them
into ideologically committed Zionists (and such training was an ideal use
of time while kibbutz youth waited to leave Europe). Negative assessments
of survivor youths notwithstanding, a closer look at the youths who chose
to join the kibbutzim and their reasons for doing so reveals a relationship
that is far more complex. Although the youths were traumatized by their
wartime experiences, they were willing to become active participants in the
flourishing kibbutz framework.

With the departure of the first groups in the Bricha, only fourteen kibbutz members remained in Bytom and sixteen in Sosnowiec. While the
madrichim accompanied their first groups on the initial steps in the path
of departure, the veteran members who remained behind focused on recon-
stituting the kibbutzim.[56] They concentrated on restoring order to the
depleted kibbutzim and on recruiting members to join the second group of
youths in the kibbutz.

Baruch and Miriam Yechieli, *madrichim* of the Hashomer Hatzair kibbutz groups in Bytom and Sosnowiec. The couple led Kibbutz *Lochamei HaGetaot al shem Tosia Altman* from Poland to Germany, and then eventually to Palestine. (Kibbutz Gazit Archive, Israel)

The Choice to Join Kibbutz Groups in Sosnowiec and Bytom

The first young survivors who found the kibbutzim in Sosnowiec and Bytom generally came to the kibbutz alone, having spent the first months or year after the war recuperating and searching for family. Although from varied backgrounds, they shared the trauma of wartime experiences.

At the age of seventeen, Haim Shorrer was liberated by Russian troops from his hiding place in a forest in eastern Poland in June 1944. Three months earlier he had witnessed the murder of his entire family after their discovery in a bunker by Ukrainian collaborators and had only narrowly managed to escape. After four years in hiding and on the run, disconnected from the rest of the world, he now faced liberation, alone and with few prospects for the future. "The period following liberation was more difficult than the war itself. Once I was liberated, everyone went on their own path."[57] A Jewish man by the name of Haber adopted Shorrer and brought him to his home in Klosowa, where he sought different forms of work trying to make a living in Poland for the next year. By the summer of 1945, however, Shorrer left Klosowa and made his way to Bytom, where he joined the kibbutz led by Baruch Wind (Yechieli).

Like Shorrer, Monish Einhorn (Haran) found himself completely alone at the end of the war. Born in 1926 in Zaleszczyki on the Dniester on the interwar border between Poland and Romania, Einhorn was part of a large family that was completely wiped out during the war. Before a mass deportation of Jews from the area in May 1943, he managed to escape to the forests and survived until being liberated by the Red Army in March 1944. He escaped a German counterattack and traveled to Czernowitz, where he remained until the end of the war. He was then repatriated to Sosnowiec by the newly formed Polish government.[58] Once he arrived in Sosnowiec, completely alone and in foreign surroundings, he looked for a new home. He found it in the kibbutz led by Miriam. "Everything was new there, life was new. . . . It is difficult to describe how important it was. The kibbutz gave a framework to kids who didn't know what to do with themselves, who had no family."[59]

Shorrer's and Einhorn's stories were typical of many Jewish youths after the war in Poland. Neither Haim nor Monish were the sort of people who would characteristically have been found at a Zionist training center before the war. Haim was too young before the war to gain much experience in a Zionist group, and Monish characterized himself as more of a "yeshivah bocher" (student in an orthodox high school), less interested in joining the Zionist youth group in his town before the war than studying at the yeshivah.[60]

The young survivors who joined the second kibbutzim in Bytom and Sosnowiec (which would later compose Kibbutz Tosia Altman) came from homes that frequently made them unlikely candidates to join a Zionist kibbutz. Their wartime experiences, while traumatic, were far from uniform, and the process of finding the kibbutz differed for many of them. Yet many of those who reached the kibbutz decided to remain with it. As Miriam described, the priority was not to find youths with a Zionist background;

in fact, this was the least of her concerns: "the only goal then was to rescue the youth . . . to remove them from monasteries, to gather them; they didn't have a home. . . . The majority of them came from camps, from hiding with non-Jews . . . [and] from Ukraine, from towns, from the forest."[61] The youth movement focused on providing shelter for the various youths who would constitute the future of the movement.

A number of the kibbutz members joined the kibbutz only after first trying to rejoin Polish society. Salusia Altman (Sarah Ben-Zvi) was born in Częstochowa in 1931 to a religious family. When the war broke out in 1939 she was not even nine years old. Her family moved into the Częstochowa ghetto, but when the deportations began they were hidden in the family factory by the foreman, Jacques. After the ghetto was liquidated, her father disappeared, and she and her mother were placed in the Hasag forced labor camp. Following her liberation from the camp on January 16, 1945, she returned first to Łódź and then to Częstochowa. Although she knew other youths who were joining kibbutz groups, Altman had first sought to return to Polish society, focusing on her education before entertaining any thoughts of departure. However, her encounter with an anti-Semitic teacher led her, with the approval of her mother, to join the kibbutz in Bytom a little over six months after her liberation from the Hasag camp.[62]

Inka Weisbort also first made an effort to integrate into the newly liberated Polish state by joining the Polish army. Nineteen years old at the end of the war, she had survived a death march from Auschwitz and managed to escape from Ravensbruck in April 1945. After three months recuperating in Germany, she returned to Poland to try to find family but found no one. She tried to join a unit of the Polish army in July 1945 but was expelled when her Jewish origins were discovered. She found the sister of her stepfather in Sosnowiec, where she heard about a joint kibbutz of Hashomer Hatzair and Dror. Having few other options, she decided to join the kids all "crowded into a small apartment" in September 1945.[63] Like Salusia, her first choice was to reenter Polish society. However, her encounter with anti-Semitism and the slim prospects for a future in Poland led her to look for other social options. This was how she became a part of the kibbutz organized by Miriam.

The majority of youths found the kibbutzim through word of mouth and not by the organized activity of the movements, although the youth movements did make efforts to attract followers. Following the beginning of actual repatriation from the Soviet Union in February 1946, one practice of the Zionist activists was to meet trains of repatriates from the Soviet Union and convince youths to join them or parents to send their children to the kibbutzim.[64] For the vast majority of the youths who joined the kibbutzim, the political affiliation of the kibbutz was an afterthought, if even considered at all. As Zuckerman relates in his memoirs, the youth movements could create the kibbutzim for the youths to join, but it was up to the youths repatriated from the Soviet areas to Silesia whether and which kibbutzim they would affiliate with:

> One day, in Kraków, I met a member of the [prewar] Warsaw branch of He-Halutz Ha-Tzair. And I found out that he was in the Ichud kibbutz. I said to him: "How come you're on an Ichud kibbutz? There's a Dror kibbutz here." He said: "I'll tell you the truth: when I came to the railroad station, I met young people in a cart and young people in a taxi, and I decided to ride in the taxi. It turned out they were from Ichud and the ones in the cart were from Dror." That was how they grabbed people. The fellow, a member of our movement, forgot his movement attachment and joined anyone. . . . Our people would stand at the railroad station and, when they saw young people coming, would take them along. That was very important for the young people who arrived, since they immediately had a house, a bed, and food.[65]

Members of the kibbutzim in Bytom and Sosnowiec also found their new homes in this random manner. Fishl Herszkowitz, a Galician Jew aged seventeen at the time of liberation, had survived in hiding, fighting with a partisan group against the Ukrainians at the end of the war. He first lived with a group of Jews in the area of Husiatyn following liberation, but the constant threats from Ukrainians led him to seek family to the west. He boarded a train of repatriates and arrived in Bytom; when he disembarked, he heard about the Hashomer Hatzair kibbutz and, being nicely received by kibbutz members, decided to join it.[66]

Other young Jewish survivors who joined the kibbutz groups in Bytom and Sosnowiec also found the kibbutzim by chance, either hearing about them in the streets of town or running into old acquaintances who told them about the kibbutzim. Haim Bronstein was among a group of young survivors from Skalat who had been resettled by the Polish government in

Group portrait of the members of the Kibbutz Ichud hakhsharah in Sosnowiec, April 1945. (USHMM, courtesy of Alex Knobler)

Bytom. Wandering through the streets of the city, he happened to see a blue and white flag inside the window of an apartment and overheard voices singing inside. He recognized two old acquaintances from Skalat who had already joined the kibbutz and decided that the kibbutz presented a better option than any others available to him at the time.[67]

The recognition of a familiar face among a world of strangers was often enough to convince orphaned survivors to join such kibbutz groups. Aharon Segel was also an unlikely candidate to join the kibbutz in Bytom. He survived under an assumed identity in the Tarnopol district working as a cattle herder. Nine months after liberation he returned to his village near Skalat to discover that he was the only one from a family of seven children to survive the war.

> I was basically adopted by the head of the community, Moshe Gelbtukh, who gave me a pair of *tefilin* [ritual phylacteries], and I returned from being a devout Catholic to a devout Jew. After 6 months in Skalat we went to

Gliwice, but there was no room for me there, so Mr. Gelbtukh sent me to a *HaPoel HaMizrachi* (religious Zionist) kibbutz in Kraków. On the way we passed through Bytom, and I met someone who told me that a friend from Skalat, Haim Bronstein, was living in a secular kibbutz in Bytom. I decided that it would at least be better to be with one friend so I stayed in Bytom.[68]

Thus, Segel went from growing up in a traditional Jewish family to passing as a Catholic during the war and then returning to the Jewish religious fold only to finally join a secular Marxist-Zionist kibbutz in Bytom bound for Palestine.

Yolek Weintraub (Yoel Ben-Porat), also from Skalat, was only fourteen years old at the end of the war. He managed to survive in the forest with an uncle from 1941 to 1944; at the end of the war Weintraub was adopted by a Russian family that wanted him to convert. He instead chose to be repatriated by the Polish government and thus found himself in Bytom. There he ran into Segel, who told him that he had joined a kibbutz and that Weintraub's cousin, Haim Bronstein, was also a member of the group. Weintraub had never heard of a kibbutz before but decided that living with friends would be preferable to being on his own in Bytom.[69] In this way, the group of boys from Skalat all independently found their way into the Hashomer Hatzair/Dror kibbutz in Silesia.

Most of the young Jewish survivors who joined the kibbutzim in Bytom and Sosnowiec had either lost their entire family or had only one relative remaining. Many had survived in hiding after the trauma of witnessing the destruction of their families. Some had returned from concentration camps and death marches, while others had managed to conceal their identities or be sheltered by non-Jewish families.[70] This diverse group of youths found themselves together in the communal living format of a kibbutz in western Poland.

As with most of those who joined kibbutzim in postwar Poland, the appeal of Zionism for these youths was primarily functional in nature, having little to do with any ideological appeal. In the case of Kibbutz Tosia Altman, the kibbutz framework seems to have provided two Zionist opportunities for those who joined it: the first was the offer of departure from Europe with a future in Palestine, and the second had to do with the appeal of the kibbutz framework, which could provide a sort of replacement family while offering its members shelter, security, and education.[71] While the choice to join the kibbutz was the result of a decision that factored in social needs and the promise of departure, the choice to remain within the kibbutz had as much to do with the intrinsic psychological value of kibbutz life on the everyday level.

Life in the Kibbutz

The members of the kibbutzim in Bytom and Sosnowiec provided a snap-shot of their everyday life within the kibbutz by keeping a kibbutz diary. Members did not sign entries but instead wrote them in the first-person plural, describing events collectively. This look into kibbutz life reveals the mutually beneficial nature of the relationship between the youths and the youth movement desperate for new members.

Miriam instigated the writing of the diary with the second group while the kibbutz was still in Germany and assigned subjects to various members. The journal itself begins with the initial period in Poland (apparently members described these events as they remembered them in the months after their departure from Poland). While it must certainly be treated cautiously as a historical document that underwent editing and has sections whose authorship or genesis is unclear, it provides a rich and exceptional point of view on the Zionist experience in postwar Europe.

It is clear that while the new members had chosen to join the kibbutz, their knowledge of Zionism and of the youth movement was superficial at best. At the first meeting of the new group in Sosnowiec, Miriam, "with tears in her eyes," opened with a description of the group that had just left. "We still don't know how to sing" (any of the youth movement songs), so the group listened to what Miriam had to say, and the meeting was closed. On the second day (August 7), members of the kibbutz went to the Jewish committee office to receive their regular rations, including sugar, oil, and potatoes. Throughout the whole first week new members poured into the kibbutz, although some boys were expelled for inappropriate behavior. On the first Sabbath evening, the members sang new songs that Miriam had taught them and listened to a story she read from *The Book of the Shomrim*

Cover page of the collective diary kept by Kibbutz *Lochamei HaGetaot al shem Tosia Altman*. (Kibbutz Gazit Archive, Israel)

(the Hashomer Hatzair movement guidebook).[72] Not yet a cohesive group or aware of the kibbutz traditions, the new members kept to themselves, each retreating to his or her own corner.

In Bytom, an early diary entry described members who were steered to the kibbutz by the League for Labor Palestine who "arrived young, without any ideological awareness and unable to understand the nature of kibbutz life. They saw the kibbutz as a practical means of aliyah to Israel."[73] As in Sosnowiec, the first few days were sad because the veteran kibbutz members who had not departed with the first aliyah group missed their old friends. The new members in both kibbutzim, unaware of many of the meanings behind the Zionist activities in the kibbutz, had clearly not joined out of commitment to the socialist-Zionist ethic but instead saw the kibbutz as preferable to the meager options available in Poland. As Inka Weisbort recalled, "the negative feelings were the primary reason for joining the kibbutz: fear of loneliness, of anti-Semitism, and the threats of the outside world. . . . Positive feelings, like the better social atmosphere . . . the desire to make aliyah and . . . achieve the Zionist ideal" came only much later.[74]

Over the first few weeks, as the kibbutzim gained more newcomers, the new members learned what was expected of them. The egalitarian format of the kibbutz meant that members made decisions collectively through *asefot* (assemblies) in which they discussed decisions facing the kibbutz and voted on them. Kibbutz members were elected to leadership positions as president, treasurer, secretary, work manager, etc. In Bytom, the first *mazkirut* (secretariat) was elected once the kibbutz reached forty members. Baruch explained the tasks of the secretariat to the kibbutz, and then elections were held: Yaffa (president/treasurer), Haim Shorrer (work manager), Helia (*makhsanait*, or clothes manager), and Rivka (*ba'alat shituf*, or administrator responsible for distribution of resources).[75] The first task that faced Rivka and the group in Bytom was to collect and equally distribute clothing among the kibbutz members. This was a topic that would be addressed at many assemblies, as members often complained about receiving ill-fitting clothing. Of more concern, however, was the failure of some members to share outside income with the rest of the kibbutz. Baruch was "experienced with these problems," and when he saw that the traditional method would not work he decided to employ the "Russian method." He staged a theft in the middle of the night and in this way used the pretext to search for all of the members' hidden cash (which he then confiscated for the kibbutz treasury).[76] Haim Shorrer, recalling the event, was relieved that as a member of the secretariat he had been let in on Baruch's secret beforehand, because this gave him a chance to hide his money before the search.[77]

Difficulties with shituf (sharing resources) notwithstanding, the opening pages of the diary from its first three months in Poland reveal the beginning of a subtle process in this period: the transition from individual to collective thinking. Some kibbutz members initially had difficulty with the notion of self-maintenance (meshek atzmi) and the sharing of clothes and all wages earned at outside work, complaining about poor allocation of clothing and the need for connections (proteksiah) to get certain items. Indeed, some members acknowledged that it "was difficult to drop 'I' from one's vocabulary," but the madrichim tried to inculcate the value of collectivism in the members.[78]

Although ideological development was rather slow in the early period, the two sections of the kibbutz developed socially, learning "positive" and "negative" behavior. As members soon understood, the new social norms enforced by the madrichim and the group as a whole included the value of work (laziness was forbidden) and the importance of sharing, deciding which members would be allowed to stay and which would be expelled for failing to contribute.[79] It was in this early period that members developed pride in contributing to the collective, happy to bring money into their new home.[80]

The kibbutz members settled into a routine in Sosnowiec and Bytom, spending their days at work and their evenings immersed in cultural activities such as lectures, discussions, singing, and reading. Activities in the early period in Poland were differentiated between men and women, reinforcing traditional gender roles despite the wartime interlude. The boys in Sosnowiec found work in Singer's metal factory, while the women engaged in work necessary for the internal functioning of the kibbutz such as cooking, cleaning, laundry, distribution of clothes, and sewing. Yedziah Noigbauer, designated the work coordinator for the kibbutz in Sosnowiec, secured work in the metal factory for the boys through an acquaintance. While the boys were able to perform some outside work, the kibbutz, like others in postwar Poland, relied on outside assistance for its existence (in many cases, wartime

connections established with the American Jewish Joint Distribution Committee [JDC] were instrumental in securing funding for postwar Zionist
youth movements).[81] Baruch managed to find construction work for ten of
the boys, who earned 3.5 zlotys per day demolishing damaged buildings.[82]
In Bytom in the house on Gronwaldski 6, it "was always the girls in the
kitchen." Likewise, the girls in Sosnowiec "made sure the boys had food"
when returning from a long day of work, creating a new home and family
for the young survivors that replicated standard gender divisions.[83]

Within weeks, the population of the kibbutz in Sosnowiec rose to include
seventy-five members, all crowded into the small apartment. Boys and girls
slept in separate bedrooms, sharing the available bed space. Tremendous
labor was necessary to ensure the day-to-day functioning of the kibbutz,
with constant work in the kitchen to keep kibbutz members fed. Women
began work in the kitchen each day at 5:00 a.m. preparing breakfast for the
workers, who left for the factories early in the morning. On laundry nights
the kitchen turned into a laundry room after the evening discussion, with
the hot water being boiled in the large pots and laundry tasks beginning at
11:00 p.m.[84] Members also worked to maintain the cleanliness of the kibbutzim, although the boys' rooms always tended to be messier than those
of the girls. As described in the diary, "all the clean and dirty clothes are
mixed together. Soap, tooth powder, brushes, are thrown in all corners of
the room. . . . After the boys room comes the turn of the shower. . . . Here the
mess is at its peak."[85] Needless to say, housework was not the most popular
assignment among the kibbutz members.

Still, the sense of camaraderie created by living and working together
was highly therapeutic for the young survivors. For the women involved in
sewing, the group activity provided them with a forum in which to talk
about their experiences during the war and in the camps.[86] As Monish Einhorn described, the kibbutz was extremely important to the youths who had
only recently emerged from the Holocaust. "The kibbutzim gave a framework
to kids who didn't know what to do with themselves, who had no family."[87]
The young men worked and earned money together, providing for their new
family. Miriam and Baruch were certainly the "mother" and "father" of their
respective groups in Sosnowiec and Bytom, despite being only three or four
years older than most of their chanichim.

The cultural activities constituted an important part of the daily experience for the youths in Sosnowiec and Bytom, as they acquired the Zionist tools necessary for their future. Miriam and Baruch taught the members about Zionism, socialism, and the history of Israel. The young women who participated in the sewing group in Sosnowiec had the opportunity to talk and to practice new Hebrew words they had learned while sewing (the main language of the kibbutz was Yiddish). They also learned Hebrew in lessons, sang songs in Hebrew and Yiddish, and danced. As Inka Weisbort recalled the cultural activities, "Manya [Miriam] held discussions in the evening, we sang songs in Hebrew (which I had sung with the movement in the ghetto), and we sang folksongs in Yiddish. . . . Manya also told stories about Eretz Israel or read from Jewish books. . . . We dressed nicely for Oneg Shabbat, had a festive meal."[88] Members were also sent to participate in wider youth movement seminars, and the kibbutz in Sosnowiec hosted a seminar for one hundred members in September 1945 where they learned about Zionism, the geography of Palestine, and the socialist-Zionist ideology. After the Holocaust, the young survivors were thirsty for knowledge; for many this was the first kind of formal education they had received in six years.

While education and cultural life in the kibbutz could satisfy their desire for knowledge, some members were also empowered by participating in the process of teaching themselves or being trained at the seminars to lead other groups. Monish, for example, became *mazkir* (secretary-general) of the group in Sosnowiec. As he had obtained more education in the years before the war, especially in Jewish culture, he organized a number of cultural activities. He held a reading group in Yiddish of Jewish literature during which he led participants in reading the stories of Sholem Aleichem and helped to teach Hebrew with the knowledge he had gained in his time in the yeshivah. He also taught the group about Marxism. In this way the kibbutz format almost immediately provided its members with the opportunity to take on leadership roles and assume responsibility in the group despite no prior experience.

The almost daily assemblies held to discuss questions facing the kibbutz also enabled members to assume responsibility in their collective life. For example, debates arose over whether outside workers in Sosnowiec should receive larger rations of food because they worked harder at the factory outside of the kibbutz or whether smoking, which was technically forbidden in

Hashomer Hatzair, would be allowed within the kibbutz.[89] In the end, the members voted to allow smoking.[90]

Despite the satisfaction that members derived from life in the kibbutz, the members in Sosnowiec and Bytom continued to be exposed to the harsh reality of their continued existence in Poland. Those who traveled by train to leadership seminars or worked outside the kibbutz in factories experienced the daily anti-Semitism that continued to be suffered by Jews in Poland. In Sosnowiec after a blood libel, the building of the kibbutz was surrounded by an angry mob of Poles, which according to one kibbutz member had to be dispersed by Soviet soldiers.[91] Quite frequently, rocks were thrown and windows were broken in the kibbutz apartments. However, now the members of the kibbutz could take comfort in another aspect of kibbutz training, *haganah atzmit* (self-defense), which was also a source of pride. In Sosnowiec, Miriam explained to the kibbutz group that in order to defend themselves, the kibbutz would be acquiring guns; three members, Yedziah, Leon, and Bolek, were selected to be responsible for the weapons (new automatic rifles known as TT2s). The group practiced how to respond to an attack against the kibbutz, and two members were placed on guard duty each night (the guards were always of the same sex, in accordance with the proper nature expected of a Hashomer Hatzair kibbutz). The kibbutz in Bytom also practiced self-defense, acquiring weapons and official permits for the kibbutz.[92]

Over time, the kibbutz members began to learn the Zionist nature of life within the kibbutz. Contact with the wider Hashomer Hatzair and Dror movements facilitated access to resources and also influenced determinations over the size and membership of the kibbutz. On September 8 four members of the Sosnowiec group traveled to Łódź to participate in a movement conference.[93] As they described the experience in the diary, it was the process itself of participating in the larger movement, of meeting other youths with similar backgrounds and seeing the expanding support network that was growing around them, that was far more important than anything they learned at the seminar. They even described being disappointed with the lectures and the house where the seminar was held, but they were still impressed with the enthusiasm and passion of the other chanichim. The ideological debates at the seminar on the League for Labor Palestine and socialism, while lively, were difficult to understand.

The word "division" [*pilug*] which was heard countless times in the discussion, was completely foreign to us, as was the reality of conditions in Palestine. With admiration we watched the participants in the seminar who were well-versed in the complexities of the issues. The opinions varied . . . in every way, the picture of the future was foggy and the answers that were given (over our future and the future of the movement in Palestine) did not make it any clearer.[94]

Thus, it was quite clear that members of the kibbutz had little knowledge of the ideological debates that had suffused Polish Zionism in the interwar period and soon reemerged despite the unity efforts following liberation. When Hashomer Hatzair decided to break off from the other Zionist youth movements in the fall of 1945, Miriam and Baruch informed the members of the kibbutzim in Bytom and Sosnowiec of these developments, but the youths had little understanding of the ideological differences that distinguished them from Dror or other movements.[95] Only those members who had participated in movement seminars had any idea of what the differences between the movements were, and even they were confused by the notions of ideological division. Even though Miriam and Baruch used this opportunity to explain the specifics of the Hashomer Hatzair ideology and educational program, members were more concerned with division within the kibbutz itself than with any division between the movements, perhaps indicating an allegiance that was far more connected to the new "family" than to the movement as a whole. Still, members noted in the diary that they could discern a shift after the kibbutzim officially became a part of Hashomer Hatzair in early October, as one or two members chose to leave the kibbutz to join Dror rather than remain in Hashomer Hatzair. All in all, they wrote, "the kibbutz began to breathe new air . . . and a sense of satisfaction could be felt in the atmosphere."[96]

Despite the increasing sense of comfort, after two months in the kibbutz the members began to grow impatient, constantly asking the madrichim when they would depart. Miriam in turn looked to the Bricha activists in Katowice for guidance on their date of departure from Poland. At the end of October 1945 both groups received the news they had long been waiting for: they would finally be able to leave Poland. Almost immediately the groups sprang into action, preparing the necessary items for their journey and splitting into six groups of ten individuals, each with a leader to guide them in their travels. Both groups left members behind in order to organize the next group of kibbutzim. However, this time both Miriam and Baruch would escort their chanichim on the path of departure, accompanying them through their journey to Germany. On Sunday, October 28, 1945, the Sosnowiec group held its final assembly before departure. Miriam opened the meeting with a few words:

> We are completing an important period in our lives. We are leaving the blood-soaked soil of Poland and are leaving on the path of *hagshamah* [fulfillment, or turning ideal into reality]. We are leaving Poland in the guise of Greeks returning to their homeland from the concentration camps. Because we do not know Greek we will use Hebrew words familiar to us from the songs we learned to sing. We must be careful to avoid revealing our identities.[97]

The Sosnowiec group departed on October 29, 1945, taking a train from Katowice to Prague, where they were joined the next day by Baruch's groups arriving from Bytom. Some questioned why they had to continue to conceal

Members of the Hashomer Hatzair Zionist youth movement cross the border from Poland into Czechoslovakia on their way to Prague. (USHMM, courtesy of Rose Guterman Zar)

their identities after so many years in hiding (and the station master at the Czech border questioned why "Greeks" would choose to go to Prague instead of Bratislava), but they did and thus managed to cross the border and reach Czechoslovakia. (The Bricha movement often supplied members false Greek papers to facilitate travel through Europe for its groups.) After nearly two weeks in Prague, living with a bunch of *spekulantim* (black market operators whom the members identified as speculators), the group arrived in Munich, where the members began the next stage of their journey as a united kibbutz in the DP camps of Germany.

The Growth of the Kibbutz Movement and the Bricha

The two kibbutz groups in Sosnowiec and Bytom were a small part of the semiorganized movement of Jewish departure from Poland that would come to be known as the Bricha. Over the course of 1945 and 1946 the movement would continue to grow, with some 110,000 Polish Jews choosing to depart Poland with the Bricha. Of these, some 33,600 were youths organized in kibbutzim such as those in Sosnowiec and Bytom (table 1).[98]

Regardless of what their rationale was for joining the kibbutzim, however, these groups formed the backbone of the Bricha and assisted in pushing the problem of Jewish refugees to the center of British and American governmental attention. While the movements viewed the kibbutzim as a method of enlisting followers and expanding the ranks of the Zionist parties, the youths who joined the kibbutzim tended to stay because of the psychological support they derived from the communal structure, which proved highly therapeutic for many of the survivors.

A number of factors contributed to the decision made by these youths to join and remain with the kibbutzim. The major benefit of kibbutzim for Jewish youths after the war was psychological, not physical; while the kibbutz groups frequently could not succeed at being self-sufficient, they did give youths a sense of purpose in their lives. In the kibbutzim, youths learned Jewish history, Hebrew, youth movement folk songs, principles of socialism, and more. The communal setting created a sense of family and tended to emphasize the positive potential of a Jewish future despite the dark Jewish past. The kibbutzim provided pride in being Jewish and offered goals for the

The Bricha from Poland according to Movement Membership

Movement	Kibbutz Members	Children	Families and Individuals	Total	Percentage
Dror	6,616	1,176	10,919	18,711	16.77
Hashomer Hatzair	4,350	709	9,064	14,123	12.66
Gordoniah	4,031	686	8,625	13,324	11.96
Nocham	710	46	221	977	0.88
Pachach	918			918	0.82
Total	16,625	2,617	28,829	48,071	43.10
Ichud HaNoar Hatzioni	7,825	1,419	14,361	23,065	21.16
Mizrachi	3,457	870	8,941	13,268	11.90
Total	11,282	2,289	23,302	36,873	33.06
Revisionists	2,596	392	4,480	7,468	6.70
Agudes Yisroel	1,305	284	6,021	7,610	6.82
PZ Smol	1,790	230	3,494	5,514	4.94
Coordinac-ja (Children)		997	45	1,042	0.93
Others (HaOved, Jungbor, Poalei Zion Right)		92	4,870	4,964	4.45
Total	5,691	1,995	18,910	26,598	23.85
Grand Total	33,592	6,901	71,041	111,542	100.00

Source: Yochanan Cohen, *Ovrim kol Gvul: Ha-Brichah, Polin 1945–1946* (Tel Aviv: Zemorah-Bitan, 1995), 469.

future, and they also represented an alternative to the established Jewish committee and a way of life that was not dependent on the official community framework.[99] In this way, the kibbutzim ended up being highly therapeutic for the young survivors, placing them with a similar community of youths who had undergone wartime trauma. The activity within the kibbutzim, both in daily work and in education, could help to avert the depression, anxiety, and anger that were certain byproducts of the posttraumatic stress that many of these survivors were perhaps facing.[100]

These factors may have then played a role in contributing to the increasing popularity of the kibbutz framework for Jewish youths in postwar Poland. According to the calculations of Engel, the Zionist youth movements were highly successful in capturing a growing percentage of surviving Jewish youths in Poland after the war. Whereas in the spring of 1945 only 7.5 percent of the total Jewish youth in Poland had joined the kibbutzim of Zionist youth movements, by the fall this number had grown to 17 percent. Between June and November 1945 the number of Jewish youths living in the kibbutzim of youth movements grew by at least 500 percent.[101] Among the youth movements that emphasized pioneer training (Hashomer Hatzair, Dror, and Gordoniah), the number had increased to 7,167 members by the spring/summer of 1946 from as few as 800 the winter before.[102] Over the course of 1946, the young members of the kibbutzim departed Poland in the Bricha, many of them bound for Palestine via the American zones of Germany, Italy, and Austria.

It was not only the pioneering movements of the Left that were able to organize all of the youths under their canopy in the kibbutzim. In fact, the pioneering movements that composed the League for Labor Palestine (Dror, Hashomer Hatzair, and Gordoniah) were so successful in their efforts to organize youths in kibbutzim and thus assert control over the Jewish street that the other major Zionist movements were left with no choice but to duplicate their methods.[103] (Other options available to Jewish youths still included affiliation with social aid groups opened by Jewish committees, the Bund, and the Communist Polish Workers' Party or simply living independently.) This quest for members would in turn assist in swelling the numbers of Jews departing in the Bricha. Thus in August 1945, the Ichud Party decided to join forces with the Bricha to prepare the youths under its auspices for departure from Poland within the Bricha framework. The Ichud had already commenced a policy in the spring of 1945 of organizing its youths in kibbutzim; by the beginning of August, it had six hundred youths in its kibbutzim.[104] In August 1945 significant developments in the internal relations of the Bricha were also addressed during the conference in London. Cooperation was maintained between the various parties that composed the Bricha, with the right-wing Ichud and Revisionists also cooperating with the Bricha framework, although the Labor wing and its youth movements continued to compose the core of the Bricha.[105] The success of the pioneering movements led both Ichud and Left Poalei Zion to seek to replicate their methods in the organization of youths and cooperation with the Bricha in an effort to maintain a following in the highly competitive Jewish street.[106] The impressive ability of the pioneering youth movements to assert control over the Zionist movement in Poland by the end of 1945 boded well for their ability to seize control of the She'erit Hapletah in post-war Europe.[107]

Youth movements emerged for an increasing number of survivors as leaders with a vision for the future and the ability to fill daily needs on a level on par with or perhaps surpassing that of the local committees. This in turn was also crucial in making known to the Jewish public that the Bricha was a safe and viable way out of Poland.

It was this growth in kibbutz membership that enabled Zuckerman to proclaim in London in August 1945, "Friends! Poland can provide one thousand chalutzim each month. The Jewish youth is completely oriented toward aliyah. 1500 Jewish youths are located today in kibbutzei-hakhsharah, and thousands more will join: it is not only that they are preparing themselves for aliyah to Eretz Yisrael, but that they strive to make aliyah with all their might, and *they will go up.*"[108]

In the seven months from the end of March 1945 to October 1945, the Zionist youth movements managed to erect a system that fulfilled the everyday needs of Jewish youths and that served as a legitimate alternative to the existing Jewish committees. This independence also enabled the youth movements to function freely without any reliance on or responsibility to the communal institutions (again, close connections to the JDC built before and during the war ensured an important source of funding). The growth in membership in the kibbutzim of the youth movements suggests that their organization, access to resources, appearance as a gathering place for youths, and promise of departure all enabled them to organize Jewish youths after the war more successfully than any other organization. The Jewish youths in Poland in turn found them to be welcoming homes that could provide them with camaraderie, education, and above all warmth that they sought after the war.

Conclusion: Perceptions of the Quality of Polish Jewish Youths

Despite the emerging success of the kibbutz model, the youth movements were quite aware that they had shifted their focus in the task of aliyah from training the elite of Jewish youths for aliyah to enlisting as many followers as

possible for departure. From the perspective of many of the youth movement activists, this entailed a sacrifice of quality for quantity. The youths who
composed the postwar kibbutzim and the youth movement leadership in
Palestine clearly had rather different understandings of Zionism. Evaluations
of these youths in the kibbutzim by youth movement and Jewish Agency
emissaries tended to assess the potential of these survivors to buttress their
numbers in Palestine to function as the vital added weight that could tip the
balance to the creation of the Jewish state. The different movements in turn
were also looking to increase their own ranks in order to enhance their
political power within the Yishuv.[109] The descriptions of the survivor youths
by the youth movement emissaries were far from flattering or optimistic.
They emphasized the demoralization, isolation, and indolence of the survivor youths.[110] Hashomer Hatzair activists expressed serious concerns over
their ability to educate the thousands of refugee youths who filled the kibbutzim. In the words of one activist, "One needs a great deal of strength of
spirit in order to create from this material a new type of man. . . . It will take
quite a few days and months [of] effort for them to be like us."[111]

    This was a sense that was expressed not only by Zionist activists arriving
from Palestine but also by youth movement organizers in Europe. At a meeting of Hashomer Hatzair leaders in Bratislava in November 1945, Mordechai
Rosman's evaluation of the quality of postwar Polish Jewish youths was
highly unenthusiastic as he assessed the rapid ideological training that the
movement would have to undertake after years of war.[112]

> After 6 years of destruction without education the Jews have become a peo-
> ple of beggars without culture, a youth without any education, sick, diseased,
> and broken. . . . The available Jewish resource has changed. . . . Deep changes
> have also taken place on the spiritual level among the youth; this youth comes
> from the forests, the ghettos, the camps influenced by lying, deceit, forgery,
> cannibalism, a lack of love and faith. . . . It is clear that the educational center
> of the movement has moved to Palestine; kibbutzim who move to Palestine
> after 6 year of camps and ghettos and only 6 months of education and
> hakhsharah will not manage to have the same level of education as our mem-
> bers obtain [in Palestine]. . . . The kibbutzim are far from being Hashomer
> Hatzair kibbutzim; while organization of the movement has taken place,
> ideological completion is lacking.[113]

Rosman's doubts notwithstanding, the youths who joined the kibbutz groups in Bytom and Sosnowiec certainly did not view themselves in this way, as broken beggars influenced by lying, deceit, forgery, and cannibalism. While they seem to have been aware of the fact that they had much to learn to become good *shomrim*, they were in no way failures as kibbutz members. They actively embraced the roles provided for them by the kibbutz framework, and their eager and enthusiastic participation must have also suggested to youth movement leaders the potential of the kibbutz in both recruiting and rehabilitating survivors. The diary reveals that the emphasis on labor and education described in Weinberg's educational manifesto was put into practice. Of equal if not greater significance for the kibbutz members themselves was the psychologically therapeutic value of the kibbutz experience, providing work, family, and structure while simultaneously empowering members of the kibbutz with educational, social, and leadership skills in the embrace of a new national identity.

It would seem that in the case of Sosnowiec and Bytom the kibbutzim had begun a process of learning the ways of a Hashomer Hatzair kibbutz. Despite persistent questions over their value as the human material with which the Zionist movement would be reconstituted, they chose to remain in the framework of the kibbutz and, like the thirty-three thousand other kibbutz youths who departed Poland in the Bricha, were a vital component in the success of that movement of departure. The youth movement itself was forced to moderate its expectations in order to ensure the success of the Bricha. The Zionist ideological development of the members may have still been a work in progress, but the framework of the kibbutz and the promise of departure were appealing enough to keep the survivors who joined in Sosnowiec and Bytom traveling on to Germany. Over the course of their time in Germany the kibbutz members continued to absorb the lessons of the movement. The enlisting of the young survivors in the kibbutzim after the war and their absorption into the movement were part of the larger transformation of the Zionist youth movements in Europe that had begun during the Holocaust in Poland.

11
Kibbutzim and Hakhsharot in Germany

3

"But We Had Not Counted on the Palestine Passion of Our Population"

Jewish Displaced Persons in Kibbutzim in Postwar Germany, 1945–47

Infiltration of Jews into the US zone will continue. If the borders are closed they will evade control points and come in thru underground railroad channels. Estimates of the potential infiltration are almost impossible. However, there are, according to the guesses of some of the Jewish leaders, still 60,000 Jews in Poland and 250,000 Polish Jews in Southeastern Russia. . . . Evidence indicates that a large number of these 310,000 will make their way into Germany. . . . There is no doubt that some of the groups are well organized. Especially is this true of the kibbutz groups. . . . There is no environment in eastern or middle Europe where these people care to live. Jewish leaders, in Europe, Zionists, non-Zionists, politically conservative or radical, orthodox or non-orthodox—in fact Jewish community leadership almost in its entirety are filled with a compulsion to lead their people to Palestine.

John Whiting, United Nations Relief and Rehabilitation Administration
American zone administrator, January 1946, in Schwarz Papers

By January 1946, months before the Kielce pogrom in July, the international aid organizations responsible for the welfare of the Jewish displaced persons (DPs) realized that an increasing number of Jews in the Bricha, or the new underground railroad, would continue to infiltrate the American zone of

Germany. The United Nations Relief and Rehabilitation Administration (UNRRA) along with the American Jewish Joint Distribution Committee (JDC) would do their best to assist the preexisting forms of Jewish group organization, the kibbutzim in particular.[1]

The willingness of American officials to accommodate these kibbutzim would have significant political implications. Following Earl Harrison's blistering report in August 1945 that criticized American treatment of Jewish survivors and his suggestion that the Jewish DPs be granted one hundred thousand certificates to enter Palestine, the British Foreign Ministry agreed to dispatch a joint Anglo-American Committee of Inquiry (AACI) in the fall of 1945. After some negotiation over its task and composition, the AACI was authorized to study the DP situation and estimate the number who wished to journey to Palestine, with a report to be issued within six months.[2] For the time being, however, American administration officials in Germany continued to admit large numbers of infiltrees (many organized in kibbutzim of the Zionist youth movements) from the East.

Among these infiltree groups were the two kibbutzim led by Miriam and Baruch Wind (Yechieli), whose members were largely unaware that their presence in the American zone and that of thousands of other youths arriving in kibbutzim from Poland would play a substantial role in the diplomatic drama that would unfold before them. Administrators assigned to finding a solution to the Jewish DP situation perceived the Zionist enthusiasm demonstrated by the youths in the kibbutzim as a sure sign that the DP population desired final settlement in Palestine. Nonetheless, although the members who joined the kibbutz groups in Poland had made the decision to travel with the group to Germany, their membership in the kibbutz did not mean that they were the ardent Zionists they were perceived to be. In fact, their knowledge of Zionist ideology, history, and culture was rudimentary at best, and their decision to remain within the framework of the kibbutz depended more on the structure and security offered by the kibbutz framework as well as the emotional and psychological support it provided to them.

The time spent by the kibbutzim in the American zone, while challenging the patience of the kibbutz members who may have expected a speedier departure for the Land of Israel, would prove critical in deepening the Zionist enthusiasm of the membership. Those who chose to remain with the kibbutz engaged in a process of transforming themselves from pragmatic

Zionists who had joined the kibbutz for the offers of shelter and camaraderie in Poland into individuals eager to acquire the tools necessary for their future lives in Eretz Israel. The relative stability of the German DP camp context allowed the kibbutz members to immerse themselves in the cultural work of education and training that could strengthen their commitment to the movement and the individual kibbutz. While the ultimate goal of the Zionist movement was to use the youths as potential immigrants to Palestine, the ability of kibbutzim to serve as alternative educational and vocational frameworks demonstrates the functionality of the Zionist framework outside of Palestine. Using materials created by young Jewish DPs themselves including the diary of Kibbutz Tosia Altman, correspondence between the kibbutz groups and the youth movement leadership, letters from kibbutz members, and journals and newspapers written by kibbutzim and youth movements, it is possible to gain a fuller understanding of how Jewish youths in kibbutzim lived within the Zionist movements.

In Poland, the kibbutz group had focused primarily on planning for departure and creating a cohesive kibbutz group. Once the kibbutz had arrived in Germany, the educational and cultural work necessary to prepare the kibbutz for life in Israel took place in two venues: the DP camp and the training farms that would be opened by the movements in Germany with the assistance of American authorities, the Central Committee of Liberated Jews, and Zionist movement emissaries from Palestine. The period spent by the kibbutzim in Germany is thus central in the postwar history of the Zionist movement on two levels: first, the arrival of increasing numbers of Jewish DPs in the American zone of Germany over the course of 1946 created a situation in which a diplomatic solution to the Jewish refugee problem would become urgent, and second, the time spent by the youths in the kibbutzim was used to deepen Zionist enthusiasm, prepare them for their future lives, and rebuild the European Zionist youth movements.

Zionist Youth Movements in the American Zone at the End of 1945

When the two kibbutz groups from Sosnowiec and Bytom arrived in the Landsberg DP camp near Munich in the second week of November 1945, they followed the earliest Hashomer Hatzair kibbutzim to arrive in the American zone of Germany, including groups from Sosnowiec, Bytom, Krakow, and Warsaw. In the same week, the Nocham movement marked a triumphant moment with the opening of Kibbutz Nili.[3] At the time Kibbutz Nili was officially opened, Nocham counted close to twelve hundred members in its ranks.[4] The kibbutzim arriving from Poland were seen by the leaders of Nocham as the reservoir for the expansion of the youth movement in Germany. For this reason, its leaders continued to emphasize the importance of unity and harmony in an effort to organize the youths of various movements under the umbrella of one united movement. Although this effort would not prove successful because individual kibbutz groups chose to remain within their movements rather than join Nocham, the foundation laid by the early leadership of young postwar survivors in the DP camps of Germany would facilitate this flourishing of Zionist youth movements in the American zone.

Under the auspices of the Bricha, thirty-three thousand kibbutz members left Poland, with sixteen thousand of this number being youths organized in the kibbutzim of the pioneering movements Dror, Hashomer Hatzair, Gordoniah, Nocham, and Pachach (a group of former partisans and soldiers), as well as an additional eleven thousand members arriving in the general and orthodox Zionist movements Ichud Noar Zioni and Mizrachi/ Bnei Akiva, respectively.[5] The vast majority of these kibbutz groups arrived in the American occupation zone of Germany, swelling the population of kibbutz groups in the DP camps.[6] Whereas at the end of 1945 the pioneering movements together counted approximately three thousand members in Bavaria, by the beginning of 1947 their ranks would almost quadruple in the U.S. zone of Germany, growing to some twelve thousand members in pioneering kibbutz groups alone (not counting several thousand who had already left for aliyah or moved on to Austria and Italy).[7] Although Nocham sought to represent all Zionist youths in Germany, over the course of 1946 the various other youth movement apparatuses began to expand independently in the DP camps. These included Dror and Hashomer Hatzair from the League for Labor Palestine, Ichud Noar Zioni from the central General Zionists, Betar (the Revisionist youth movement) on the Right, and the leftist Jungbor (the Borochov youth of Left Poalei Zion).[8] By the middle of 1946, only the kibbutzim of Gordoniah continued to join the ranks of Nocham.[9]

Hashomer Hatzair and the Growth of the Pioneering Youth Movements

At the Hashomer Hatzair meeting in Bratislava held during November 17–19, 1945, the movement had for the moment decided to cooperate with the Nocham framework while maintaining the independent functioning of its kibbutzim. Obviously, such an arrangement would be difficult if not impossible to maintain. Following the decision in Bratislava, Hashomer Hatzair began to organize a movement framework in the American zone of Germany. This entailed creating a central leadership (*hanhagah rashit*) in Bavaria as well as moving a kibbutz to Bergen-Belsen in order to establish a presence in the British zone. The central leadership would be led by a triumvirate that included Mordechai Rosman and Michael Deshe.[10] With the arrival of more groups from Poland, the central leadership worked to create organization among the movement in Germany, maintaining correspondence with the various kibbutz groups, requesting frequent updates on their status and activities, and keeping records of membership with lists that recorded place and date of birth as well as level of education and family status. These records as well as the regular updates provided by the kibbutz groups offer fascinating insights into the experiences of the youths organized in the Hashomer Hatzair kibbutzim in the DP camps of Germany.

Among the first wave of Hashomer Hatzair kibbutz groups to arrive in the American zone of Germany were Miriam and Baruch's first kibbutz groups from Sosnowiec and Bytom and the first kibbutzim from Warsaw and Krakow. Other kibbutz groups would continue to arrive after the kibbutzim from Sosnowiec and Bytom over the course of 1946, including groups that had been organized in Częstochowa, Łódź, Katowice, and Opole, to name a few, as well as kibbutzim from Czechoslovakia, Romania, and later Hungary. The archives of the Hashomer Hatzair movement in Germany have preserved records on at least fourteen different kibbutzim in the American zone. The kibbutz groups were initially named after the town where they were organized. The decision to name many of the kibbutzim after the movement's resistance fighters who had died during the war was only taken at the first Hashomer Hatzair movement conference in postwar Germany at Biberach on December 10, 1945.[11] There several of the kibbutzim were renamed after Hashomer Hatzair resistance fighters such as Mordechai Anielewicz (the first groups from Sosnowiec and Bytom), Chaviva Reik,

Yosef Kaplan (first from Warsaw and Krakow), Tosia Altman, Aryeh Vilner, and Zvi Brandes.[12] Other kibbutzim carried symbolic names such as Le-Shichrur (Toward Liberation), BaDerech (On the Way), and BaMa'avak (In the Struggle).[13]

Statistical information on the demographic composition of the Hashomer Hatzair kibbutzim in the American zone reveals the strategy of the pioneering youth movements (Hashomer Hatzair, Dror, Gordoniah-Nocham) of recruiting the younger strata of the DP population into their kibbutzim in an effort to draw in what they regarded as the most desirable candidates for life in kibbutzim in Palestine. The nonpioneering kibbutzim, including those of HaOwed, Left Poalei Zion, Poalei Zion Right, and Poalei Agudat Israel were often composed more of families and focused less on adhering to a rigorous communal lifestyle. Studies done on kibbutzim organized in Poland indicate that the pioneering youth movements sought to include primarily those under the age of twenty-five.[14] Pioneering youth movements divided their kibbutzim into two classes: kibbutz yeladim (children) and kibbutz bogrim (young adults). Those under the age of thirteen who had been included in the Koordinacja, which "redeemed" Jewish children from Polish families, were then placed in children's homes.[15] The children's kibbutzim included those aged thirteen through sixteen.[16] The youth movements tried to limit membership in the kibbutz bogrim to those ages seventeen to twenty-five. Such assessments are borne out by the data collected on selected Hashomer Hatzair kibbutzim in Germany in the summer of 1946 (table 2).

Among the children's kibbutzim, the kibbutz named LeShichrur, organized in Łódź and located in the French zone in the town of Jordenbad, numbered twenty-six members (equally divided between boys and girls) with an average age of 15.[17] Similarly, Kibbutz Aryeh Vilner, composed of two children's groups from Poland, many of whom had been removed from children's homes there, counted seventy members between the ages of 11 and 15 in March 1946.[18] Finally, the so-called veterans' kibbutzim (kibbutz vatikim) were composed of former prewar youth movement members and their families. Among these kibbutz groups, which included married members and children, were Kibbutz Bechazit (On the Front), with twenty-five members aged 25–36, of which four were married couples with five children under the age of 13.[19] The kibbutz vatikim in Schlifing, on the other hand, had an average age of 31.75 and included thirteen families and seven infants.[20]

Age and Composition of Selected Hashomer Hatzair Kibbutzim in Germany, 1946

Kibbutz	Average Age	Male:Female Ratio
Kibbutz Tosia Altman[a]	16–18 years	24 men:33 women
Kibbutz Chaviva Reik[b]	19.84 years	34 men:17 women
Kibbutz Zvi Brandes[c]	18.5 years	60 men:33 women
Kibbutz LeShichrur[d]	23 years	31 men:9 women
Kibbutz BaMa'avak[e]	21.5 years	31 members (ratio unclear)
Gailingen Hakhsharah[f]	21.9 years	23 members (ratio unclear)

[a] Kibbutz Tosia Altman report to Hashomer Hatzair leadership in Germany, June 1946, Eschwege, Haganah Archives, Ha'apalah Project (HAHP), 123/HaShomer Hatzair/410 (at Giv'at Chaviva, Hashomer Hatzair Archives, file 8.13.2), Correspondence with Kibbutzei Hakhsharah, pp. 314–17. Elsewhere the age range is given as sixteen to eighteen years old.
[b] HAHP, 123/HaShomer Hatzair/410, pp. 34–41; a for brief history of the kibbutz, see p. 70. Monish Einhorn later became madrich of this kibbutz.
[c] HAHP, 123/Hashomer Hatzair/410, pp. 282–89.
[d] Kibbutz Leshichrur report to leadership, August 12, 1946, HAHP, 123/Hashomer Hatzair/410, pp. 234–36.
[e] HAHP, 123/Hashomer Hatzair/410, pp. 98–101. Kibbutz BaMa'avak in Wildbad also counted six members over the age of forty.
[f] Jewish Agency questionnaire of the Hakhsharah in Gailingen, Gottmadingen Strasse, YIVO, DPG, Roll 108, Folder 1512, pp. 872–981, based on twenty-three individual surveys conducted by the Jewish Agency.

Although the various Zionist youth movements were divided by ideological differences, the daily experiences of their members shared much in common. Like the kibbutz groups of Hashomer Hatzair, the Dror and Gordoniah groups followed similar patterns in their departure from Eastern Europe with the Bricha and in their experiences once in Germany. Preparation for life in Palestine dominated the activities of most of the movements; what distinguished them was their idea of what the future Jewish state would look like. Dror and Hashomer Hatzair, for example, emphasized the need to create a socialist society in the new state; Poalei Agudat Israel and Bnei Akiva worked toward the creation of a state that would be a synthesis of the religious ideals of Torah with a Zionist ethic.[21] Generally, these groups were also formed in Poland (usually as one group in a specific town; later kibbutz groups arrived from Czechoslovakia, Hungary, and Romania). During their time in Germany they interacted with the central leadership regularly, compiling activity reports, paying dues to the movement, and relying on the movement for educational materials, the movement newspaper, and questions of aliyah and internal movement in Germany. After spending the first few months in a DP camp, part of the kibbutz would move to a kibbutz hakhsharah (agricultural training farm) in order to gain experience with agriculture before departure. Such was the experience of Baruch and Miriam's first kibbutz groups from Sosnowiec and Bytom (which later formed Kibbutz Mordechai Anielewicz), living in various DP camps before relocating to the movement farm in Eschwege. Kibbutz Chaviva Reik first lived in the DP camp at Pocking (Pine City) before moving to the farm at Eschwege. On the other hand, the kibbutz named after the United Partisans' Organization (Fareinigte Partizaner Organizatsye) of the Vilna ghetto, which did not arrive in Germany until the summer of 1946 after spending its first five months in Opole and Katowice, came directly to the farm in Holzhausen, near Munich, on June 20, 1946.[22] Over time, certain members would be selected for aliyah, while others would remain, continuing to learn and train while in Germany. Those who did not depart were often left to hold places and supplies for new groups of kibbutzim arriving from the East.

Adjusting to Daily Life in a DP Camp: Activity Reports

As Hashomer Hatzair organized its kibbutzim in the American zone, members did increasingly begin to sense how the movement became an important part of their everyday lives. Individual kibbutz groups were responsible for contributing regular reports (dinim ve'cheshbonot) to the movement leadership in order to inform them of the composition of the kibbutzim, their everyday activities, and their progress culturally, socially, and educationally.

The descriptions of life in the DP camps provided by the diary of Kibbutz Tosia Altman and the reports of the kibbutzim reveal the daily patterns of life within the kibbutz as well as those departures from the norm—aliyah of members, movement meetings, seminars, cultural activities, etc.—that members deemed worthy of note or believed that the central leadership would be interesting in learning about. The reports also provided kibbutzim with an opportunity to voice complaints and concerns to the leadership, which they did with frequency depending on the perceived severity of problems within the kibbutz. While such reports certainly convey the experience of the individual kibbutzim as they related to the central leadership of the movement, often in response to specific requests for information from the movement, taken together with the diary of Kibbutz Tosia Altman they can be helpful in understanding the nature of the kibbutz experience in postwar Germany. Although kibbutz members may have taken into consideration the audiences for which they were writing in composing their descriptions of kibbutz life, together the sources provide a reasonable and consistent internal perspective on the functioning and experience of Hashomer Hatzair kibbutzim in Germany.[23]

The diary was written with the guidance of Miriam and Baruch and begun once the kibbutz had reached Germany.[24] While it is clear that periods of time were not recorded in the diary, it does not seem that the diary was intended to record only positive experiences and events in the kibbutz history. Indeed, in many cases crisis periods, episodes of kibbutz abandonment, the departure of key members, and other difficult situations are recorded within the diary. Likewise, the reports sent by the kibbutzim to the movement leadership, including those sent by Kibbutz Tosia Altman at the time, record various difficulties such as poor living conditions, inadequate supplies, discontent and departure of members. At the same time, kibbutz groups seem to have understood that there was an equation between their cultural development and their potential to be selected for aliyah, meaning that reports may have emphasized educational and cultural initiatives within the kibbutz to present their kibbutz in a positive light to the leadership. In the case of Kibbutz Tosia Altman, the diary recorded events as they transpired to the kibbutz as a collective while highlighting what were perceived to be the most interesting aspects of kibbutz life, generally holidays, celebrations, and cultural activities.

The Difficult Arrival of Kibbutz Tosia Altman in the American Zone

In their departure from Poland with the Bricha, the kibbutz groups shared similar experiences, traveling together with forged documents that frequently labeled them as Greeks. They were forced to deceive train conductors, station agents, and customs officers as to their ultimate destination and often had to sneak across borders at night with the assistance of Bricha operatives.[25] For many of the Hashomer Hatzair kibbutz groups organized in Poland, regardless of age or composition, the period of arrival in Germany marked a difficult stage of transition in which members had to grow accustomed to the vagaries of life in a DP camp. The kibbutz groups often encountered opposition from other Zionists in the camps suspicious of groups affiliated with other movements and also had to deal with poor living conditions, delayed access to rations, and other difficulties associated with adapting to life in a new place.

Miriam's group from Sosnowiec began its first day in Germany inauspiciously, as members were quickly initiated into the intermovement rivalry that would characterize much of the period. On November 12, 1945, the sections of the Sosnowiec kibbutz met in Munich at the Deutsches Museum, from where they were directed to the Landsberg DP camp by the Zionist organization. Landsberg was the largest Jewish camp, holding five thousand Jewish refugees at the end of 1945. Cultural life was beginning to flourish there as the Jewish groups organized activities in the camp.[26] Miriam entered the camp and requested a place for a Hashomer Hatzair kibbutz. A soldier of the Jewish Brigade by the name of Bar-Yosef responded that it would be impossible to accept such a group; the members would have to be divided into two groups. As noted in the dairy, the meaning of such a suggestion was clearly understood by the members of the kibbutz after being explained by Miriam: "They [the Zionist leadership of the camp] want to break us apart and prevent the establishment of the Hashomer Hatzair movement here. All of the slogans about unity and harmony between the movements will not prevent us from accomplishing our goals."[27]

The United Zionist Organization (UZO) had grown increasingly wary of the Dror and Hashomer Hatzair kibbutz groups arriving from the East, suspicious that they had little intention of integrating into the Nocham movement framework.[28] (And indeed, these kibbutz groups were for the most part intent on maintaining an independent framework.) Nonetheless, with the assistance of Mishka Zacks, a Hashomer Hatzair comrade with connections on the Landsberg camp committee who worked for the UNRRA, Miriam's kibbutz managed to sneak into the camp and find a place to sleep at a Dror kibbutz. The tension between the Hashomer Hatzair kibbutz and the Zionist leadership in the camp did not dissipate after arrival, however, and for the first two days the kibbutz was unable to acquire the necessary ration cards to secure food and clothing.[29] While it is unclear whether this delay was a function of administrative inefficiency or political pressure, the youths in Kibbutz Tosia Altman clearly interpreted it as a sign of political opposition. Such a perception only served to reinforce the sense of allegiance to Hashomer Hatzair for kibbutz members.

Part of the difficult transition to life in a DP camp was the less than ideal housing available in the camp. Miriam's kibbutz managed to find an unused cabin (perhaps a former barrack) in the DP camp that, despite its miserable condition, was preferable to crowding together in one building with two other non–Hashomer Hatzair kibbutz groups. Two days after the move to the new barrack Baruch's kibbutz from Bytom arrived, and the Hashomer Hatzair leadership decided to join the two groups in order to form one large kibbutz. The cabin was filled with trash and rats, and the members of the kibbutz spent the first two days cleaning it up. They took doors, beds, windows, stoves, and whatever else they could find in the camp for the bunk, because they "understood that if they did not take it, someone else would."[30] There was no plumbing in the building, so members initially had to wash up using the early season snow outside and a bathroom in the yard that they shared with the Dror kibbutz. Thanks to their connection with Mishka Zacks from the UNRRA, they were eventually able to get electricity in some of the rooms and light to facilitate evening activities, although initially they were forced to rely on candles.

The cabin was long and narrow with a hallway down the middle (a diagram is included in the diary). The bunk was divided into six smaller rooms for boys and four rooms for girls; a dining room, kitchen, washroom, reading room, and storage room; and an administrative office where Miriam and Baruch lived. The mattresses in the bedrooms were crowded one on top of the other, leaving little room for much else. A small stove heated each room, filling it with smoke in the process. One room was designated for members with scabies, an allergic reaction caused by burrowing mites under the skin. Not surprisingly considering the conditions in which the members were forced to live, this highly contagious affliction turned out to be prevalent.[31]

Poor conditions notwithstanding, the kibbutz members slowly grew accustomed to the new situation and began the process of kibbutz life there, holding their first joint kibbutz meeting and electing a new mazkirut. At the first

Excerpt from the Diary of Kibbutz *Lochamei HaGetaot al shem Tosia Altman*. On the left is a drawing of the group's living quarters in the Landsberg DP camp. (Kibbutz Gazit Archive, Israel)

joint meeting Miriam warned them of the difficult challenges they would face in Germany, urging them to be strong in the face of efforts to break the unity of the kibbutz, which now numbered 110 members. "Nonetheless, we must withstand such efforts and without a doubt, each of us will need to be dedicated to protecting the sanctity of the kibbutz. We will stand before such efforts as one united body."[32] In order to begin anew the "normal life" of the kibbutz, however, it was urgent that the kibbutz reestablish the institutions of the kibbutz as they had begun in Poland, and first and foremost among these were the mazkirut and the cultural committee. Monish Einhorn was elected mazkir, and a number of other members were selected to the positions of treasurer, work coordinator, pantry manager, cultural committee administrator, house mother, and others. Yedziah was designated foreign minister, a position that required making the necessary connections outside of the kibbutz to secure any number of essential items (such as a pot acquired from a German woman outside of the camp) as well as positions of employment within the camp.

Almost immediately after arrival in Landsberg, Yaffa, a member of the kibbutz from Sosnowiec, was selected to participate in the conference in Bratislava on November 18, 1945. Upon her return, she reported back to the rest of the kibbutz on her encounter with soldiers from the Jewish Brigade and on the lectures she heard on the current political situation in Palestine. She was most impressed, however, by the unity of the movement and by the feeling of being a "member of one large family, with one large shared goal before it. In these unforgettable moments I felt for the first time identification, closeness and a love for the movement which not long ago I did not even know. I was overcome by a feeling of contentment, that the event had led me along the correct path."[33] Yaffa's report back to the kibbutz must have conveyed some sense of belonging to a larger movement family, but it did not seem to provide the necessary solace (or provisions) to remedy the trying situation that the kibbutz faced in Landsberg.

Crisis within the Kibbutz

Despite entries in the diary that suggest that this renewal of organizational and cultural work within the kibbutz (and contact with the wider movement) fortified members "prepared to face the difficulties of the future," it is clear that the difficult transition to Landsberg took a toll on the kibbutz. According to one entry in the diary written shortly after arrival in Landsberg, a number of members decided to depart the kibbutz group, and out of thirty prospective members (aged seventeen to eighteen) who arrived from Prague to join the kibbutz, only five decided to stay.[34] As it was explained in the diary, many of the Prague children (*Prager Kinder*) decided not to remain with the kibbutz because "they could not understand our arrangements in the kibbutz. How was it that we didn't have private money, what was shituf [cooperation] at all? On the new arrivals, the 'chalutzim,' the place did not make a good impression. A wooden cabin, crowded rooms and they immediately started to confer secretly among themselves." The next morning most of the Prague group scattered in the camp, some finding private apartments, some "establishing themselves in comfort in the 'salons' of Nocham. . . . Our kibbutz was not prepared to tolerate this."[35] For most of the group of new arrivals from Prague, the restrictions of kibbutz life and the spartan conditions of Kibbutz Tosia Altman were too much to absorb in the adjustment

to the DP camps. All in all, some fifteen original members from Poland
(13–14 percent) decided to leave the kibbutz within the first two weeks in
Landsberg. Some members such as Tzipporah and Liza discovered acquaintances within the camp and chose to join them instead, leaving the kibbutz
for personal rather than political reasons. The fact that so few of the new
arrivals from Prague chose to stay makes the decision of those from Poland
who remained with the group all the more worthy of investigation.

The difficulty of the transition to Landsberg left the kibbutz in a perceived state of crisis. Indeed, it seems that while the period in Poland was
marked by efforts to attract new membership, the period in Germany for
many kibbutzim would be defined by efforts to maintain membership and
deepen loyalty to the movement. The madrichim had tried to teach the
members of the kibbutz while they were still in Poland that individual decisions were no longer solely personal; they now had to be considered in light
of their impact on the collective. After three months of living together as a
collective group, members were not only taught such lessons directly by the
madrichim, but the directives were also reinforced by more subtle forms of
peer pressure in order to encourage members not to abandon the group.
Miriam and Baruch did not hesitate to rely on other, more coercive, methods in order to force members to weigh the consequences of departure from
the group.

In response to the departure of members, the cultural committee sensed
a need to take drastic action to convince members to remain within the kibbutz. The committee initially conceived of staging a mock trial of the Zionist movement, but it was decided that such a project would not excite the
membership enough to remove them from the crisis of low morale that had
beset the kibbutz. Miriam and Baruch secretly came up with the idea of put-
ting Monish, the secretary of the kibbutz, on trial for supposedly opting
to leave the kibbutz in order to pursue a musical career in Frankfurt with a
cousin.[36] Miriam and Baruch asked Monish to pretend that he had truly
found a family member and had decided to leave the kibbutz in order to
pursue his own interests. The madrichim thought that such a trial would be
ideal in order to stimulate discussion in the kibbutz and overcome the boredom that had begun to set in.

Monish agreed to participate in the charade and was apparently quite
successful in deceiving his fellow kibbutz members, for their reactions were

extreme. In the diary in a personal entry written after the mock trial, Monish describes the treatment he faced from members stunned by his alleged betrayal. He endured shouting, curses, and even spitting. His closest friends seemed to become his greatest enemies. Yehudit stated that she simply "won't allow it," while Paula's reaction was personal: "I no longer respect him as a person, even if he does end up staying."[37] Another female member questioned, "How could he take on the position of mazkir when he always knew that he was going to leave?" Friends who previously would loan him a hat or clothes now refused. Others came to him in tears begging him to stay, while Hinda and Tzintza sat in their room "as if they were sitting shiva [the week-long mourning period observed by Jews after a death], wiping tears from their eyes."[38]

Monish agreed to stand trial, and the dining room of the kibbutz was turned into a courtroom with space provided for the prosecution, defense, a judge, the accused, and the witnesses; the rest of the room was reserved for the audience. Arguing in his own defense while enduring shouts and catcalls from the audience, Monish blamed the faults of the kibbutz and the Zionist movement for his decision to leave. His defense attorneys, Yehudit and Ruth, still unaware that the trial was a farce, also blamed the Zionist movement and the institutions of the kibbutz. Ruth, who was also the administrator for sharing, blamed the idea of shituf, asking "how is it possible that each individual not have his own pajamas and be forced to wear those of another?" Yehudit suggested that the work assignments in the kibbutz were not properly delegated and that a person needed "connections" (*proteksiah*) in order to secure favorable positions. Monish indicted the whole concept of collective decision making in his own defense: "If I need to smoke a cigarette, the kibbutz will decide only five per day; if I want to go to the movies, do I have to wait until everyone is ready to go together?!" Finally the prosecution (Inka, Hinda, and Salusia) spoke, "dismantling the house of cards that I [Monish] built in my charges" and defending the kibbutz and the Zionist movement.[39] After a period of questioning from the audience, the judges left to deliberate and returned with a verdict that was intended to be binding: "Whether by or against his will, Monish must recognize the fact that Zionism is the only way to establish (and resurrect) the nation and the kibbutz the only way to actualization. He must stay in the kibbutz!" Monish read a statement accepting the verdict of the court, and "all of a sudden, my

worst enemies once again became my best friends. . . . I even received two
rations of chocolate."[40] Afterward, the members discovered that Monish
had in fact been acting.[41] The reactions of the members seem to have tended
toward happiness and relief; there is no reference in the diary or in subsequent recollections to any sense of having been manipulated by Monish or
Miriam and Baruch.

The episode of the trial so soon after the arrival and unification of the
kibbutzim from Sosnowiec and Bytom points to a number of questions that
the kibbutz group would have to face in Germany: How would members
be encouraged to remain with the kibbutz now that other potentially more
attractive options were open to them? Why should they choose to stay with
Hashomer Hatzair as opposed to any of the other movements promising
aliyah and perhaps better connections to achieve this goal? Why would certain members choose the kibbutz over the prospect of migration to another
country or the option of settling in Germany?

The complaints about the kibbutz and shituf suggest that for many of the
members, these ideological goals were only worthy of sacrifice when considered in light of the greater value of the kibbutz as a new family. Departure
from the kibbutz, even if shituf and the lack of individual freedom were to
blame, was an inexcusable betrayal. The pressure to conform and follow the
dictates of the kibbutz remained strong. The trial stood out in the memory
of the kibbutz members as a significant event in regard to the development of
the kibbutz. Miriam recalled it many years later as a great success, and Monish was surprised by the ease with which he was able to slip into his role, as
if he were "descended from a great line of actors."[42] However, the episode of
the trial also points to the tensions that could easily boil to the surface when
the kibbutz was faced with the crisis of one of its leaders' departure. Those
arguing in his defense were quick to blame the narrow constraints of shituf
and collectivism; his accusers were less concerned with his choice to leave the
Zionist path than his decision (especially as mazkir) to abandon the kibbutz
family, the ultimate act of betrayal.

Was the trial successful? It did reveal the degree to which the members of
the kibbutz were susceptible to coercive tactics of ensuring continuing loyalty to the kibbutz group. And it also revealed the intense need that many
of the members felt to preserve the integrity of their new family following the
wartime loss of their own families. In terms of the goals of the madrichim,

Miriam and Baruch were successful in using the trial as an educational tool to demonstrate to the membership the importance of maintaining the kibbutz. The psychologically manipulative impact of the episode on the kibbutz is striking. Yet there is no indication that any of the members were sufficiently put off by the manipulation to leave the kibbutz; on the contrary, the episode seems to have reinforced the reasons for remaining with the group for members who may have questioned the kibbutz framework. Nonetheless, it is also of note that the reasons put forth by the members for remaining within the kibbutz had little to do with the ideological basis of the kibbutz or the youth movement. On the contrary, Monish's accusers first vilified him for abandoning his comrades in the kibbutz before defending the concepts of collectivism and the goal of aliyah.

After approximately six weeks in Landsberg during which the kibbutz stabilized and began a daily routine, the kibbutz received instruction from UNRRA representatives in the camp that it was time for them to move to better living conditions in the new camp of Leipheim, ninety kilometers away. The kibbutz members, defiant and perhaps suspicious of the command from an outside authority, refused to leave their current situation, overcrowding and rats notwithstanding. However, after Mordechai (from the leadership), Mishka (from the UNRRA), and Yedzia (from the kibbutz) returned from Leipheim with a positive recommendation on the new living situation, they agreed to leave Landsberg. On December 23 they set out for Leipheim with the first transport of DPs from Landsberg, taking with them all the kitchen items and articles collected in the storehouse (shoes, coats, blankets, etc.) that they feared would be hard to come by in the new camp. They arrived at the camp and were greeted with DDT powder and immunization shots.[43] They moved into building number 9, a two-story, whitewashed new home (a diagram is included in the diary). There was only one problem: they had to share the building with a kibbutz from Dror. Baruch worked to have them split up, and Kibbutz Tosia Altman managed to occupy the whole building by itself. Twenty different rooms housed boys and girls separately and included a kitchen, dining room, and office and other kibbutz essentials.[44] Despite their initial reservations, the period at Leipheim ended up being a fruitful one for the kibbutz, providing the group with a tremendous opportunity to engage in intensive cultural and educational activities while undertaking various work assignments within the camp. During their time there, the kibbutz managed to transition from crisis to productive educational training.

Becoming Part of a Larger Family

As Shaike Weinberg noted in his educational program for Hashomer Hatzair madrichim working in Europe after the war, one of the most important tasks of the movement leaders was the "cultivation of a spiritual connection to the movement through a deepening of patriotism to the movement—the most important educational weapon without which one cannot speak of success in educational activity at all, not to mention in the area of ideas."[45] He rejected prewar methods of cultural education such as scouting, which had been emphasized in movement education, in favor of methods that would be more relevant to the young survivors joining the movement. The creation of a framework that would be appealing enough for youths to decide to join the movement was only the first step on the Zionist route from Europe; the kibbutz framework would also have to prove sufficiently satisfying and worthwhile to keep youths in the movement.

In fact, from a very early point in their arrival in Germany, the leadership worked to make the kibbutzim feel as if they were a strong part of the movement, instructing them early on that there was a clear difference between their kibbutz and the rest of the Zionists in the American zone. For Kibbutz Tosia Altman, they also now understood that a Dror kibbutz was quite different from their own, even if they were forced to share an outhouse with them.[46] Competition between the movements seems to have been perpetuated by the leadership and understood by the members not as a function of differing ideology but rather as a matter of group cohesion versus otherness.

Kibbutz members were made to feel a part of the larger movement through participation in local movement meetings and conferences. The leadership of Kibbutz Tosia Altman accompanied Miriam and Baruch to the first Hashomer Hatzair conference in Bavaria at Biberach on December 10, 1945. The participants heard Mordechai Rosman (also one of the first organizers of the Bricha movement in Poland) lecture on the current situation in the Zionist movement and in the Hashomer Hatzair movement and learned about past glories of the movement during the war. One of the main decisions taken at the meeting was to name the kibbutzim after fallen heroes of the movement.

The subsequent entry in the diary portrayed the excitement of the members of Kibbutz Tosia Altman when they learned of their new kibbutz identity. Mordechai Rosman, who had been a member of a prewar kibbutz with Tosia Altman, told them stories about her life and her heroism in the ghetto. "We were all enchanted by her personage . . . and thus the kibbutz decided in an assembly to accept the decision of the meeting and call our kibbutz from now on Kibbutz Lochamei HaGetaot al shem Tosia Altman [Ghetto Fighters' Kibbutz named after Tosia Altman]."[47] The movement, by linking the identity of the individual kibbutzim with the heroism of wartime resistance fighters, cemented the identification of Hashomer Hatzair with its central leadership role in the ghetto resistance in the minds of the young survivors.

Making members feel like part of the larger movement did not necessarily remedy everyday problems faced by kibbutz members within the DP camp, however. The process of deepening loyalty to Hashomer Hatzair and the Zionist idea was a process that would take place on the everyday level within the kibbutz. Such cultural immersion would be necessary for members to overcome the various difficulties that life in a DP camp presented to kibbutz members. The reports sent by the individual kibbutz groups to the central leadership document the unfolding of this process from week to week.

Surveys on Kibbutz Activity in the DP Camps

In March 1946 the Hashomer Hatzair central leadership in Germany complained to the kibbutzim named after Mordechai Anielewicz and Yosef Kaplan that they had yet to receive surveys and regular reports on the current situation of the kibbutz "despite repeated requests for materials."[48] The movement leadership preferred regular reports for contact rather than occasional visits by movement representatives to the kibbutzim. As they noted in their request, the reports could be written in Yiddish or Hebrew, but "it is important that you touch upon all areas of life in the kibbutz, social situation, cultural work, accomplishments, learning of Hebrew, connection with the movement (contact), movement activities, etc."[49] In other correspondence with the kibbutzim, the movement requested that they provide regular reports on the composition of the kibbutz, including information on the level of education of members, any illiteracy, the number of classes they held regularly, the number of books available to members, and the frequency of kibbutz meetings.[50]

In response to the request, Kibbutz Yosef Kaplan in Jordenbad sent a survey written in Hebrew "on all areas of activity."[51] The kibbutz, which at the time (March 16, 1946) numbered 112 members, was composed of the first kibbutzim organized in Warsaw and Krakow as well as the kibbutz from Gdansk and the group from Łódź. As they noted in the report, "despite the age differences between the members and the very small rooms, social conditions are good in the kibbutz." The kibbutz was proud to record its success in joining the diverse groups together and noted that "little difference is felt between the groups." Economic conditions were good, as the "clothing and shoe question" had been solved. Notably, however, "the main problem in the kibbutz is *lack of work*: only 7 percent of the members are occupied in outside work, the rest are involved in housekeeping and other internal forms of work. Despite various efforts we have still not been able to find work outside of the kibbutz."[52]

In many cases, the best way to avoid demoralization and charges of laziness was to keep kibbutz members busy. Yet despite the best efforts of the kibbutz and the camp administration in their creation of workshops for vocational training, there was not always work to be had.[53] The members of Kibbutz Tosia Altman in Landsberg and Leipheim often took on forms of work that others in the camp were reluctant to perform, working as potato peelers (*kommando kartoszki* in Polish) in the camp kitchen, forming a sanitation group to clean bathrooms in the camp, moving furniture, and working in the camp laundry.[54] Such forms of work gave members of the kibbutzim positive reputations as industrious young refugees willing to take on the "hardest and nastiest assignments" and made them less likely to fall into the demoralization and laziness that American administrators feared.[55] Nonetheless, as was the case with Kibbutz Yosef Kaplan, there was usually not enough such work to go around. The rest of the kibbutz members were thus frequently occupied with internal forms of work such as housekeeping, cleaning, laundry, sewing, and acquisition of goods for the kibbutz. The members of Kibbutz Chaviva Reik in Pocking worked in the vocational school and the camp kitchen and operated a tailor shop for other camp residents.[56] Not surprisingly, much of the work was performed according to standard gender roles commonly in practice in the Zionist movement: in Kibbutz Chaviva Reik at the farm in Eschwege, for example, the women were occupied with housekeeping, cleaning, and cooking, while the men were occupied with outside work and manual labor.[57] This was also the case in Kibbutz Tosia Altman; in Leipheim, female members (Bluma, Ruth, and Tzilah) handled housekeeping, administration, kitchen work, and sewing, while the men worked as tailors or in the camp. As noted in the Kibbutz Tosia Altman diary, "every day our women sweated from 8 am in housekeeping. . . . One girl had to mop the long hallway. The girls who were cleaning would get angry at the [male] members who got in their way."[58] Kibbutzim also seemed to derive a considerable amount of their income from speculation on the black market, usually through the sale of cigarettes acquired by official rations but not smoked in the kibbutz. This, however, was a form of work that both men and women could perform.[59]

These forms of work and speculation brought the kibbutzim into contact with rest of the DP camp. As part of their training, kibbutz members also took on the tasks of security and defense in the camps; in Leipheim, Baruch established a local militia for defense and order to prevent theft in the camp. While there was not a strong need to defend against any particular enemy in the DP camps, defense (*haganah*) was seen as an important part of kibbutz training for life in Palestine and the many potential threats that could be encountered there. According to the Kibbutz Tosia Altman diary, "only the members of the kibbutzim joined the militia."[60] The security committee was composed of members from Hashomer Hatzair, Dror, and Pachach; their first mission was to maintain order in the camp dining room. Defense was a task that each of the kibbutzim, including Kibbutz Aryeh Vilner, Kibbutz Yosef Kaplan, and Kibbutz United Partisans' Organization, also undertook in their respective camps.[61] In the schools (vocational and regular) the kibbutz members also encountered other camp members, although such schools continued to be attended for the most part by kibbutz members. Kibbutz Tosia Altman also worked on the local camp committee in Leipheim and did various service jobs in the kibbutz, including cleaning, repairs, and cooking.[62]

While they initially had to dine in the camp dining hall, over time kibbutzim gained the right to dine on their own, sending members to the camp kitchen to obtain food and bring it back to the kibbutz.[63]

The Difficulties of Kibbutz Life in the DP Camp

Despite such efforts to keep the kibbutzim busy, however, kibbutz members were forced to face numerous difficulties associated with inadequate living conditions and the social complexities of collective life. The kibbutzim confronted on a daily basis mundane problems such as social conflicts within groups, boredom, and issues of gender relations as well as the more serious matters of illness and death. For example, Kibbutz Tosia Altman designated a room in its new building in Leipheim as Mitzrayim (Egypt) for those unfortunate members still afflicted with scabies. Five girls were the first patients, and they were quarantined for one week without contact. Even before their departure from Landsberg, Baruch tried to convince those members with scabies not to be embarrassed to admit that they had it and to remain in Landsberg for treatment. Nonetheless, no one wanted to remain in Landsberg without the rest of the kibbutz. Shortly after their arrival in Leipheim, however, it became clear how many individuals from the kibbutz were suffering from scabies, as they immediately had to create a quarantine room in the new home. The afflicted members were confined to bed all day and forced to rub a "stinky black ointment that smelled like sulfur" all over their skin. Members were prevented from having any contact with the afflicted, an especially difficult sentence for the "carousels" (this was the word used for couples) in the group: as noted in the diary, it was difficult to prevent Mishka from sitting by Sonia, Haim by Hanka, and Azriel near Tzipporah. Still, despite the restrictions, Baruch forced the smelly comrades to participate in his Zionism lectures in the evenings, where the members who reeked of sulfur were greeted with snorts and pinched noses. After a few weeks all of the afflicted healed and returned to their rooms.

Other kibbutzim dealt with more serious life-threatening illnesses, with many members still not fully recovered from the diseases they had encountered during the war. Kibbutz Ma'apilim Zvi Brandes (named after Zvi Brandes) lost two members to illness within the span of a month in early 1946. Moshe Schwartz, a twenty-year-old survivor of the notorious death marches

from the Stutthof camp in northern Poland, joined the kibbutz in Częstochowa despite not having fully recovered from his wartime illnesses. He
departed with his kibbutz from Poland on the path for Palestine, but, as
noted in a report to the leadership, "it was discovered that the days of suffering had not departed from his body and they found signs of tuberculosis."
He was transferred to the hospital in Feldafing, where he spent eight weeks.
His condition worsened, and on "Thursday, January 24, 1946, at 9 am, Moshe
left this world." His comrades wrote that "we found comfort next to his grave
but only with the continuation of our path in order to realize his will and
dream to reach our homeland will we find solace."[64]

Illness seems to have been a condition common to kibbutz members, as
it was for many among the DP population. Kibbutz Tosia Altman noted soon
after moving to Leipheim that in addition to the five sick members within
the kibbutz, five more were at a hospital outside Leipheim. As it reported in
a letter to the leadership, "the most important question is the issue of the
sick, who need better treatment . . . so far the kibbutz has done its best to
help the sick members. . . . The situation cannot remain like this, it leads to
a weakening of the social group and more sick members."[65] Emissaries from
Palestine also testified to poor health among the DPs. Miriam Warburg
described the difficult health conditions in Föhrenwald at the end of October 1945: "Our main problem is the fight against tuberculosis. Even for our
worst cases we have not yet found sufficient places in the sanatoriums in the
neighborhood, and the infected mix freely with the whole camp."[66] In a June
1946 letter, Haim Hoffman, head of the Jewish Agency delegation to Germany, expressed concern at the still rising rates of TB, numerous heart problems, and the poor diet lacking in vitamins that was available.[67]

Other problems expressed by kibbutzim fell under the category of social
relations. Some of the kibbutzim sent requests to the central leadership with
concerns over gender imbalances in the kibbutz; it seems that there was a
general belief that women in a kibbutz could have a stabilizing influence on
the behavior of the young men.[68] (This could also be a way of ensuring that
young men remained within the kibbutz framework rather than leaving it
to find partners.) The kibbutz in Gabersee, for example, complained to the
leadership that it needed more women.[69] The Hashomer Hatzair Kibbutz
LeShichrur, which arrived from Lublin and Warsaw in the summer of 1946,
was particularly imbalanced between men and women, with thirty-one men

and only nine women. This, they feared, could have a negative influence on social life in the kibbutz. "The most difficult is the question of girls in the kibbutz, because there are no young women in the kibbutz; this influences the attitude of the boys. The kibbutz needs to be completed by adding some girls."[70] Similarly, Kibbutz United Partisans' Organization in Holtzhausen (which counted fifteen women and thirty-nine men) noted that because of the almost three-to-one ratio of men to women, "we focus a lot of energy on playing games and especially sports . . . it would be much healthier for us and for the movement to have more girls. We suggest sending 2–3 members to Poland to bring about 20–30 women to the kibbutz."[71]

In this regard Kibbutz Tosia Altman seems to have been unique, for it was consistently populated by more women than men. For example, in the summer of 1946 out of fifty-seven members counted, there were twenty-four men and thirty-three women; an earlier count listed twenty-seven men and forty-two women.[72] It is unclear why this was the case; perhaps the fact that the kibbutz had a female leader during its early period in Poland helped to attract more women to begin with. For the most part, the general gender imbalance in the kibbutz groups comported with the Zionist image of young, male pioneers who were meant to become new Jews.

Kibbutz United Partisans' Organization seems to have been particularly troubled in the sphere of social relations. Natan, an emissary from Hashomer Hatzair, described with particular concern in a letter to the central leadership the social situation in the kibbutz at Holtzhausen. He detailed problems with theft between members and constant complaining about one another, concluding that "each person looks out only for himself." He suggested "the poor nature of the kibbutz [was] because not enough cultural work had been done with them," work he had endeavored to begin.[73]

The situation in Kibbutz United Partisans' Organization seems to have improved little after this, for the subsequent correspondence detailed problems with their recently departed madrich, Menasheh, who had left the kibbutz in a "manner that was very far from decent [menschlech]. . . . When he left he took with him kibbutz property, including a radio, pictures from the archive, books, and shoes, all items he was never given permission to take." The mazkirut sought the assistance of the central leadership in having these items returned.[74]

Thus, it is clear that a number of challenges faced the kibbutzim in their time in Germany. In addition to poor conditions and problems of illness, they had to face the crisis of members who chose not to remain in the kibbutz and overcome the difficulties associated with boredom and possible demoralization in the DP camp. Kibbutzim struggled with the problem of departure from the kibbutz and tried to come up with solutions to avert kibbutz abandonment. (Nonetheless, abandonment was not necessarily portrayed as a bad thing; in this way, the weaker elements of the movement, less dedicated to the cause, could be eliminated before their arrival in Palestine.)[75] Kibbutzim also complained of lack of work or in some cases unfair delegation of work or resources. Compounding such problems were the tensions that accompanied the realization that the stay in Germany may be prolonged beyond the expected duration. As the emissary Natan had suggested in the case of the problematic Kibbutz United Partisans' Organization, the ideal solution to such problems was cultural work through the immersion of the kibbutz youths in the education and ideology of the movement.

Cultural Work in the Kibbutz

The goal of the time spent in Germany by the kibbutzim was not merely to keep members busy, although this was a good way of preventing excessive dwelling on the past. The best way to deepen loyalty to the movement was to continue the intensive cultural work that had begun in Poland. This was in a sense part of the immersion process that kibbutz members underwent in preparation for their journey to Palestine so that they could begin to feel as if they were there before they had actually arrived. As recommended by Shaike Weinberg in the educational program, a number of educational methods and activities with a "kibbutz, human, and pioneering" stamp could be utilized in order to effect a radical shift in the behavior of the youths. These recommendations reflected attention to the perceived physical, mental, and social problems among the youths. The cultural program that Weinberg suggested directed work in seven key areas, including vocational and agricultural training, socialization, general education to make up for lost schooling, instruction in Jewish history, culture, the history of the Zionist movement, the history of Hashomer Hatzair, and the history of socialism and Jewish activity in the socialist movement.[76]

Despite efforts to secure various forms of employment in the DP camps and within the kibbutz, kibbutz members were left with a considerable amount of down time. The kibbutz used this time for cultural activities. Kibbutz Yosef Kaplan described for the leadership the cultural work that was taking place in its kibbutz in the March 1946 report, detailing three levels of Hebrew instruction and classes in Hebrew literature.[77] Aside from the mandatory Hebrew groups, there were also required math groups for learning accounting and algebra that met five days a week from 2:00 in the afternoon until 6:30 in the evening. After dinner, the kibbutz held its regular assembly for the discussion of questions related to things the members had learned or issues to be resolved in kibbutz life.

Kibbutz members also participated in week-long seminars held within the kibbutz. During seminars, the kibbutz received visits from a representative of the movement who lectured the kibbutz on various topics. Kibbutz Tosia Altman opened its first seminar in the kibbutz on December 21, 1945, with the participation of Mordechai Rosman, Zelig Shushan (an emissary from Palestine), and Levi Schwartz from the Jewish Brigade, who passed on "the knowledge that had been bequeathed to them by the prewar members of the movement."[78] The seminars were composed of lectures on various themes in Zionist history, discussions on the future of Palestine, and other topics. In the evenings, the kibbutzim met for parties and discussions dedicated to various problems.[79] The kibbutz in Jordenbad also heard lectures on Zionism, Jewish history, the geography of Palestine, and historical materialism from the madrich and from shlichim sent to the kibbutz to participate in seminars.[80]

The language in which the kibbutz report sent to the leadership was written (Yiddish, Hebrew, or Polish) also gave the leadership some clue as to the developmental level of the kibbutz, and it was clear that linguistic training remained a much-needed task in the kibbutzim. Changes in the language of the report also provided evidence of the changing demographic nature of a kibbutz, with the arrival of new members from the East and the departure of more veteran members for aliyah, training farms, or movement work. Thus, it was not uncommon to see one kibbutz's reports change from

Hebrew to Yiddish and then to Polish depending on the level of Hebrew education of the membership. The first three reports of Kibbutz Yosef Kaplan, for example, from March to May 1946 were written in Hebrew (with a few mistakes); the fourth one, written on May 20, 1946, was written in Yiddish; and by the beginning of July the report was written in Polish.[81] This prompted a response from the central leadership to the kibbutz: *"you need to learn Hebrew!"*[82] On top of this, the kibbutz reported to the leadership that it had a sizable library in Yiddish and Hebrew that many members (who only had knowledge of Polish) could not use.[83]

In addition to the informal education taking place within the kibbutz, younger members of kibbutzim also attended schools in the DP camps, as was the case with Kibbutz Tosia Altman in Leipheim. Nine of the youngest members were chosen at a kibbutz meeting to attend the six hundred-student school funded with UNRRA resources. As described in the diary, however, one of the major problems in the school was a shortage of teachers and lack of materials; youth movement leaders and emissaries from Palestine frequently constituted the bulk of teachers in the schools.[84]

For the majority of kibbutz members, however, education continued to take place within the framework of the kibbutz. Members returned to the kibbutz after completing the work that was done during the day (either in or outside of the kibbutz) for the start of cultural activities. Following the first seminar in Leipheim, the members of Kibbutz Tosia Altman wrote that they were "enthusiastic" to be taking part in such activities.[85] At 4:00 p.m. the Hebrew groups began, with six classes divided on the basis of level that were conducted in an "intensive manner." After a break for dinner, the kibbutz split into two groups, one on the history of settlement in the Yishuv led by Miriam, and the other on the history of Zionism taught by Baruch.[86] After the evening classes the kibbutz held assemblies devoted to discussions of current political events, reviews of lessons learned in the seminar, or important issues facing the kibbutz. As in Poland, members could also raise concerns about the functioning of the kibbutz, providing a forum for self-criticism within the group. The assemblies were also a time for members to ask questions about sexual problems and sex education. Other free time was devoted to the writing of the kibbutz newspaper, usually by the female members of the kibbutz. Presumably, cultural time was also devoted to the writing of the kibbutz diary, although this is not mentioned within the diary itself.

מנר' י. אָבִישׁי / נ. לוֹין / ד"ר י. פָּרֶץ / ד"ר פ. שֶׁרְנוֹרוֹדְסְקָה־

יְסוֹדוֹת

סֵפֶר לִמּוּד הַלָשׁוֹן הָעִבְרִית לַמְבֻגָּרִים

הוצאת
דזשׇאִינט

Printed in Germany by the American Joint Distribution Committee, Kassel Office. U.S.A.-Zone. 1947.

Cover of a Hebrew language primer printed by the American Jewish Joint Distribution Committee in Germany. (USHMM, courtesy of Morris and Lala Fishman)

Hebrew songbook published by the United Pioneering Youth movement, Nocham, in honor of its first anniversary. The book was used in the Feldafing DP camp. (USHMM, courtesy of George Fine)

The daily activities of the kibbutzim were thus run on a schedule deter-mined by the youth movement, as was the calendar of holidays and celebra-tions in the kibbutz. Beyond daily activities, kibbutz members seemed to particularly enjoy celebrations of Jewish and Zionist movement holidays as well as the weekly commemoration of the Sabbath in an Oneg Shabbat (literally "enjoyment of the Sabbath"). The Oneg Shabbat, held on Friday evenings, was a time to have discussions of literature and readings of books and newspapers and a chance for members to present plays and perform-ances. A successful Oneg Shabbat could keep the kibbutz discussing it for several days afterward.[87] These were common to the kibbutzim of all the youth movements regardless of the level of religious observance. In fact, Hashomer Hatzair as a Marxist-leaning socialist group was decidedly secu-lar, yet the movement calendar continued to run according to the familiar Jewish holidays. The weekly Oneg Shabbat certainly did not imply obser-vance according to Jewish tradition; both Kibbutz Yosef Kaplan and Kib-butz Tosia Altman noted the Sabbath as a popular time to go to the movies in the DP camp, an activity that the Jewish religion prohibits on that day.[88]

The celebration of holidays within the kibbutzim tended to blend Jewish and Zionist motifs; in many cases, Jewish traditions were appropriated by the movement in order to emphasize wartime heroism. On the last night of Chanukah (December 6, 1945), Kibbutz Tosia Altman held a party to cele-brate the holiday (with guests from the UNRRA and representatives of the camp) and to bid farewell to the first *olim* (immigrants to Palestine) from the kibbutz. The activities within the kibbutz combined a focus on the future with constant reminders of the past, especially Hashomer Hatzair's leading role in wartime resistance. The holiday commemoration "reminded [members] of their fathers' homes," and thus speeches on heroism were given by Baruch and Mordechai. The kibbutz sang songs from the "dark days" in the ghettos, forests, and in hiding that "described the many graves in which our families were buried. The songs told the stories of the Jewish child, on the Jewish home in Poland and Lithuania, on Janusz Korczak, who went to his death without abandoning the children he taught. The songs told the stories of the ghetto fighters whose deaths in bravery rivaled the deaths of the Maccabees."[89]

The observance of Jewish holidays thus incorporated motifs of wartime resistance while continuing to focus on the Zionist future in the Land of

Israel. In honor of Chanukah in the Föhrenwald camp, Miriam Warburg (an emissary for youth aliyah) reported showing a youth aliyah film on Palestine to the residents of the camp in the big hall:

> The hall can only hold 500 people and special tickets were issued for a first and second sitting. The Jewish police were called in to see that no more than 500 people were admitted for each performance. But we had not counted on the Palestine passion of our population. In spite of the police, 800 people managed to squeeze in for the first performance. And when the show was over—and they received it with great enthusiasm—nothing could induce them to leave the hall to make room for the second lot. They started to sing and dance the hora (in spite of the dangerous overcrowding) and the second show simply could not take place.[90]

Warburg arranged for a few shows in order to enable everybody to see the film and bring "the land of their dreams at least a little nearer to the Jews."

Zionist youth from the Hashomer Hatzair children's home in the Lindenfels DP camp marching through the streets of Lindenfels. (USHMM, courtesy of Rose Guterman Zar)

Following the show, she reported, "all the Zionist youth marched through the camp with huge torches. There were about 700–800 young people, and it was a grand sight. This was the first time that the camp had stopped to be a refugee camp; it became a joyful Jewish village."[91]

Other holidays such as Tu Be-Shevat, the fifteenth day of the Jewish month of Shevat, and the traditional New Year for the Trees, or Yom Tel Hai, the day commemorating the death of early Zionist hero Josef Trumpeldor at the Battle of Tel Hai in 1920, were again opportunities to educate the kibbutz members about the heroism of Zionist leaders and strengthen connections to the Land of Israel. On Tu Be-Shevat, kibbutz groups celebrated with hikes in the forest, planted trees with the Jewish National Fund, and performed plays in their DP camps.[92] A few weeks later, Kibbutz Yosef Kaplan held a party in Jordenbad with other residents of the camp to commemorate Yom Tel Hai. They celebrated the day with a flag ceremony in the forest, haganah exercises, and games.[93] Kibbutz Tosia Altman spent the evening of Yom Tel Hai learning about the heroism of Trumpeldor, singing songs, and discussing the concept of bravery.[94] Other noteworthy dates were the anniversaries of the deaths of such Zionist luminaries as Theodor Herzl, Haim Nachman Bialik, and Yosef Haim Brenner.[95]

Yom Tel Hai was followed a few days later by a more lighthearted celebration of the Jewish holiday of Purim with a comical rendition of the kibbutz's play *Haganah*.[96] The Föhrenwald camp newspaper noted the celebration of a "Purim-Ownt [Purim evening] with the Hashomer Hatzair kibbutz in which the madricha of the kibbutz, Mirjam, . . . gave a speech on the heroes of the present-day Purim, the fighters from the Warsaw, Vilna, Bialystok, and Częstochowa ghettoes, as well as the partisans and the front-line fighters, who with their blood defended the honor of the Jewish people just as once before did Mordechai and Esther defend Jewish honor before King Ahashuerus."[97]

The first Passover following liberation was also a momentous one, as the traditional meanings of exodus and redemption took on a new significance, and in May the kibbutzim marked the holiday of Lag Ba'Omer with hikes, games, and bonfires.[98] The kibbutzim also marked the socialist holiday of May 1, which for Kibbutz Tosia Altman constituted an opportunity to "celebrate the defeat of fascism" with kibbutzim of Dror and Pachach, although the members were careful not to mark May 1 too vociferously so as not to arouse opposition in advance of the elections to the twenty-second Zionist Congress (from the local residents of the camp in Eschwege).[99] It is unclear whether this concern for overt displays of socialism had more to do with internal Zionist politics or fears of demonstrating sympathy for communism before American administration authorities. Similarly, Kibbutz Yosef Kaplan marked May 1 with a celebration, although in its case the kibbutz noted being able to do so with the other residents of the camp at Jordenbad.[100] The anniversary of liberation on May 8, 1946, was commemorated one week later.

Many of the kibbutzim also noted writing their own internal newspapers, an activity that in the case of Kibbutz Tosia Altman complemented the writing of the kibbutz diary and gave members an opportunity to record events as they happened within the kibbutz. The kibbutz in Jordenbad, for example, had at least two internal newspapers, *Chayenu* (Our Life) and *Hedim Ba-Kibbutz* (Echoes in the Kibbutz), in which members recorded the collective goals of the kibbutz: to live the life of heroes, to leave for aliyah, and to thus "realize our dream that we have dreamt for so long."[101] As in the reports sent to the leadership, members of Kibbutz Yosef Kaplan also recorded the cultural work taking place within the kibbutz in a section titled "What's New in the Kibbutz?" The arrivals of new members and departures of old ones were recorded, and correspondence from members who had immigrated to Palestine or were involved in movement work elsewhere in Germany was transcribed into the newspaper. Such letters could also serve to give members hope of departing for Palestine in the near future. The newspapers also reported on the most recent movement news from Germany and Palestine, highlighting prominently the struggles of the Jewish Agency in Palestine against the British.[102] Kibbutz Tosia Altman and Kibbutz Aryeh Vilner also wrote their own internal newspapers, as did kibbutzim belonging to other youth movements.[103]

Like Nocham and Dror, the Hashomer Hatzair movement leadership also tried to maintain a sense of belonging to a larger community by publishing its own movement newspaper, which was distributed to all of the kibbutzim in the American zone. The newspaper, titled *Hashomer Hatzair*, was published in Munich (twenty issues appeared between March 1946 and October 1947). The newspaper was dedicated to keeping members informed of current political debates in Palestine, issues facing the movement there

and in Germany, ideological concerns, the history of the movement, and the
past glories of the movement during the war. The movement intended for the
newspapers to be read by the kibbutzim during evening time designated for
cultural activity.[104] According to Hashomer Hatzair, the newspaper "should
not only be a newspaper for the movement but also a newspaper *of* the
movement." For this reason the leadership sought to encourage "members of
the kibbutzim to participate in the writing of the newspaper."[105] The movement promised kibbutzim that it would publish articles written by members
in the movement newspaper.[106]

The newspaper, which was written in Yiddish, was intended to put
members in touch with leaders of the wider movement in Palestine as well.
Articles were published based on speeches by Meir Ya'ari (Hashomer
Hatzair leader in the Yishuv), Abba Kovner (resistance leader of Hashomer
Hatzair in Vilna), Ya'akov Hazan (Ya'ari's close associate), and other leaders.
In the first volume of the newspaper Shushan, the emissary from the Yishuv,
described his encounter with the survivors in Europe in an article titled
"The Meeting with the Comrades in the Diaspora." He assured the young
survivors who had "seen what it is to wander on the ruins of Jewish life, on
the cemeteries of your parents, sisters, and brothers," that they were "not
alone in your struggle. You are comrades in a large movement 'Hashomer
Hatzair.' Your shoulder joins together with all of the shoulders of Hashomer
Haztair in the entire world." According to Shushan, the Jews from Palestine
not only understood what it was that the surviving youths had gone through
but also shared their sense of terror and loss. He expressed their pride in
finding youths to continue the path of the halutzim before them. "And when
I come to you and I see what you have demonstrated to create, how you have
already instilled content to your life, when I see the devotion to the kibbutz,
to comrades, I see exactly in you the light that I see in the windows around
us."[107] Such an essay, intended to be read to the members of kibbutzim during the Oneg Shabbat or in kibbutz discussions, captured the nature of the
encounter between the survivors and the Yishuv. The topic of wartime suffering was not taboo for Zelig, the movement emissary, but he used it to
instill a sense of pride and responsibility in the members of the kibbutzim
who still joined in the struggle for freedom. These youths carried the responsibility of those who had died to continue along the path of *halutziut* (the
pioneering way). This was a path in which they would not have to struggle

Meir Ya'ari, leader of the Hashomer Hatzair youth organization in the Yishuv, during his visit to Lindenfels DP camp. (USHMM, courtesy of Rose Guterman Zar)

alone, however; they were now part of a larger family, the worldwide movement of Hashomer Hatzair. Such an approach pointed to the method of the movement in reframing the misery and destruction of the war as a basis for the rebirth of the Jewish people (and of the movement now dependent on the survivor youths). A passage such as this may have helped to infuse their recent trauma with an uplifting and potentially productive source of meaning.

Kibbutz members were also reminded of the ongoing political struggle between Hashomer Hatzair and the UZO in case there was any question as to which movement they belonged. Mordechai Rosman, in an article titled "About the United Zionist Organization," wrote that "it is difficult to believe, but a fact, that the so-called United Zionist Organization in Bavaria is closed for a part of the Jewish public in its place and, especially, for large parts of the Jewish pioneering youth."[108] Jewish unity during the German occupation, he suggested, was led "primarily through the pioneering Jewish youth organizations." The other organizations had made a mistake, for together with Dror, Hashomer Hatzair was the strongest pioneering force among the Jewish youths. Rosman assured the youths that the movement would fight for them to reach the shores of Palestine. Ya'akov Hazan, in a speech given to the He-Halutz organization in Palestine, also described "the guilt in Bavaria. . . . Jews there are boycotting other Jews because they belong to different movements. . . . One of our kibbutzim arrived in Landsberg and was ignored by the Jews there."[109] The inclusion of such a speech in the newspaper not only drew attention to the political division taking place among the Zionist groups in the DP camps of Germany but also let the members of the kibbutz (probably Kibbutz Tosia Altman) know that movement leaders in the Yishuv had not forgotten them and were dedicated to fighting for their cause.

In addition to noting the connection to Palestine and making members feel a part of the community there (in time if not in space), a greater part of the newspaper continued to emphasize the heroism of Hashomer Hatzair in leading wartime resistance. As was noted in the second edition of the newspaper (April 1946) dedicated to the third anniversary of the Warsaw Ghetto Uprising, "Our movement was among the first to make the call for rebellion."[110] The cover was graced by a drawing of the ruins of the Warsaw ghetto, and the first page profiled Mordechai Anielewicz, including a selection from his last will and testament to the world: "How happy am I that I am one of the first Jewish fighters in the ghetto." The volume also included part of Abba Kovner's appeal to the Jews of the Vilna ghetto "not to go like sheep to the slaughter" as well as the hymn of the United Partisans' Organization, "Zog Nit Keyn Mol."[111] Articles by ghetto fighters Ruzhka Korczak, Abba Kovner, and Chaya Klinger detailed their wartime activity in the resistance. Later editions of the newspaper continued this emphasis with profiles of other resistance leaders after whom Hashomer Hatzair kibbutzim were named, including Yosef Kaplan and Tosia Altman (third and fourth editions) as well as leaders such as Frumka Plotnicka and Abba Kovner.

The newspaper also kept members informed of ongoing activities within the DP camps of Germany as well as throughout the wider worldwide movement. Each month a literature section provided work by Yiddish authors such as Itzik Manger, Sholem Aleichem, and others to be read within the kibbutz. Informational material on upcoming holidays and the Zionist movement was also distributed through the newspaper.[112]

Kibbutz members were also included and integrated into movement activities in more direct manners such as through training seminars that prepared newer members to replace those who departed for aliyah.[113] Seminars typically lasted two to three weeks; the April 25, 1946, seminar in Jordenbad trained forty-five members and included lectures covering the history of Israel, Zionism, the settlement and geography of Palestine, socialism, the Arab question, Hebrew literature, the Jewish problem, and scouting lessons.[114] Other movements also held similar seminars. Nocham's first seminar was held at Greifenberg in January 1946, and Dror held seminars in February and August of that year.[115]

Those members who had been selected to participate in seminars were often placed in leadership positions as madrichim and teachers in order to direct the movement after the departure of certain members for aliyah. Thus, for example, from Kibbutz Tosia Altman, Monish, Fani, Inka, Brachah, Salusia, Sarah, and Malka followed up on their participation in seminars to be teachers and madrichim for other kibbutzim. Monish became the madrich of Kibbutz Chaviva Reik in Halle (Bavaria), the Czech kibbutz that had not had a madrich before him. In fact, he met his future wife in the kibbutz.[116] Two young women from Kibbutz Tosia Altman (Inka and Fani) became the madrichot of a children's home in Feldafing, while two younger female members from another kibbutz became the madrichot of Kibbutz Aryeh Vilner.[117]

The members who participated in seminars and went on to lead other kibbutzim became the most involved in working to pursue the wider goals of the movement, demonstrating the degree to which they had become inculcated in movement practice. Two members of Kibbutz Yosef Kaplan, Shraga and Monik, detailed the work they were doing in Bad Reichenall with newly arrived Hashomer Hatzair kibbutzim from Poland whose quality and education they assessed as "very weak. It will be very difficult to bring one of the kibbutzim to normal living conditions."[118]

At times the concerns of the movement could come into conflict with the needs of the kibbutz, raising questions of primary loyalty on the part of members, who were forced to sacrifice the needs of the kibbutz for the movement as a whole. In many cases, those selected to participate in seminars or in movement work were the most educated or most talented members of the kibbutz, and their departure from the kibbutz could have a negative impact on cultural work within the kibbutz. Thus, Kibbutz Yosef Kaplan was concerned at the beginning of May that with the movement seminar taking place (with the participation of fourteen members from its kibbutz), "cultural

Cover page and excerpt from the Hashomer Hatzair newspaper, April 1946, commemorating the three-year anniversary of the Warsaw Ghetto uprising. The image depicting a ghetto roundup includes a call to resistance by the underground organization in the Vilna ghetto, the United Partisans' Organization: "Let us not go like sheep to the slaughter." (USHMM, courtesy of Sharon Muller)

דער ווערשטער אויפרוף

אָנגעשריבן דורך אבא ראוועער
אויסגעגעבן דורך פאר. פארטיג. אָרג.

לאָמיר נישט גיין ווי שאָף צו דער שחיטה!

ייִדישע יוגנט גלויב נישט די פארפירער פון די אכציק טויזנט
ייִדן אין ירושלים־דליטא איז געבליבן נאָר צוואנציק טויזנט. פאר אונ־
זערע אויגן האָט מען אומגעבראכט די עלטערן, ברידער און שוועסטער.
וווּ זענען די הונדערטער מענער, געכאפטע אויף ארבעט דורך
דער שטאטישער פּאליציי? וווּ זענען די נאקעטע פרויען און
קינדער, ארויסגעפירטע אין גרוילעקער נאכט פון דער פראוואקאציע?
וווּ זענען די ייִדן געכאפטע אין יום־כיפור? און ווי זענען אונזערע
ברידער פון דער צווייטער געטאָ? וועמען מען האָט ארויסגעפירט

work has stopped completely; the Hebrew lessons are not taking place everyday and not in a consecutive manner. This is because all of the active elements are busy with the seminar, and the classes in the younger kibbutz are led by kibbutz members at the seminar."[119]

On the other hand, some kibbutzim put in requests for seminarists in order to elevate the cultural level of the kibbutz. The kibbutz named after the United Partisans' Organization in Holzhausen testified to problems educating the members in the subjects of Zionism, Palestinography, and the history of the movement (although knowledge of socialism was not a problem). As a member wrote, "in truth I don't have strength or materials. I haven't been to a seminar, and before the war I was only a 'tzofeh boger' [advanced scout]. Can you send some *seminaristim* [seminar graduates] to help with the activities?"[120] At times, those in leadership positions were frequently no better educated than others in the kibbutz.[121]

Members were also empowered by the manner in which they were put into positions of responsibility through participation in the movement. Movements not only relied on kibbutz members for education but also used them to ensure continued daily functioning on a financial level. Haim Shorrer from Kibbutz Tosia Altman recalled meeting Mordechai Rosman in Munich. Rosman gave Shorrer his first movement job, delivering cash for the Bricha. "I was sent with a bag full of dollars on a train to deliver it—this was how the Bricha operated, transferring funds in cash. I told Mordecai that he was the first person to put full trust in me. . . . This is what the leaders did, they put trust in you and gave you responsibility."[122] For young survivors, such responsibility also helped to provide meaning and made them feel a part of something significant after the war.

Finally, as alluded to by Shorrer, a large part of the relationship between the kibbutzim and the movement was also financial; the kibbutzim reported monthly budgets to the leadership detailing their income and expenses and contributing regular dues to the movement for its continued operations to facilitate work in the DP camps, in Germany, and throughout Europe. The April budget for Kibbutz Yosef Kaplan in Jordenbad, for example, detailed income and expenditures for the kibbutz between April 3 and May 9, 1946: 19,000 marks came into the kibbutz through the UNRRA, the movement leadership, and most importantly (15,000 marks) through the sale of tobacco. The kibbutz reported spending 15,000 marks on travel, storage, medicine, and other assorted items. The remaining 4,000 marks were saved for future expenses and/or transferred to the leadership.[123] In the rations provided by the UNRRA and the JDC, the kibbutzim received cigarettes; since most of the kibbutzim theoretically forbade smoking on principle as behavior unbecoming a pioneer, they were able to sell cigarettes on the black market and use the income for kibbutz expenses and to contribute dues to the movement.[124] In its May budget, Kibbutz Ma'apilim al shem Zvi Brandes reported an income of 10,500 marks, 7,000 of which were from the sale of cigarettes.[125] In the diary, Kibbutz Tosia Altman noted that in a trip to Stuttgart in March to perform a play for camp residents there, "Miriam and Azriel went to sell the cigarettes that they brought with them because the prices there were very high. With the money they bought butter for the sick [kibbutz members]." Upon their return to Leipheim they were greeted by an American military police officer, as was always the case. "They received us as good guests, checked our packages and papers. Upon each of us they found a container of butter. They were angry, but there was nothing they could do and they let us go. We came home happy."[126] The sale of cigarettes on the black market thus also became a method of acquiring much-needed luxury items.

Aliyah: The Prospect of Departure for Eretz Israel

Above everything, however, the focus of nearly all activity within the framework of the kibbutz was the prospect of aliyah to Palestine, or Eretz Israel. Kibbutz Tosia Altman's first encounter with Palestine took place on a cold winter day during Chanukah in Landsberg. As Hanka stood outside the cabin of the kibbutz on guard, she observed an automobile pulling up with two passengers, one dressed in civilian clothing and the other in the uniform of the Jewish Brigade, and thought to herself, "Oh, now something is going to happen!" Almost immediately the secretariat convened to select the first olim from the kibbutz for aliyah. The prospect of members finally moving to Palestine was met with excitement and joy in the kibbutz: "Is it really possible? Will the first members of our kibbutz truly immigrate to Palestine?" Six members of the kibbutz were selected for departure (Yedziah, Leon, Haim Sack, Hila, Monzik, and Efraim), but because at the time the kibbutz was not even officially part of the Zionist organization in the Landsberg DP camp (owing to their early difficulties following arrival at the camp), they had to leave secretly to become part of the aliyah allotment from another camp (Föhrenwald and Feldafing). After some lobbying Hashomer Hatzair was granted eight official certificates, and three more members were selected in addition to the original six.[127]

During the first Chanukah celebration, Kibbutz Tosia Altman held a ceremony to mark the departure of its first representatives for aliyah (olim) to Palestine. "The word 'olim' had been a foreign one to us but now we had our very own olim from our kibbutz. . . . As the first olim from our kibbutz they carried a very heavy responsibility." Members spoke heartfelt words in which they emphasized the sense of unity and cooperation within the kibbutz. "The party ended with a tempestuous *hora* that swept everyone up in its excitement. This was perhaps the first *hora* in our kibbutz that was so full of a *joie de vivre*, a *hora* that emphasized the unity of the kibbutz, the connection between the members. For many days afterwards, the members continued to move under the influence of this hora." Nonetheless, those who were left behind were saddened by the emptiness in the kibbutz, "as if half the kibbutz had just left." The members were torn by conflicting emotions; they were overjoyed at seeing their first comrades leave for Palestine but saddened by the loss they felt in the dilution of their kibbutz. The tension between loyalty to the goals of the movement and loyalty to the primary group of affiliation, the kibbutz family, was a conflict that would reappear numerous times during the kibbutz's stay in Germany as members were selected for aliyah or "borrowed" by the movement for "essential movement work."[128]

The decision to select certain members in the kibbutz for aliyah was called *berurim* (selection). In the beginning of January, when Kibbutz Tosia Altman was already in Leipheim, the group received a message from the central leadership to prepare for a "large aliyah" in which perhaps twenty to twenty-five members would be designated for departure. The kibbutz members were beside themselves with excitement and joy. "Everyone thinks to himself, who will be selected? . . . The secretariat met together with the madrichim and it was decided to hold discussions in which members would be selected in groups of ten."[129] Ruth described the atmosphere surrounding the selection in a separate entry in the diary:

Today on January 10, 1946, in the dining room, a very important assembly is taking place. Finally the much hoped for day has arrived. It is up to all of us to determine the members who will be designated for aliyah. We all assembled here in order to discuss each individual member independently. Not everyone can be among those selected this time and each of us hopes that perhaps his name will be included in the list of the olim. The heart pounds.[130]

Despite the "close connections that link[ed] the members of the kibbutz together," it was difficult to decide who would be "uprooted" from the kibbutz and who would remain. Miriam read from the list of members alphabetically, and, as Ruth wrote in the diary, "we each judge him. We are brothers and sisters. We 'dissect' the comrade down to the smallest foundations and peek inside the depths of his soul, we judge his actions and issue a ruling." Members worked to recall other's first days in the kibbutz in order to assess the righteousness of each member's actions, but Ruth noted that this difficult task also served to bring the kibbutz together, to remind them that "the kibbutz is our home, and in it are all of our brothers and sisters to whom we feel so close." Each member's level of education and dedication to the kibbutz and the movement was assessed, although (somewhat ironically) those deemed most indispensable to the kibbutz became less likely candidates for selection. Hours passed as each name was read and judged; the entire decision process lasted three days. Finally, three members (Yehudit, Rachel, and Azriel) were nominated to be the aliyah committee in order to make the final decision on the olim on the basis of the preceding discussions. The kibbutz then held a party as it awaited the decisions of the aliyah committee. Miriam read the list of the twenty members (ten men and ten women) who had been selected for aliyah. Nonetheless, despite the drama of the selection process, this group did not leave for aliyah for another three months, at the beginning of April.[131]

Still, the prospect of aliyah dominated much of the kibbutz's time in Germany, and hence quite a bit of attention was devoted to preparing for it. In submitting reports to the kibbutz leadership, the kibbutzim had a vested interest in portraying the high "pioneering quality" of their kibbutz in order to make kibbutz members worthy of aliyah. This did not discourage kibbutzim from sending complaints to the leadership on "cultural activity" within the kibbutz or in detailing ongoing disputes between members or even with a departed madrich. While the central leadership informed the kibbutzim of an upcoming allotment of members for aliyah, it was up to the individual kibbutzim to decide which members should be selected for departure. Prospective immigrants (olim) were divided between movements, with each youth movement allotted a percentage of aliyah candidates.[132] For example, in early April 1946 five hundred spaces were secured for members of pioneering groups on an aliyah of seven hundred people; Hashomer Hatzair was allotted 15 percent of the "pioneering" spaces, or seventy-five people.[133] While the individual kibbutzim could decide who would leave, the leadership suggested that the most active members be left for movement work.[134]

By the summer of 1946, after Kibbutz Tosia Altman had moved to the training farm in Eschwege, half of the original members who had arrived in November 1945 had departed for aliyah (some had made it to Palestine, while others were stuck at various points along the way). Groups were selected for aliyah in a similar way over the course of 1946, with more than fifty members leaving in four groups between December 1945 and July 1946.[135] The process of aliyah therefore resulted in turnover within the kibbutzim, with new groups taking the places of those who had departed. Aliyah could be disruptive to the individual kibbutzim; in the case of Kibbutz Tosia Altman, the kibbutz had to elect a new secretariat because a number of the leaders had been selected for departure. In other cases, kibbutzim expressed concern that aliyah disrupted the social equilibrium of the kibbutz. Aliyah thus seemed to have a paradoxical effect on the kibbutz. On the one hand, it was the goal of their entire time in Germany, that for which they were constantly training. On the other hand, however, the departure of key members could weaken camaraderie and cultural work in the kibbutz. Kibbutzim were asked to select members worthy of aliyah while simultaneously making an effort to "leave an active group" who could be "candidates for seminar, movement work." Still, the thought of aliyah served to inspire kibbutz members, and as Kibbutz Tosia Altman noted in a report to the leadership, after many months in Germany, "Aliyah brought a new spirit in the kibbutz and encouraged the members to improve their work in the kibbutz."[136] As the culmination of efforts to deepen Zionist activity and the ultimate purpose of cultural work in the kibbutz, aliyah served to inspire members to continue their work and perhaps more than anything else helped to retain those members who chose to remain within the kibbutz.

Conclusion

A number of common themes emerge from the experiences of the Hashomer Hatzair kibbutzim as described in the diary of Kibbutz Tosia Altman and the correspondence of other kibbutzim from their time in the DP camps in occupied Germany, perhaps helping to explain why members chose to remain within the kibbutz. It seems that the decision to remain within the framework of the kibbutz resulted from a number of factors that demonstrated a transformation within the kibbutz over time. From the beginning, on the psychological level the continuing peer pressure and techniques employed by the madrichim and leadership persuaded members not to leave the group. The kibbutz granted structure and work, giving members something to do every day and reintroducing them to a daily schedule based on the time frame and calendar of the movement. However, the favorable situation in the DP camps of Germany also gave the kibbutz members time to engage in learning and education, providing members with access to knowledge for which they hungered. The kibbutz also offered a basis for identity, as membership in the movement provided a sense of belonging to a larger group and a larger family; the identification of the kibbutz with the wartime heroism of the ghetto fighters only served to strengthen this basis of identity. Finally, through the promise of aliyah staying with the kibbutz carried the additional incentive of an expedited route to a future life in Palestine. While the initial psychological and structural factors kept members in the group, the time in Germany offered the movement and the members an opportunity to deepen their attachment to Hashomer Hatzair and the ideals for which it stood.

Throughout the experiences of the youths in the kibbutzim a common tension emerged, however, one in which the members had to balance their preparation for a future life in Palestine with the difficulties of everyday existence in the present. Departure for Palestine was certainly not guaranteed; as they waited for a diplomatic solution or their chance to be selected for aliyah, members had to work to avoid depression and a growing sense of impatience with their situation. In their cultural work, kibbutz members acquired the necessary Zionist tools to qualify them for aliyah; such exercises simultaneously filled the function of keeping kibbutz members occupied, thereby lessening the potential for boredom, laziness, and demoralization. In classes and by reading newspapers and listening to lectures, kibbutz members learned the politics and geography of Palestine while still facing the reality of continued life in Germany. The appropriation of Jewish tradition and the transformation of a traumatic past into a source of heroic pride perhaps provided members with the psychological balm necessary to continue life in the wake of such tragedy. (Still, in some cases, individuals decided to try life outside of the kibbutz, choosing to live independently or join friends and family in other groups.)

Just as importantly, on the diplomatic level the high visibility of the kibbutzim and their manifestations of Zionist enthusiasm demonstrated to outside observers a perceived state of "Palestine passion" on the part of the Jewish DPs. The apparent importance of Zionism for the increasing numbers of arriving DPs confirmed the necessity of the Zionist solution for representatives of the AACI. After beginning their work in Washington and London in January 1946, members of the AACI visited the DP camps and Poland to assess the Jewish situation beginning in February. In a March report the committee suggested that "children are being conditioned to believe that Palestine is the only place in the world where Jews can live."[137] R. E. Manningham Buller, a British AACI member, taking note of the success of the Zionist organization (presumably of kibbutzim), commented that "one cannot fail to be impressed with the unanimity of the demand for entry into Palestine. To what extent this is due to Zionist propaganda one cannot precisely determine. . . . The fact that when they are in groups, they are so well looked after, fed and clothed and their transit organized for them is surely an inducement to them to comply with Zionist wishes in stating the country for which they wish to go."[138] Richard Crossman (also a British AACI representative and Labour Party member of Parliament) was slightly less suspicious of Zionist propaganda: "Even if there had not been a single foreign Zionist or a trace of Zionist propaganda in the camps these people would have opted for Palestine."[139]

Regardless of any concerns over manipulation, on April 20, 1946, the AACI recommended "(A) that 100,000 certificates be authorized immediately for the admission into Palestine of Jews who have been the victims of Nazi and Fascist persecution; (B) that these certificates be awarded as far as possible in 1946 and that actual immigration be pushed forward as rapidly as conditions will permit." This was the conclusion that the AACI came to

A large crowd of Jewish DPs participate in a demonstration protesting British immigration policy to Israel at the Neu Freimann DP camp in Munich. They stand beneath a Yiddish banner that proclaims, "We want to go back to our home in the Land of Israel." (USHMM, courtesy of Jack Sutin)

not only because of a lack of any other options but also because the committee genuinely believed that this was the truest expression of the Jewish DPs' desires. "Furthermore, that is where almost all of them want to go. There they are sure that they will receive a welcome denied them elsewhere. There they hope to enjoy peace and rebuild their lives." The committee based these findings in part on surveys conducted among the DPs. However, the committee also firmly believed that based on what it had observed among the Jewish DPs, they were a group ardently preparing themselves for a Zionist future. Many among the DPs were seen as reluctant to work. "On the other hand, whenever facilities are provided for practical training for life in Palestine they eagerly take advantage of them."[140]

Despite the recommendations of the AACI, however, over the course of 1946 and into 1947 diplomatic efforts stalled, and it became clear that for the majority of the youths in the kibbutzim life would continue in Germany and not on the path to Palestine. As more and more infiltrees arrived from Poland, kibbutz groups moved to hakhsharot in the American zone of Germany, where they would continue life within the youth movement awaiting selection for aliyah.

4

Farming Blood-Soaked Soil

Agricultural Training in Germany

Four months into their stay in Germany, the members of Kibbutz Tosia Altman had acclimated to their new surroundings, growing accustomed to the rhythms of life in the camp for displaced persons (DPs). They had managed to overcome the initial crisis of dwindling membership and enjoyed the educational and cultural opportunities that kibbutz membership provided them. In early March 1946, however, Miriam informed the kibbutz of a new change in their collective life, one that would bring them into contact with life in Germany as they had not confronted it before. At an early spring meeting of the mazkirut following a routine visit from Mordechai Rosman and Moshe Laufer of the central leadership, "Miriam revealed the secret: an agricultural farm has been established near Frankfurt, and our kibbutz has been designated to travel there." After a brief discussion, the members came to a unanimous decision: "Tomorrow the first twenty-five members must depart. . . . We all agree."[1] The adjustment to farming the German soil "soaked in blood"[2] constituted the final eight-month chapter of their stay in Germany.

Unlike the residents of the first hakhsharot of Buchenwald and Nili, who initiated their own move to a farm, the members of Kibbutz Tosia Altman

155

were to be sent to the farm through a decision of the youth movement. Miriam explained to the members the importance of the move to the farm, focusing on the "connection to the land" and emphasizing the hakhsharah experience as "preparation for life in Palestine."[3] Members were apparently excited by Miriam's explanation (or reluctant to break up the kibbutz), and the diary notes that "everyone asked to travel to the farm." Nonetheless, only twenty-five members could be selected initially, for the kibbutz also had to hold the space in the Leipheim DP camp until another kibbutz arrived from Poland. After much discussion, the first pioneers were selected, and as was noted in the diary, the kibbutz now "marched toward that which in the future would be the crucial aspect of our lives in Palestine."[4]

The departure of the twenty-five kibbutz members was hard on those left behind in Leipheim, who immediately sensed their absence in the cultural and social life of the kibbutz. For those who moved to Eschwege the transition would be difficult but for different reasons altogether. Subsequent reports sent by members from the farm to the central leadership complained of the division of the kibbutz group and of insufficient time to engage in cultural work. While the diary may have recorded the move as essential in the march toward Palestine, it is unclear whether the young farmers actually experienced it this way. The move to the farm perhaps signified a step on the path to aliyah, but it also marked a collective life increasingly governed by the needs of the youth movement and the wider Zionist enterprise.

The Creation of the First Farms

The first training farms to be opened in postwar Germany in the summer and fall of 1945 were the creations of concentration camp survivors who sought the assistance of American Jewish chaplains in acquiring land for their farms. The desire to move to farms was a direct result of the poor conditions in abundance in the DP camps following liberation, with life on a farm presenting a far more appealing option than continued existence in the camp. Initially, the move to farms was not overwhelmingly supported by the Zionist DP leadership. Some members of the United Zionist Organization (UZO) voiced concerns at the first conference, in October 1945, that moving Jewish youths away from DP camps could detract from the camps' cultural life. Furthermore, they argued, it was necessary to leave kibbutz members in the DP camps so that newly arriving kibbutz groups would have a model for future behavior.[5] Others suggested that Jewish youths in the DP camps not only had a responsibility to realize their own Zionist development but also needed to serve as role models for the wider Jewish community; for this reason, they should leave some of their numbers within the DP camps. Ultimately, the UZO and Nocham reached a compromise in support of the farming project, agreeing to leave some kibbutz members in the DP camps to accommodate new arrivals and contribute to cultural life in the camps. The acquisition of farms expanded with the support of American administration authorities and the Jewish Agency so that by the end of 1945, nine kibbutz hakhsharot functioned in the American zone.[6]

The promotion and expansion of farming by outside groups reflected a transformation in the farming project. The later opening and movement of Jewish youths to farms would be determined by the choices and actions taken by the Jewish Agency, the Central Committee of Liberated Jews, the United Nations Relief and Rehabilitation Administration (UNRRA), and the Zionist youth movements (with the official approval of the U.S. Army). This change would influence the lives of Jewish youths in kibbutzim in very real ways. Although farming could be justified by members of kibbutzim as necessary for *hagshama* (realizing the Zionist dream) in preparation for life in Israel, it was now weighed against the appeal of the educational and cultural initiatives that the kibbutzim had begun in DP camps. Unlike the early members of Kibbutz Buchenwald, who moved to a farm soon after liberation, many of the youths in kibbutzim had spent months in the kibbutz framework, integrating into the youth movement through immersion in cultural work. Still, kibbutz members agreed to move to the farms in order to remain within the kibbutz framework and promote their chances of reaching Palestine even if agricultural work detracted from the educational and cultural opportunities they enjoyed in the DP camp. The willingness of thousands of kibbutz members to farm German soil advanced the agendas of various groups in the American zone, each of which saw some significance in the farming project, a significance that generally had little to do with the intrinsic value of agricultural training.

Context and Continuity with Prewar Hakhsharot

The elevated status of agricultural work in the Zionist youth movement was not new to the postwar context. The goals of the youth movements in moving youths to farms echoed prewar statements regarding the purpose of hakhsharah. In independent Poland (1918–39), the pioneering Zionist youth movements were central in fulfilling the aims of the larger Zionist movement.[7] The Zionist youth movements in interwar Poland aspired to realize the ideological pronouncements of their parent movements through the practical application of this ideology. The productive training of the Jewish people through the creation of an agricultural and working class in Palestine was one of the primary goals of Labor Zionism. The pioneering ethos of the Second Aliyah (1904–14), as typified by the example of A. D. Gordon, strove to instill in the Jewish people "the principal ingredient for national life": the habit of labor.[8] Through the hakhsharah kibbutz, the pioneering Zionist youth movements endeavored to educate Jewish youths through physical labor in the belief that this could stimulate the rebirth of the Jewish people; throughout the 1930s, this model spread to most places of Jewish settlement in Poland.[9] The He-Halutz movement, which sought to unify the divided ideological strands of Zionism under the common umbrella of agricultural training for aliyah to Israel, had one hundred thousand adherents at its height (1930–35), with approximately sixteen thousand members in hakhsharot in Poland (not including Galicia).[10] The number of members declined with the onset of the Arab Revolt in Palestine (1936–39) and the concomitant decline in immigration.

During the early years of World War II as well, youth movements sought to continue the activities of kibbutzim and hakhsharot under German occupation. Membership in Zionist youth movements was expanded in certain cases under German occupation, accompanied by intensified educational activity.[11] The youth movements sought to reopen kibbutzim and hakhsharot in Warsaw, Łódź, Będzin (Dror), and Hrubieszow (Betar), and Hashomer Hatzair sought to revive the kibbutz in Częstochowa.[12]

After the war the pool of labor recruited for this process differed greatly from its prewar predecessors. Far from representing the elite of the Zionist youth movement as had those who populated the prewar hakhsharot, young survivors after the war were perceived by Zionist activists from Palestine as demoralized and lazy.[13] Still, the Zionist youth movements believed that Zionist education, and agricultural work if possible, could heal this "broken youth."[14]

At the first Nocham conference, held at Kibbutz Nili on February 25, 1946, the largest Zionist youth movement in Germany highlighted the renewed focus on hakhsharah. In fact, the general resolutions of the conference were almost exclusively devoted to hakhsharah. The movement declared that all of its aliyah kibbutzim were obliged to undergo agricultural hakhsharah of two years and requested that the Zionist Histadrut in Palestine require all of the Jewish youths in kibbutzim to fulfill this duty.[15]

The summary of the conference in the youth movement newspaper reinforced this focus on the move of youths to agricultural training, where the "question of hakhsharah dominated discussion." At the time, Nocham counted hakhsharot in Gersfeld, Geringshof in the Hesse Nassau region, Forkenhof, Zettlitz, Ansbach, Kadolsburg (Nili) in Franconia, and Erding in Upper Bavaria. Along with these existing farms, "future hakhsharot in Föhrenwald, Deggendorf, and near Landsberg [would] be able to accommodate thousands of chalutzim in order to prepare them for their future lives of work and creation in Eretz Israel. Only the intensification of the hakhsharah work will once and for all solve the problem of mixed hakhsharah among the youth of Nocham."[16] As their prewar predecessors had done, the postwar chalutzim would be expected to complete both physical and spiritual training, ideally before their arrival in Palestine. It would seem that the two-year requirement, however, could also be completed in Palestine following a kibbutz group's departure on aliyah.

The other pioneering youth movements also endeavored to achieve this goal. Hashomer Hatzair described the move to training farms as preparation for agricultural work in Eretz Israel and moved its first kibbutz groups to a training farm in March 1946.[17] At the Ichud Hanoar Hazioni movement conference held in Erding during April 9–10, 1946, the movement also highlighted its focus on hakhsharah. After explaining its reasons for breaking off from Nocham, which it believed failed to represent all Zionist youths in Germany, the conference resolved that "the central leadership of the movement will work to establish branches in all of the DP camps in order to instruct the youths in pioneering values [*chalutziut*] and to move them to agricultural hakhsharah."[18] Dror, Bnei Akiva, and Betar, which similarly

rejected the "monopolistic" tendencies of Nocham, also worked to open their
own training farms in Germany in the spring of 1946.[19]

Although the move to hakhsharah fit into a familiar prewar system for
the youth movements, for Jewish youths living in kibbutzim in the DP camps
of postwar Germany agricultural training may have nonetheless seemed like
an entirely foreign concept. Unlike their prewar predecessors, who viewed
themselves as the avant-garde of Jewish youths in Poland, the Jewish youths
in the kibbutzim of postwar Germany had joined for practical and psychological reasons. Additionally, while the first farms were joined by survivor
youths eager to escape the poor conditions in the DP camps, conditions did
begin to improve in the Jewish DP centers following the publication of the
Harrison Report. Thus, the move to a training farm removed DP youths
(more and more of whom had arrived from Poland) from the atmosphere of
the Jewish DP camp, which, while feared by outside observers as a source of
demoralization, was a comparatively safe bastion of Jewish security on what
had not long ago been the territory of their greatest enemy. What then was
motivating the timing of this creation of hakhsharot if the Jewish youths in
the kibbutzim were no longer able to initiate the move to farms on their own?

Administrative Support for the Expansion of the Farming Project: A Convergence of the UNRRA and Jewish Agency Goals

The early success of Zionist farms turned farming into a bureaucratic endeavor, one that required the political support and cooperation of a number
of groups in the American zone of Germany, including the U.S. Army, the
UNRRA, the Jewish Agency, the American Jewish Joint Distribution Committee (JDC), and the Central Committee as well as the young Jewish pioneers in kibbutzim of the youth movements required to inhabit and work
these farms. The success of the farming project depended on the interplay
of all of these different groups in the American zone of Germany, each of
whom saw value in employing young Jewish DPs in agricultural labor. While
an apolitical group such as the United Nations endorsed Zionist projects
because of their productive and rehabilitative capacity, the Jewish Agency
continued to maintain its bottom-line goal of creating a state in Palestine and
hoped to employ farms as training centers and holding stations for future
immigrants. Similarly, the Agricultural Department of the Central Commit-

tee of Liberated Jews viewed farming as a means of assisting the Zionist project while training Jewish youths for future lives as farmers. The goals of these groups thus came together to facilitate the expansion of the farms. The farming project provides an enlightening view into the manner in which various groups could attempt to utilize and act on behalf of the Jewish DPs in methods that were alternately instrumental, political, altruistic, and therapeutic.

Following David Ben-Gurion's visit to the U.S. zone in late October 1945 and his consultations with Generals Dwight Eisenhower and Walter Bedell Smith, the UNRRA and the JDC decided to pursue a more active policy in securing land for agricultural training for Jewish DPs. Throughout the fall of 1945, UNRRA and JDC representatives had worked to secure appropriate land for hakhsharot and assess the viability of specific farm locations.[20] The aid agencies continued to operate under the assumption that this would be the ideal manner in which to remove Zionist youths from the demoralizing atmosphere of the DP camp, where Jewish DPs could end up occupied in laziness or worse. Jack Whiting (UNRRA zone director) suggested in January 1946 that a greater emphasis be placed on training in farm schools and industry, as "we know that there are at least several thousand youngsters who are at present occupied only in idleness and who could be placed in factories, schools, or on farms." Whiting made note of the presence of the emissaries that Ben-Gurion had promised from Palestine, who could assist in the project and get it started as soon as possible. "Agronomists, teachers, etc. are now available from the Jewish Agency and it would be a waste of their time as well as a waste on the displaced persons' lives not to get such programs under way."[21]

At the first meeting of the Jewish Council in March 1946 (with representatives from the UNRRA, the U.S. Army, the JDC, the Jewish Agency, and the Central Committee), Whiting reaffirmed his support for the idea of moving Jewish youths in kibbutzim out of the DP camps and onto farms to enable them "to train themselves for their future life work . . . in agriculture."[22] Furthermore, Whiting believed that such training would be highly beneficial because it would maintain morale and thus prevent a descent into unemployment, "petty thieving, black marketing, loose morals, etc." The farms could also relieve overcrowding and produce fresh foods that, according to Whiting, "are so much desired and so necessary for these people who have

suffered persecution for many years. In this connection it is notable that
X-ray screening in its very beginning is showing a high rate of TB instances
which can only be combated by fresh air, fresh milk, eggs and vegetables."[23]
Thus, Whiting indirectly advocated a Zionist position but not out of an overwhelming love for the idea of Jewish state. Rather, Zionism came to represent a solution to immediate problems: DP demoralization, crime, black
market activity, overcrowding, poor hygiene, and tuberculosis. The high visibility of the kibbutzim in the DP camps and their manifestations of Zionist
enthusiasm continued to convince the UNRRA and American authorities
of the need for agricultural training farms.

The UNRRA's support for training farms corresponded well with the
Jewish Agency's diplomatic goals. The UNRRA would be assisted in its
efforts to secure land and instructors for farming projects by representatives
of the Jewish Agency operating in Germany. Shlichim from the Jewish Agency
attached to Haim Hoffman's delegation worked to ensure the expansion of
the project. The first delegation of twenty Jewish Agency emissaries, technically working under the auspices of the UNRRA, had arrived in Germany
in mid-December 1945. According to Hoffman, the delegation worked in five
key areas in its mission to Germany:

> a) organization of aliyah in the framework of allocated certificates by the
> British government as well as aliyah by our own means; b) organization of
> the group of East European Jews in the American zone of occupation; c) pio-
> neering agricultural hakhsharah and vocational hakhsharah for the masses
> of refugees; d) political instruction of the She'erit Hapletah and their prepa-
> ration before the Anglo-American Committee of Inquiry; and e) assistance
> in the camps, for all that is necessary, in the organization of the lives of the
> refugees specifically in education and Zionist instruction.[24]

The first twenty emissaries who arrived in Germany at the end of 1945
secured positions in the DP camps of Landsberg, Föhrenwald, Feldafing,
Deggendorf, Leipheim, Pocking, Freiman, and Struth, where they focused
their efforts on organizing cultural and educational work and in preparing
kibbutzim for hakhsharah. One of the shlichim also traveled directly to Kibbutz Nili in order to instruct the youths in farming practices.[25]

In March 1946 the Jewish Agency mission established its Hakhsharah
Department to organize the acquisition of land for the movements and the

kibbutzim, to obtain equipment for the hakhsharot, and to inspect the equipment, health, and sanitation in the settlements.[26] Based on the number of Jewish Agency emissaries assigned to farms versus those assigned to DP camps, it seems that the focus of Jewish Agency activity was disproportionately on chalutzim on farms. By the end of 1946 out of 53 emissaries in Germany, 11 were assigned to hakhsharot with a population of 3,172 (a ratio of 1:290), while 42 were assigned to DP camps with a population of 133,000 (a ratio of 1:3,200).[27] The Jewish Agency hakhsharah office was also created in order to ensure the fair allocation of training farms to the various Zionist youth movements in Germany. In addition to assisting in efforts to secure land for hakhsharot, the Jewish Agency worked together with the UNRRA to designate consultants to the various training farms in order to provide instruction and ensure proper training.[28] Jewish Agency emissaries were also active in providing general education to DPs by offering instruction in UNRRA-established schools.

With the arrival of more shlichim over the course of 1946, the Jewish Agency team expanded its efforts to assist in the opening of hakhsharot. For political reasons the Jewish Agency believed that such farms could not only prepare youths for life in Palestine through agricultural training but could also prove valuable by increasing the visibility of DP Zionism and isolating the pioneering avant-garde from the rest of the DP camp. For the most part, however, Jewish Agency workers adopted a largely instrumental view of survivor youths as unsuitable for true agricultural labor in Palestine. Haim Hoffman lamented the lack of adequate training for the new farmers: "Before the war we would send the youths to train first on a farm as a hired hand or to train with a farmer before they were sent to a Hehalutz farm. But in Germany we could not do this, and so responsibility for the farms was given to people who had absolutely no experience in agricultural work; many of them had done little work at all and arrived in the farms weakened by their wartime experiences."[29]

The added value of agricultural training therefore lay in its therapeutic power. As Liuba Leck conveyed to Dror-Hehalutz Hatzair in Jerusalem, "it is clear, that the fact that the 'hakhsharah' has organized thousands of youths, and incorporated *human dust* into a pioneering Zionist framework, there is to this—in light of the [DP] camps, which are full of destructive factors and elements—tremendous value."[30] To Leck, the ultimate value of farms was their ability to isolate youths from the demoralizing atmosphere of the DP camp as it existed in early 1946. Hoffman shared this view of the farms, which while not agriculturally valuable could successfully transform their residents into suitable Zionist material. As he suggested in the spirit of A. D. Gordon, by removing them from the DP camp, it was "the contact with nature, work with their hands [that] healed their bodies and their souls. After a short time, a different type of person was created from the residents of the camps who was even closer to the Eretz Israeli type of person."[31]

Members of the Jewish Agency team thus worked to determine the amount and type of support needed by the farms to ensure their success. Shmuel Zamri (agricultural adviser to the Jewish Agency) seems to have spent much of 1946 evaluating the performance of already existing hakhsharot and assessing the viability of new areas for the creation of farms.[32] In certain cases the assistance rendered by the UNRRA was insufficient to supply all of the needs of the farms. For this reason, Zamri also reported to the JDC regarding the needs of farms in the U.S. zone.[33] In this way the UNRRA, the Jewish Agency, and the JDC were able to work together to successfully support the operation of Zionist farms.

Whereas the UNRRA saw Zionist training farms as a practical solution to potential overcrowding and demoralization, the Jewish Agency saw an opportunity to advance its diplomatic agenda. Neither of these would have been possible, however, had there not been a sizable population of youths willing to engage in agricultural work.

The Expansion of the Farming Project: Diplomatic or Demographic Necessity?

A brief overview of the timing of the farm creation suggests that it was not necessarily a response to overcrowding occurring within the DP centers. When Kibbutz Tosia Altman and Kibbutz Mordechai Anielewicz prepared the farm in Eschwege for its official opening in April 1946, there were already twenty-seven agricultural training farms open in the U.S. zone.[34] The concerted efforts of the UNRRA, the Jewish Agency, the youth movements, and the kibbutz members were thus successful in creating many farms in advance of the sizable influx of Jews from Poland later in 1946.

Appendix A and appendix B provide charts that reflect the growth in the Jewish population in the U.S. zone of Germany between April and October 1946 as well as the development of hakhsharot in the American zone. These statistics suggest that in April 1946 when the Jewish DP population had risen only 6 percent from January 1946 (from 49,695 to 52,669), almost twenty farms had been opened in this period. The 3,600 inhabitants of hakhsharot constituted 5 percent of the total U.S. zone population, not insignificant when considering that in January fewer than 900 (or one-quarter of the June number) lived on farms. The population of hakhsharot increased by 400 percent, while the population increase during this period (January–June 1946) for the zone as a whole stood at 59 percent.

Beyond productively employing the youths living in the kibbutzim, part of the stated UNRRA rationale for moving Jewish DPs out to training farms was to alleviate the anticipated overcrowding that would develop with the arrival of increasing numbers of infiltrees from the East. Interestingly, the peak of farm creation far preceded the sizable influx of Bricha infiltrees in the summer of 1946. This is most noticeable in the demographic calculations made between June and September 1946. Whereas the 3,600 youths living on farms in June 1946 constituted nearly 5 percent of the Jewish DP population, by October 1946 this population had been halved to 2.5 percent.

The growth and development of farms was thus the result of a convergence of necessity and political motivation. The presence of a sizable population of Jewish youths willing to move to farms coupled with the realization on the part of Zionist activists that such farms could have real political value determined the timing of the creation of the farms. Over the first half of 1946, the youth movements were quite successful in opening numerous training farms. As a Nocham representative wrote in the movement newspaper in June 1946 announcing the "mobilization to hakhsharah," twenty hakhsharah locations had been established, and many more were planned to provide physical and spiritual training "geared to the constructive building of a community, in the ideals of collective life and collective construction." The movement mobilized to establish "hakhsharah groups in all places where Jews are to be found, whether in camps or in small communities."[35]

As the UNRRA well understood and as the pioneering youth movements desired, the agricultural training farms were to be inhabited by those deemed to be from the segment of the DP population that displayed a pioneering ethos to the greatest degree, the Zionist avant-garde organized in the kibbutzim. And indeed, demographic surveys of those living on the hakhsharot consistently reveal their inhabitants to have been from the younger segments of the population. At the end of 1946 the population living in the hakhsharot continued to be younger than that of the average Jewish DP population. Out of a population of 3,032 living in hakhsharot surveyed by the JDC at the end of 1946, 85.8 percent (2,603) were between the ages of eighteen and forty-four, and an additional 9.7 percent (294) were under the age of seventeen. Thus, more than 95 percent of the residents of hakhsharot were under the age of forty-four, most presumably in their twenties (although this age was not specifically surveyed by the JDC). This was slightly higher than the 90 percent under the age of forty-four for the U.S. zone as a whole.[36]

It is clear that during the course of 1946 these agencies worked together to move Jewish youths to training farms for a variety of reasons, all of which corresponded in their belief that this was the best thing to do for the DPs whether out of a political, ideological, or therapeutic rationale. Despite views of survivor youths as "human dust," the Jewish youths who moved (or were moved) to the farms also had to engage in this process actively, for American administration authorities were growing increasingly sensitive to the needs of the German economy and were thus reluctant to appropriate good land from German owners. Ultimately the youths themselves would have to make the farms successful by turning out an agricultural crop, which they worked hard to do. How did the kibbutz youths, with next to no experience in agriculture, adapt to this dramatic shift in their daily schedule and surroundings? Would they take to the land as Zionist pioneers, or would they reject farming as impractical and, even worse, as a betrayal of their families who had been killed by the German murderers?

Kibbutz Tosia Altman Goes Farming

The first group of Kibbutz Tosia Altman members arrived in Eschwege on March 16, 1946. They were disappointed to find that instead of a farm they were confronted with a former Luftwaffe airfield filled with plane parts. Compounding their disappointment, Moshe Laufer (of the Hashomer Hatzair central leadership) informed them that for the first week they would have to live in the DP camp at Eschwege until they had finished cleaning the airbase. Upon arrival they were greeted by American authorities who disinfected them with DDT, and they met their fellow farmers, the members of Kibbutz Mordechai Anielewicz. After they had a much-needed night's sleep, the next day began with work in the kitchen and cleaning and a less than enthusiastic first impression:

> Before we came here we imagined to ourselves that on a farm can be found cows, horses, fields, etc. as is normal on every agricultural farm. How much was our disappointment to find in this place a large airport with broken plane parts scattered about, different building materials, machine parts, and the like. The building was abandoned and dirty. We were asked to clean it and bring things in order and change the place around the abandoned airfield into a blooming agricultural farm.[37]

Group portrait of members of the Ghetto Fighters kibbutz hakhsharah at the Eschwege DP camp, where Kibbutz *Lochamei HaGetaot al shem Tosia Altman* farmed until the end of 1946. (USHMM, courtesy of Nina Szuster Merrick)

The members of Kibbutz Tosia Altman worked together with Kibbutz Mordechai Anielewicz to clean up the airbase, collecting the trash left behind by the German air force inside the main building and on the airfields that would become crop and pasture land. The kibbutz members lacked tools to clean up, especially needing large machinery supplied by the UNRRA to remove the broken plane parts, motors, and barrels of gasoline left behind and prepare the fields for plowing.[38]

After ten days the major clean-up work was completed, and the UNRRA vehicles were taken away. The living space was prepared in the main building, with broken windows replaced and a proper water heater put in place.[39] While the broken planes and barrels of gasoline seemed like more of a hassle than anything, the kibbutz soon turned these relics to their advantage, with sales of the gasoline on the black market used to supplement the kibbutz income.[40]

Farmland: The Shape of the Farm

In the first days after their arrival, the new farmers in Kibbutz Mordechai Anielewicz and Kibbutz Tosia Altman surveyed their new estate. The members of Kibbutz Tosia Altman were aware of the irony implicit in the mission they were to undertake in their new surroundings: "As was noted, the place was used as a German military airfield. Here were parked many airplanes. From this place they took off and sowed tragedy and destruction for humanity, for many, many people. On this place we built now our hakhsharah."[41]

The hakhsharah was allotted eighty hectares of land, one-third of which were various buildings including the main residential space.[42] The main dwelling house, which stood on the corner of the land, was a large two-story building with a wide entrance and glass doors. Opposite the doors, the kibbutz members created signs that identified the farm as belonging to the Hashomer Hatzair Ghetto Fighters' kibbutzim. Both floors of the building had rooms of various size divided between males and females (the boys' room for twelve boys continued to be a *balagan*, or a dirty mess) and a large dining room that they decorated with pictures of Theodor Herzl and Hayyim Nachman Bialik and used for kibbutz assemblies. Downstairs were the kitchen, a reading room, a room used to accommodate agricultural tools, and rooms for Kibbutz Mordechai Anielewicz. Not far from the kitchen there was a room for milking cows, and opposite were the buildings of the animals the farm would acquire, including cows, horses, sheep, chickens, and pigs. Two-thirds of the farm was taken up by fields, which were rotated between plowing and sowing. The unworked fields were used to collect hay for the animals. The fields were bordered on one side by a river, and the hakhsharah kept a vegetable garden as well.[43]

Other Farms in the American Zone

The youth movements intended to move kibbutz groups to training farms that with some preparation would be similarly suitable for agricultural work. Still the shape of the land and the nature of the farms varied considerably in the forty hakhsharot eventually created in the American zone of Germany. Some of the farms functioned completely independently, while others were assisted in their work by German laborers. Farms were appropriated from German owners and former Nazis or were opened on land that had belonged to Jews before the war. For example, Kibbutz Nili at Pleikhershof occupied the former estate of Julius Streicher, while Kibbutz Buchenwald moved to a prewar Bnei Akiva hakhsharah in Geringshof. The American authorities and Jewish farmers engaged in a process of denazifying all types of Nazi land from various elements of the defeated regime. The farm at Fulda was opened on Hermann Goering's land, the Hochlandslager farm was situated on a former Hitler youth camp, and, as noted, Eschwege occupied a Luftwaffe airbase.

Shmuel Zamri, in his work as agricultural adviser for the Jewish Agency, surveyed many of the hakhsharot created in the American zone, assessing the land allocated for the farms and their viability as self-sustaining settlements. For the April 1946 survey, he visited nine of the twenty farms officially in existence, which had some 1,500 residents (an average of 167 residents per farm).[44] The living conditions on the farms could vary considerably, with some young halutzim moving into old castles (such was the case in Aschbach), while others moved to small farmhouses or dilapidated buildings as in Fojta and Losau near Prebitz.[45]

In many cases, advance teams from the kibbutz groups were sent to prepare the farms before their official opening. Such was the case at Eschwege, where the members of Tosia Altman and Mordechai Anielewicz cleared the farmland of refuse and cleaned the main residence in order to make the farm suitable for use as an agricultural hakhsharah. Just as importantly, the preparation of the farm for its official opening was as much about making the new location suitable for demonstrations of Zionist enthusiasm on the part of the young pioneers and newly minted farmers.

The Official Opening of the Farms

The youth movements and the Jewish Agency as well as the young farmers on the hakhsharot understood the symbolic value of their farms on the confiscated German land. This visibility was not only intended to be demonstrated in surveys or newspaper reports but was also put on display at the official farm openings, attended by officials of the U.S. zone administration. This significance was not lost on the residents of the farm at Eschwege.

Approximately one month after the first members of Kibbutz Tosia Altman and Kibbutz Mordechai Anielewicz arrived at the abandoned airbase at Eschwege, the farm held its official opening, which was attended by representatives of the UNRRA, the JDC, and the Jewish Agency. The members described the occasion in the diary:

> The date is April 16, 1946. In the meantime we have reached some order in the place. The trash and the many barrels have been cleaned from the yard, the fields have been plowed and the time has come to hold a festive and official opening of the kibbutz. It was on a beautiful spring Shabbat day, when all around everything is green and in the scenery the sheep and the cows blend in. And in the kibbutz there is noise and excitement.[46]

The members marched to the field for inspection dressed in clean shorts and white shirts and holding the movement flag. Shlomo Charchas (from the central leadership) devoted his speech to the theme of preparing the kibbutz youths for aliyah through the move to the farm. In the evening a number of official speakers including the head of the nearby UNRRA team in Zamberg and Zelig, the emissary from Palestine, spoke of the good work the youths were doing in establishing a hakhsharah. The members of Kibbutz Tosia Altman put on performances of some of their plays for the many guests who attended the festive evening. Immediately after the official opening of the farm at Eschwege, the Hashomer Hatzair movement held its first meeting on the farm, timed to coincide with the third anniversary of the Warsaw Ghetto Uprising on April 19, 1946. The schedule of the conference included a speech on the Warsaw ghetto, discussion of the situation of Jews and Zionism, a seminar on social and instructional problems in kibbutz groups, and a meeting of madrichim from the movement.[47]

Farther south in the American zone, not long after the Eschwege opening, the joint movement farm at Hochland near Föhrenwald was opened to coincide with the holiday of Passover. The Hochland farm housed nearly three hundred members from four youth movements: Nocham, Dror, Hashomer Hatzair, and Hanoar Hatzioni. On the night of the Passover seder a large celebration was held to which hundreds of guests from various other kibbutzim and the nearby Föhrenwald camp came along with numerous official guests. According to Haim Hoffman, the opening of the farm also symbolized a transformation of the survivors for the outside observers. "Guests from the administration of UNRRA were also present at the party, who, seeing the boisterous youth full of enthusiasm, could not believe the sight before their eyes that these were the same broken and exhausted refugees which they had taken care of in the camps."[48]

An article in *BaMidbar*, the weekly newspaper of the Liberated Jews in Föhrenwald, also depicted the opening of the farm on Passover as a great holiday celebration, with a military-style march and parade by the kibbutz youths.[49] As the writer described in the newspaper, the march was led by a soldier, and "one of the most touching moments was the unfurling of the blue-and-white flag." The kibbutz choir sang songs, and the farm opening was attended by Henry Cohen, the UNRRA director of Föhrenwald; members of the Jewish Agency delegation; representatives of the Central Committee; and the local camp committee.

The timing of the Hochland farm opening on Passover also contributed to the symbolic significance of the day. The theme of Jewish liberation from Egyptian slavery nearly one year after the liberation of the concentration camps resonated with all of those in attendance. "Never have the words from the Haggadah [the traditional liturgy read during the Passover seder]: '*She-bechol dor vador omdim alenu lechalotenu*' [that in every generation they stand before us to eradicate us] had so much meaning. Even stronger, however, was the meaning of the words '*Hashata ocho, leshana habah beara Israel*' [This year, we are still here; next year in the Land of Israel]."[50] Following a speech by Dr. Hoffman, the formal seder service concluded with the Zionist anthem "Hatikvah," although this did not conclude the festive portion of the evening. The pioneering youth then danced the hora around the fire late into the night. As the *BaMidbar* reporter commented, "the seder will always stay in the memory of those who attended it."[51]

The Farm As Youth Movement Center

The training farms served a functional purpose for the youth movements, operating as a location to concentrate youth movement activities. Like the other farm openings, the first Nocham youth movement conference held on Kibbutz Nili was a highly symbolic event, intended to represent the Zionist enthusiasm of the young farmers to numerous outside attendees. Leo Schwarz described the first conference, held on February 17, 1946, in which the kibbutz welcomed numerous guests to the farm, including the leadership of the Central Committee as well as Haim Hoffman, Chaplain Abraham Klausner, and Leo Schwarz.[52] For the youths on the farm, it represented an opportunity to show off their collective accomplishments as the movement discussed the expansion of the farming project. The first conference held there generated a great deal of excitement, in particular for Baruch Cheta, leader of the kibbutz:

> He jostled his comrades out of bed and barked orders with the energy of a drill sergeant. To play host to a hundred young guests and Zionist leaders was an adventure that gave him new verve, and he was determined that his kibbutz should prove worthy of its name "Nili," the musical initial letters from the biblical verse, "Israel's victory should not be belied." For these youths, hustling into their long boots, riding trousers and open shirts were neither scrawny dreamers nor brands drawn from the Nazi fire, but young veterans of the Baltic and Polish forests, partisans and underground fighters imbued

with the pioneering ideals of the chalutzim who dedicated themselves to fructifying the soil of Palestine.[53]

The conference, which was attended by more than two hundred members of the movement and representatives from various bodies in liberated Germany, was highly meaningful for those who participated, who, as noted in the *Nitzotz* newspaper:

> All felt a sort of internal satisfaction of a feeling of revenge, because they were gathered precisely [*davka*] on the estate of the great Jew-hater, Julius Streicher. The pioneering youth honored the memory of their brothers who had bequeathed the call to realize the creation of the Jewish state in Palestine to the survivors. In the singing of HaTikvah they symbolized their readiness to achieve the will of the preceding generations, the generations of chalutzim, who worked and struggled in all conditions and who, in their deaths, had also sanctified their people.[54]

Many of the official guests spoke at the conference, commending the efforts of the young pioneers on the farm and praising the continuation of the

Group portrait of members of Kibbutz Nili in Pleikhershof, Germany. Those in the front row hold a portrait of the labor Zionist ideologue A. D. Gordon. (USHMM, coutesy of Ruchana Medine White)

Zionist struggle on the fiftieth anniversary of the publication of Herzl's *The Jewish State*.[55]

American authorities, UNNRA officials, and the JDC not only surveyed the agricultural training farms, where they witnessed the "Zionist enthusiasm" of their residents, but also screened the hakhsharot to determine the level and success of the farming work taking place on the farms.[56] From the kibbutz members' perspective, the continuing process of haksharah was a chance to demonstrate to the movement leadership their worthiness as candidates for aliyah. Once the initial excitement had passed after the farm opening, the new farmers had to adapt to life on the hakhsharah and learn the new daily schedule, one that would involve a great deal more physical labor and less time for cultural work. How did the Jewish youths adapt to the schedule of farm labor, and how did they describe the transition in their journals, letters, and correspondence?

The Nature of Kibbutz Life on the Farm

The move to the farm changed the dynamics of kibbutz life in multiple ways, most obviously through the change of location, living conditions, scenery, and daily schedule. The members of the kibbutzim also had to grapple with unforeseen changes in the morale of the kibbutz that accompanied the move to farms. While many greeted the move with excitement and pride, they soon encountered tension and apathy among their members on the farms. The move to a farm also changed the nature of kibbutz life by forcing individual kibbutzim, whose core group had been molded during their time since joining the kibbutz, to join and cooperate with other kibbutzim in the operation and management of farms.

The farms often had space for multiple kibbutzim, forcing groups that had adapted to living independently to extend the nature of collective life to outside groups. The farms at Struth, Hochland, and Greifenberg not only accommodated multiple kibbutzim from the same movement but were also used by members of Dror, Hashomer Hatzair, and Hanoar Hatzioni together.[57] Even in cases where kibbutzim came from the same youth movement, however, the primary loyalty remained first and foremost with the family that had been formed within the initial kibbutz group. At the farm in Eschwege numerous Hashomer Hatzair kibbutzim shared time there, with

Kibbutz Tosia Altman and Kibbutz Mordechai Anielewicz sharing the space with Kibbutz LeShichrur and BaDerech. Later Kibbutz Chaviva Reik from Pocking (led by Monish) moved to the farm, which it shared with LeShichrur.[58]

The encounter with other kibbutz groups on the farm was eye-opening for the members of Kibbutz Tosia Altman. Although they had previously come into contact with other kibbutzim both from their movement and from others, they were perhaps unaware of the extent to which their group could differ from others. For Kibbutz Tosia Altman, the contrast between their conduct and that of Kibbutz Mordechai Anielewicz was striking, and "the two social frameworks on the farm led to conflicts. There was no shortage of reasons: we worked very hard, they less so. In the other kibbutz the members could, for example, not come to the assemblies of the kibbutz, not vote on decisions, and disobey the mazkirut and the madrichim. Slowly we were influenced by this."[59]

The members of Kibbutz Tosia Altman also blamed this contact with the other kibbutz group for a crisis of low morale that occurred upon the move to the farm. Interestingly, they attributed these problems to an external locus of control, namely the other kibbutz, and not to any problems inherent within their own group. A few members were "influenced by this gloomy atmosphere," demonstrating a lack of respect for the kibbutz secretariat and Miriam and blaming problems on others "not before their faces . . . one can hear members saying expressions that are taken from the life in the camps."[60] This deterioration in the morale of the kibbutz was reminiscent of the situation upon arrival in Landsberg, although this time the kibbutz faced the crisis of members questioning the authority of Miriam as leader of the kibbutz. The influence of the other kibbutz (Miriam's former group) may have been a factor in the kibbutz apathy as was the period of adjustment to the new surroundings. The time spent by the advance team of the kibbutz on the farm before the arrival of Miriam and the rest of the kibbutz may have also led some members to assert their independence. After years of uncertainty, change, and tremendous loss, members were not well equipped to handle disruptions in their daily lives.

This tension between different groups on the farm was not unique to Kibbutz Tosia Altman. Kibbutz Buchenwald also experienced difficulties in accommodating new kibbutz groups arriving on their farm. The arrival of some former chanichim of Jechezkel Tydor from Bergen-Belsen to Gering-shof, who viewed themselves as more deserving of aliyah certificates for their prewar Zionist activity, contributed to the tension on the farm. In addition, the inability to accommodate the more religious residents on the farm led to the creation of a new hakhsharah at Gersfeld with the formation of Kibbutz Hafets Hayim. Furthermore, there was tension on the farm between the survivors of German origin and the newer arrivals from Poland.[61] These tensions perhaps had as much to do with the differing wartime experiences of the members as they did with the perceived threat to primary group loyalty on the part of the members of individual kibbutz groups.

Such difficulties notwithstanding, the encounter with other kibbutz groups forced members to learn to cooperate as they worked together to clean the farm and begin agricultural work there. They were forced to subordinate the needs of the kibbutz to the needs of the movement and of the farm. Various forms of work on the farm were shared between the kibbutz groups. Various branches of the farm competed for use of the kitchen, leading to a great deal of overcrowding and disorder. As described in the diary, "cooking began very early and then many different people would come into prepare food for the cows, pigs, chickens, etc.; all these different people upset Tzipporah. . . . It is true that the food did not always taste good and the kitchen was in general a source of many problems."[62]

The members of the kibbutzim also had to cooperate in the cleaning of the main farm building. Housekeeping work (sidur habayit) entailed washing the floors in the hallway and cleaning the shower and the bathrooms. "This work was not pleasant because for the most part the dirtiness was great and thus so was the work."[63] Still, it was necessary to keep the main building clean, for this reflected on the cleanliness and organization of the farm as a whole. Inspectors from the nearby DP camp, the UNRRA, and the Central Committee came to evaluate the functioning of the camp and the sanitary and hygienic quality of the farm. "More than once we were embarrassed by the lack of cleanliness when we were visited by administrators in the camp or visiting committees. The female members who were responsible for cleaning were also in charge of preparing the dining room for meals and also serving and cleaning the tables—all of this three times a day."[64]

The continuing inspections by UNRRA, Jewish Agency, and Central Committee teams motivated the kibbutz members to keep the farm and the residence clean, although, as noted, it was the female members of the kibbutz who continued to be responsible for most of the cleanup work. When it came to eating, the different kibbutz groups were able to have separate dining rooms, which allowed them to maintain some level of kibbutz independence. This was not the case on every farm, but the main building at Eschwege was large enough to accommodate several dining areas.[65] Nonetheless, the move to the farm certainly did not lead to complete isolation for the kibbutzim, as they encountered other groups and were frequently visited by outside guests for inspections and to showcase the accomplishments of the Zionist groups on the farms. These visits from outside groups also ensured that the kibbutzim were aware of the visible importance of their presence on the farm.

Learning to Farm: The Agricultural Department of the Central Committee

The youths who moved to the farms obviously needed to receive a great deal of help to become farmers. They received this assistance from Jewish Agency instructors and the Central Committee's Agricultural Office established during March–April 1946. The UNRRA and the JDC also provided assistance in the form of rations and farm equipment. The farms were often staffed by a member of the youth movement leadership who worked to ensure the successful functioning of the farm. Kibbutz Tosia Altman received help from Moshe Laufer of the Hashomer Hatzair central leadership, whom Miriam later described as in fact not very knowledgeable about farming.[66] While these farms theoretically had enough land for cultivation of crops and grazing farm animals, the Zionist youths moving to the hakhsharot were not prototypical farmers, ready and willing to take to the soil. In practice, the application of this plan would require a considerable amount of effort to justify concentrating Zionist youths away from the DP camps on valuable German soil. And in many cases, moral concerns notwithstanding, the farms relied on outside assistance from German agricultural laborers to continue functioning.[67]

While the various bodies (the UNRRA in particular) could marshal arguments to convince the U.S. Army to allocate land for farms, this did not guarantee that the farms would remain open once created. In order to justify the creation of farms, Jack Whiting of the UNRRA had to prove to the U.S.

Army that they could be viable and would not be a waste of valuable German soil, even though the kibbutz youths generally had very little experience in agricultural techniques. Whiting estimated in March 1946 that out of the five thousand he anticipated who would want training, only 5–8 percent would have any previous farm experience.[68]

As the American occupation force began to focus more and more on the reconstruction of the German economy and on Germany's food supply, the potential damage that could be caused by Zionist farms was viewed less favorably.[69] Therefore, the Central Committee and the Jewish Agency were keen to ensure the continued successful functioning of the hakhsharot. Success was not only determined by economic viability but was also understood by the two Zionist organizations to be a measure of the productive Zionist education of the kibbutz youths. The sphere of activity of the Central Committee, and specifically its Productivization Department, mandated that it work to facilitate the "professional education of Jewish youth" in the DP camps.[70] In this regard, the official creation of agricultural schools and farms with the assistance of foreign aid organizations, including the UNRRA, the Jewish Agency, ORT, and the JDC, fell under its purview, although it was the youth movements that provided the necessary manpower. After receiving complaints from the military government over the inefficient functioning of agricultural settlements, the Jewish Agency and the Central Committee formulated a plan to reorganize hakhsharot.[71] The two agencies worked to create a uniform program of agricultural training and instruction for all the farms while seeking to improve living conditions and efficiency through regular joint inspections.

The Central Committee supplemented the instructional materials and agronomists provided by the Jewish Agency through its Productivization Department, founded in April 1946. At the same time, the department also commenced publication of its *Landwirtschaftlecher Wegwajzer* (Agricultural Guidebook) under the editorship of Jacob Olejski and Nochum Sienicki, with volume 1 issued in May 15, 1946. To fill the need that had developed with the growth of the agricultural project (by the end of April 1946, there were twenty-seven hakhsharot in the American zone, with 2,270 members working on them),[72] the *Landwirtschaftlecher Wegwajzer* was created as a monthly publication dedicated to professional instruction of Zionist youths in the latest scientific agricultural techniques.

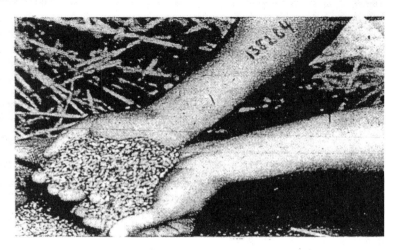

קאצעמישע הענט בײ דער הײליקער ארבעט

"Concentration Camp Hands Engaging in Holy Work." (*Landwirtschaftlecher Weg-wajzer*, The Agricultural Guide, November 1947, Jewish Periodicals Collection, USHMM/YIVO)

The program advanced in the pages of the *Landwirtschaftlecher Wegwajzer* by the Productivization Department supported a Zionist position but one that reflected the tensions inherent in providing Zionist agricultural educa-tion for youths whose ultimate priority was departure from the land they were to work only temporarily. In the first volume of the *Landwirtschaftlecher Wegwajzer*, Sienicki provided "directions for the organization and work of the agricultural hakhsharah."[73] According to Sienicki, "due to the uncertainty accompanying the present condition, it is not possible to create a strict program of work and organization of the agricultural hakhsharah," so he proposed a series of provisional guidelines. Because it would be difficult to foresee the duration of the She'erit Hapletah's stay in Germany, the agricultural effort of the Central Committee in Germany would focus more on education, theoretical and practical work, and "productivization" of the DP youths. One of the primary goals of the Productivization Department's agricultural plan, in accordance with its overall Zionist thrust, was to ensure that "upon their arrival in Palestine our youth do not go to become merchants in the cities but instead participate in the agricultural development of the land." Sienicki recommended providing theoretical and practical instruction to the young farmers in training as well as supplying farms with an agricultural library. He also suggested that each hakhsharah member "obtain in his own disposition a piece of land, let's say 100 meters sq., on which he makes a purely individual work on a beloved choice.... For example, through cultivation of tomatoes, cucumbers, cabbage, etc."[74] As with the rest of the prevailing Zionist discourse in the DP camps, the presentist educational and rehability goals of the leadership had to defer to the overarching priority: settlement and support of the Zionist cause in Palestine. In the case of the training farms, they would have to be successful enough to justify their continued existence and instill in the Zionist youths a love of agricultural work, but at the same time they were only temporary way stations on the journey to Palestine, where youths constantly dreamt of eventual aliyah.

In its first year of activity, the Central Committee Agricultural Office and the Jewish Agency were thus quite busy in providing training and instruction to kibbutz members who moved out to training farms. A report in the tenth volume of the *Landwirtschaftlecher Wegwajzer* summarized the accomplishments of the Agricultural Office of the Central Committee in the year since its founding in November 1946.[75] In the year and a half following the creation of the office (later renamed the Agricultural Department) of the Central Committee, it organized courses in theoretical agriculture, veterinary care, mushroom and fish cultivation, and tractor and machine usage while providing exams and certification upon successful completion of each course. The office also secured supplementary supplies for the hakhsharot and furthered education through the creation of agricultural libraries. Nonetheless, paradoxically, the ultimate goal of the hakhsharot—aliyah—continued to drain the farms of labor and manpower, thereby making the work of the office that much more challenging.

Turning into German Farmers:
The Life of a Young Zionist Pioneer in Germany

Although the kibbutz members on the farm at Eschwege had a support network designed to facilitate the operation of an agricultural training farm, they had to engage in the agricultural work on their own. Once the cleanup had been completed and the farm was officially opened, the kibbutz members set themselves to become farmers on their German hakhsharah. From the descriptions in the diary, the correspondence, the movement newspapers, and the surveys of the Jewish Agency and the JDC, it is clear that the farms were not merely new living centers where the youths in the kibbutzim continued their DP camp routines. The farms and the farmers actively engaged in the process of farming, taking the tasks of tending to livestock (sheep, pigs, chickens, horses, and cows) and raising and harvesting crops quite seriously. Work assignments were designated by the work organizer (*sadran avodah*), although members were not always content with the assignments they received. The work list compiled by Shaike, the work coordinator, for Kibbutz Chaviva Reik conveyed the variety of work performed by the members at Eschwege, which included everything from milking cows and tending pigs to mending shoes and arranging travel off the farm.[76]

The work done on the kibbutz was divided between the same self-maintenance work for the kibbutz itself, including cooking, cleaning, and organization of kibbutz supplies; although in theory agricultural work was the domain of both sexes, many of these maintenance tasks continued to be filled by women. The tending of livestock, however, marked a new experience for many of the kibbutz members, one that they noted as a momentous occasion in the life of the kibbutz. Members of Kibbutz Tosia Altman described the arrival of the first sheep to the farm in the diary as an "event [that] caused great excitement and emotion in all of us." The flock of sheep began with 14 head delivered to the kibbutz in a truck; soon thereafter 35 more sheep arrived, and by the time the kibbutz left the farm there were 187 sheep living in the sheep pen. The livestock was acquired through both

Jewish youth feed pigs on the Kibbutz LaMatara hakhsharah in Germany in preparation for their immigration to Palestine. (USHMM, courtesy of Henryk and Juta
Bergman)

official and unofficial means. Certain animals were provisioned by the Agricultural Department and the UNRRA, while others were acquired directly
by the kibbutz through cash they had earned through the sale of gasoline
(from the airfield) on the black market.[77] Eliyahu Raziel was designated
first shepherd of the flock, but he grew tired of the work and was replaced
by Bracha and Salusiah. When they also tired of "instilling culture and tradition" (i.e., proper domestic behavior) in the sheep, a professional shepherd
from the surrounding German population was hired to conduct the first
shearing, and this soon solved the problem of who would watch the sheep.[78]
While the kibbutz members could be designated to certain jobs, this did not
mean that they were necessarily proficient in the work or had to enjoy it.

The kibbutz soon also acquired pigs, chickens, and cows.[79] The chicken
coop began with 5 hens and a rooster, which soon produced 126 chicks; the
kibbutz members determined that they needed a real coop with a secure fence
and a roof to ward off predators (rats and hawks) and also needed incuba-
tors for the chicks. By the fall, the farm had enough birds to slaughter some

A young Jewish man holds onto a cow while a woman milks it on the Kibbutz LaMatara hakhsharah. (USHMM, courtesy of Henryk and Juta Bergman)

in order to share with members who were still in the hospital.[80] Shortly after the kibbutz's arrival at the farm, the cow barn was opened with three cows (this was after the American committee forced the kibbutz to move the cows away from their living quarters). Work in the barn began each day at 5:00 a.m. when the cows were first fed and then milked; milking took place three times a day. The kibbutz soon acquired pitchers and a centrifuge and managed to produce butter; "the eating of homemade butter caused great joy among the chevreh." Although Miriam did not know how to churn the butter, girls who had survived the war living in Polish villages had suggestions for how to improve the process.[81] The milk and butter from the dairy were shared within the kibbutz and given to the DP camp kitchen at Eschwege as well. Eventually the herd grew to such a size that the farm had to hire German laborers to build a new cowshed with a capacity for fifty cows.[82] Other farms had varying quantities of livestock depending on the size of the farm.[83]

Turning the deserted airfield at Eschwege into an efficient agricultural center capable of raising and harvesting crops would prove to be more complicated than utilizing the farm for tending to livestock, however. The farm

Group portrait of Jewish youth holding farming tools in the Kibbutz LaMatara hakhsharah. (USHMM, courtesy of Henryk and Juta Bergman)

operated by the kibbutzim at Eschwege boasted two vegetable gardens and greenhouses that raised such crops as tomatoes, cabbage, squash, onions, carrot, green peas, beets, and lettuce. The fields of the converted airstrip meanwhile were used for the cultivation of several hectares of wheat, oats, potatoes, turnips, and hay. While theoretically the members were to be assisted by the Central Committee's Agricultural Department in cultivation, in practice they again had to turn to Germans for expertise and assistance. As was noted in the diary, "there were generally not any seeds to be found. The wife of the German agronome would fix different seeds, like onions, carrot, green peas, beets, lettuce, cabbage, etc.," that were then planted by the members of the kibbutzim in the farm's two vegetable gardens.[84]

The airstrip that had been covered with Messerschmidts and barrels of gasoline ("reminders of the fascist regime") was turned into cropland by the kibbutz groups working on the farm. Shortly after their arrival the farm acquired an Ursus tractor with the assistance of the UNRRA in order to prepare the fields for crops.[85] Sowing and harvesting of crops such as potatoes, beets, and peas required the assistance of the entire kibbutz as did the gathering of hay, which corresponded with the beginning of spring.[86] The first hay harvest collected eighty-four wagon loads of hay. This was followed by harvests of wheat (12 hectares), potatoes, a second hay harvest, and oats.[87] When autumn came the kibbutz began to collect the onions, turnips, and carrots. During a whole week they collected four tons of onions that were sorted according to size; carrots were also gathered and placed in the basement in dry sand. The most difficult work was in collecting the potatoes. The machine for collecting the potatoes was harnessed to two oxen or horses. The machine worked slowly, burrowing and turning out the potatoes. Members walked behind with baskets to pick up the potatoes and place them in wagons; tons of potatoes were then sorted by members for weeks afterward.[88] At the same time the tractor plowed the fields for the planting of wheat, oats, and grain. The kibbutz planted 6.75 hectares of winter seeds and 8 hectares of wheat in 1946. Thus, over the course of 1946, the farmers at Eschwege successfully harvested tons of potatoes, onions, wheat, oats, turnips, and other crops.

Farming Streicher's Estate

Like the farm at Eschwege, Kibbutz Nili on Julius Streicher's estate in Pleikhershof could also boast of its agricultural success on the six-month anniversary of its opening. As Yosef Heller, a member of the group of halutzim working on Kibbutz Nili, described in the Nocham newspaper in June 1946, the initial work to prepare the land was difficult, but they could look with pride upon the fruits of their productive labor: "The time until the aliyah to Eretz Israel we would not wait behind the wires of the camps, but only to be productive, learning the agricultural work, in order to know how to plant our lives in an Eretz Israel kibbutz." The first members of Kibbutz Nili moved to Pleikhershof, where they found poor conditions, a deserted farm, and miserable livestock. As a group determined to be fully independent, the members of Kibbutz Nili had the German workers removed from the farm, and the kibbutz members took over all of the work. Nonetheless, the initial period was rather difficult, but over time the members managed to create a *makhlava* (dairy) for milking cows, a cheese press, and branches for cultivation of sheep, chicken, geese, fish, and bees. They also tended crops in their fields and vegetables in the garden. After six months of work gaining theoretical and practical training, they could state with confidence that their accomplishments would not go unrewarded. "The time, which we have spent here against our wishes, has given us a lot. Our members, who desire to make aliyah to Israel and wish to go to settlement, wish to have the necessary professional education and wish to possess the necessary qualifications in order to build the future of our people."[89]

For the members of Kibbutz Nili, agricultural work on the former estate of "our greatest enemy" was understood as a necessary evil required of pioneers preparing themselves for a future in Palestine.[90] The publication of this testimonial in the Nocham movement newspaper was clearly intended to demonstrate the hard work performed by the pioneers on the farm dedicated to the Zionist cause and prepared to take on any task in order to build the Jewish state. In this sense, it must certainly be read with an awareness of its propagandistic value. Still, it seems clear that the members of Kibbutz Nili did engage in an extensive array of agricultural work, from independent milk and dairy production to the cultivation of a diverse array of livestock and crops.

As Leo Schwarz described in his visit to the farm at Pleikhershof, the chalutzim had trained the horses to respond to Hebrew commands, and the kibbutz had amassed an impressive collection of chickens and cows. "The cows were housed in a veritable mansion. There were fifty-eight of them, with bulging udders, in separate, immaculate stalls." His host was proud of the milking operation on the kibbutz. "Come in the milking room and have a drink of our fresh milk and cream. Delicious, eh? Imagine what it will be like when we have our own milk from our own cows on our own land!"[91]

The farm at Hochland also occupied the members of the Dror Kibbutz Hannah Senesh in shoemaking, carpentry, tailoring, and other forms of artisan work that prepared the youths for aliyah through vocational training.[92] Surveys conducted by the JDC and the Jewish Agency attested to similar usage (to a varying extent) on other hakhsharot throughout Germany. While Streicher's farm and the farm at Eschwege, at eighty-two and eighty hectares, respectively, were comparatively larger than most of the other farms, almost all tended to livestock and engaged in crop cultivation.[93] The JDC and the Jewish Agency, which sought to promote the underlying value of the farming project, continued to conduct surveys that demonstrated the viability of the farms. In a survey of agricultural usage by Jewish DPs for 1946, Georg Muentz of the JDC estimated that on average, 56 percent of available land was used for the sowing of crops such as corn, clover, flax, vegetables, and fruit, while 40 percent of land was taken by meadows, woods, and ponds (the other 4 percent was unplowed). This compared favorably with Bavarian farmland usage, which showed that "the land on Jewish farms is used more intensively than on an average German farm."[94] According to Muentz, this argued strongly for the rational economic basis of Jewish farms. The survey of the sample eleven hakhsharot also suggested that land cultivation was not the only vital element of Jewish farming; tending to cattle and other forms of livestock also composed an important part of the agricultural training program of the hakhsharot.[95]

The Jewish youths who moved to the farms were thus willing to engage in agricultural work on the farm in order to prepare themselves for "the future in the Land of Israel" and were even aware of the symbolic value that such work could represent to outside observers. They could rationalize working on a former Luftwaffe airfield of harvesting crops on Streicher's and Goering's estates with knowledge that this served the continuing goal of hakhsharah atzmit, self-preparation for aliyah to Israel. How did they perceive this move collectively, however? Did they sense that it added anything to their experience in Germany? Most basically, how did the move to the farm affect their everyday life, and did it add or detract from their cultural work as a kibbutz?

The Transition to the Farm: Collectively Adapting to Change

While seemingly an ideal progression in their Zionist education and a move presented as desirable by various groups in the American zone ostensibly working in their best interest, the move to the farms could be difficult for the kibbutzim on a number of levels. To the kibbutz members, agricultural training was not only a disruption of the routine they had established in the DP camp but was also an indication of the lengthening duration of their stay in Germany. The difficulty or ease with which a kibbutz transitioned to the farm seemed to be influenced by the nature of members' experiences prior to arrival on the farm. Despite feeling excitement with their agricultural accomplishments, Kibbutz Tosia Altman reported to the central leadership of Hashomer Hatzair serious difficulties associated with the move from Leipheim to the farm at Eschwege.

The kibbutz had trouble adjusting to the rhythm of life on the farm under new conditions and reported that the move had a harmful effect on the kibbutz through the departure of key members and the disruption in the social life of the kibbutz.[96] Moreover, the cultural life and regular routine of Kibbutz Tosia Altman were also negatively affected by the move to Eschwege. The new schedule imposed upon the kibbutz by the needs of agricultural work certainly had an impact. Both kibbutzim worked until seven in the evening, and the mazkirut struggled greatly with the social question in order to return the kibbutz to normal life. As the kibbutz reported, "despite the best efforts of the mazkirut to improve cultural life in the kibbutz, there are still numerous disturbances in the [cultural] work."[97]

For Kibbutz Tosia Altman, part of the struggle with adapting to the farm seemed to relate directly to its positive experience in the Leipheim DP camp, which kibbutz members described as "the nicest time in the kibbutz." As they reported to the leadership, even though economic conditions were poor there, they enjoyed their cultural immersion and benefited from "the chance to get to know the reality of life in Israel and its difficulties. During the whole time in Leipheim the kibbutz was engaged in an intensive cultural activity which involved discussions over various problems, parties, a strong drama group, etc."[98] The move to the farm from Leipheim certainly transformed the kibbutz, and "with our arrival in Eschwege, life in the kibbutz took on a second character." While members took interest in the new type of work they were introduced to, they complained that the difficult farm work left them with little time for "cultural and ideological work" and overall hampered the social life of the kibbutz.[99] After finally settling into the new environment of the Leipheim DP camp and engaging in the flourishing of Jewish culture there and throughout the zone, the kibbutz members struggled with the transition to a new setting in which they were unfamiliar with the agricultural work and missed the daily routine of their cultural and ideological education (despite any improvements in their economic situation).

Other kibbutzim more immediately saw the move to a farm in a positive light. This was certainly the case with the first farms created in the American zone by Kibbutz Buchenwald and Kibbutz Nili, which had chosen to make the move to a farm on their own. The kibbutz named after the United Partisans' Organization in the Vilna ghetto, which traveled directly from Poland to an agricultural training farm in June 1946, also reported to the central leadership members' satisfaction with their new home: "Spirits are high and everyone is happy with the work (which is not too hard). In these ten days we have been browned by the sun, we sing and discuss at night until 1 am. And no less important we are eating very well—meat, drinking milk, eating cheese, butter, vegetables."[100] Unlike Kibbutz Tosia Altman, their move to the farm took place directly upon their arrival in Germany, so they had no other experiences with which to compare aside from those in Poland and in transit. Their group was also not separated upon arrival, perhaps as part of an effort to fully isolate youths from the atmosphere of the DP camps.

For the movement, transferring kibbutzim from the DP camps to farms was an opportunity to concentrate a number of kibbutz groups in one place, making the farm a focal point of movement activity and reestablishing the prewar hakhsharah framework. From the perspective of the youths in the kibbutzim, the DP camp was not always a source of demoralization, but to the youth movement it did present a danger of distraction and potential kibbutz abandonment if a better option presented itself to the youths in the camp. While good for the aims of the movement, such transitions were not always pleasant for the members of the kibbutzim, who disliked having to be separated from their newly formed close-knit family or having to share resources with other groups.

The Continuing Value of Cultural Work

In contrast to the descriptions of farming in the kibbutz diary and in the movement newspapers, in the correspondence with the central leadership (in the form of kibbutz reports) there was little mention of agricultural work except to convey the degree to which it disrupted cultural endeavors of the kibbutzim. The Hashomer Hatzair kibbutzim seemed to focus disproportionately on their cultural work, although agricultural labor now seemed to take up the majority of members' days. The disruption in educational and cultural work was resented by the members of Kibbutz Tosia Altman following their move to Eschwege who, in complaining to the leadership, seemed to genuinely fear the loss of any educational advances they had made as a group in the DP camp. In the reports to the leadership they mentioned the lack of consistency with the education begun in Leipheim and the disturbances caused by the agricultural work that continued late into the day.[101] The return to normality following the transition to the farm was measured by the amount of cultural education the kibbutz could accomplish. This belief in the central importance of the cultural education suggests that the kibbutz members either truly enjoyed the cultural work, believed that it was most important in readying them as candidates for aliyah, or were astute enough to realize that this was what the leadership wanted to hear. Regardless, its importance relative to the agricultural work was clear.

Once the members of Kibbutz Tosia Altman had begun a regular schedule, they reported more success adjusting to their new lives and returning to the cultural work they had enjoyed before. Nonetheless, some six weeks after their arrival at Eschwege, the amount of work required of them was still considerable. "The field of work remains almost without an end; the farm administration committee continues with control over work in the farm and in the kibbutz and the group is occupied throughout the eight hour day with many different forms of work."[102] Still, they could report that "in the realm of social life, things have improved in recent days." A new mazkirut worked to improve the atmosphere in the kibbutz through a renewed effort to expand the cultural life as much as was possible in the new setting. In addition to Hebrew and seminar groups, members of the kibbutz who attended the movement seminar would instruct the kibbutz on the geography of Palestine. The kibbutz tried to accommodate the new reality by encouraging members to educate themselves when they had the time through the creation of a library and reading room where members could read books and newspapers.[103]

After the arrival of the remainder of the kibbutz from Leipheim in mid-June, the kibbutz reported to the leadership that the cultural life of the kibbutz had returned to normal. It was reported that the members had adjusted to the daily work schedule and that educational groups had indeed been resumed in Hebrew, socialism, economics, and Palestinography. The kibbutz continued the tradition of holding an Oneg Shabbat on Friday evenings and holding assemblies to discuss the various problems facing the kibbutz.[104]

Although the members of Kibbutz Tosia Altman may have complained about the disruptions to their cultural work following their move there, life on the farm also contributed to their cultural work and brought new meaning to the celebration of Jewish holidays outside, in nature. For example, on the Jewish holiday of Lag Ba'Omer (May 19, 1946, the thirty-third day after Passover), the members of the kibbutz decided to spend the holiday, traditionally celebrated outdoors, with hikes in the fields and the forest. They marched to a nearby campsite (the UNRRA forbade them from marching directly through the town) where they held a discussion, sang songs, danced the hora, and played scouting games along with other kibbutz groups and students from the school in the Eschwege DP camp.[105] The kibbutz similarly described the occasion in a report to the central leadership and noted participating with groups from Pachach and Betar. The Betar group that they happened to meet on the way to the campsite decided to celebrate with them, a notable occurrence between two groups theoretically in opposition to one another. The members of the Betar group behaved and followed all of Miriam's instructions.[106]

Two weeks later (June 5, 1946), the kibbutz celebrated the pilgrimage holiday of Shavuot, also known as Hag HaBikkurim (Feast of First Fruits), a harvest holiday, that provided them with an opportunity to show off the produce and animals they had cultivated until then.[107] They created a "festive holiday atmosphere" with singing and dancing and put on a performance in honor of the holiday. They also hosted two Hashomer Hatzair kibbutz groups from Lampertheim and Zeilshem, who journeyed to the farm to celebrate the holiday. In this sense, Jewish holidays continued to be celebrated within the kibbutz with a blend of Jewish and Zionist motifs, although now the youths in the kibbutz had the opportunity to celebrate on their own farm, in nature, in a manner similar to how they imagined the pioneers in the Land of Israel would celebrate on their kibbutzim.[108]

Cultural Work on Other Farms

After six months of farm activity, members of Kibbutz Nili also pointed to their cultural work as one of their greatest sources of pride. "To speak or write about Kibbutz Nili and not mention the cultural committee is almost impossible, because Kibbutz Nili has for its fame to thank the work of the culture committee; there is not one corner of kibbutz life, on which the cultural committee did not leave its stamp."[109] Yerachmiel, a member of Kibbutz Nili, described in the Nocham movement newspaper the challenging assignment that the cultural committee had before it in the kibbutz. "The committee had a difficult but important task—to educate and implant our pioneering ideals in people, who came from all corners of Europe, from various sectors of society, speaking various languages and who were demoralized in the labor and concentration camps." Difficulties with various languages, backgrounds, and horrific wartime experiences notwithstanding, Yerachmiel wrote that on the farm a transformation had taken place among the members, who "only a short time ago looked with distrustful eyes upon one another, not knowing anything about Zionism, chalutziut, the working Eretz Israel." Today these members "feel in our kibbutz a warm home and a true pioneering warm atmosphere. . . . They all beat and breathe the spirit of the Yishuv and from the wall of the dining hall resonate the slogans of pioneering life."[110]

Like Kibbutz Tosia Altman, the members of the kibbutz on Streicher's farm were divided into groups according to level and met several times a week to discuss questions and problems of "Zionism, pioneering, socialism, the kibbutz movement, Palestinography, instruction, general knowledge, and political press overview." Several Hebrew groups, in which all members participated, also met daily. Kibbutz Nili also seemed to maintain a weekly schedule similar to that at Eschwege, holding an Oneg Shabbat every Sabbath dedicated to "Jewish and Zionist" problems and personalities. Artistic performances were also put on at these weekly gatherings, which attracted guests from the surrounding area as well as residents of the farm.[111] The members of Kibbutz Nili were quite proud of the publication of the Passover Haggadah, which was published with original "pioneering content according to the pattern of the kibbutzim in Israel." As in many other kibbutzim, members of Nili wrote their own wall newspaper, *Kadimah* (Forward), that appeared every two weeks. Yerachmiel wrote with pride that "the appearance and content of the newspaper articles present the highest cultural levels of achievement of our members." Kibbutz Nili also had to balance its time between work, learning, and celebrating (singing and dancing), but all were activities that helped them to "prepare for the life which awaits us in Eretz Israel."[112] This summary of Kibbutz Nili's agricultural work would demonstrate to readers of the youth movement newspaper that the kibbutz members on the farm were not only engaged in dull agricultural labor all day but were also able to maintain education and leisure time, all geared toward preparing them for aliyah. For members who may have feared leaving the DP camp, such a piece could reassure them that life on a training farm could be a mixture of business and pleasure.

The Farm and the Youth Movement

The youth movements also used the farms to host kibbutz groups from the wider movement, turning the farms into focal points of movement activity. This not only provided the movements with a place to concentrate youth and direct their activities but also gave kibbutz members a sense of pride in showing off their accomplishments on the farm. Like the first movement conference held at Kibbutz Nili, such a focus also continued to reinforce their sense of belonging to a larger movement family.

The movements also held training seminars for madrichim on the farms. In June 1946 the newly created hakhsharah kibbutz at Teublitz hosted one hundred members of Nocham at a regional meeting of the movement. Such meetings, like the seminars described in chapter 3, constituted opportunities to meet other "brothers and sisters" from the various kibbutzim in order to learn together, with time set aside for discussions and the requisite singing and dancing.[113] Kibbutz Nili was also later used by Nocham for such events as a conference of madrichim held during July 1946.[114] During the summer of 1946 (and even more so in 1947), the youth movements used the training farms as summer camps for the younger members of the youth movement branches in the DP camps. The first Hashomer Hatzair *moshavat tzofim* (scouts' camp)—described in the next chapter—opened in Hochland on July 20, 1946.[115] The Dror movement also used Hochland for seminars and scouting, hosting training sessions on the hakhsharah in 1946 and 1947.[116]

The movement conferences were often timed to coincide with Jewish holidays, giving the members of kibbutzim in the DP camps an opportunity to enjoy the holidays with special celebrations on the farms. During the holiday of Sukkot (Feast of Booths), the farm at Eschwege hosted members from each kibbutz and movement branch at the first Hashomer Hatzair northern regional conference.[117] Members of Kibbutz Tosia Altman also traveled to the farm at Hochland near Föhrenwald (occupied by Kibbutz Shmuel Breslaw) to participate in a movement conference and greet Meir Ya'ari (the Hashomer Hatzair movement leader) in his visit to the DP camps from Palestine.[118] In this way, the hakhsharot continued to function as places to unify kibbutz members training together in preparation for aliyah while reinforcing their membership in the larger youth movement.

Revenge and Redemption: The Encounter with Germany

Perhaps more than any other aspect of their postwar experience, for the youths who moved out to the farms the new setting brought them into more direct contact with the reality of Germany and the surrounding German population than life in a the solely Jewish DP camp did. Some farms relied on Germans for farming expertise and nearby towns for basic services. As the members of Kibbutz Buchenwald discussed in their diary, this raised moral concerns for them such as whether it was permissible for them to farm on "cursed German soil" at all or whether male members should be allowed to pursue sexual relations with German women. While they could rationalize farming in Germany as essential to the creation of a Zionist future, intimate relationships with Germans would be strictly forbidden. The members of Kibbutz Tosia Altman were well aware of what farming on a former Luftwaffe airbase represented: "Let us not forget that in fact the working of the land that was soaked with Jewish blood awakened in us a problem and we had to overcome our emotions and take upon ourselves the responsibility of the task of hakhsharah in agricultural work."[119]

Likewise, Kibbutz Nili faced the task of working the former estate of Julius Streicher, a symbolic irony that was not lost on them. As they began work on the farm in November 1945 they replaced the German inscriptions around the property with Hebrew names such as Shoshana, Chaviva, and Zivia. "The buildings on Streicher's farm were renamed Hulda, Hanita, Degania [places of Jewish settlement in Palestine], *refet* [cowshed], *urvah* [stable], *lul* [chicken coop], etc. In Streicher's former office was located the mazkirut, in which one could hear the sounds of the Hebrew and Yiddish language."[120] Among the most amusing aspects of this symbolic reappropriation was the renaming of the Kibbutz Nili dogs. As Leo Schwarz described on his first visit to Kibbutz Nili:

> They followed him [Baruch Cheta] toward a large doghouse. "Julius! Julius!" he shouted. An enormous, hairy dog leaped out, frightening the visitors. Running at his heels came a big black bitch. The lad put his hands into their mouths, stroked their heads, and they ambled about together. Their names now are Julius and Streicher. They obey and protect us! It's a pity to humiliate innocent animals with such swinish names. But we couldn't resist the temptation.[121]

Above all, the occupation of Streicher's farm was a serious matter, and on the six-month anniversary of the farm opening Kibbutz Nili noted with pride its occupation of Streicher's estate: "And destiny wished that we should make our hakhsharah on the farm of our greatest enemy, Streicher, *which at the same time was a great moral satisfaction for us.* It did not scare us that we found ourselves far from Jewish kibbutzim, in a region of German people. We go forward and strive to build our land by all means and through all hardships."[122] Destiny had brought them to occupy Streicher's farm, and they made the most of the symbolic value of Jewish youths working Nazi soil. Their isolation from other Jews in Germany, surrounded by German people, was a badge of pride in their collective effort to prepare themselves for departure from Europe and demonstrate their readiness for aliyah.

The residents of Kibbutz Tosia Altman also had a more direct relationship with Germans than simply on the symbolic level. A German agronomist and his wife instructed them on virtually all agricultural matters on the farm. Farm residents also hired German laborers to build the cowshed and work as a shepherd. And perhaps most importantly, the members of Kibbutz Tosia Altman recalled selling items on the black market to Germans; in addition to the regular sale of cigarettes while in the DP camps, the members of Kibbutz Tosia Altman sold what they could from the airbase, including airplane parts and unused barrels of gasoline, all of which facilitated the successful functioning of the farm.

Conclusion

Various sources attest to the overall success of the effort to move kibbutzim arriving from Poland out to hakhsharot in the U.S. zone. While certainly influenced by Ben-Gurion's visit to the zone in late October 1945, the creation of forty agricultural training farms in the U.S. zone of Germany with more than thirty-five hundred residents by the end of 1946 was dependent on cooperation among a number of different groups that each saw something useful in the Zionist endeavor. Through these sources, we can begin to get a sense for how Zionist options were appealing less for ideological reasons and more for pragmatic ones to many of the groups functioning in the DP camps. Supposedly apolitical groups such as the United Nations and the JDC as well as Jewish chaplains endorsed Zionist projects because of their productive and rehabilitative capacity. Likewise, the U.S. Army took a functional view of training farms, which for a time were seen as a solution to the problems of infiltration and overcrowding. The Jewish Agency always maintained its bottom-line goal of creating a state in Palestine and hoped to employ farms as training centers and holding stations for future immigrants. Meanwhile, for Jewish youths who had been liberated in the concentration camps of Germany or who arrived over the course of 1946 in the kibbutzim of the Bricha, the experience of farming in postwar Germany provided them with the opportunity to work collectively with their new families in the kibbutz, spending their days working, singing, and learning away from the DP camps until they could leave Germany. The very dilemma that Zionist agriculturalists on the Central Committee had to struggle with—that is, how to balance the present effort to make farms viable and productive with the ultimate goal of facilitating aliyah—was the very reason the farms succeeded. While not necessarily the intent of U.S. authorities, the productive upside of Zionism as represented in such training farms facilitated a situation that assisted in the ultimate creation of the Jewish state.

In many ways, however, the opening of the training farms was most successful in serving the political ends of the Zionist movement by demonstrating enthusiasm on the part of the Jewish DP population and training new cadres of young pioneers. The pioneers themselves seemed to enjoy most those aspects of the farm that continued to contribute to their cultural life through the celebration of holidays, hiking, and the symbolic nature of agricultural work and as focal points of movement activity where they could participate in events with the larger movement family. The timing of the farm creation also suggests that the farms could not have been opened without the active participation of the youths on the kibbutzim. The hakhsharot had to be fully functioning farms that could justify the diversion of resources from the German economy. They were not merely holding centers for overcrowded DP camps but were opened and continued to function in such a time and manner that suggests that largely untrained Jewish youths ended up being vital to their success.

The farming project also demonstrates the manner in which, within a short time, Jewish youths could become the object of outside agendas, with numerous groups seeking to make use of the youths or believing they were acting in their best interest. Despite decreased control over their own movements and activities, the youths in the kibbutzim continued to believe in the kibbutz framework and the support system it provided as well as the educational and recreational activities they enjoyed within its context. In the difficulty of transition, kibbutz members sought a return to their new state of normal: life with the kibbutz group as a whole engaged in cultural work. Kibbutz members did not question the value of these cultural endeavors or the social group they now called home.

Kibbutz members also seemed to be aware of the symbolic value they carried farming the blood-soaked German soil. The renaming of Streicher's cattle and dogs, the transformation of a Luftwaffe airfield into a farm, and the working of Goering's land were powerful symbols of redemption in the year following the war's end. Yet kibbutz members did not want to engage in such behavior one day longer than they had to, as their ultimate goal continued to be departure from Germany. Kibbutz members continued to play their part, training for their future lives in the Jewish state, doing what they could to improve their chances of finally leaving.

III
Leaving Germany for the Land of Israel

5

"Between Hope and Disappointment"

Jewish Displaced Youths and Aliyah

By the end of 1946, the Jewish displaced persons (DPs) in general and the youths in particular demonstrated a Zionist enthusiasm that was evident to the DP population and outside observers. Nonetheless, membership in Zionist organizations, while offering the psychological, social, educational, and vocational rewards detailed in the previous chapters, had failed to accomplish its ultimate goal for the majority of DPs in Germany, that being departure from Europe. While the youths could decide whether to remain within the framework of the kibbutz, the timing of departure from Germany was largely out of their control. Aliyah was determined mainly by external factors: access to certificates, requests made by the parties and the movements, and the regulations of the British mandatory authorities. As the members of Kibbutz Tosia Altman discovered, departure for aliyah did not even necessarily mean arrival in the Land of Israel. The length of time it took to remove Kibbutz Tosia Altman's 110 members from the American zone was indicative of the wait facing young kibbutz members who ostensibly stood at the front of the immigration line. Although the members of Kibbutz Tosia Altman were indeed able to leave Germany by the beginning of 1947, the vast majority of Jewish DPs in the American zone were forced to wait for relief, making 1947 the longest and most trying year since liberation.

Over the course of 1947 the hopeful prospects for immigration that had followed the Anglo-American Committee of Inquiry report waned. Zionist activists in the DP camps feared that any prior enthusiasm for the Zionist enterprise would diminish along with the declining chances of departure. The arrival of large numbers of children and families in the Bricha from Poland and Eastern Europe also seemed to change the nature of the DP population. While the earlier arrivals had been considered for their pioneering capacity by the youth movement activists from Palestine, the families arriving from the East were more likely to be burdened by the responsibilities of children, spouses, and the concomitant considerations for the future. Likewise, 1947 became the year of the baby boom within the DP camps, as many young Jewish DPs made the choice to create new families while they still lived in Germany. For many DPs, young and old alike, other options such as immigration to the United States, Canada, South America, or Australia would also have to be considered.[1] Zionist leaders in the youth movements, the camps, and the Jewish Agency worked to counteract this trend, although their communications over the course of 1947 betrayed a rising sense of urgency and a willingness to consider any aliyah option at any cost. Still, during this year the Jewish DPs played a crucial role in a number of episodes that would prove critical in the creation of the Jewish state, namely the *Exodus* Affair and subsequent United Nations support for the Palestine partition plan. Most directly, as a result of the hostilities that broke out in Palestine at the end of 1947 and the beginning of 1948, Jewish DPs enlisted for military service in Palestine (and Israel after May 1948), contributing a substantial number of frontline fighters to the Haganah and to Israel Defense Forces.[2]

A number of scholars in Israel have been critical of the Zionist enterprise in this context, suggesting that Zionists in the Yishuv cynically made use of the survivors to accomplish their own goals by forcing refugees onto rickety immigrant ships bound to be captured by the British and conscripting young Holocaust survivors into military service in the 1948 war. From the DP perspective, many were prepared to leave Germany at almost any cost by this time; in this sense, they may have been ready to make use of themselves as political tools in order to accomplish their goals of departure. It would seem that by the end of 1948 the DPs and the Zionist movement had entered into a mutually beneficial relationship with a result that accomplished each of their long-term goals: the creation of a Jewish state that could absorb the large number of Jewish refugees in Europe. But was the cost paid by the DPs greater than the one they had anticipated? And was the goal that of the entire DP population or merely the younger segment of it?

The Departure of Kibbutz Tosia Altman

The final chapter of Kibbutz Tosia Altman's stay in Germany did not conclude until the last members of the group departed the American zone. While the members of Kibbutz Tosia Altman succeeded in turning Eschwege into a functioning farm, their agricultural work was meant to be temporary, only intended as a means of achieving a long-term goal. The prospect of aliyah to Israel continued to dominate discussions and activity within the kibbutz, with cultural work focused on preparing them for life in Israel. The youth movement publications such as the *Hashomer Hatzair* newspaper also devoted themselves almost completely to events and developments in Palestine, usually leaving the final page of the paper for movement news from Germany.[3] Feature articles described political and social developments in Palestine, the struggle against the British Mandate, and the history of the Yishuv in Palestine. Letters from kibbutz groups that had already left described the process of aliyah, providing glimpses of what kibbutz groups could expect once they were fortunate enough to be chosen to leave. Through letters written directly to the kibbutzim and letters published in movement newspapers, kibbutz members were able to maintain contact with those who had left. The news was not always encouraging; in fact, reports of kibbutz groups being forced to split on arrival in the Yishuv was one of the primary factors that prevented youth movement unity in the DP camps. Other letters published in movement papers realistically chronicled the difficulties with adjusting to the difficult work on a kibbutz in Israel. Nonetheless, such letters reinforced the potential for members to reach Israel and therefore encouraged them to work that much harder to prepare themselves for life there.[4]

השומר
הצעיר 9

הוצאת הסתדרות "השומר־הצעיר" בהעפלה

עמק יזרעאל

HAIFA

עשינה ורחם כנים לגאולתו בידי הקרן הקימת לישראל • תרס'א - תש'ה

16 נאוועמבער   1946

Hashomer Hatzair newspaper, November 1946, highlighting the accomplishments
of the Jewish National Fund in the Jezre'el Valley in the Yishuv. (Jewish DP Periodicals Collection, USHMM/YIVO)

Aliyah of Kibbutz Groups

The British government's restriction on immigration to Palestine was the primary factor limiting access to departure. The limited number of certificates available meant that the aliyah of kibbutz groups was squeezed to a slow drip. Beyond this, the youth movements were sensitive to the quality of the olim (immigrants to Palestine) who would be allowed to join the ranks of the kibbutzim in the Yishuv. In the requests to compile lists of candidates for aliyah, the central leadership instructed the kibbutzim to exclude those who were most active in the movement or on the farm.[5] This perhaps contradicted the effort to work hard in order to earn a spot for aliyah, because those who were most capable or most important to the continued functioning of the youth movement in Germany were least likely to be selected. In the internal debates held within the kibbutz to select members for aliyah, such factors were weighed by the kibbutz collectively, and indeed the most active members often remained in Germany to work with other kibbutz groups.

In general, staggered departure was the norm for the kibbutzim of all of the movements, as it was rare for an entire kibbutz group to be able to depart at one time. The eighty members of the group constituting Kibbutz Buchenwald who left Germany in August 1945 were a rare exception; even then members were left behind to continue the operation of the farm and hold the hakhsharah point for Nocham. All of the Hashomer Hatzair kibbutz reports to the leadership discussed the departure of sections of the kibbutz.[6] Beyond the limits on immigration certificates, there were a number of other reasons for this slow departure, including the logistical difficulties of arranging transport for hundreds of youths at one time. Moreover, the youth movements wanted to ensure the continuity of their influence in the DP camps and were reluctant to give up barracks or farms they already occupied. The movements in Palestine were also sensitive to integrating Holocaust survivors into preexisting kibbutzim in Israel; they wanted to avoid creating a separate stratum of survivor groups within the movement and believed that breaking survivor kibbutzim into small groups within the movement would facilitate integration and adaptation.[7]

Of the original 110 members of Kibbutz Tosia Altman who had arrived in Germany in November 1945, 40 had departed German soil for aliyah by

July 1946, some eight months after their arrival.[8] In addition to these 40 were 11 members waiting for departure in Bergen-Belsen, whose difficulties with aliyah are rather instructive in demonstrating the challenging immigration process kibbutz members faced after the war. Being chosen for aliyah rarely meant arriving in Palestine; it simply represented an opportunity to be on the move once again.

The Belsen Group

On June 9, 1946, Kibbutz Tosia Altman received a notice from the central leadership to send eight members to the camp at Belsen in the British zone where they would depart with five hundred other youths for aliyah, a rather large shipment of immigrants. As described in the diary, the kibbutz held a meeting to select the new olim, and the group traveled to Belsen to depart with the rest of the aliyah group. From Hanover they traveled in the direction of the Belgian border; that night they reached Dusseldorf, where they met the larger group. They waited for two days near the Belgian border for permission to cross but were then sent back to a camp in the British zone, where they eventually waited six weeks for departure. In the meantime five more members of Kibbutz Tosia Altman had joined them. They finally left this camp and were sent to Belsen by the central leadership, where they spent another month waiting for immigration certificates. Two and a half months after their initial departure from Eschwege, unable to secure certificates, the group returned to the farm frustrated but still "living with the constant thought of aliyah."[9] Their return to the kibbutz allowed them to record their experience in the diary. The group finally left for good at the end of September 1946, almost four months after their initial selection for aliyah.

Likewise, the third large group of twenty-five members, *plugah gimmel* (C group), designated to depart in July 1946 did not have an easy time in its efforts to leave Germany for Palestine. The group consisted of both newer and older members; those who were "most active, sick, and most responsible on the farm were not considered." As was customary, the kibbutz held a festive party to bid the members farewell with singing, dancing of the hora, and a rendition of "Tekhezekna" (the movement anthem).[10]

All the same, the path of the C group was also filled with the twists, turns, and manipulations of the immigration system necessary for a successful attempt at departure from Germany. Together with members of Kibbutz Mordechai Anielewicz, the selected members of Tosia Altman traveled to Zeilsheim, where they stayed with a kibbutz from the Nocham movement. They were instructed by the Jewish Agency *shaliach* there to register at the Hebrew Immigrant Aid Society (HIAS) office in order to obtain departure visas to Bolivia. The Bolivian visas would enable them to leave Germany; once they did they would be directed by the Bricha on the path to Palestine. In Frankfurt they met with a representative of HIAS, who could not understand why they would possibly want to go to Bolivia.[11] They explained their ostensible reasons for wanting to move to South America, and after three weeks they received their visas. In the meantime another kibbutz had taken their spots, and they had to wait another seven weeks before they could leave. Beyond causing great disappointment and tension within the group, some members decided that it was not worth the wait and abandoned the kibbutz altogether.[12] While it is unclear which members chose to leave the kibbutz, members' frustration over the inability to leave Germany, which only continued to grow over the course of 1947, would be a serious problem facing the youth movements.

The rest of Kibbutz Tosia Altman waited for departure in Eschwege, with another group of thirteen leaving for aliyah in August (before the Belsen group managed to leave in September). They continued with the upkeep of the farm and the regular kibbutz schedule, commemorating Jewish and Zionist holidays and the first birthday of the kibbutz.[13] On December 5, 1946, the kibbutz received the news for which it had been waiting for more than a year: the remaining members of the group should prepare themselves for departure. "Our joy knew no bounds. We began our preparations for aliyah, but first we thought about our departure party."[14] At the same time, some of the members went to participate in the twenty-second Zionist Congress in Basel during December 10–12, 1946.[15] Beyond preparing a party to celebrate departure with the other residents of the Eschwege farm, the preparation for aliyah required practical and financial organization on the part of the kibbutz members. Hinda, who was responsible for preparing bags and clothes for the departing groups of olim, bought materials from the German

population in Eschwege and prepared the materials for each departing aliyah
group. After the final departure notification, Chanka, Yedziah, Malkah, and
Miriam worked to prepare backpacks for the members of the kibbutz to
take with them on their path to Israel. All of the possessions of the kibbutz
that could be taken were emptied from the *makhsan* (storage space) and organized in backpacks. Each member also received new shoes and a coat from
the United Nations Relief and Rehabilitation Administration (UNRRA).[16]
Preparation for departure not only required practical planning; there was
also the cost associated with organizing travel for such a large group. Kibbutzim that remained were also asked to help other kibbutz groups departing for aliyah, both with preparation of materials and with financial
contributions.[17]

On December 29, 1946, the members of Kibbutz Tosia Altman held their
final departure party. Yosef (Tzunik) Richter, Miriam's brother, spoke and
said that "in the history of the Jews there is no example of young people like
us, who only yesterday we left concentration camps, bunkers, and forests
and now we have taken upon ourselves the responsibility for the future of
the people."[18] The shaliach, Yehoshua Bruk, praised the kibbutz as "the last
of the first kibbutzim created after the war to leave for aliyah" and congratu-
lated them as they received the symbol of movement graduates, "the Chazak
ve-Ematz" (literally "strong and brave," from Deuteronomy 31:7).

On January 5, 1947, the kibbutz left forever the farm, "which we established, developed, and (in which) we invested great energy. Here we were
educated and trained for different forms of work and therefore this period
will remain engraved in our hearts. She [the farm] sealed on us the signature
of productive work."[19] Their efforts on the farm were temporary, but the
members sensed that the work had left a permanent impression and in ensuring their departure from Germany had been worth any physical or emotional hardship. They took a train from Eschwege via Frankfurt to the
south. It was far too cold (28 degrees Fahrenheit) to traverse the Alps for
Italy (a common border crossing route for Bricha groups), so they joined
their comrades in Kibbutz Shmuel Breslaw at Hochland and awaited their
departure. For many of the kibbutz members the ten days at Hochland
waiting to leave constituted a long-awaited vacation in which the working
conditions were easy and the members were allowed to sleep late. Finally,
on January 16, 1947, they left Hochland, traveling via Leipheim, and recalled

"the nice and quiet lives we had there." They were met in Ulm by agents of the Bricha and by Monish, Yedziah, and Tzunik, Miriam's brother, who wished them farewell.[20]

At dawn on the morning of January 17, 1947, the kibbutz reached the Austro-German border on trucks driven by members of the Bricha. As was noted in the diary, "we left forever the cursed Germany, in which we resided for 14 months, beginning in November 1945 until January 1947. Beautiful and rich experiences were our part during this period, but everyone was united in his/her thoughts on the difficult path that lay before us." The kibbutz spent two months in Italy before leaving for Palestine. On the way, they were intercepted by British forces and were deported to Cyprus, where much of the kibbutz spent one more year before departing for Palestine in March 1948.[21]

As Yehoshua Bruk, the shaliach from Palestine, noted upon the departure of Kibbutz Tosia Altman, the kibbutz was "the last of the first groups" to leave Germany.[22] The departure of Tosia Altman not only signified the end of its fourteen-month stay in the American zone, but its departure (and that of other early kibbutz groups) symbolized a larger shift in the nature of the Jewish DP population in Germany. These changes would influence the character of the Zionist youth movements that worked to adapt to the growing number of families with more babies and children among the Jewish Germans. Although Zionist emissaries and youth movement activists may have fretted over the pioneering nature of the first wave of kibbutzim arriving from Poland at the end of 1945, the contrast between the first and second generation of youth movement members threw into sharp relief the commitment of the first group to the Zionist path. The kibbutzim that arrived from Poland in the Bricha at the end of 1945 and beginning of 1946 embraced the Zionist educational opportunities in the kibbutz and willingly moved to the hakhsharot established in the American zone. As the prospects of an immediate departure from Germany faded and overcrowding grew in the DP camps, the Zionist youth movements observed a decline in morale and decreasing willingness to participate in the existing framework on the part of Jewish DP youths. The manner in which the Zionist youth movements were forced to adapt to the newer arrivals over the course of 1946 and 1947 suggests that the character of the first generation was far more suited to the pioneering lifestyle of kibbutzim in Palestine than they had ever admitted.

Changing Demography and Changing Movements

While the youth movements certainly controlled many aspects of daily life for the youths who inhabited their kibbutzim, hakhsharot, and branches within the camps, the movements themselves were forced to react to changes in the nature of the population in order to maintain their continued appeal and guarantee membership. The dynamic relationship transformed the youth movements as they adapted to the changed DP population in 1947. By the end of 1946 the Jewish DP population in the American zone of Germany had swollen to more than 145,000. This constituted a 356 percent increase over the nearly 40,000 Jews in the zone at the beginning of the year.[23] With this tremendous growth in the size of the Jewish DP population, the demographic characteristics and, most noticeably, the age structure of the population shifted as well.

As Georg Muentz noted in his American Jewish Joint Distribution Committee (JDC) population survey for 1946, the first screenings in November 1945 revealed no children under the age of six, 3 percent between the ages of six and seventeen, and only .2 percent over age sixty-five.[24] Following the first wave of infiltrees arriving in Bricha groups at the end of 1945, the Jewish age structure changed little on the older and younger poles, with only 1.2 percent under age five and the same proportion of elderly. According to Muentz, "this lack of change was due to the fact that most of the incomers were young people who survived the time of the Nazi regime hidden in the forests or in concentration camps."[25] Still, the impact of arriving kibbutzim and children's homes could be felt in the 9 percent recorded between the ages of six and seventeen, as the proportion of children and young adults continued to grow.

The big influx in the summer of 1946 "brought a fresh human element" with repatriates from the Soviet Union and people who decided to leave Poland and elsewhere in Eastern Europe after trying to stabilize their lives there.[26] The arrival of Bricha infiltrees led to a noticeable shift in the Jewish DP population (see appendix A). At the end of November 1946, 23,594 children (aged zero to seventeen) were counted, with 17.5 percent of the total 134,541 surveyed, a 7 percent increase over the beginning of the year. Of the children, 31.7 percent were between the ages of fourteen and seventeen (7,494), 29.7 percent were between the ages of six and thirteen (7,024)

Demographic Comparison of Jewish DP and German Population in Bavaria[a]

For Each 1,000 of Population	Births	Deaths	Natural Increase	Marriages
Jewish DP population	14.1	0.8	13.3	16.7
German population of Bavaria (post-1945)	3.7	4.3	0.6	1.4

[a] Jewish population, U.S. zone Germany, November 30, 1946, JDC, YIVO, LS 9, 57, p. 682.

and a remarkable 38.5 percent (9,076) were under the age of five. A new investigation on December 31, 1946, revealed that the Jewish population was composed of 20.3 percent children (aged zero to seventeen) and 79.7 percent adults (out of the total population, 8.5 percent were between the ages of zero and six (4.5 percent under age one), 11.8 percent between the ages of six and seventeen, 68.1 percent were between the ages of eighteen and forty-four, and 11.6 percent were forty-five years old and over.[27] The proportion of young and older adults between the ages of eighteen and forty had declined, while the number of children under the age of seventeen grew from under 5 percent of the population to 20 percent by the end of 1946. The percentage of babies had skyrocketed, as the Jewish DP population underwent a veritable baby boom. Twenty-two percent of all children under the age of seventeen were babies under one year old (to be precise 22.3 percent, or 5,349 of 23,989 out of total of 118,875 surveyed, were babies).[28] The Jewish population demonstrated a much higher marriage and birth rate than their German counterparts (table 3).

The historian Atina Grossmann has noted this trend as a "conscious affirmation of Jewish life" after the Holocaust and a form of biological revenge.[29] Regardless of the intent or symbolism of this baby boom, the birth of babies had practical implications for the DP population. All of these babies had parents who were no longer unattached and presumably free of responsibilities. Whereas such individuals may have easily grasped at earlier immigration opportunities, the needs of a spouse or child now also had to be considered.

The kibbutzim arriving as part of the Bricha were thus no longer inhabited exclusively by orphaned youths who had joined the kibbutz in Poland as a source of security, shelter, camaraderie, and family. The Bricha increasingly came to be seen as a safe means of departure from Poland, and the kibbutzim that were the vehicles of this departure counted among their members more families with children as well as unaccompanied children who had been sent ahead by their parents in order to leave Poland. Susan Pettias, the child infiltree officer of the UNRRA at the children's center in Rosenheim, noted this trend among the kibbutzim:

> In some groups there is a percentage as high as 50% or 60% who have parents. Apparently the families gave the children up to the Kibutz [sic] for one of the following reasons: 1. To enable them to more quickly get out of Poland as unaccompanied children are given priority. 2. Feeling that better physical care and provision would be administered to such groups. 3. Hoping that by being unaccompanied that the children would be given priority for entrance to Palestine.[30]

After families learned that children would not move through Germany immediately, some appeared to claim their children, causing "emotional conflicts within the child who had become strongly attached to the group." She further noted that the decision about releasing children to relatives was complicated because relationships were often unclear, and the "children are confused themselves about values of attachments and loyalties to groups" in contrast to the unknown emotional needs met by a relative. Beyond assessing where children would better have their emotional needs met, it was also difficult to assess whether the children would be safer with individuals "in comparison to the responsible care of agencies, especially in Palestine."[31] Nonetheless, she worked to determine the child's wishes and eliminate any pressure that may have existed from kibbutz groups.

This change in the age and familial composition of the Jewish DP population was also reflected in the shape and number of the kibbutzim in the DP camps. A survey of Föhrenwald kibbutzim taken at the beginning of 1947 revealed that many more kibbutzim contained whole families with small children.[32] Far from shaping the Zionist nature of the population to their liking, the youth movements had to shift their focus in order to maintain a continued appeal among Jewish youths. The Zionist youth movements now faced a DP population that was still young but whose priorities and responsibilities had changed, with many more married people with families in the population. The departure of the kibbutzim led to a general weakening of the hakhsharot and a need to reevaluate the prior emphasis on farming and agricultural training. The youth movements de-emphasized agricultural training in hakhsharot and stressed educational work within the DP camps, targeted at younger children and families.

1947: "Between Hope and Disappointment"

Jewish DPs in Germany thus faced 1947 with a declining sense of hope for immediate aliyah and increasing willingness to explore other migration options, although even these were limited.[33] Had immigration to the United States been a realistic option after the war, it is quite conceivable that a majority of Jewish DPs would have made the choice to move there. Nonetheless, when President Harry S. Truman set out American policy on the absorption of DPs and refugees from Europe at the end of 1945, he limited the scope of American capacity to existing immigration quotas. For the Jewish DPs, a majority of whom were Polish citizens, this provided little reason for hope, as the annual immigration quota for Poland was 6,524. Immigration restrictions to the United States, Canada, and Australia were not relaxed until after 1948 and the creation of the State of Israel. Although youths in kibbutzim such as Tosia Altman managed to leave Germany between liberation and the beginning of 1947, they were a minority of the total Jewish DP population, most of which remained stuck in the DP camps. Between the end of the war and the spring of 1947, only 9,500 people managed to leave the U.S. zone via illegal immigration, the majority of them in kibbutzim shepherded by the Bricha.[34] The British policy instituted in August 1946 of sending illegal immigrants to Cyprus rather than the detention center in Atlit near Haifa diminished DP hopes of reaching Palestine even more. Enthusiasm over a potential breakthrough at the twenty-second Zionist Congress in December 1946 gave way to disappointment; by 1947, the Jewish DPs were caught in a spiral of dwindling morale and progressive overcrowding in the DP centers, with hopes for departure seeming increasingly bleak.[35] Observers also had reason to fear that DPs would fall into a pattern of idleness and demoralization: whereas 25 percent of Jewish DPs

Jewish DPs sailing to Palestine aboard the Aliyah Bet ship *Tel Hai* in March 1946 climb the mast of the ship to hoist the Zionist flag. (USHMM, courtesy of Alex Knobler)

were employed (vs. 36.25 percent of Germans working at the time) in February 1946, no more than 15 percent of the more than 50,000 infiltrees who had arrived between August 1946 and January 1947 had managed to find employment, dragging the rate even lower.[36]

Furthermore, American policy had shifted in an effort to limit the number of infiltrators into the American zone. General Lucius D. Clay (American commander as of March 1947) published an order stating that any Jews who arrived in the zone after April 21, 1947, would no longer be accepted in the DP camps and would be denied food from American sources. While the borders of the zone would never actually be closed to Jewish refugees, the financial burden fell primarily on the JDC, and housing shortages intensified as American efforts came to focus increasingly on German reconstruction.[37] Again Zionist activists feared the worst, assuming that any Palestine enthusiasm that may have existed was sure to decline as the waiting time grew and departure seemed hopeless. The exit of the first generation of Zionist kibbutzim seemed only to add to Jewish Agency and youth movement fears over a lessening Zionist influence over the Jewish DP camps.

Avraham Gevelber, emissary of the Jewish Agency, noted the changing nature of the Zionist project in a survey on kibbutzim and hakhsharot conducted in the spring of 1947 after the departure of the first wave of kibbutzim. While kibbutz members arriving from Poland at the end of 1945 and throughout 1946 were willing to move to farms created in the American zone, with the departure of the kibbutzim that had first moved to the farms the whole project seemed now to be at risk. New kibbutz groups in the DP camps showed little desire to move to farms: "a greater problem now however is how . . . to ensure the continued existence of the farm. . . . There is a danger that many of the farms will have to be closed. All of our efforts are dedicated to strengthening the current situation, with the cooperation of all of the pioneering movements in the duty of agricultural training."[38]

As Gevelber observed, the kibbutzim now arriving from Poland "included whole families and in them ages from three to sixty. . . . It is difficult to suggest that there is a great possibility of educational activity and instilling of pioneering movement values in these kinds of kibbutzim." For this reason, he anticipated that the majority of the kibbutzim would again be located in the DP camps, where a great deal of time and energy would have to be invested in instilling basic Zionist education in the kibbutzim so as to shield them from the negative influence of the camps, where "with the continued settlement the unemployment has grown and with it the degeneration whose influence is difficult on the kibbutzim."[39]

In the view of Zionist activists, the kibbutzim arriving in the American zone had to overcome a number of obstacles: mixed age composition, the demoralizing atmosphere in the DP camps, and feared loss of hope at chances of aliyah were chief among the concerns of the youth movements. Still, kibbutz groups in the camps could engage in productive work and vocational training both in ORT workshops and in workshops set up within the kibbutz groups themselves.

Georg Muentz in his report for the JDC on kibbutzim in the DP camps also corroborated this view of a change within the composition and nature of the kibbutzim, noting that the kibbutz had come to be viewed increasingly as a vehicle of departure from Europe for all segments of the Jewish population, "who join the kibbutzim merely in order to obtain a possibility of cheap and organized emigration. Whole families with old people and small children come to join the kibbutzim which thus lose their former character of collectives. They become assembly centers for small but closely kept together groups of relatives. The family interest is overwhelming the influence of the political organization and her ideology." Zionist groups tried to overcome this state of affairs, but only with limited success among younger boys and girls. Muentz also echoed the concerns of the Zionist groups that such a state within the kibbutz groups could lead to demoralization and impatience with the immigration process. Terming the internal life of the kibbutz as "unhealthy," he suggested that the monotony of DP camp life and the pressure of living together under close conditions could lead to "growing demoralization and organizational decomposition." To overcome this, he suggested providing the possibility of real work and the assurance that they would emigrate in a certain length of time.[40]

The demographic change that had taken place in the DP population and the overwhelming success of the Bricha in recruiting the Jewish public in Eastern Europe as a whole to depart via kibbutzim forced the Zionist youth movements to adapt to this new situation. While Zionist enthusiasm remained a characteristic of the larger DP population, time, overcrowding, and the addition of other responsibilities had a negative effect on the pioneering nature of the DP youths. A whole new line of obstacles, beyond those that traditionally interfered with illegal immigration, greeted the efforts of the Zionist movements, including "pregnancy, little children [and] illness."[41] The Zionist youth movements in the DP camps were thus faced with a contradictory situation: they had to develop new programs in order to keep youths occupied, interested, and patient but at the same time had to prepare them to be ready to go at any moment if aliyah beckoned. Still, the promise of immigration continued to be the most important benefit they could provide.

The Zionist youth movements intensified work in the camps by training additional madrichim, focusing on educational work, publishing new materials, opening summer camps, and creating cultural activity centers within the DP camps where youths could play games and sports, read, hold discussions, dance, and engage in other forms of recreation. The movements did not completely abandon the farming program but began to work together to solidify the farms that already existed. The five major pioneering movements (Nocham, Dror, Hashomer Hatzair, Hanoar Hatzioni, and B'nei Akiva) joined to form Brit Ha-Irgunim Ha-Halutzi'im (Pioneering Groups Organization) on January 29, 1947, in order to strengthen their agricultural work and intensify educational efforts in the camps and hakhsharot.[42] Such a collaborative effort revealed movements eager to cooperate in order to better facilitate the process of aliyah, perhaps indicating an awareness that earlier divisions would have to be overcome in order to maintain Zionist enthusiasm within the DP camps. Activists in the various pioneering youth movements that had created agricultural hakhsharot, in particular from Nocham, Dror, and Hashomer Hatzair, were well aware that the departure of the kibbutzim from the hakhsharot greatly threatened the farming project.

Nocham's March 1947 movement survey detailed the coming difficulties facing the movement. Although there were still two thousand members on thirty-eight training centers (and fifteen farms), it had become increasingly clear to movement leaders that members in kibbutz groups in DP camps were reluctant to replace those who had left hakhsharot for aliyah. As the report summarized, "The big question now [is]: Where will the reserves of the movement come from?" The survey noted that the problems the movement confronted, including an emptying of the hakhsharot, a lack of educators and educational material for activities, and the need to train more activists to work with the youths. To deal with the new situation, the most immediate needs were more teachers, more books, and more money with which to expand movement activities.[43]

According to movement leaders, the new arrivals from Poland, Hungary, and Romania did not have the dedication or the drive of the earlier generation that had created farms such as Kibbutz Nili, as the apparent incentive of aliyah also seemed to dwindle. The Zionist option seemed to have less immediate reward despite the potential upside of living in a collective kibbutz group. These groups of youths generally joined kibbutzim in order to first and foremost leave Poland (or Hungary and Romania) or, as noted by Pettias, were placed there by their parents, who hoped to join them in Germany later.[44] The movement would do what it could on its own to accommodate the changes, but it would also be dependent on assistance from the Yishuv in the form of emissaries, books, and financial support, a sign of increased Yishuv involvement in youth movement operations.

Anticipating the changes that would take place following the departure of the rest of the hakhsharah groups, the movement convened a conference at Teublitz in April 1947, at which members discussed "the duties of the movement and every member with regard to the fact of needing to dismantle the hakhsharot and the continued existence of Jewish youth in Germany."[45] Henceforth, the movement would only work to maintain those sites that maximized agricultural training for all of the members of the kibbutzim in residence. Bearing in mind the demographic situation, Nocham sought to accommodate families of youth movement members while working to remove them from the DP camp environment. Accordingly, the Teublitz conference noted "the need to concentrate families, who are not leaving with the *ma'apilim*, in special hakhsharah points outside of the camps."[46]

The May 1947 survey of Nocham activity in Germany also took note of the changing situation among its kibbutzim and the implications that this would have for the movement in trying to maintain a continuing appeal for the youths in Germany. With the departure of the more experienced kibbutz members for aliyah, the movement leaders feared that "with the conditions of today, at a time when there is no replacement for the emptying hakhsharot, the meaning of this departure, with a lack of people . . . raises a whole line of problems."[47] Those who were already in the DP camps seemed to be less interested in moving out to the existing hakhsharot. Over the course of 1947 those hakhsharot that did remain open came to be populated primarily by new arrivals from Hungary and Romania who filled the agricultural points that movement members living in the DP camps no longer wished to fill. "We worked from the assumption that they were qualified for pioneering work and the pioneering capabilities of the Romanian immigration would not be less than that of the Polish repatriation in its day . . . we enlisted our most talented members for this [education] work and in many of the places the work was left to the shlichim."[48] Nocham leaders thus seemed to acknowledge that among the existing membership already in Germany the appeal of agricultural training had either declined or that those members most interested in training had already been integrated into the pioneering framework. Those unaffiliated youths living in the DP camps were unlikely to find the idea of farming away from the DP camp appealing. The new arrivals from Romania would have to replace those groups that had already left for aliyah.

As of February 1947 Dror also noted that with the departure of their earlier kibbutz groups, which "lessens our influence and abilities in the camps. . . . Our first task will be to establish new branches in the camps."[49] At the time Dror counted seven hundred members in twenty-two branches in the DP camps, although it worked to continue to establish more branches in the camps. As Dror made an effort to expand its presence among the youths in a camp, the other movements worked to keep pace.

The youth movements thus collectively turned away from focusing on moving the pioneering youths out of the camp and returned to focusing on children within the DP camps. For the younger segment in the DP camps, this meant less of an encounter with Zionism in the form of the kibbutzim that had arrived from Poland. Jewish youths in the DP camps, more of whom were under the age of seventeen, participated in *snifim* [movement offices] and *kenim* [movement branches] opened in the camps as well as in the children's homes.[50]

The movements also began to focus on training a new cadre of madrichim for movement work in order to bolster their presence again in the DP camps. Nocham held a five-week seminar in Muencberg to train madrichim in the beginning of 1947, while Dror and Hashomer Hatzair also held training conferences to educate new leaders in instructional techniques geared toward youths living in the DP camps, both orphaned and those living with

A gymnastics show at the children's home of the Lindenfels DP camp in Germany. The school was administered by the Zionist youth organization Hashomer Hatzair, which trained the youth for their new lives in Palestine. (USHMM, courtesy of Rose Guterman Zar)

the parents.[51] Dror leaders voiced concerns that the madrichim who had accompanied the kibbutz groups from Poland were not up to the task of intensive movement work in Germany. "The madrichim who came with them from Poland are tired and ill, and there are not enough of them to do the work. We are facing a lack of madrichim ... [to] organize and work with the branches."[52] In order to rectify this perceived educational weakness, Dror moved quickly to organize special seminars for madrichim working with branches in the DP camps, and a regional mazkirut was organized to work directly with movement kibbutzim and branches in the region.

At its May 1947 meeting, Nocham also decided that "after the dismantling of the hakhsharot ... the central focus of movement work from this point forward will be on strengthening educational work in the youth movement branches." New madrichim were recruited from among youth movement members and trained in special seminars to work with youths, even though the movement lacked "games, sporting equipment, uniforms, diversions all of the other things that the kids love that will be sure to attract them."[53] In May 1947 Nocham counted twenty-seven branches in the DP camps with twelve hundred younger members and created a special department to focus on work in the DP camps.

Like Nocham and Dror, Hashomer Hatzair also noted a decline in the activity of its kibbutzim over the course of 1947. The movement had renamed itself Hashomer Hatzair Be-Ha'apalah at a founding conference on February 14–15, 1947, in Bad Reichenhall. According to Mordechai Rosman, one of the leaders of the movement, the creation of a political party was the logical progression from a youth movement. The name of the new party was significant: this was part of an effort to redefine the character of the She'erit Hapletah as immigrants to Palestine, standing at the forefront of *ha'apalah* (clandestine illegal immigration) and the struggle for the state. The party's slogan was "HaBonim Yibanu, HaMeginim Yagenu, Ha Ma'apilim Ya'apilu" (the builders will build, the defenders will defend, and the clandestine immigrants will conquer [the shores of Palestine]). It was more than symbolic that this youth movement now viewed itself as the political leader of the She'erit Hapletah in this struggle. The need to create a political party representing the broader DP public also represented an awareness that Hashomer Hatzair could no longer appeal to the pioneering vanguard of the DP population; changes in the population necessitated a broader appeal to the Jewish DPs as a whole in the DP camps.

Immediately following the founding conference of the renamed movement, members got down to the business of the setting the agenda for the coming year. Madrichim from youth movement branches and children's homes discussed the priorities of the movement. Like Nocham, Hashomer Hatzair was struck by the need to accommodate the increasing numbers of children under the age of seventeen living in the DP camps. With that in mind, movement work would focus on expanding the existing kenim and deepening educational activity within the framework of the DP camp branches.[54]

Despite the decline in farming activity, the existing farms were thus still used for movement conferences, seminars, and the celebration of holidays.[55] During May 10–11, 1947, the movement held a conference at the Eschwege farm, with seventy members representing the eighteen Hashomer Hatzair kibbutzim in Germany. According to a report of the conference published in the movement newspaper, the largest problem that stood before the conference was the drafting of new guidelines for the movement to address "the new situation that was created as a result of the ha'apalah . . . which brought a standstill to activity in a large part of the kibbutzim," while segments of kibbutz groups prepared for departure. The suspense of preparations for aliyah had a rather negative impact on the daily activity of the kibbutzim and left many of the members unable to focus on anything but immigration.[56] As Mordechai Rosman argued at the conference, it was now the responsibility of the kibbutzim to dedicate themselves to the educational activity of the movement while they waited for aliyah. The resolutions of the conference declared that the kibbutzim would continue the struggle to break the British blockade of immigration to Palestine while deepening educational work in the movement, which would aid in resolving the tension and lack of activity within kibbutz life. Existing kibbutzim were instructed to make room for new arrivals, absorb the new groups from Hungary and Romania, and assist in their education.[57]

Summer Camps

In the summer of 1947, Jewish DP youths also witnessed the expansion of a phenomenon that had begun on a more limited basis in 1946: summer camps for Jewish children in the DP camps. The movements converted agricultural training farms into summer camps where children and young adults would be instructed for two weeks on pioneering and scouting skills. The summer camps represented an opportunity to remove children from the DP camp environment while immersing them further in the ideology of the youth movement.[58] The youths and children in the branches in the DP camps were the intended campers, but the youth movements first sought to convince parents to send their children to the two-week camps. Movements advertised their appeals to parents in the wide-circulation newspapers. Hashomer Hatzair BeHa'apalah encouraged parents to consider the "importance of sun and fresh air" in removing children from the atmosphere of the DP camps. "The movement can help prepare the children in the spirit of working-life in Eretz Yisrael. . . . Send your children to us, away from the DP camps, from the stinking DP camp air . . . and let him enjoy the time away from the camp in the clean air, in the fields, in the forest, among friends."[59]

Other advertisements emphasized the camping experience as a chance join in the building of the land and an opportunity to participate in the "struggle for our rights."[60] Whereas in the earlier period movements may have made a direct appeal to youths, parents now determined the choices made by the increasingly younger segment of the population.

Nocham announced the opening of its camps in the May 1947 volume of the movement newspaper:

> To the summer camps!: The time of the summer camps is approaching. In July hundreds of the members of the movement will go to the *moshavot*. This will certainly be the most interesting part in the life of the movement. We will spend two weeks together in the fields and in the forest, in games and in hikes, we will get to know one another . . . and we will read together the new publications which stand before us on the way to ha'apalah and hagshamah [realization of the Zionist ideal].[61]

Before the summer camps opened Nocham held a training camp for counselors at Kibbutz Nili, where they gained "real camp experience" with tents,

Jewish youth at a DP summer camp in the Grunewald Forest, 1947. (USHMM, courtesy of Mayer and Rachel Abramowitz)

forest life, and scouting to prepare for life in Israel.[62] The summer camps, it was hoped, would do important work in connecting the youths to the movement, the pioneering lifestyle, and ha'apalah for an expected 750 members, half of the movement. The big question remained, however, "how much will we be able to instill this spirit in the youth?"[63] Nocham ultimately opened camps for all three age levels: *b'nei midbar* (under thirteen), *ma'apilim* (ages thirteen through sixteen), and *magshimim* (ages seventeen and over).[64] Dror also managed to organize six summer camps for 1,220 children and youths between the ages of six and seventeen. Their daily schedule included sports, games, contests, hikes, arts evenings, discussions, lectures, etc. The movement now pinned its hopes on the success of the summer camps, which could serve as a springboard to intensive educational-ideological activity leading to the eventual formation of aliyah groups with and without children.[65]

The youth movements thus tried to keep both children and parents engaged, seeking to remain relevant in the new demographic and political situation that had developed. Summer camps were a clear effort to remove from the DP camps youths who were otherwise unwilling or now unable to leave the DP camp environment for life in a hakhsharah. According to the JDC, a total of eight thousand Jewish DP children were sent to summer camps supplied by the JDC in the U.S. zone during the summer of 1947.[66]

By the fall of 1947, the movements did register success in expanding activities in the DP camps. In September 1947 Dror noted a tremendous growth in the number of members in snifim within the DP camps. The movement counted more than 3,360 members, almost evenly divided between kibbutzim and children's branches. There were 1,600 members living in twenty-three kibbutzim (fourteen kibbutzim in DP camps) and 1,760 children in thirty-seven DP camp branches.[67] Still, the efforts of the movements only took them so far in pleasing the Jewish public. As a leader of the Dror movement noted, "no efforts at instruction or education on the part of the Zionist movement could be satisfying because one answer is requested from the mouth of every person: aliyah."[68] Youth movements also had to deal with complaints from individual kibbutz members, who feared that they would be left behind and never be selected for aliyah.[69] The increasing impatience and continuing frustration over lack of aliyah put the Jewish youths and the youth movements in a very difficult position. For the youths who had joined kibbutzim and put all of their faith in the hope of eventual aliyah, the lack of opportunity must have been all the more frustrating. They continued to occupy themselves with activities to prepare for life in Palestine, but who knew if such time and effort was worthwhile or would ever by repaid? Nocham summed up the difficult situation it faced going into the second half of 1947 in the face of their major challenges: the British offensive to break the ha'apalah operation on one side, Revisionist opposition on the other, and perhaps most crucially "the postponement of aliyah for 2–3 months, which on the face of it may not seem so long, *has turned into a difficult struggle for the pioneering movement in Germany.*"[70] If all the DPs in Bavaria were impatient for departure, then the chalutz movement grew even more anxious. As the report summarized:

> We should add to this the continuing expectations of the hakhsharah groups sitting for nearly two years in Germany and the extraordinary tension that derives from the potential for aliyah that could be close at hand—then we can understand what is in the souls of those members who heard the news barring their departure . . . we should not be surprised therefore that we now see conflicts within the groups, a cynical relation to everything and on top of all of this: Azivot [kibbutz abandonments].[71]

As the Zionist youth movements and the youths in the kibbutzim and branches in the camps faced the second half of 1947, it seemed as if the departure for which they had now waited for more than two years would not be forthcoming. The youth movements did all they could to maintain support and enthusiasm, but the future did not look promising.

Focus on Ha'apalah

For the Jewish DPs, young and old alike, the common goal remained immigration and departure from Germany. The Zionist youth movements could offer education, work, training, camaraderie, and social diversions, but as time waxed on the DPs' desire for a resolution to their stateless condition only continued to grow. The DPs were losing patience with the promises of the Zionists, despite their guarantees of aliyah and promises to fight on behalf of the She'erit Hapletah for their historical right to settle in Palestine.

Aliyah remained the word in everyone's mouth, but it was reserved for those kibbutz groups fortunate enough to join ha'apalah groups. Even so, during the first four months of 1947, the British government had intercepted eight vessels carrying a total of 9,237 persons.[72] Thus, as was the case with the members of Kibbutz Tosia Altman, for the majority of those who did manage to leave Germany, Aliyah Bet usually meant an extended stay in Cyprus.

The movements tried to keep the focus of DP youths on aliyah and ha'apalah and recounted stories of successful immigration in the DP press. Nocham devoted almost entire volumes of the movement paper to ha'apalah, including pictures of ma'apilim, articles on the importance of the illegal immigration movement, stories about individual ma'apilim, and letters from movement members who had tried to land in Palestine but were sent to Cyprus.[73] The July 1947 volume of Nocham opened with a picture of a ha'apalah ship on the front cover and explained how ha'apalah could "be the way to save thousands of Jews." The youths who had survived the war had a duty to "lead the way and hold the flag that floats over the ships on the ocean."[74]

The same volume also included a profile of the Kovshei HaYam hakhsharah in Deggendorf. The plugah group there began to get organized in April 1947. The group was small in the beginning and faced numerous challenges beyond difficult daytime work and nighttime guard duty, including threats from the Revisionists who branded them communists before American authorities. As more members joined the hakhsharah (by July they numbered fifty), the group increased cultural work with Hebrew lessons and Shabbat parties. Group members received their first tour of a ship on May 5 and soon began sea lessons in three groups. While one group obtained theoretical instruction, the others engaged in exercises and technical jobs. In the theoretical classes, the members learned subjects such as boating, motor construction, and electrical work on the ship as well as received lessons on rudders, swimming, and ship signaling. In the afternoons after lunch on the boat, they learned mathematics, geography, English, and German. In the evenings and on Shabbat they continued with their cultural work. In the opinion of their instructors, the group was progressing nicely; they were also visited by guests from the Jewish Agency and the Nocham administration, who were suitably impressed with their development. As Chaim Barlas from the Jewish Agency announced on his visit to the group, "After my visit in the

עתון התנועה בגרמניה

Nr. 7 (12)   מינכן, ד' שבט התש"ח — 15 יאנואר 1948   פרייז 1 מארק

תחי המדינה העברית!

פתחו

שערים-

ויבואו

גאולים!

Nocham movement newspaper, January 1948. The headline reads, "Long Live the Jewish State! Open the Gates and the Redeemed Will Come!" (Jewish DP Periodicals Collection, USHMM/YIVO)

camps of the She'erit Hapletah I have seen here in your plugah a point of light. It gives me pleasure to see how young men and women have found the appropriate way and understand how to correctly prepare for their future in Eretz Israel." The plugah was ready to accept more members and awaited another group to expand the hakhsharah.[75]

The members of the Nocham movement could write with great pride of the accomplishments of the Deggendorf sea hakhsharah. However, the decision to create a hakhsharah to train members in maritime knowledge was clearly an indication of the emphasis that the movement put on preparing members for ha'apalah by any means. It also demonstrated a need to display the movement's dedication to ha'apalah and thus the removal of Jews from Germany. Nocham was willing to invest considerable time and money in the operation, which it described as "one of the largest operations in our movement."[76] In the summer camps as well the movement maintained the focus on ha'apalah, instructing members on what to expect when their eventual departure would take place.

Maintaining Membership through the Promise of Ha'apalah: The Exodus Affair

In this sense, beyond their efforts to appeal to youths in the DP camps through education, sports, games, and camping, the ultimate recruiting tool continued to be hope of departure through the promise of aliyah. As the situation grew increasingly desperate, the largest ploy to keep hope alive in the DP camps took place in July 1947. The preceding month, Bricha agents in France had requested five thousand DPs from Germany to participate in an unspecified illegal immigration operation.[77] The request for additional olim inspired great enthusiasm within the ranks of the youth movements and in the DP population in general.

In the summer of 1947 rumors of a mass departure on a large illegal immigrant ship swirled around the DP camps. Generally such rumors had proven false in the past, although on this occasion such a ship did in fact exist.[78] The Bricha organization had acquired a large passenger ship, *The President Warfield*, in Baltimore that it intended to use for a massive departure of illegal immigrants from France to Palestine.

In its July report (before the *Exodus* drama unfolded) Nocham noted that "we did receive the news we had been waiting for and over the span of ten days, some six hundred members were able to leave for aliyah, including 350 from hakhsharah groups and 250 youth (under seventeen years of age)." Presumably these members were bound for *The President Warfield* in southern France. As the movement report noted, "this aliyah instilled a new breath of hope."[79]

Thousands of immigrants were organized in the DP camps of Germany for transfer to France at the end of June 1947. A French transit visa for seventeen hundred people was forged and copied by Bricha agents in Germany in order to facilitate the transfer of more than five thousand DPs. On July 7, 1947, a total of forty-five hundred people snuck across the German border via Mulhousse and Strasbourg. They boarded *The President Warfield* on July 10 in Sete in southern France. All of the passengers bore entry visas to Colombia although they had no intention of sailing across the Atlantic. Their goal was to sail east toward Palestine.[80]

The story of what transpired thereafter has been described in a number of places and will not be treated in depth here. In brief, the ship departed Sete on July 11, 1947, with 4,052 men, women, and children.[81] On the way to Haifa, the ship's name was changed to *Exodus 1947* (*Yetziat Eyropah 1947*). The ship was intercepted by British warships, and the passengers fought them until they were subdued. The British resolved to teach the illegal immigration movement a lesson, and rather than allow the passengers to disembark in Palestine or even Cyprus, they decided to force the DPs to return to France. The transfer of the DPs to prison ships in Haifa Harbor took place within full view of the United Nations Special Committee on Palestine (UNSCOP) commissioners touring Palestine at the time, a notable diplomatic coup on the part of the Zionist enterprise. Although the prison ships were returned to France the passengers refused to disembark, and the French government refused to force them to do so. The passengers even went so far as to stage a hunger strike to arouse sympathy for their plight. The ship's passengers were finally returned to Hamburg, a practical defeat for the DPs in their effort to depart German soil but one of the greatest victories for the Zionist movement in their ongoing diplomatic struggle against the British blockade. The symbolic value of Holocaust survivors being forced to return to former Nazi soil was not lost on the world press or on the UNSCOP commissioners debating the future of Palestine.

In her work on the role of Holocaust survivors and the emergence of the State of Israel, Idith Zertal has presented the *Exodus* Affair as a prime example of Yishuv Zionist manipulation of the survivors to further the needs of the state in the making. She concludes that "the messages sent from the ship to the Mossad [l'Aliyah Bet, the Zionist organization that organized the clandestine immigration] center in Palestine . . . prove that those involved on the Zionist side were aware of the tremendous political effect of a ship carrying thousands of Holocaust survivors being denied access to their 'national home.'" While the Zionists (meaning the Yishuv activists) were not so adept as to be able to anticipate every twist and turn of the entire affair, she suggests that they were shrewd enough to gain maximum political benefit from the plight of the Jewish DPs. "This does not mean, however, that every step was planned in advance by the Zionists. The opposite is true. They made intuitive and effective use, as the incident developed, of the 'weapon' they had at their disposal—the survivors themselves—and quickly and cleverly exploited the opportunities the British so clumsily presented them during the course of the affair."[82] It was "the Zionists" (or, more specifically, the Mossad l'Aliyah Bet agents) who prevented the DPs from disembarking in France, but even more so the whole affair was orchestrated from afar by the Yishuv's Zionist establishment. "The role of the people on the shore, headed by the Mossad agents, was secondary in the *Exodus* drama. Aided by various elements in the Jewish community—party representatives and youth movement members, Jewish Army veterans, community aid and welfare institutions—*the Yishuv operatives produced the campaign for the Exodus refugees and organized from afar the unfolding events.*"[83]

Various elements of the entire affair, however, suggest that the DPs on the boat played a vital role in the diplomatic success of the affair. The struggle against the British troops who boarded the ship in Haifa, the organization and implementation of the hunger strike in France, the singing of "HaTikvah" as British and French agents boarded the ship all could have been orchestrated by Zionist activists from the Yishuv but also had to be carried out by the DPs on board the ship. Schools, newspapers, celebrations, and even weddings were organized on the boat. In fact, a closer look reveals that a substantial number of the more than 4,000 passengers on *Exodus* were members of Zionist youth movements from the German DP camps who had been trained and were waiting for just such an opportunity to leave German soil. The passengers were not merely a random cross-section of the Jewish DP population. For example, of the more than 4,000 passengers on the ship, an estimated 1,000 were deemed eligible for *aliyat hanoar* (youth aliyah) and hence under the age of seventeen.[84] Of these 1,000, 813 were counted as belonging to the Zionist youth movements in Germany.[85] They played a critical role in the manifestations of Zionist enthusiasm on board the ship, and their enthusiasm was emblematic of the DPs' willingness to leave Germany at almost any cost by the summer of 1947. This was in a sense a re-enactment of what they were unable to do in 1939.

Subsequently, the *Exodus* Affair received a great deal of attention in the DP camps and was highlighted in the youth movement newspapers. Coverage in the movement papers focused on the heroism of the youth movement members and the passengers of the ship who stood up to British tyranny and refused to surrender their Zionist passion. Hashomer Hatzair BeHa'a-palah reported that the episode "open[ed] a new black page in British Labor government treatment of the victims of Nazism."[86] The August 1947 volume of the movement paper included a profile of the ship and educational instruction in teaching about the episode to movement branches. An editorial on the incident proclaimed that "we will follow in their path until we achieve complete liberation!"[87] The movement papers also recounted with pride the participation of their members in the affair. Nocham listed 450 members who took part (November 1947 issue), while Hashomer Hatzair highlighted the starring role played by Mordechai Rosman in the affair.[88] A letter from Rosman featured in the paper promised "to continue in the war and not rest until arrival in Israel." He addressed the members of the movement with a description of the struggle against the British soldiers. A photo (taken from another newspaper) of Rosman being removed by 4 British soldiers from the British prison ship *Runnymede Park* carried the title "Iron Man of the Exodus Carried Ashore" with the caption: "Mordechai Miry Rosman, fanatical Zionist for 20 years and self-styled 'commander-in-chief' of the Runnymede Park, is carried ashore by troops after the desperate fight in the ship's hold when illegal Jewish immigrants refused to disembark peacefully at Hamburg."[89] The central role played by Rosman emphasized Hashomer Hatzair's struggle to enable Jewish immigration to Palestine.

Jewish New Year's card, November 1947, bearing the photo of a young DP couple and their child, along with a drawing of the Aliyah Bet ship *President Warfield* (later renamed *Exodus 1947*). (USHMM, courtesy of Marsha Rozenblit)

The October 1947 volume of *Nocham* argued that "after *Yetziat Eyropah* we must continue with Ha'apalah at all costs." The episode demonstrated "the stubbornness of She'erit Hapletah . . . that no means can stand in the way of our desire to reach Eretz Israel . . . and nothing can stand in the way of our one and only land of the future: Eretz Yisrael."[90] A poem composed at Port De Bouc (disembarkation point of the ship) by a passenger on the ship described seeing the Zionist flag "held in the hands of the children of She'erit Israel." The episode was linked both with the recent tragedy of the Jewish people in the Holocaust and the distant past as a new attempt at exodus from slavery. The song of *Exodus 1947* was like the "Song of Sea" sung by Moses and the Israelites following the crossing of the Red Sea and the biblical Exodus from Egypt.[91]

Nonetheless, the whole episode must have also been quite depressing for the Jewish DPs in Germany, who would have looked at the success of the immigration attempt as evidence that their plight was not hopeless. The defeated return of the DPs to Germany, any symbolic diplomatic victory notwithstanding, must have increased misgivings as to whether the Zionist path would ever lead them out of the German wilderness. Nocham *madrichim* reported hearing doubts from movement members at a seminar that corresponded in time with the *Exodus* Affair; still they believed that the timing of the seminar was serendipitous because it could be used to strengthen the beliefs of those who began to question the path of ha'apalah.[92]

Conclusion

The year 1947 was decisive for the Zionist movement and the youth movements. Conditions worsened in the DP camps as hope for a diplomatic breakthrough dwindled. Youth movements struggled to maintain membership through the assurance of social, emotional, and physical support as well as the promise of an opportunity to leave Germany for Palestine. The youth movements directly sensed the transformation in the nature of the DP population with the arrival of more children and families from the East. They worked to adapt to changes in the population and fought to recruit and retain members.

Over the course of 1947, the Zionist movement stepped up its challenge to British immigration restrictions to Palestine through the most available weapon it had: Jewish DPs who were willing to board illegal ha'apalah ships and submit themselves to severe hardship in order to reach Palestine. By and large these passengers, 70 percent of whom were captured and deported to Cyprus, came from the kibbutzim of the Zionist youth movements. While the *Exodus* Affair may not have resulted in the actual arrival of new immigrants to Palestine, it did have significant political and diplomatic ramifications that far exceeded the impact of forty-five hundred new arrivals to the Yishuv. In its report to the United Nations General Assembly submitted on September 3, 1947, UNSCOP recommended that "The General Assembly undertake immediately the initiation and execution of an international arrangement whereby the problem of the distressed European Jews, of whom approximately 250,000 are in assembly centers, will be dealt with as a matter of extreme urgency for the alleviation of their plight and of the Palestine problem." As the members concluded, "the distressed Jews of Europe, together with the displaced persons generally, are a legacy of the Second World War. They are a recognized international responsibility. Owing however to the insistent demands that the distressed Jews be admitted freely and immediately into Palestine, and to the intense urge which exists among these people themselves to the same end, they constitute a vital and difficult factor in the solution."[93]

Thus, it is clear that the emphasis on ha'apalah and the role played by the Jewish DP youths in the effort influenced the decisions of the Special Committee. This also meant that 1948 would be a year quite unlike any that had preceded it.

6

"Youth: Fulfill Your Duty to the People"

Encountering the Demands of Citizenship

The United Nations Partition Plan

Following the disappointment of the return of the *Exodus* passengers to Germany, the youth movements resumed their daily and monthly schedules, holding seminars and movement conferences and reinforcing their dedication to continued hakhsharah and ha'apalah. Educational activities in the kibbutzim and the branches integrated the *Exodus* Affair into the teachings, highlighting the heroism of the participants in the struggle against the British. Still, it seemed to the displaced persons (DPs) that they would have to settle in for another long winter without any break on the diplomatic front. The extent to which they could control their own destiny was limited. They could wait and prepare for an eventuality that seemed as if it would never come. And then on November 29, 1947, following the recommendations of the United Nations Special Committee on Palestine (UNSCOP), the United Nations (UN) voted to adopt the Palestine Partition Plan, sending the Jewish DP camps into frenzied celebration. As Haim Hoffman reported, "the UN's decision was met with a wave of joy in the DP camps. They danced in the camps and their happiness knew no boundaries. All of

235

the difficult divisions for or against the partition were forgotten. Only the revisionists looked at it as a day of mourning."[1]

The Jewish DP press reported the wave of celebrations that spread through the DP camps and indeed throughout the Jewish world. The headlines of the *Jidiscze Cajtung* (formerly the *Landsberger Lager Cajtung*), the largest DP newspaper in circulation, tried to capture the excitement of the moment. The top headline read "The Yishuv Greets the UN Decision with Joy" and just under that "Spontaneous Demonstrations by the She'erit Hapletah."[2] The newspaper reported the announcement of the Central Committee to mark the occasion: "On the ruins of the Diaspora will arise the Jewish state, which will represent the most beautiful ideals of our people and will give the possibility to return the Jewish masses of the historical past and the coming future. With the help of the Jewish state the Jewish camps in Germany will be liquidated and the Jewish people will return to the family of free nations after 2000 years." The Central Committee reported that spontaneous marches and demonstrations took place in all of the DP camps and that the Jewish community of Berlin decided to hold special evening services in all of the community synagogues to commemorate the occasion.[3]

Furthermore, it seemed that a massive immigration to the new state was imminent. The *Jidiscze Cajtung* reported in the next edition that David Ben-Gurion had announced a plan to bring 1.5 million Jews to the state in the next ten years. The special adviser for Jewish Affairs in the zone, Judge Louis E. Levinthal, suggested that as early as February 1948 immigration would begin from the DP camps of Germany to Israel. He estimated that as many as 600,000 Jews could be absorbed by Israel in the next six years.[4] Dr. Gustav Landauer, head of the Jewish Agency's youth aliyah division, reportedly spoke of a massive aliyah of 80,000 youths to Israel, with 20,000 young immigrants to be brought to the state in the next year. Most immediately, 2,000 youths would be brought from Cyprus as soon as the funds and resources were made available.[5] The moment for which the Jewish DPs had waited for so long had arrived; the possibility of aliyah was no longer theoretical or only available for the select few in the kibbutzim of the youth movement. Soon it seemed it would be available to all in a massive immigration from the DP camps.

The excitement in the DP camps was tempered, however, by the announcement of a second piece of accompanying news. Arab riots had broken out to protest the decision, and the Yishuv had initiated plans to defend itself. The December 19, 1947, volume of the *Jidiscze Cajtung* announced that the Haganah and the Yishuv were prepared to counter the organization of the Arab Legion. Defense forces had "begun a mobilization of those aged 17–25. . . . Jewish formations have already begun to work in Tel Aviv and Petach Tikvah, and in Jerusalem they have helped the British to put down an Arab demonstration. . . . The Jewish police is working together with the 'Mishmar Ha-Am,' the unofficial militia."[6]

The Jewish DPs did not observe developments in Palestine merely as passive third parties. As the newspaper discussed preparations to defend the homeland against Arab enemies in the wake of the partition decision, plans were already underfoot to integrate Jewish DPs between the ages of seventeen and thirty-five into the effort to defend the Jewish state in the making. Although 1947 had been a year marked by failure, disappointment, and growing impatience, the looming struggle in Palestine finally presented an opportunity to mobilize the younger segment of the DP population to join the Zionist struggle. Years of Zionist enthusiasm demonstrated to emissaries from Palestine a perceived willingness to join the fight. Desperation to leave Germany at almost any cost led many to participate in a war so soon after the conclusion of the last one, although the eagerness of the DP population as a whole to migrate to Palestine under any circumstances may have been overestimated.[7] Although Jewish DPs cheered the Palestine resolution as a potential solution to the fate of the wider DP community, the young adults among the DPs would be called upon to make the dream a reality.

The Conscription Campaign in the DP Camps: The Beginning of Haganah Operations

The Haganah first began operations in Europe in 1946, as Nachum Shadmi (Kramer) had traveled there in February 1946 to investigate the possibility of creating a manpower reserve to aid the Yishuv in any future fight it may have.[8] When Shadmi arrived in Europe in 1946 he was uncertain of what he would find among the DP population. He was soon pleased, however, by the degree of cooperation he received from the Zionist youth movements in the creation of Haganah schools, and he became convinced that in Europe he would find a pool of willing and able-bodied soldiers to participate in the fighting in Palestine. The initial purposes of the Haganah organization in Europe were to investigate the remnants of Nazi resistance; to organize self-defense among the Jews in Europe, especially partisans and resistance fighters; and to train groups for service in Eretz Israel.[9] The first Haganah training school was opened in Wildbad (near Nuremberg), where twenty-two students (primarily members of hakhsharot) received training in hand-to-hand combat, sports, and ideological education from Haganah agents in Germany. Upon completion of the month-long course, graduates returned to their camps and hakhsharot in order to train others. In a sign of the holy work they were undertaking, trainees had to swear an oath of allegiance to the Haganah with one hand on a gun and the other on the Tanach, the Jewish Bible.[10]

Although operations began on a limited basis in 1946, Shadmi expanded the focus of Haganah operations throughout Europe in 1947 despite less than enthusiastic support on the part of leaders in the Yishuv. Shadmi was unable to obtain the financial assistance he needed from the Yishuv and failed to convince those responsible for Aliyah Bet that it was in their best interest to give preference to his trainees. Nonetheless, with his return to Europe from Palestine in June 1947, he continued to organize the manpower reserve. He convened a meeting in Germany at the end of June in which he informed the Haganah operatives of his plan to recruit the survivors for military service in Palestine and facilitate a total aliyah of the DPs within one year.[11] Between May and November 1947, Haganah operations spread to eleven countries in Europe and three in North Africa. The largest delegation included twenty-four emissaries sent to Germany and Austria under the command of Ze'ev (Glazer) Gal in Munich. Four Haganah offices were opened in Germany (in Munich, Frankfurt, Stuttgart, and Regensburg), and one was opened in Austria. The offices in Germany were led by Dov Neshri (Adler) in Frankfurt, Arieh Nir (Nisht) in Regensburg, Mordechai Ben-Ari in Stuttgart, and Pinchas Meromi in Munich.[12] Activity in Germany focused on two areas: organizing Haganah activities for DPs in the camps and opening a training school for madrichim to train hundreds of Jewish youths in weapons, Hebrew, and ideological training. The coordination of work in different parts of Germany involved sending arms to branches, conducting instruction in camps, opening of a central information (*hasbarah*) office, and the later organization of conscription (*giyus*).[13] In August 1947 the second course of Haganah officers opened in Hochland (on the site of a former Hitler youth camp); the course lasted six weeks, and twenty-seven students took part. Three hundred students passed through the Haganah training schools in Hochland and Wildbad by the end of 1947, fanning out to the DP camps in order to train other potential recruits in military techniques and serve as a Haganah presence among the She'erit Hapletah in the camps.[14] As many as five hundred commanders (*mefakdim*) were trained from among the DPs, and this network of DP officers would later play a vital role in implementing the conscription operation.[15] The Haganah schools also trained students in the use of guns and grenades, although few weapons were actually available.[16] Haganah schools were visited by Yisrael Galili (head of the Haganah command), Yig'al Allon (Palmach [the offensive force of the Haganah] commander), Shadmi, and others who gave the students ideological support and told them what to expect once they reached Israel.

As Shadmi recalled after the 1948 war, the Haganah activities varied throughout Europe but were especially successful in Germany and Austria thanks to the assistance of the Central Committee and the American Jewish Joint Distribution Committee (JDC). Furthermore, he noted,"*in this work we cooperated especially closely with all of the Zionist youth movements (despite their political divisions). . . . It was clear to us that without these movements we would not be able to operate.*" Through this framework the Haganah managed to organize more than forty thousand youths within two months. In addition to this, Shadmi noted, they succeeded in recruiting several thousand older Jews in the DP camps of Germany and Austria.[17] Shadmi's success in organizing Haganah activities among the DPs would prove especially fruitful when the survivors were called upon to join the fighting in Palestine/Israel.

The Giyus Operation in the DP Camps

Although the implementation of the conscription operation required Shadmi's initiative and the arrival of Haganah instructors and recruiters from Palestine, the success of the operation also depended upon the organization and enthusiasm of the Central Committee and its subsidiary regional and local committees as well as the manpower provided by the Zionist youth movements and political parties.

Why would Shadmi have believed that he had the right, and perhaps the obligation, to recruit Holocaust survivors for fighting in Palestine? The youth movements and political parties representing the DPs consistently presented a profile of intense Zionist enthusiasm among their constituencies. The DP desire to make aliyah, as represented among the youths in the kibbutzim, could thus have been interpreted as a willingness to join in the fighting. The performance of the DPs in the *Exodus* Affair, young and old alike, would surely have reinforced Shadmi in the belief that the She'erit Hapletah would be a vital and reliable resource in the fighting that would take place over Palestine. Shadmi anticipated the need of the Yishuv for a large reserve in October 1947 in a report to his superiors: "it seems as if a large war is approaching. . . . I therefore intend that we will need to enlist all of our forces in order to assist in the war in Israel. It will be our duty to enlist all of the youth here."[18] The UN decision of November 29, 1947, gave added impetus to the Haganah's activities. Witnessing the enthusiasm of the Jewish DPs following the UN decision, Shadmi believed that he could enlist between ten thousand and twenty thousand soldiers from Europe within six to eight months.[19]

Nonetheless, the leadership of the youth movements may have professed one position on behalf of their constituency while fearing another situation altogether. As had been the case over the course of 1947, the youth movements continued to fear declining morale and waning enthusiasm for Zionism by their chanichim. A February 1948 *Nocham* survey suggested that "many factors point to the conclusion that in the last two months, Zionist enthusiasm is in decline among the She'erit Hapletah."[20] While the fall had seen a rallying effect due to the *Exodus* Affair, "the excitement over the heroism of *Yetziat Eyropah* has faded. . . . Fatigue and disappointment have taken away from the spiritual strength of the She'erit Hapletah." Fortunately, the UN decision had rescued things to a certain extent, although increasing numbers seemed to be turning to vocational training from ORT to improve their emigration prospects:

Who knows where things would have reached were it not for the decision of the U.N.? This awakened a great deal of excitement in the camps. . . . This declined too though. Passivity. The influence of this on the youth is a major question. . . . *The question is: how do we break this complacency? How will we bring the youth who are shirking their duty to fulfill their obligations?*

The remedy for this still has not been found. We still need to strengthen our educational apparatus. The new period requires new paths and completely different methods.[21]

Thus, at the beginning of 1948 Nocham detected complacency, passivity, and an unwillingness to participate in movement activities on the part of its members and the general DP population. And this was precisely at the time when the Yishuv called on the She'erit Hapletah in its time of need.

It is quite possible that Nocham's search for "new paths and completely different methods" was met by the conscription campaign as a way to remind young Jewish DPs of their duty to Palestine. The search for new paths paralleled arguments by the Zionist Jewish DP leadership, who concluded that the general DP population was overwhelmingly Zionist but perhaps needed to be "shaken up" in order to remember this fact. On March 15, 1948, at the first meeting with the new adviser on Jewish affairs to the American zone, William Haber (also the brother of Samuel Haber, JDC U.S. zone director), participants from the Central Committee voiced considerable concern over the morale of the DPs after more than two and a half years of dwelling in the DP camps, with the possibility of at least another year.[22] While there was general consensus among the parties at the meeting that emigration for Palestine would be the best solution, the Central Committee was most consistent in its firm belief in the need for immediate departure. At the meeting with Haber, David Traeger, head of the Central Committee, argued that now was the time that "the Camps must be shaken up and the people must be reminded of their mission with respect to Palestine."[23] Traeger reassured those present that "the Central Committee [was] endeavoring to work along this line." In fact, Traeger had no doubt as to the underlying Zionist enthusiasm of the DP population and concluded that "the fact that approximately 90 percent of those eligible to vote participated in the election for the Congress of the Central Committee shows the dynamic interest of the people in Palestine." Political participation thus represented an automatic assumption of Zionist affiliation on the part of voters. In a sense, however, this was unavoidable, as all the represented parties in the Central

Committee elections came from the Zionist camp, with the notable exception of Agudat Israel.[24] If the Zionist enthusiasm of the DP population was
as evident as believed, this would have also indicated to the leadership the
legitimacy of implementing a conscription and taxation campaign, which
could prove to be the ideal method by which to remind the people of their
mission with regard to Palestine. Nonetheless, the need to shake up the
camps perhaps also indicated that while people may have voted Zionist,
they were frequently more concerned with other issues of daily life such as
locating or starting families or obtaining food and work. From the leadership's perspective, emigration was presented as a solution to the authorities'
two major problems: black market participation and the fear that vocational
training would immerse DPs in the German economy, making departure
from the camps even less likely.[25] As the Central Committee representatives
attested to the strong underlying enthusiasm of the DPs for the Zionist
cause, it is thus not surprising that the Haganah would have viewed the DPs
as ideal candidates for reinforcements to the depleted forces of the Yishuv.

The effort to remind the people of their mission with respect to Palestine
began at least as early as mid-February 1948, as the Central Committee,
the Zionist Federation, the Jewish Agency, and seven of the main political
parties and their youth movements active in the DP camps (excluding the
Revisionists), joined together to form the Exekutive Far Bitachon Le'Am
U-Moledet (Executive Committee for Security for the People and the Homeland).[26] In circular number 1, addressed "to the entire She'erit Hapletah,"
the executive committee announced its formation, which coincided with the
initiation of a wide, all-inclusive campaign on the part of the She'erit Hapletah to assist the Yishuv in its struggle, to "lead a normal, nationally independent life." The proclamation called upon local committees in camps, in
cooperation with the executive committee in Munich, to implement a "material and financial campaign for security" as rapidly and broadly as possible.
Thus, while the operation would devolve upon the entire DP population, considerable agency was given to local committees in the organization of camp
campaigns, with the expectation that contact would be maintained with the
executive committee in Munich.

At a February 29, 1948, meeting in Paris between representatives of the
Haganah, Mossad l'Aliyah Bet, and Bricha and members of camp commit-

tees to discuss the giyus operation, Shadmi emphasized three key aspects of the plan: the obligation to enlist on the part of eligible DPs who "are Israeli citizens not allowed to reach Israel," the need to secure resources, and priority in aliyah to be given by the Bricha and Mossad to enlisted individuals.[27] The resolutions of the Paris meeting called upon:

1) The Jewish youth in the countries of Europe and in the camps of the She'erit Hapletah to enlist for aliyah and defense [Haganah], and to join the ranks of the fighters and the builders who stand on the decisive battle for the future of the land and the people

2) Every young man and woman between the ages of 17 and 32 to be prepared for immediate and organized aliyah to Eretz Israel

3) The Zionist parties and youth movements in the countries of Europe and the She'erit Hapletah camps have the *obligation* to focus all efforts and energies in education and organization for the immediate Giyus, to empower your best members for this activity and to fill the maximum quotas which will be placed upon you by the Giyus centers.[28]

Jewish youths in the DP camps of Germany and throughout Europe between the ages of seventeen and thirty-two were expected to enlist in order to join the fight, but it would be the responsibility and indeed the obligation of the youth movements and parties to concentrate all of their powers on a successful and immediate conscription campaign. It is worth noting that the call to the youths to enlist focused on every young man *and* woman. This was also manifested in the courses of the Haganah training schools and in the Haganah training in the kibbutz groups, in which men and women both participated.

In each camp, the Merkaz le-Sherut Ha'am of the Jewish Agency in Munich advocated that a corner for *sherut ha-am* (service to the nation) be set up, where slogans calling on DPs to "fulfill your duty to the people" and suggesting that "not one deserter should be found among us" were to be distributed.[29] This language of national duty indicated the implicit responsibility of citizenship that had been assigned to the DP population in the Central Committee's presentation of their Zionist enthusiasm. Posters published by the Jewish Agency, the Central Committee, and the Zionist Federation called

בירגנער־קאָמיטעט פֿאַר   נױס למען המולדת   בירגנער־קאָמיטעם פֿאַרן

אין שטוטגאַרט

1948   שטוטגאַרט, דעם

Sample conscription (*Giyus*) form, issued by the Citizens Committee for Conscription for the Homeland in Stuttgart, 1948. The form calls on conscripts to "offer your duty to the people!" (YIVO)

upon the entire Jewish people to "stand in a united front," as the Haganah in the war and in the creation of the Jewish state, "in order to open the gates of aliyah and defend the future of the Jewish people."[30]

In the general DP and youth movement press as well, the Zionist leadership worked to create an atmosphere of duty and obligation to enlist. In the *Jidisze Cajtung*, the creation of the Magbit LeBitachon Ha'Am was announced, calling upon all Jewish DPs to contribute "to the fund for the security of the people and the fatherland." The She'erit Hapletah was reminded of the difficult situation facing the Yishuv. As Haim Hoffman made clear at the meeting to create the fund, "the She'erit Hapletah needed to participate in the present strengthening of [those defending the Yishuv].... The struggle for the Yishuv is the struggle for the near future of the She'erit Hapletah."[31] In this way, Jewish DPs and the Yishuv were engaged in the same fight to defend the same larger Jewish community. The newspaper reported on the heroism of the Israeli youths who had already mobilized to defend the Jewish homeland, 85 percent of whom, it was noted, were between the ages of seventeen and twenty-five (suggesting that fighting was a job for the youth). As part of this Jewish national community, Jewish DPs would be expected to defend the homeland as well. The headline of the March 2, 1948, *Jidiscze Cajtung* instructed Jewish DPs to "prepare yourselves to serve the nation and the homeland."[32] An announcement directed at Jewish youths and signed by all of the major movements instructed them to "prepare for your duty to the People."[33]

While announcements in the general press targeted the wider DP population, the youth movements worked to recruit their members over the age of seventeen, who were obligated to report for duty. Interestingly, the campaign to recruit members for the fighting began even before the resolutions at the Paris meeting, suggesting that the youth movements took the initiative upon themselves to begin a conscription campaign.

On February 21, 1948, Hashomer Hatzair BeHa'apalah circulated a call to all of its members in the movement branches announcing the beginning of recruiting to fight in Palestine to help the Haganah, which was "bravely undertaking Jewish *holy work.*" As the party suggested, "the whole Yishuv has gone to support the Haganah. . . . *The Jewish youth is prepared to sacrifice itself for the people and the fatherland.* . . . The struggle of the Yishuv is the struggle of the entire Jewish people." The time had come for the She'erit Hapletah and the DP youths especially to do their part in the struggle: "We must mobilize, all of our members between the ages of 17 and 30. . . . The Giyus will last as long as the gates to the land will not be open to the whole She'erit Hapletah."[34]

In this regard, each branch was asked to submit a list of all those required for conscription by the end of February and prepare them for departure. The March 10, 1948, circular of the movement continued the pressure, announcing that the "duty of the hour is: GIYUS!" The party had always stood at the front of the pioneering camp, and the current situation was no exception. Hashomer Hatzair members had to serve as an example in "fulfill[ing] the vital duty for the people and the land."[35] As part of the general call for national service, Hashomer Hatzair created a central mobilization committee composed of five people to review all members who were required to fulfill their duty to the people. The obligation to fight in Palestine was equated with the heroic performance of the movement in the wartime ghetto fighting: "Twice in the history of our movement we have been required to take weapons into our hands. Once in the ghettos where one of our greatest chapters was written with blood . . . we have now been called once again."[36] No one was exempt from the obligation to report, even members of the mazkirut of kibbutzim and movement branches. If any member was unable to report, he or she had to provide a reason and receive permission from the conscription committee of the movement. All members reporting for conscription had to be cleared through the movement before appearing before the general giyus committee of the local DP camp. In this way, the youth movement could keep track of its enlisted members before they reported to the general board of the camp.[37]

While movement division had dominated youth movement politics in the first two years and more after liberation, the needs of 1948 brought the movements together in drafting members for the conscription campaign. Bnei Akiva, Dror, Hanoar Hazioni, Nocham, Hashomer Hatzair, and Noar Borochow came together to issue joint calls to the youths to enlist.[38] This collaboration between the youth movements and the local DP camp committees was crucial because although the individual movements recruited members for the Haganah, it seems that official conscription took place through the camp committees.

The lower age range of the giyus obligation meant that some residents of children's homes and youth kibbutzim were also technically obligated to enlist in the draft. This fact was not lost on the leadership of the youth aliyah in Palestine and Germany, who declared that their eligible members must enlist. At the end of February 1948, the youth aliyah division of the Jewish Agency published a bulletin in the DP camps announcing that "all graduates of aliyat hanoar are required to fulfill GIYUS at the end of hakhsharah." Madrichim were requested to submit lists of boys and girls three months before the completion of their term of hakhsharah (ranging from one and a half to two years) so that they could be drafted once their term was completed.[39] As time was of the essence, for those groups where more than half of the members were over the age of sixteen, the hakhsharah period would be reduced to one and a half years so the members could be eligible for conscription earlier.[40] In the meantime, these groups were instructed to begin preparations by initiating training in guard duty and self-defense. An allowance was made for orphans who refused to leave their younger siblings behind.

The Central Committee and the local camp committees, beyond publicizing the need to provide support for the Yishuv, were also active in executing the giyus and *magbit habitachon* (security tax) campaigns in the individual camps. Shortly after the publicity campaign was initiated within the DP camps, local camp committees and Central Committee members commenced discussion of the practical implementation of the conscription operation in certain camps, in advance of the Third Congress of the She'erit Hapletah held at the end of March 1948. For example, at Feldafing near Munich, one of the largest DP camps in the American zone, an invitation to discuss giyus with various members of the Feldafing community and Yechezkel Eife (a member of Left Poalei Zion and a representative from the Central Committee of Liberated Jews) was sent out on March 16, 1948.[41] At the meeting on March 19 (two weeks before the Third Congress of the She'erit Hapletah), Eife declared the policy of the Central Committee of Liberated Jews already to be to dismiss from work those persons who were of giyus duty age so they could receive military training. A giyus commission was formed at the meeting, with representatives from the camp committee, the ORT school, the youth movements, and the Haganah.[42] In addition, it was agreed that while contributions of one hundred dollars per person were satisfactory, more stringent measures would need to be employed to implement the taxation campaign in Feldafing in order to raise two hundred dollars per person and achieve the desired goal for the camp.[43]

Conscription and preparation for war dominated discussion at the Third Congress of the She'erit Hapletah in the U.S. zone, which took place at Bad-Reichenall from March 30 until April 2, 1948. Representatives from the U.S. Army, the JDC, Agudat Yisrael, the Jewish Agency, and the Haganah in Europe were in attendance.[44] The DPs were called upon to fulfill their "national duty," which attended membership in the Jewish state. Nachum Shadmi, in his address to the congress, called for "each man and woman, from 18 to 35, to be in the ranks of the Haganah . . . with no excuses."[45] The congress declared that "the She'erit Hapletah would stand together with the Yishuv . . . and do all in its power to mobilize all forces and material to achieve a rapid and final victory."[46] To this end, the congress called upon "all men and women between the ages of seventeen and thirty-five to fulfill their duty to the people," and that all those "who failed to fulfill their [giyus] duty

1948. U.S ZONE-

Program cover of the Third Congress of the She'erit Hapletah in the U.S. Zone, which was held in Bad Reichenhall from March 30–April 2, 1948. The cover includes the emblem of the *She'erit Hapletah*, a felled tree with a map of Palestine sprouting from it. (USHMM, courtesy of Abraham Atsmon)

would be excluded from social and political life." The congress also called upon the She'erit Hapletah to support the *"mi'fal habitachon*, the fund for Jewish arms and security in Palestine."[47]

While certain aspects of the conscription and security tax campaign operations certainly began prior to the Third Congress, in April the application of the giyus resolution began in earnest throughout all the camps. Circular number 31, sent from the Central Committee in Munich on April 11, 1948, to the various camp committees, outlined the implementation of the giyus resolution. The circular called upon the camp committees to support the work by the Va'adot Le-sherut Ha'am (Committees for Service to the Nation) and to assist them in their work in any way possible. Those between the ages of seventeen and thirty-five who failed to enlist by April 15 would be subject to dismissal from work. The circular also requested that lists of workers, with birth dates included, be compiled and sent to the Organiza-

View of the dais at the Third Congress in Bad Reichenhall, March 30–April 2, 1948. The Yiddish banner on the podium reads, "The Fatherland calls: offer your service to the people." (USHMM, courtesy of Alex Hochhauser)

tion Department of the Central Committee.[48] In addition to working to ensure compliance with the conscription demand, the Executive for Security for the People and the Homeland also sought to coordinate the collection of funds in the individual camps to support the giyus operation in Europe and the "fighting Yishuv."[49] The contribution of approximately three hundred thousand dollars from the DP population in Germany alone enabled the giyus operation to continue functioning well into August.[50]

As Shadmi suggested after the war, he was quite pleased with the display of Zionist patriotism and duty on the part of the Jewish DPs. Haim Hoffman also remembered the episode as a heroic chapter in the history of the period that demonstrated the Zionist enthusiasm of the She'erit Hapletah:

In the camps an atmosphere of enlistment was created, of public comment, of praise for the parents of conscripts and scorn for those who avoided conscription, until the point where it was difficult for a young person to walk in the camp. And many came. The pioneering movements sent off their oldest groups [of bogrim] and these enlisted until the last man, except for a few madrichim who were released from the draft so that they could continue with the educational activity. The hakhsharot were closed. The Hebrew Gymnasiah in Munich moved up exams by three months. In this way the circle of conscripts grew day by day. The giyus project continued all of the months of the spring and into the summer, and in the end—7800 conscripts from all the zones of Germany. . . . Among those who enlisted were public leaders of the She'erit Hapletah, including four members of the Central Committee: Dr. A. Blumovitch, A. Melamed, M. Rosman, and Arieh Retter, and with them the head rabbi of the refugees in the British zone, Dr. Helfgott and many others.[51]

In Hoffman's opinion, "the chapter of the volunteering of She'erit Hapletah for fighting in the War of Independence is perhaps the most wonderful chapter in the history of the She'erit Hapletah, a chapter which does not detract from the glory of the people of Yetziat Eyropah, 1947."[52]

All of this suggests that the Yishuv representatives of the Jewish Agency and the Haganah were quite pleased by what they saw in the conscription campaign in the DP camps, which brought nearly eight thousand soldiers to the aid of the Yishuv. Still, the perspective of the Yishuv agents reflects an instrumentalist usage of the DP population as a manpower reserve to fulfill the needs of the Haganah fighting in Palestine. They first and foremost evaluated success on the basis of assistance rendered to the Yishuv, not on its benefits to the DPs themselves. How did the youths themselves respond to the call to enlist? Did they stream to the giyus centers, enthusiastically marching to join the fight? The judgment on this account seems to be far more mixed.

At the beginning of May 1948 Nocham summarized its previous two months' worth of efforts to enlist its members. Not surprisingly, the movement concluded that "the most active participants [in giyus] are the kibbutzim."[53] As was suggested would happen in Paris in late February, "the need to defend Eretz Israel turned into the dominant issue facing the movement. . . . The task became the collective responsibility of all those in the camps, falling upon every young man and woman in She'erit Hapletah." Like the other pioneering movements, Nocham felt that as one of the leading forces in the She'erit Hapletah, it needed to stand at the forefront in organizing this task. Had its members been equal to the task? Although the "number of those willing to enlist and the total who enlisted were very high," the total number of "shirkers" reached into the hundreds. The groups most eager to enlist were from the hakhsharah centers: Nili, Kibbutz Buchenwald (Geringshof), Ichud (Zeilsheim), Kovshei Hayam, and one group from the children's home Yehuda Maccabi (Bayrische Gemeine). This led the movement to conclude that "once again those groups in hakhsharot and children's homes demonstrate their superiority over the frameworks in the camps, which were influenced by the negative atmosphere of the DP camp." The work was far more difficult in "encouraging" members from the kenim within the camps to enlist, although "dozens" had been drafted from these frameworks.[54] All in all, the movement counted 175 members who had been drafted from the American zone (300 including the British zone) by late April, a slow start for the movement of nearly 2,000 members. (It must be noted, however, that the majority of conscripts would not be able to leave until after May 1948 anyway).

Hashomer Hatzair also tabulated its number for giyus, with the members of kibbutzim representing the best source of conscripts. The kibbutz in Hochland listed 40 members (including 15 women) ranging in age from eighteen to twenty-eight as eligible for giyus. All told, approximately 250 members were counted as eligible for giyus among Hashomer Hatzair members in Feldafing, Hochland, Pritzler, Ulm, Neu Ulm, and Funk Kaserne. While giyus was intended to be the ultimate goal of the movement and the focus of all activity, it could still generate problems for madrichim of groups with mixed-age composition. As the madrich of Ken Bozlow argued, although he understood the importance of the giyus, the departure of older members deprived the movement of a future generation of leaders for the younger children in Germany.[55] Nocham also reported that giyus put the movement in the difficult position of preparing for the summer and the continued functioning of the summer camps while dealing with the loss of vital members and leaders to giyus.[56]

Nonetheless, overall the youth movements had the most success in recruiting their members to enlist in the Haganah. According to one report from Austria, while the activity in the camps was not successful, the youth movements there were able to fulfill their quotas.[57] Still, there not was a mass outpouring of willingness to enlist, aside from those members of kibbutzim and hakhsharot who had already been awaiting aliyah for more than a year. The notion of national duty was not always successful in garnering full support for the campaign. Camp committees employed coercive measures such as denial of additional food rations and dismissal from work to encourage those who were reluctant to participate in the draft. Nocham, in its May 1948 report, noted that despite the presence of shirkers the readiness to enlist *le-sherut ha'am* (service to the nation) "became nonetheless a massive operation, with a sizable number of individuals ready to enlist." Any disciplinary measures against those who refused to enlist from within the youth movement were not cited in the report. Ironically, the fact that Nocham and the other movements had to prepare for the increasingly difficult task of continued activity within the DP camps (with the departure of many key members) meant that those youth movement members who chose not to enlist perhaps had a valid service to the movement that they could continue to perform in the camps, especially for members of "pre-giyus age."[58]

As Hoffman recalled, "there were also ugly events in this chapter. There were people who resisted conscription, youths who escaped to cities and towns, and informants who told the authorities about coercion in the camps." He suggests that the DP camp leadership desired to employ harsher measures against shirkers than the Yishuv agents wanted. "We had disputes with the ZK [Zentral Komitet, or Central Committee] and committees over what kind of sanctions to hold against the shirkers. . . . We were in favor of social sanctions (prohibit from serving on committees, prohibit future aliyah) but opposed to financial sanctions. . . . The committee disagreed with us and saw us as too liberal but ultimately accepted our suggestions."[59] While Hoffman may have been reluctant to frame the Yishuv activists as too harsh on the Jewish DPs, this would have been in line with the hierarchy functioning in the DP camps at the time, with the local camp committees and the Central Committee having ultimate say over rations and work assignments within the camps. Beyond denying employment and hence rations, coercive measures also included the publication of lists of nonsupporters in the press and in immigration offices so that they would suffer the appropriate consequences.[60] In his report on the progress of the giyus in the camps, Yehuda Ben-David, a Haganah commander from the Yishuv, relates that initially the "giyus of the 'first thousand' was not easy, and in fact, the organization only managed to enlist 700 people." Nevertheless, "an atmosphere of overall obligation to enlist was created. . . . It was this atmosphere which would later bring the many thousands who enlisted to Israel."[61]

Some individuals managed to dodge recruitment, while a number of Bund members reported evidence of physical and emotional coercion employed by the Zionist leadership in the giyus and magbit habitachon initiative, including organized violence perpetrated in the name of so-called Zionist terror.[62] In addition to complaints raised by the few members of the Bund in the DP camps, there were complaints from camp committees over the loss of vital employees and teachers, and the JDC felt compelled to reprimand the local committees for denying rations to DPs.[63]

Even among those students listed in the Haganah classes in the DP camp Haganah schools, where zeal to enlist would presumably be at its highest, enlistment was not without difficulties. Of the fifty-two students listed in Course #10 in early June 1948, twelve had already made aliyah in order to join the fighting. Another six had been discharged for failing to return from vacation or simply refusing to enlist. By far the largest number refusing to join the draft at the time cited familial reasons (which would perhaps also be best understood) as the basis for their refusal to enlist. Some refused to leave brothers, sisters, husbands, and wives behind, while one student's mother refused to allow him to leave.[64] In much the same way, the youth aliyah division had made an allowance for those members who refused to leave behind younger siblings. This reluctance to enlist on the part of those with surviving family members is understandable: why would Jewish DPs who had only recently emerged from the Holocaust leave behind the only family they had to join in the fighting in Palestine? It is quite possible that those most reluctant to enlist were also from the older segment of the requested age range (those twenty-five years old and over), a fact supported by data on the soldiers who participated in the fighting in Israel.

DP Soldiers in the Haganah

A total of 20,239 people were conscripted in Europe by the Haganah between January and July 1948.[65] Of those who arrived in 1948, 292 were killed in the fighting.[66] One major critique of those who have argued that the Yishuv manipulated Holocaust survivors to serve their own ends has been that DPs conscripted to fight in the 1948 war died in overwhelming numbers during the fighting in 1948. An analysis of those who served and were killed reveals this not to be the case.

Kibbutz Tosia Altman lost three of its members in the 1948 War of Independence, all of whom were conscripted after arrival in Palestine. Yitzhak Schnitzer, born in 1926 in Poland, was a member of one of the first aliyah groups to reach the Yishuv in 1946. He joined a group from Kibbutz Tosia Altman that settled in Kibbutz Ein Hamifratz. When fighting broke out after the UN resolution, he was part of a group of kibbutz members sent to reinforce Kibbutz Dan. He was killed at the age of twenty-two on May 1, 1948, during an attack on the kibbutz. Meir Grinberg, born in 1925, arrived in Israel in 1947 with another aliyah group from Kibbutz Tosia Altman. Along with other members of the group, he was also sent to reinforce the defenses of Kibbutz Dan in the Huleh Valley in the north of the country. He fell on June 15, 1948, at the age of twenty-three in a battle with Syrian forces. Mordechai Feldman, born in May 1925, reached Israel in 1947 after a period of detention in Cyprus. He enlisted in December 1947 and became part of a brigade that specialized in explosives and accompanied convoys to western Galilee. He was killed escorting the Yechiam convoy on March 27, 1948.

Among those other members who fought in and survived the war was the former mazkir of the kibbutz, Monish Einhorn, the subject of the mock trial in Landsberg. He arrived in Israel from Cyprus in March 1948 at the age of twenty-two (on a youth aliyah visa that listed him as seventeen years old). He joined a group of Kibbutz Tosia Altman at Kibbutz Ha-Zoreah and enlisted in the army. He was injured during the battle at Megiddo against the Iraqi forces and the Arab military leader Kawukji but survived the war (and lives today in Jerusalem).[67]

The members of Kibbutz Tosia Altman who participated in Israel's 1948 war fit the prototype of young soldiers in the war. The three who died enlisted in 1946 and 1947, while Monish joined the armed forces in 1948. All were aged twenty-two or twenty-three at the time of the war. This was in line with the profile of the average Haganah soldier at the time. Of those soldiers who arrived in Israel in 1948, 72.5 percent were born between 1923 and 1930, while 67.4 percent of the 1940–47 arrivals and 78.5 percent of

An Israeli artillery unit gathers by a howitzer during the Israeli War of Independence, 1948. Among the commanders of the unit was Samuel Schalkowsky, a Holocaust survivor from Kovno. (USHMM, courtesy of Sam Schalkowsky)

Sabras (native-born Israelis) fell into this age range. Likewise, the average age of those who died was twenty-two years old for the 1948 and 1940–47 arrivals and twenty years old for the Sabras.[68] Counteracting the myth that 1948 arrivals died in disproportionate numbers as "cannon fodder" in the war, Emmanuel Sivan has calculated the number who died (as a percentage of the total number of soldiers from each group). According to his calculations, 292 (1.4 percent) of the 1948 arrivals died as opposed to 1,170 immigrants who arrived between 1940 and 1947 (5.1 percent) and 1,239 Sabras (5.6 percent).

Total Giyus of men and women by year of immigration:
1940–47 group: 23,800
1948 group: 21,755
Sabras (native-born Israelis): 22,100[69]

Sivan suggests that one of the major reasons for fewer 1948 arrivals actually perishing in the war is that the majority of the 1948 arrivals came later in 1948 when the risk was lower.[70] Over the course of 1948, 118,000 immigrants arrived in Israel; 68,000 of these came after August 1948 when the major combat danger was lower (of the 50,000 who arrived between December 1947 and July 1948, 23,000 arrived after May 1948). The giyus numbers also make this clear: of the 21,755 1948 arrivals conscripted, one-quarter arrived between January and June 1948, one-third in July and August, and more than two-fifths between September and December 1948.[71]

Further research also suggests that a total of 858 new immigrants (1945–48 arrivals) were killed by the end of January 1949, which was 18.9 percent of the 4,517 killed until then in the war (tables 4 and 5).

Thus, while it is clear that the contributions of the Giyus Hutz La-'aretz (conscription outside of Palestine) soldiers (twenty-two thousand out of eighty-two thousand total soldiers in the war) were extremely significant, it is not the case that these 1948 conscripts were merely sent to die as cannon fodder in numbers that surpassed those of native-born Israelis.

Jewish DPs did indeed play a vital role as a manpower reserve for the forces of the Yishuv in the war. The majority of those who served as soldiers in the war were between the ages of eighteen and twenty-five, not coincidentally in the same age range as the majority of members of kibbutzim in the DP camps. Although the draft in Germany focused on those between the ages of seventeen and thirty-five, more than 70 percent of the 1948 soldiers were between the ages of eighteen and twenty-five. The kibbutzim provided the majority of participants in the Haganah training schools and

Soldiers Killed in 1948 War according to Year of Immigration[a]

Year	Number of Soldiers Killed	Percentage of New Immigrant Soldiers Killed
1945	112	13%
1946	242	28.3%
1947	233	27.1%
1948	246	28.7%

Twenty-five soldiers were killed whose year of immigration was not known.

[a] Markovizky, *Gachelet Lochemet*, 195.

Soldiers Killed in 1948 War according to Country of Origin

Country	Number Killed	Perecentage of New Immigrant Soldiers Killed
Poland	321	37.5%
Romania	218	25.4%
Hungary	96	11.1%
Czechoslovakia	79	9.2%
Bulgaria	58	6.8%
Germany	29	3.4%
Soviet Union (including Lithuania, Latvia, and Ukraine)	23	2.7%

in the ranks of those recruited by the Haganah. This also suggests a need to revisit the nature of the relationship between the DP population and the fighting in the 1948 war. It seems that it was not the DP population as a whole that was counted on directly for support in the war but rather the younger segment of the population, especially those between the ages of eighteen and twenty-five. The Zionist enthusiasm and activity on the part of the youths and their desire to reach Palestine made them ideal candidates to fill this manpower gap in the Haganah forces.

Conclusion

When at the end of 1947 the Jewish DP population as a whole was called upon to fulfill its national duty in order to defend the Yishuv against Arab attack, this duty fell upon the segment of the population that had consistently demonstrated the greatest level of Zionist commitment: the youths. Those aged seventeen to thirty-five were ordered to enlist through proclamations supported by the political leadership of the She'erit Hapletah. More than 70 percent of those who participated in the fighting were between the ages of eighteen and twenty-five.

The youths who populated the kibbutzim, hakhsharot, camp branches, and children's homes made a statement as to their membership in the Zionist movement. It was this membership, as a form of citizenship for stateless individuals, that would eventually bring with it the responsibilities of conscription and taxation (with a division of responsibility on the basis of age in the camps). It is in this context that Zionism must be viewed as a uniquely functioning transnational political system that could force its stateless adherents to confront the very real duties of citizenship while still residing on foreign soil. A dynamic Zionism could thus fulfill both the needs of the DPs and the Yishuv, albeit in different ways. For the young DPs in the kibbutzim, Zionist affiliation could be a functional Zionism that addressed their most pressing postwar needs while also responding to the reality of post-Holocaust existence. At the same time, it indicated to the Yishuv a willingness to defend the homeland they had never seen.

Nonetheless, these were not the conditions that the majority of youths envisioned bringing them to Palestine. They saw Palestine as a place of final refuge, not as an opportunity to engage in more fighting. It is not surprising that they would have taken the opportunity to go to Palestine, whether out of explicit or implicit coercion. Yet, it is in a sense tragic that for many the only way to leave Europe and reach the Holy Land was through the outbreak of another war.

Conclusion

Zionist Function and Fantasy in the Aftermath of the Holocaust

Sixty years after the creation of the State of Israel, at a time when the need for a Jewish state can be thrown into question, it is worth reexamining the period immediately after the Holocaust when the creation of a Jewish state was by no means a foregone conclusion. While most literature on the Jewish survivors of the Holocaust in postwar Germany is in agreement on the fact that the She'erit Hapletah demonstrated an abundant Zionist enthusiasm that influenced the course of diplomatic debates over the creation of the State of Israel, there has been considerable debate as to the source and depth of that Zionist enthusiasm. The positions explain displaced persons' (DPs) Zionism either as an obvious conclusion to the Holocaust that manifested itself instantaneously in political enthusiasm or as a foreign import imposed by agents from abroad on the mass of helpless Jewish refugees, neglecting to consider the decisions faced by Jewish survivors in the aftermath of the war. Both these poles reflect a largely monolithic view of Zionism, asking how it ultimately benefited the creation of the state in Palestine rather than focusing on the function that Zionism filled for the diverse DP population while they were still in Europe, regardless of whether the state was ultimately created or not. Furthermore, studies of the Jewish DP population tend to describe the group as an undifferentiated mass, although it is apparent that the Jewish DPs were a population with a distinctive demographic makeup that influenced its political and cultural choices. Just as the nature of the DP population was transformed during 1945–48, a dynamic Zionism was capable of accommodating groups with various needs in the immediate postwar period.

This study has investigated the behavior of young Jewish DPs against this background in an effort to determine the meaning and appeal of Zionism to young DPs and the reasons for its success. It seems clear that the Jewish DP population manifested pronounced demographic tendencies that influenced the political, social, and cultural characteristics of the surviving population. The overwhelming youth of the DP population directly correlated to the Palestine passion that could be witnessed among the She'erit Hapletah. The most visibly Zionist segments of the population, actively engaged in public demonstrations of Zionist activity, were the organized kibbutz youths, who came to represent the collective future of the DP population as a whole.

As this study has suggested, understandings of youth and the responsibilities and expectations that could be projected on this amorphous segment of the population were highly varied. The Jewish DP leadership, the U.S. Army, the United Nations Relief and Rehabilitation Administration (UNRRA), the American Jewish Joint Distribution Committee (JDC), Jewish Agency emissaries from Palestine, and the Zionist youth movements all had differing assessments of the Jewish DP youths and what would be best for their future. For those DPs who chose to live in the DP camps in Germany, these assessments often shaped the range of possibilities open to them. Even among those who fell into the age range of fifteen to thirty, many chose to get married, have families, return to school, and/or migrate to America and other promised lands, all choices that would seem incongruous with the pioneering lifestyle of the Zionist youth movements. And it must be noted that contrary to the beliefs of Yitzhak Zuckerman in postwar Poland, Zionism or Zionist youth movements were by no means the way of all youths. Not all youths chose to join the kibbutzim, and not all youths who joined the kibbutzim remained with them. Nonetheless, a consensus developed in the DP camps among the She'erit Hapletah and outside observers that the youths, and especially those who chose to join the youth movements, represented the future of the surviving Jewish people. The kibbutz youths who committed themselves to a future in Palestine did so not only on behalf of themselves but also on behalf of the She'erit Hapletah as a whole.

From an early point in time, the Jewish DP youths were invested with a tremendous degree of responsibility by the Zionist political leadership of the Jewish DP population. As Samuel Gringauz, head of the Landsberg DP camp, suggested soon after liberation, the actions of the youths would demonstrate to the world the commitment of the She'erit Hapletah to continue with life. Jewish DP youths would serve as the agents of both creativity and revenge for the DP population as a whole.[1] However, the entreaties of the leadership to adopt a Zionist position to avenge Jewish deaths and lead the surviving population did not compel the youths to adopt such a position. For a large number of those between the ages of fifteen and thirty, Zionism and the collective lifestyle of the youth movement kibbutzim seemed to offer the best answers to their most pressing postwar problems.

Nonetheless, the first thought of most Jewish survivors upon liberation was not questioning how long it would take to reach the Land of Israel. Far from making life-altering decisions on the basis of conclusions to ideological considerations, survivors were forced to confront immediate problems of a practical nature soon after liberation. The thought that had preoccupied and sustained most survivors during the course of the war concerned the question of what had happened to family, to loved ones from whom they had become separated during the war. For some the answer was clear after witnessing the murder of their families. Others returned to what was left of home in order to reunite with or bury what remained of family. Most soon realized that they had no family to return to and, as orphans, were largely on their own.

For these youths, the early kibbutzim organized by the camp survivors in Germany and the Zionist youth movements in Poland provided the warmth, camaraderie, shelter, and security they yearned for after the war. The recent survivors of trauma and tragedy preferred to put their lives back together in a supportive environment in the company of fellow survivors. The Zionist ideological aspects of the kibbutz were secondary. Still, by joining a kibbutz these youths were making a statement of membership in a Zionist organization. And membership in the kibbutz came with the opportunity for education in Jewish and Zionist history as well as the ideology of the movement they joined. (While many had abandoned the religion of their youth, the

Jewish aspects of the kibbutz continued to hold appeal as a meaningful part of their identity.) The Zionist opportunity, however, was not merely defined by its end goal—the creation of a Jewish state in Palestine—but instead came to be understood as the community provided by the kibbutz, the education it offered, the structure, and the chance to work as well as the hope for departure from Europe.

Although the members did not necessarily join for ideological reasons, this did not preclude the growth of Zionist enthusiasm. On the contrary, as members remained within the kibbutz, they learned more about their youth movement, the history of the Zionist movement, the ideas and beliefs that their movement stood for, and their new partnership in a legacy of wartime heroism. The time spent in the DP camps was put to good use by deepening their Zionist education and training. The kibbutz also provided a cultural outlet for dramatic performances, music, dancing, and writing, all of which were part of the Zionist immersion. Gradually their understanding of Zionist ideology grew as they became more enthusiastic about the lives they could build once they reached the Land of Israel.

The Zionism of the youth movements in the kibbutzim filled another function for the young members: the traumatic individual past of the survivors was replaced with the shared experience of wartime heroism in the ghetto revolts. Regardless of what members' experiences had been in the war, whether in the forests, in hiding, in the Soviet Union, in concentration and labor camps, or in the ghettos for that matter, the kibbutz members now adopted the collective heroic identity provided by membership in the group. The kibbutzim of Hashomer Hatzair and other movements were named after fallen resistance heroes and celebrated holidays commemorating ghetto uprisings. Members learned about the bravery of their predecessors in the movement, whose legacy they now continued through participation in the struggle to create the Jewish state.

Zionism in this way not only reframed the past but also provided a new way to understand DPs' present situation. Kibbutz members came into contact with Germans on the farms and in economic exchanges; the acquisition of estates for farming and the participation of German farmhands reveals that Jewish DPs did not live in a German-free vacuum in the American zone. Although their contact with Germans may have been more limited than those who lived in cities, they were still confronted with the reality of continued existence among their former enemies. The Agricultural Department of the Central Committee worked to instill a love for the soil among the youths; the blood-soaked German soil would have to serve as a surrogate for the soil of agricultural labor in an abstract sense. Still, farming German soil provided emotional meaning for Jewish DPs on a number of levels. The DP youths on Kibbutz Nili in Pleikhershof linked farming to revenge, finding satisfaction in working the land on Julius Streicher's estate while he stood trial in nearby Nuremberg. The renaming of farm buildings and livestock with Hebrew names was part of a consciously symbolic revenge for youths empowered by membership in a kibbutz and the Zionist youth movement. While Zionism could allow them to transcend their current situation through a focus on the future, when they did face Germany and Nazism they were now armed with the tools to do so. At the same time, the young farmers could take pride in their collective accomplishments, as farming provided some tangible product to their time and efforts in Germany.

Nonetheless, the presence of the Jewish DPs in postwar Germany constituted a unique challenge to understandings of citizenship and statehood in the mid-twentieth century. The centrality of citizenship to the organization of modern states was a fundamental component necessitating the repatriation of refugees in post–World War II Europe. This certainly had an impact on the formation of a new national identity among the Jewish DPs and its ready acceptance by the Allied occupying powers. The story of the Jewish DPs represented a prime example of the unacceptability of statelessness within the international filing system of citizenship and pointed to various possibilities for dealing with this situation.[2] For individuals dealing with the problem of statelessness and struggling to obtain some form of citizenship (even while still on German soil), Zionism proved successful in filling this perceived lack in state membership. In the classes and seminars and from the DP press the youths learned about current events in Palestine; through study of the Jewish people, Jewish history, Hebrew, the geography of Palestine, cultural activities, and farming they acquired the tools necessary for their future life in the Land of Israel. Zionism could empower these young survivors by offering a solution to their stateless condition, providing them with membership in a nation before they actually arrived in Palestine and making them feel like part of a larger national community. They were updated on events in Palestine and learned about the history they shared with their compatriots on the kibbutzim of the Jezre'el Valley or western Galilee. In the kibbutz they trained for life in their future country, essentially beginning the process of absorption even before they had arrived. Through active participation in the Zionist framework of the kibbutz, they were learning to become citizens of the state in the making. When the time came to fulfill their civic duty as their fellow citizens who had already enlisted in the Haganah were doing, many young Jewish DPs filled the duties of citizenship through giyus and taxation. When the DP leadership ultimately called upon the DP population to support the 1948 war, this duty once again fell upon the young adults in the DP camps between the ages of seventeen and thirty-five (even though 70 percent of those who fought were under age twenty-five).

This Zionism was also appealing to American authorities responsible for handling the DP situation because it suggested that they would not be in Germany indefinitely. Support for farming could be justified because the young DPs were busy training for their future lives in Palestine. With the emergence of the Cold War, the Jewish DPs increasingly became a thorn in the side of the U.S. Army in its attempts to foster the full rehabilitation of German society. Indeed, American attitudes toward Jewish DPs were often shaped by concerns that Jewish black marketeering functioned as a negative influence on the reconstruction of the German economy.[3] American authorities could support Zionism as a productive use of DPs' time that would not detract too much from the German economy and seemed to ensure the eventual departure of Jewish refugees from Germany. Jack Whiting from the UNRRA and Irving Heymont of the U.S. Army—just to name two— wholeheartedly supported the creation of training farms for the youths whom they believed were anxious to prepare for the future lives in Palestine. Furthermore, these demonstrations led international observers from the Anglo-American Committee of Inquiry and the United Nations Special Committee on Palestine to conclude that Palestine was the only solution for the DP population as a whole.

In this regard, the charges of a cynical manipulation of the Jewish DP population are difficult to reconcile with the evaluations of Zionist enthusiasm among the DP population by contemporary observers. UNRRA authorities, JDC workers, and Zionist emissaries testified to demonstrations of Zionist enthusiasm on the part of Jewish DPs. By and large these examples tended to describe the DP youths in the kibbutzim of the youth movements. In describing the commitment of the Jewish DPs to settle in Palestine, the Central Committee leadership focused on the youths in the kibbutzim. Likewise, even the Zionist emissaries, who at times focused on what was lacking from the pioneering quality of the DP population, observed with wonder the displays of enthusiasm from the youths. As Miriam Warburg described the scene on the first Chanukah in Föhrenwald when a youth aliyah film on Palestine was shown in the big hall of the camp, the "Palestine passion" of the young population convinced her of their desire to reach the Jewish homeland.[4]

The very nature of the Zionist youth movements, which sought to shape the DP youths in their own image, was transformed after the war as a result of direct contact with the survivor youths. The enlisting of the young survivors in the kibbutzim after the war and their absorption into the movement were part of the larger transformation of the Zionist youth movements in Europe that had begun during the Holocaust in Poland. The youths in the kibbutzim believed that through their cultural work in the kibbutz and training on the farms they were actively preparing themselves for their futures. Nonetheless, it is also clear that the range of options open to them was certainly shaped by membership in a kibbutz. While the choice to join the group had been their own, once they became part of the larger movement decisions such as where to live in Germany or the timing of departure for aliyah were determined by the movement. Some who were dissatisfied with life in the kibbutz chose to leave, making their own arrangements for emigration and the future. It is also clear that for many of the youths who remained in the kibbutz, their understanding of Zionism was transformed over the course of their time in the kibbutz and the youth movement. Many had joined the kibbutz with next to no knowledge of Zionism; by the time they left Germany, many were prepared to take up arms to defend the homeland they had never lived in.

Unlike previous studies of postwar Zionist youth movements, this study provides the perspective of the youths who made up the movement.[5] While the movement and its activists had various expectations of the surviving youths, the youths also had expectations of the movement. Despite reservations of the quality of surviving youths, the movements were ultimately dependent on these youths to reconstitute the European branches of the movements and to provide the human reservoir that had nearly been eradicated by the war. Some of the kibbutz groups under the auspices of youth movements became broadly enough defined that they could accommodate families with children or individuals who were no longer youths but who still identified themselves with the youth movement. And in many cases, members of youth movements came of age once they were already in the youth movement, learning a trade, falling in love, and starting families within their kibbutz groups. While movement activists from Palestine focused so much attention on maintaining the pioneering nature of the youth movements, the survivor youths who composed the reconstituted movements forced emissaries to adjust definitions of who could qualify as a pioneer. In the end, leaders such as Haim Hoffman and Nachum Shadmi had to acknowledge that the efforts of the Jewish Agency and the Haganah in Europe would not have been successful without the active participation of what had once been deemed demoralized and broken youths.

While outside observers often perceived them as homogeneous, the youths who joined the kibbutzim were a diverse group with varied experiences before and during the war. Some had been exposed to Zionist youth movements; others were in families that were religious, secular, or communist. During the war they had survived in hiding, camps, resistance, or the far reaches of the Soviet Union; the kibbutzim of the youth movements took in these young adults with varied experiences and seemingly elided divisions between them. These variations in the composition of the Jewish DP population also came to be reflected in seemingly contradictory depictions of DP behavior as either remarkably active and creative or powerless and passive. Sources created by the DPs themselves and by outside groups observing the Jewish DPs betray highly inconsistent assessments of the population.

Contradictions in representation and in explanations for DP behavior suggest a need to be wary of the sources created by outside groups charged with the task of caring for the DPs who thus tended to view them as social welfare cases. Alternately, some Zionist activists were biased by preconceived notions of what type of human element could have emerged from the Nazi camps and tended to view the DPs as human material unfit for pioneering work. Thus, it is unsurprising that analyses of the DP population written from those perspectives (be they American administration sources or Israeli agents) at times tend to depict the DPs as powerless and apathetic.

It is quite possible that there were those among the DPs who fit this description, but this was not predominantly the case among the youngest and most active part of the population.

Sources created by the kibbutz youth themselves, such as the diary of Kibbutz Tosia Altman, depict a group highly aware of their postwar situation and actively involved in rebuilding their futures. A unique source, the kibbutz diary is not the journal of an individual kept as a private recounting of personal thoughts, nor is it a Holocaust diary similar to those kept by Emmanuel Ringelblum, Adam Czerniakow, Herman Kruk, or Victor Klemperer.[6] The act of writing the diary collectively had the function of reinforcing collective identity and strengthening group cohesion by creating a shared past; at the same time the creation of a shared past was a project actively shared by the group members in the writing of the diary. The elimination of individual thoughts and feelings was part of the effort to sublimate individual needs to those of the collective and by extension the youth movement and the Zionist movement. The diary is of great value in providing details on daily life within a kibbutz after the war; inasmuch as the diary is also a reflection of social and ideological pressure imposed on the members of the kibbutz to conform to collective and movement values, its value is also significant. It is also important to note what is left out of the diary: there is little discussion of members' experiences during the war, just as there is no mention of members' individual histories. Nonetheless, testimony by kibbutz members suggests that members did in fact share their experiences with one another in order to provide support. This must certainly have been one of the therapeutic aspects of the kibbutz, and its absence in the diary is noteworthy. Whether members were discouraged from writing about their past experiences in the diary and encouraged to focus on the present and the future, this suggests that material that is withheld from the writing of a diary is just as significant in the controlling and containing of emotional experience, be it individual or collective. Likewise, the reports sent to the youth movement leadership and the articles in the youth movement newspapers reflected a consistent focus on daily activities and preparations for the future; discussions of past trauma were integrated into education on the youth movement.

Taken together with the other sources created by kibbutz and youth movement members after the war, the perspective of Jewish youths on their experiences in the aftermath of the Holocaust indicates that they were forced to grapple with significant practical concerns after the war that could not be addressed merely by a convincing ideology. An attention to methodology thus throws into question conclusions pointing to ideology as the basis for life-changing decisions or studies that focus primarily on the leadership of the Central Committee of Liberated Jews in an effort to understand the origins of DP Zionism. It is predictable that the editorial pieces and committee debates they held would tend more to ideological explanations for the Zionist conclusion. A leader such as Samuel Gringauz, who never in fact immigrated to Israel, could reflect on the Jewish situation and suggest reasons why Jews needed to settle there. These were not necessarily reasons for himself as an individual but, importantly, were for the Jewish DPs as a community.

For the youths in the kibbutzim, the ideological pronouncements of Gringauz mattered little. Nonetheless, ideology provided a significant foundation for a distinctive form of DP Zionism that factored in the postwar political contributions of the DPs on the diplomatic level by appealing to various groups interested in ameliorating the DP situation. On the ground, DP Zionism could succeed because it made sense on both the ideological and practical levels; without pragmatic solutions to the most pressing needs of the young survivors, Zionism could not have attracted and maintained the membership that it did.

It is clear that the DPs played an important role in the creation of the State of Israel so soon after the war. However, even without the retroactive knowledge that the State of Israel would ultimately be created, Zionism was highly successful in filling a positive function for DP youths in the aftermath of the Holocaust by providing a secure environment for vocational training, education, and rehabilitation and a surrogate family that could ultimately restore their belief in humanity. For the wider Jewish DP population, Zionism filled a symbolic need that had arisen for the Jewish people in the wake of tragedy even if not all would make the Zionist dream their reality. For many of the youths who joined the kibbutzim and journeyed to Israel, it was the search for a new home that ultimately brought them to a new homeland.

Appendix A
Demographic Data
on Jewish DPs

The following chart reflects the growth in the Jewish population in the U.S. zone of Germany between April and October 1946:

The Change of Jewish Population in the U.S. Zone of Germany

	April 1946	May 1946	June 1946	July 1946	August 1946	September 1946	October 1946
Pop. at beg. of month	52,669	64,519	67,691	75,517	91,410	115,898	138,551
minus emigration	− 123 =	− 1,904 =	− 974 =	− 840 =	− 907 =	− 606 =	− 221 =
	52,546	62,625	66,717	74,677	90,503	115,292	138,330
Influx	11,973	5,076	8,800	16,733	25,395	23,259	2,747
Pop. at end of month	64,519	67,691	75,517	91,410	115,898	138,551	141,077
Monthly increase in %		7	12	21	27	20	2
vs. Jan. 31, 1946	32%	42%	59%	92%	143%	190%	196%

(YIVO, MK483, DPG, Reel 3, Folder 29, p. 63)

Statistics are based on JDC calculations. Constant shifts in the size and location of the Jewish DP population made it difficult to gather accurate and reliable data on the actual size of the population at any given point in time. Population statistics should hence be analyzed in terms of overall trends in population change.

Growth of Hakhsharot in the American Zone

Date of Survey	Number of Hakhsharot	Number of Inhabitants	Total Pop. in U.S. Zone (hakhsharah pop. as % of total population)
Jan. 27, 1946 (LS 9, 57, 576)	8	870	49,695 (1.75%)
May 31, 1946 (LS 2, 20, 835–41)	26	2,337 (or 2236)	67,491 (3.46%)
June 30, 1946 (LS 2, 21, 1024)	35	3,661	75,517 (4.84%)
Sept. 30, 1946 (DPG 3, 29, 53)	36	3,515	138,551 (2.54%)
Oct. 31, 1946 (DPG 3,30, 200)	36	3,442	141,077 (2.4%)

According to JDC calculations; note that the JDC definition of "hakhsharah" may differ from other sources.

Age Structure of Jewish Population in the U.S. Zone (November 1945–January 1947)

At End of Month of:	Total Population Investigated	Under Age 1 (As % of Total Pop. Investigated)	Aged 1–5	Aged 6–17	Aged 18–44	Aged 45 and Over
November 1945	900	0	0	3.1%	85.8%	11.1% (over 40)
February 1946	30,156		1.2% (0–5)	7.6%	80.1%	11.4% (over 40)
August 1946	49,861		5.5% (0–5)	8.7%	85.8% (includes over 45)	
November 1946	134,541	3.2%	3.5%	10.8%	72.3%	10.2%
December 1946	118,875	4.5%	4.0%	11.8%	68.1%	11.6%
January 1947	139,037	8.6% (0–5)	11.5%	71%*	8.8%	

(YIVO, MK 488, LS 9, 57, p. 715)

*For January 31, 1947, 56,639 men (aged 18–44) and 42,041 women (aged 18–44) out of 98,680.

Appendix B

Hakhsharot in the American Zone of Occupation in Germany

According to a report by Avraham Gevelber to the Jewish Agency regarding kibbutzim, Munich, April 10, 1947, Central Zionist Archives, S6/1911:

1. Shtelitz—Nocham; 93 residents (aged 19–32); land belonged to Jewish man before the war and was given to our members in order to establish an agricultural training school; 20 hectares of agricultural land and 4 hectares of forest; twelve cows in the cow barn
2. Zeckendorf (Bamberg District)—Nocham; 76 members; average age 23 years; farm also belonged to Jewish owner; 17 hectares of agricultural land; five cows in the cow barn
3. Boxdorf (Regensburg District)—Nocham; soon to be passed to *Noar Borochow*; 25 members; seventeen cows in the cow barn; five milking cows; 20 hectares of agricultural land; two oxen, two horses, chickens, etc.
4. Zettlitz (Bamberg District)—Nocham; 50 members; age range between 16 and 30; 20 hectares of land; eleven milking cows in the cow barn; three horses, chickens, etc.

5. Lossau (Bamberg District)—Nocham; 80 members; 54 hectares of land; fifteen milking cows in the cow barn; eight oxen, goats; the workable land includes three farms

6. Prebitz A (Bamberg District)—Nocham; 48 members; land includes two farms of a former Nazi; 100 hectares of land; of this 14 hectares are forest; in the cow barn are eleven milking cows and five calves; three horses and four oxen

7. Prebitz B (Bamberg District)—Bnei Akiva; 60 members between the ages of 17 and 27; former Nazi farm; 40 hectares of land: of this 10 hectares are forest; in the cow barn five cows and eight calves; seven oxen, chickens, etc.

8. Oberschwarzbach (Bamberg District)—Nocham; 30 members between the ages 18 and 37; farm taken from a Nazi; 25 hectares of land, of this 3 hectares are forest land; in the cow barn are six cows, two oxen, one horse

9. Windisch-Liebech (Bamberg District)—Agudat Israel; 50 members; the age is between 16 and 40; the farm belonged to a Nazi and was appropriated by the Army; 35 hectares of land; fifteen cows in the cow barn

10. Funkendorf (Bamberg District)—Agudat Israel; 22 members aged 17–30; 16 hectares of land; four milking cows, three calves, etc.

11. Fojta (near Pegnitz; Bamberg District)—Lochamim Ivriim (partisans' group); 67 members (of these 50 percent are invalids from the war); ages are between 25 and 40; 76 hectares of land; in the cow barn are thirty-two heads and of these ten are milking cows; also seven oxen, two horses; the land is made up of two farms

12. Streicher's Farm—Kibbutz Nili (Bamberg District)—Nocham; 120 members aged between 18–30; 82 hectares of land; forty-seven heads in the cow barn of these are twenty-five milking cows; two tractors, oxen, horses, etc.; there are also fish pools

13. Wildbad—Hashomer Hatzair; 80 members; 7 hectares of land; the farm is new and organized; they plan on setting up a larger cow barn

14. Bernstein—Hashomer Hatzair; 80 members; the age is between 18 and 27; 53 hectares, of which 25 are farmland; ten heads in the cow barn

15. Aschbach—(Bamberg District; thirty-two kilometers from Bamberg) Bnei Akiva; 60 members, aged 17–25; farm taken from a Nazi; 30 hectares of land; in the cow barn are seven milking cows; two horses; there are also pools for fish

16. Forkenhof (Bamberg District)—Nocham; 59 members; average age 25; the farm belonged to a Nazi and was seized by the Army; 49 hectares of land, 9 hectares of which are forest; there are seven milking cows in the cow barn; two horses and four oxen; good living conditions

17. Passau—Nocham; 30 members average age 17–24

18. Nettenberg—Hanoar Hazioni; 70 members (of these 53 are men); all members aged below 30 years old; farm belongs to a German who lives and works there

19. Teublitz—Nocham; 55 members aged between 20 and 30; the farm belongs to a German and the members work on it as students

20. Mainkofen—Hanoar Hazioni; 120 members in good living conditions; the land is large and beautiful but Germans work on it; our members participate in the work as students

21. Deggendorf (Bamberg and Regensburg Districts)—Kibbutz Kovshei Hayam—Nocham; 38 young male members; they receive training in fishing and in handling boats in the river

22. Dorfen-Baumgarten—Betar; 40 members; 9 hectares of land with twelve head of cattle

23. Reithofen (Munich District)—Hanoar Hazioni; 60 members; the average age is 18; 90 hectares of land for agricultural work; forty-seven heads in cow barn; thirty-eight milking cows; forty chickens; two tractors

24. Bertel-Gras—Hanoar Hazioni; 40 members; age between 20 and 22; 30 hectares of land; twenty heads in the cow barn

25. Firstbach—Hanoar Hazioni; 50 members; the average age is 20; 50 hectares of land (9 hectares of which are forests)

26. Rotschweigen (near Dachau; Munich District)—Hanoar Hazioni; 80 members; 90 hectares of land; the members work alongside Germans on the farm

27. Alzstreit (Eisolzried; Munich District)—Hanoar Hazioni; 40 members; average age of 27 years; they work together with Germans although recently relations have been poor

28. Leiphof (near Dachau; Munich District)—Hanoar Hazioni; this farm was formerly a part of the Dachau camp; 40 members with an average age of 25 years; the members work under the supervision of a German manager

29. Greifenberg (Munich District)—Nocham and Hanoar Hazioni; approximately 120 members; the members are of the age of aliyat hanoar, 15–18; the agricultural work only includes a small cowshed and a garden; with the assistance of ORT workshops (carpentry, shoemaking) have been established here

30. Hochland—(Munich District) Nocham, Dror, and Hashomer Hatzair; approximately 250 members; 40 hectares of land but only 9 hectares can be used for agricultural work; 40 members are employed in workshops on the hakhsharah

31. Holtzausen (near Landsberg; Munich District)—Dror; 80 members; average age is 20; the majority of hakhsharah work is done at an ORT workshop here

32. Deisen—Dror; 40 members; in the summer the members work in fishing on the lake under the guidance of German instructors; in the winter they work in ORT workshops (electronics, ceramics)

33. Weilheim—Betar; 40 members; small operation

34. Struth—Dror and Hashomer Hatzair (Bamberg District); children's home; vegetable garden and cowshed

35. Indersdorf—Dror; children's home; vegetable garden and cowshed for the older members

36. Geringshof—Nocham; 80 members; large agricultural estate

37. Eschwege—Hashomer Hatzair; 210 members; the farm encompasses 80 hectares of agricultural land; a cow barn with thirty-two heads and of these twenty-five are milking cows; the members work in an independent manner

38. Holtzhausen—Hashomer Hatzair; 85 members; three more hakhsharot (one Hashomer Hatzair and two Dror) have been closed in the French zone in recent months.

Notes

Introduction

1. M. Winogrodzki to Nathan Schwalb, June 18, 1945, Haganah Archives, Ha'apalah Project (hereafter HAHP), 123/Maccabi/0012, Box 20, Folder 4, letters to Nathan Schwalb in Hechalutz Geneva Office, pp. 88–89.

2. In June 1945 Ruth Kliger and David Shaltiel, two Paris-based representatives of the Jewish Agency for Palestine, told the heads of the political and immigration departments of the Jewish Agency Executive in Jerusalem that up to 95 percent of the survivors were under thirty-five years old. Kliger and Shaltiel to Shertok and Dobkin, June 11, 1945, Central Zionist Archives (CZA), S6/3659. A survey of Jewish DPs in Bavaria taken in February 1946 found that 83.1 percent of their number was between the ages of fifteen and forty, with more than 40 percent between the ages of fifteen and twenty-four and 61.3 percent between the ages of nineteen and thirty-four. Jewish Population in Bavaria, February 1946 (YIVO, MK 488, Leo Schwarz Papers, Roll 9, Folder 57, p. 581). A study by the JDC in the U.S. occupation zone in Germany more than one year after liberation found 83.1 percent between the ages of six and forty-four (YIVO, MK 488, LS 9, 57, p. 682; Jewish Population, U.S. zone Germany, November 30, 1946).

3. Winogrodzki to Nathan Schwalb, June 18, 1945, HAHP, 123/Maccabi/ 0012, Box 20, Folder 4, letters to Nathan Schwalb in Hechalutz Geneva Office, pp. 88–89.

4. The origins of the term "She'erit Hapletah" are biblical, specifically in the writings of the prophets. The use of the term links the notions of destruction and redemption. According to Dalia Ofer, the Yishuv leaders invoked phrases from Micah (4:6–7) and Isaiah (II Kings 19:30–31) in reaction to reports they received related to the Holocaust. From 1943, Yishuv leaders used the term "remnant" to refer to what remained of European Jewry, still believing that Jewish survival and the realization of Zionism remained possible despite the destruction. See Dalia Ofer, "From Survivors to New Immigrants: *She'erit Hapletah* and *Aliyah*," in *She'erit*

Hapletah, 1944–1948: Rehabilitation and Political Struggle, edited by Yisrael Gutman and Avital Saf, 304–36 (Jerusalem: Yad Vashem, 1990).

5. See, for example, J. Whiting's comments as UNRRA zone director: Report from J. Whiting on Jewish DPs in U.S. zone, January 19, 1946, YIVO, MK 488, Leo Schwarz Papers, Roll 10, Folder 65, pp. 7–15; memorandum from J. H. Whiting (UNRRA zone director) to the commanding general, U.S. 3rd Army, regarding formation of Jewish Council, March 5, 1946, YIVO, LS 10, 66, p. 150. After the war, the term "kibbutz" was used to refer to groups of youths, affiliated with Zionist youth movements, who presumably lived together in a collective framework (but not necessarily on a farm). Agricultural hakhsharot were training farms where kibbutz groups worked to prepare for life in Palestine.

6. This conclusion has been noted by numerous scholars (Engel, Ofer, Weitz, Lavsky, and Kochavi, among others) who have written on the Jewish DPs, including those studies that address the role of survivors in the creation of the State of Israel. See the bibliography for a full listing.

7. "Declaration of the Establishment of Israel," in *Israel Yearbook and Almanac, 1991/92*, ed. N. Greenwood, 288–99 (Jerusalem: International Publication Service, 1992).

8. Elimelech Rimalt (member of the Knesset for the General Zionist Party) argued in 1953 that perhaps it was the "Holocaust that gave the (Jewish) people, not only (Jews) in Palestine, the supreme impetus to liberate themselves and establish their state?" Quoted in Yechiam Weitz, "Shaping the Memory of the Holocaust in Israeli Society of the 1950s," in *Major Changes within the Jewish People in the Wake of the Holocaust*, edited by Yisrael Gutman, 500 (Jerusalem: Yad Vashem, 1996). Benzion Dinur, "Galuyot ve-hurbanan," in Dinur, *Dorot u-reshumot: Mehkarim ve-iyunim ba-historyografyah ha-yisraelit* (Jerusalem: Mosad Bialik, 1978), 192.

9. According to Emmanuel Sivan, 21,755 soldiers arrived from Europe to join in Israel's War of Independence in 1948. Of these, the average age of those who died was twenty-two years old for the 1940–47 and 1948 arrivals and twenty years old for the Sabras. Emmanuel Sivan, *Dor Tashakh: Mitos, Diyukan ve-Zikaron* (Israel: Ministry of Defense, 1991), 76.

10. Koppel S. Pinson, "Jewish Life in Liberated Germany: A Study of the Jewish DPs," *Jewish Social Science* 9, no. 2 (1947): 117.

11. Ze'ev Mankowitz, *Life between Memory and Hope: The Survivors of the Holocaust in Occupied Germany* (Cambridge: Cambridge University Press, 2002), 69.

12. Evyatar Friesel "The Holocaust: Factor in the Birth of Israel?" in *Major Changes within the Jewish People in the Wake of the Holocaust*, edited by Yisrael Gutman, 519–52 (Jerusalem: Yad Vashem, 1996).

13. Idith Zertal, *From Catastrophe to Power: Holocaust Survivors and the Emergence of Israel* (Berkeley: University of California Press, 1998), 1.

14. Yosef Grodzinsky, *Homer Enoshi Tov: Yehudim mul Tsiyonim, 1945–1951* (Or Yehudah, Israel: Hed Artzi, 1998), 185.

15. Ibid., 16–17.

16. Ibid., 17.

17. See also the work of Zeev Tzahor, "Holocaust Survivors As a Political Factor," *Middle Eastern Studies* 24, no. 4 (1988): 432–44. Tom Segev, *The Seventh Million: The Israelis and the Holocaust* (New York: Hill and Wang, 1993), also takes this approach.

18. Dan Diner, "Elements in Becoming a Subject: Jewish DPs in Historical Context," *Jahrbuch zur Geschichte und Wirkung des Holocaust* (1997): 229–48.

19. While the categories of youth movement membership and adolescence were more clearly defined in the prewar period, the interruption of childhood, loss of education, and death of family radically altered the meaning of youth for these young survivors, who were often forced to embrace the responsibilities of adulthood prematurely. For a traditional conception of adolescence focused on biological, social, behavioral, and cultural factors, see Michael Cole and Sheila Cole, *The Development of Children*, 2nd ed. (New York: Scientific American, 1993), 572. For the psychological impact of persecution on young survivors, see Judith S. Kestenberg, M.D., and Ira Brenner, M.D., *The Last Witness: The Child Survivor of the Holocaust* (Washington, DC: American Psychiatric Press, 1996).

Chapter 1

1. Robert H. Abzug, *Inside the Vicious Heart: Americans and the Liberation of Nazi Concentration Camps* (New York: Oxford University Press, 1985), 54.

2. Marcus J. Smith, *The Harrowing of Hell: Dachau* (Albuquerque: University of New Mexico Press, 1972), chap. 15, "Priorities."

3. Ibid., 98.

4. Leonard Dinnerstein, *America and the Survivors of the Holocaust* (New York: Columbia University Press, 1982), 9, estimates that by September 1945 the U.S. Army had successfully repatriated six million DPs.

5. See Malcolm Proudfoot, *European Refugees, 1939–1952: A Study in Forced Population Movement* (Evanston, IL: Northwestern University Press, 1956).

6. For more on the postwar refugees, see Dinnerstein, *America and the Survivors of the Holocaust*, and Arieh Kochavi, *Post-Holocaust Politics: Britain, the United States, and Jewish Refugees, 1945–1948* (Chapel Hill: University of North Carolina Press,

2001). On the UNRRA, see George Woodbridge, *UNRRA: The History of the United Nations Relief and Rehabilitation Administration* (New York: Columbia University Press, 1950).

7. According to one source cited in David Engel, *Ben Shikhrur Li-Verihah: Nitsolei ha-Shoah be-Polin veha-ma'avak 'al Hanhagatam, 1944–1946* [Between Liberation and Flight: Holocaust Survivors in Poland and the Struggle for Leadership, 1944–1947] (Tel Aviv: Am Oved, 1996), 42n30, in the first month following liberation in Germany, approximately thirteen thousand Polish Jews returned to Poland. As noted by the CKZP, this number only counted those Jews who had chosen to register with local committees and presumably not all of those who had returned to Poland. See "Polish Jews from the West," *Dos Naye Leben*, May 20, 1945.

8. Ze'ev Mankowitz asserts that for the most part the Jews of Hungary and Romania sought to return home following liberation, while the Polish Jews (some 90 percent of those liberated) were far more divided on the issue. See his "The Formation of She'erit Hapletah: November 1944–July 1945," *Yad Vashem Studies* 20 (1990): 27.

9. YIVO, MK 488, Leo Schwarz Papers Roll 8, pp. 1032–37. Later surveys of the Jewish DP population in the American zone of Germany corroborated this information. A survey of the Jewish DP population of Landsberg (4,976 residents) taken on October 1, 1945, indicated that 75.2 percent (3,740) of residents were Polish, while only 5.7 percent (283) were Hungarian and 3.3 percent (162) were Romanian. A survey of residents of Feldafing taken at the same time indicated that a population drop from 600 to 400 from the summer to October 1945 was attributable to the sizable repatriation of Hungarian and Romanian Jews.

10. Yehudit Kleiman and Nina Springer-Aharoni, eds., *The Anguish of Liberation: Testimonies from 1945* (Jerusalem: Yad Vashem, 1995), 48.

11. Alexander Grobman, *Rekindling the Flame: American Jewish Chaplains and the Survivors of European Jewry, 1944–1948* (Detroit: Wayne State University Press, 1993), 39–40.

12. Chaim Finkelstein Letter to World Jewish Congress, July 5, 1945, WJC, file 67, drawer 242; cited in Grobman, *Rekindling the Flame*, 40.

13. See Ruth Schreiber, "The New Organization of the Jewish Community in Germany, 1945–1952," PhD dissertation, Tel Aviv University, October 1995, 11. While some 36 percent of Jews from Eastern Europe did try to live in German cities in January 1946, the continuing housing shortage and reluctance of some newly formed German Jewish communities to represent Jews of non-German descent made this option a difficult one. German Jews also suffered from initially being denied the status of persecuted individuals and were classified as enemy nationals along with Austrian and Hungarian Jews in some cases.

14. June 24, 1945, report of Abraham Klausner, "A Detailed Report on the Liberated Jew As He Now Suffers His Period of Liberation under the Discipline of the Armed Forces of the United States," in Grobman, *Rekindling the Flame*, 42–43. For more on Klausner and his instrumental role in the early organization and representation of the She'erit Hapletah, see ibid.

15. Klausner, "A Detailed Report."

16. Protocol of the Jewish Committee in Feldafing, July 12, 1945, YIVO, MK488, Leo Schwarz Papers, Roll 15, Folder 135, p. 570.

17. See Dinnerstein, *America and the Survivors of the Holocaust*, 28. Slightly different statistics can be found in Yehuda Bauer, *Out of the Ashes: The Impact of American Jews on Post-Holocaust European Jewry* (New York: Pergamon, 1989), and Proudfoot, *European Refugees*.

18. Zalman Grinberg and Puczyc to OMGUS and the UNRRA, July 10, 1945, YIVO, DP Germany, MK 483, p. 340.

19. Ibid., 342.

20. YIVO, MK 488, Leo Schwarz Papers, Roll 9, Folder 57, p. 584.

21. As Terence des Pres, *The Survivor: An Anatomy of Life in the Death Camps* (New York: Oxford University Press, 1976), 122, has argued, survivors sought support from collective affiliation often based on shared history and nationality. Postwar psychological studies also noted a predilection to collective forms of affiliation. See Paul Chodoff, "The German Concentration Camp As a Psychological Stress," *Archives of General Psychiatry* 22 (1970): 78–87. The study noted by Chodoff was performed by Editha Sterba, "Some Problems of Children and Adolescents Surviving from Concentration Camps" (Detroit: Wayne State University Conference, 1964). See also Editha Sterba, "Emotional Problems of Displaced Children," *Journal of Social Casework* 30 (1949): 175–81.

22. Mankowitz, "The Formation of She'erit Hapleita," 337–70. Mankowitz describes a number of surviving Jews from the Kovno ghetto grouped together in Dachau who wrote an underground newspaper, *Nitzotz*, in which they made plans for life after liberation.

23. A similar process also took place in Poland during the war and will be discussed extensively in chapter 2.

24. He-Halutz was created to prepare Zionist youths in Europe for life in Palestine through agricultural and vocational training. See Israel Oppenheim, *The Struggle of Jewish Youth for Productivization: The Zionist Youth Movement in Poland* (Boulder, CO: East European Monographs, 1989).

25. See Judith Tydor Baumel, *Kibbutz Buchenwald: Survivors and Pioneers* (New Brunswick, NJ: Rutgers University Press, 1997), 5.

26. Tydor's age was listed as forty-two on immigration records for Kibbutz Buchenwald at time of aliyah (August 1945). Haganah Archives, Hativah 14, Tik 943. For Tydor's role in wartime youth organization, see Baumel, *Kibbutz Buchenwald*, 5.

27. Baumel, *Kibbutz Buchenwald*, 5. Posnansky's age was listed as thirty-three in a Haganah document regarding the aliyah of Kibbutz Buchenwald. Despite the steadily worsening situation for Jews in Germany under the Nazi regime, some agricultural training farms (e.g., Ahlem, Gehringsdorf, Ahrendrof, and Gross Breesen) remained open even after the beginning of the war. Many of these were converted into forced labor camps by 1941. For more on this topic, see Eliyahu Kuti Zelinger, *Lamrot ha-kol: tenu'ot ha-no'ar ha-halutsiyot be-Germanyah ba-shanim 1933–1943* [Despite Everything: Pioneering Youth Movements in Germany in the Years 1933–43] (Giv'at Havivah: Yad Ya'ari, 1998). See also Francis R. Nicosia, "Jewish Farmers in Hitler's Germany: Zionist Occupational Retraining and Nazi 'Jewish Policy,'" *Holocaust Genocide Studies* 19 (2005): 365–89.

28. Letter from Arthur Posnansky to Nathan Schwalb, May 22, 1945, Haganah Archives, Ha'apalah Project, 123/Maccabi/12, p. 83 (in German).

29. Kibbutz Buchenwald diary, in Leo Schwarz, *The Root and the Bough: The Epic of an Enduring People* (New York: Rinehart, 1949), 310–11.

30. Baumel, *Kibbutz Buchenwald*, 22, 27.

31. Arthur Posnansky, "Bericht ueber die bisheige Entwicklung des Kibbutz Buchenwald," September 19, 1945 (Archion Ha-avodah ve-He-halutz, Hativah A 37 III, Folder 43b), in Ada Schein, "Ma'arehet ha-hinukh be-mahanot ha-'akurim ha-yehudiyim be-Germanyah ube-Austryah, 1945–1951" (PhD dissertation, Hebrew University, 2001), 162.

32. "We have still not lost hope," from the Zionist anthem "HaTikvah," in *Nitzotz*, in Kaufering Camp, Yad Vashem, M-1P, She'erit Hapletah Collection, Folder 24; see no. 3 (38), Chanukah, 1944–45.

33. See Tsemach Tsamriyon, *The Press of the Jewish Holocaust Survivors in Germany As an Expression of Their Problems* (Hebrew) (Tel Aviv: Irgun She'erit HaPletah Mehe-Ezor HaBrit, Bi-Yisrael, 1970).

34. Shlomo Frankel went on to be active in the flourishing DP press, continuing to edit *Nitzotz* after liberation and then *Das Wort*. See Ze'ev Mankowitz, *Life between Memory and Hope: The Survivors of the Holocaust in Occupied Germany* (Cambridge: Cambridge University Press, 2002), 347.

35. See Mankowitz, *Life between Memory and Hope*, 36, and "The Formation of She'erit Hapletah," 336–70. Samuel Gringauz was born in East Prussia at the turn of the century. He was deported from Kovno to Dachau in August 1944, was active in the Zionist underground in Kaufering, and was liberated with the group near

Schwabenhausen at the end of April 1945 (Mankowitz, *Life between Memory and Hope*, 174). Grinberg was a doctor who had studied medicine in Switzerland.

36. Dr. Zalman Grinberg, "Bericht an den Juedischen Weltkongress," May 31, 1945, YIVO, DP Germany, MK 483, Reel 21.

37. Mankowitz, *Life between Memory and Hope*, 31. For a transcript of the speech given by Zalman Grinberg at St. Ottilien on May 27, 1945, see YIVO, LS, MK 488, Roll 13, Folder 104, pp. 10–14. In the speech, Grinberg also recounts his experiences in the Kovno ghetto and his deportation to Germany.

38. YIVO, DP Germany, MK 483, Reel 21. Dr. Zalman Grinburg, "Appel an den judischen Weltkongress," St. Ottilien, May 31, 1945.

39. The Committee of Pioneering Youth in Buchenwald (Signed: Jochanan Goldkranz, Aron Feldberg, Tuwiah Kaminsky, Israel W.) to Nathan Schwalb in He-Halutz Geneva office, June 7, 1945 (HAHP, 123/Maccabi/12), p. 82 (in German), from Kibbutz HaMeuchad archive (Group 2, Container 21, Folder 121). The term *yevseksim* refers to the Jewish communist organization Yevsektsiya, established in the Soviet Union from 1918 to 1930.

40. Ibid.

41. Letter from M. Winogrodzki (Dachau) to He-Halutz world headquarters in Geneva, June 18, 1945, HAHP, 123/Maccabi/0012, Box 20, Folder 4, letters to Nathan Schwalb in He-Halutz Geneva Office, pp. 88–89.

42. Zionist youths who organized themselves in the French zone of Germany also noted the slow arrival of any outside Zionist group. Letter from Konstanz to Schwalb, signed by Gina Gutgold, Richard Rechen, and Henryk Prusak, July 26, 1945, HAHP, 123/Maccabi/0012, Box 20, Folder 4, letters to Nathan Schwalb in He-Halutz Geneva Office, p. 98.

43. Mankowitz, *Life between Memory and Hope*, 40–41.

44. Ratner to Zionist Executive in Jerusalem, June 9, 1945, CZA, S5/829. See in Mankowitz, "The Formation of She'erit Hapletah," 357. Bauer, *Out of the Ashes*, 39, writes that Ratner formed the Zionist group in Bavaria while he was still in a hospital bed.

45. Mankowitz, "The Formation of She'erit Hapletah," 357.

46. In ibid., 359–60; quoted from "Declaration of the Zionist Congress in Munich, Bavaria, June 25, 1945," in Z. Herring, *Between Destruction and Redemption: Struggle for the Holocaust Survivors* (Yiddish).

47. For more on the early efforts of the JDC to gain access to the DP camps, see Bauer, *Out of the Ashes*.

48. Shlomo Lazarovitch, June 6, 1945. Kibbutz Buchenwald diary, in Schwarz, *The Root and the Bough*, 312. Presumably, Lazarovitch is able to write this once the situation in Buchenwald has stabilized somewhat. Nonetheless, his references

to a life of "comparative ease" and "plenty of food" are curious unless they are understood as standing in contrast to what he perceived to be the difficult labor of establishing a farm in postwar Germany, thus demonstrating the DPs' value as Zionist pioneers.

49. Baumel, *Kibbutz Buchenwald*, 27.

50. Avram Gotlieb, June 9, 1945, Kibbutz Buchenwald diary, in Schwarz, *The Root and the Bough*, 314.

51. Baumel, *Kibbutz Buchenwald*, 25.

52. Hayim-Meir Gotlieb, June 21, 1945, Kibbutz Buchenwald diary, in Schwarz, *The Root and the Bough*, 315–16.

53. Baumel, *Kibbutz Buchenwald*, chap. 3.

54. Ibid., 44.

55. July 17, 1945, Kibbutz Buchenwald diary, in Schwarz, *The Root and the Bough*, 319–20. At the time, the kibbutz was also visited by several members of the JDC, including the director, Dr. Joseph Schwartz. Noting their monthly budget deficit of five thousand marks, Schwartz promised to help them maintain kibbutz functioning. See Baumel, *Kibbutz Buchenwald*, 49.

56. Baumel, *Kibbutz Buchenwald*, 48. Baumel also notes that tension developed between the German-born leaders of the kibbutz and those members of Polish origin who felt discriminated against by the *yekkim* (German Jews) who "act as if they are the masters and we are the workers in some work camp or other." Kibbutz diary, July 12, 1945, in Baumel, *Kibbutz Buchenwald*, 46–47.

57. July 21, 1945, Kibbutz Buchenwald diary, in Schwarz, *The Root and the Bough*, 322, and Baumel, *Kibbutz Buchenwald*, 49.

58. Schwarz, *The Root and the Bough*, 322.

59. July 21, 1945, Kibbutz Buchenwald diary, in Schwarz, *The Root and the Bough*, 324.

60. The Jewish Brigade was a Jewish military unit, composed mainly of Jews from Palestine, that served in World War II in the British Army. At the conclusion of the war the Jewish Brigade was stationed in northeastern Italy, where its soldiers first came into contact with survivors of the Holocaust. See Yoav Gelber, "The Meeting between the Jewish Soldiers from Palestine Serving in the British Army and *She'erit Hapletah*," in *She'erit Hapletah, 1944–1948*, edited by Yisrael Gutman and Avital Saf, 60–80 (Jerusalem: Yad Vashem, 1990).

61. YIVO, MK 488, Leo Schwarz Papers, Roll 15, Folder 135, pp. 557–58: meeting in Feldafing on July 1, 1945, to discuss organization of the Central Committee (among those present were Klausner, Kaspy from the Jewish Brigade, and Zalman Grinberg). It must be noted that some dissenting voices argued that not all surviving Jews desired to live in Palestine and that the Executive must in a "better

future fight not only for those Jews who desire to go to Palestine, but for all the other living Jews."

62. By and large, the pioneering Zionist youth movements targeted those under the age of twenty-five as the ideal pioneering material, although many kibbutzim included members who were over the age of twenty-five and often in their early thirties. Jechezkel Tydor, at the age of forty-two, reflects the need to have a broader definition of the term "youth."

63. Grobman, *Rekindling the Flame*, 72. Harrison was also the former U.S. commissioner of immigration and the U.S. representative on the Intergovernmental Committee on Refugees.

64. Kochavi, *Post-Holocaust Politics*, 89; Dinnerstein, *America and the Survivors of the Holocaust*, chap. 2.

65. Protocol, July 14, 1945, meeting of Executive Committee YIVO, MK 488, Leo Schwarz Papers, Roll 15, p. 141.

66. YIVO, DP Germany, MK 483, Reel 61, frame 721–27.

67. See YIVO, DP Germany, MK 483, Reel 61, frame 727.

68. The language of productivization was not new; see the interwar model of kibbutz hakhsharah as discussed in Oppenheim, *The Struggle of Jewish Youth for Productivization*.

69. YIVO, DP Germany, MK 483, Reel 61, frame 721–27.

70. At the Central Committee meeting of August 8, the JDC representative apologized for their late arrival in the camp, explaining that their presence had not been made legal by the U.S. Army until July 30. See protocol of the meeting of Liberated Jews in Bavaria (August 8, 1945, 15:00), YIVO, MK 488, Leo Schwarz Papers, Roll 15, 135, p. 581 (my emphasis). For more on Olejski, see note 91 below.

71. Baumel, *Kibbutz Buchenwald*, 50.

72. Interviews with Baumel, March 30, 1983, and June 4, 1983, quoted in Baumel, *Kibbutz Buchenwald*, 51.

73. Ibid.

74. August 5, 1945, entry, Kibbutz Buchenwald diary, in Schwarz, *The Root and the Bough*, 325.

75. September 2, 1945, Kibbutz Buchenwald diary, in Schwarz, *The Root and the Bough*, 329. Upon reaching the French port, the group discovered that only seventy-eight certificates were available. The other two members were able to reach Palestine by other means.

76. See Judith Tydor Baumel, "Kibbutz Buchenwald and Kibbutz Hafetz Hayyim: Two Experiments in the Rehabilitation of Jewish Survivors in Germany," *Holocaust and Genocide Studies* 9 (1995): 231–49. Poalei Agudat Israel was established as an organization of Haredi workers in Poland in 1922. After the war, the movement

was organized in the DP camps as a religious youth organization with a decided orientation toward settlement in the Land of Israel, a direction that garnered it considerable support among Haredi youths in the DP camps. See Yehoyakim Cochavi, *Shoresh le-'Akurim: Tnu' ot ha-No'ar be-Mahanot ha-'Akurim be-Germanyah, 1945–1949* (Giv'at Havivah: Yad Ya'ari, 1999), 172. The movement also eventually maintained a central leadership and a movement newspaper, *Ba-Derekh* (On the Way). See YIVO, Jewish DP Periodicals, Reel 30.

77. Baumel, *Kibbutz Buchenwald*, 121. Nocham (No'ar Chalutzi Meuchad, or United Pioneering Youth) was the Zionist youth movement created in the DP camps of Germany.

78. Protocol of the meeting of Liberated Jews in Bavaria (August 8, 1945, 15:00), YIVO, MK 488, Leo Schwarz Papers, Roll 15, 135, p. 581.

79. Ibid. Schalitan, who later changed his name to Shalit, was also the author of *Azoy zaynen mir geshtorbn* (Munich, 1949) on the destruction of the Jewish community of Shavli (Siauliai) in Lithuania.

80. Ibid. Melamed would go on to become a member of the Knesset after moving to Israel.

81. YIVO, MK488, Leo Schwarz Papers, Roll 15, Folder 135, p. 581; protocol of the meeting of Liberated Jews in Bavaria (August 8, 1945, 15:00).

82. Schein's "Ma'arehet ha-hinukh," her dissertation on educational institutions in the DP camps, defines the work of the Zionist groups as informal education frameworks, paralleling the development of more formal educational institutions in the DP camps.

83. Letter from Zionist organization in Bavaria to the Central Committee of Liberated Jews in Bavaria, July 28, 1945; from Schein, "Ma'arehet ha-hinukh," 162.

84. Letter from Ratner to Aliyah Deptartment, CZA, S6/1911, August 10, 1945.

85. Letter from Zionist center in Bavaria to Jewish Agency, August 10, 1945, CZA, S6/3657. The letter seems to suggest that Nocham was already in existence by early August.

86. This call for unity was in response to the division that existed between the kibbutz movements in Palestine and their youth movements there and in the Diaspora. The two main kibbutz movements in Palestine were Kibbutz Ha-Artzi (the National Kibbutz movement founded in 1927) and Ha-Kibbutz Ha-Me'uhad (the United Kibbutz Movement founded in 1927). Hashomer Hatzair was the youth movement of the National Kibbutz movement; Dror and Gordoniah were affiliated with the United Kibbutz movement. While the early leaders of the youth movements in postwar Europe strove for unity following liberation, the leaders of the movements in Palestine feared such unity, which could dilute and confuse the potential

membership reservoir for the kibbutz movements organized among the youth movement groups in Europe.

87. See Schein, "Ma'arehet ha-hinukh," 163.

88. See Pratei Kol of First Zionist Conference in Frankfurt, October 23–24, 1945, Yad Vashem Archives, MP 1, Folder 3. Yehoyakim Cochavi, *Shoresh le-'Akurim*, 34–36, sees the strong influence of the Jewish Brigade in the resolutions of Nocham and suggests that the socialist language led to later divisions with nonsocialist Zionists from Poland. He proposes that Jewish Brigade soldiers also paid special attention to the question of the youths, as many of them were formerly active in Yishuv youth movements.

89. Harrison report to Truman, August 24, 1945. See treatments in Kochavi, *Post-Holocaust Politics*, 89, and Dinnerstein, *America and the Survivors of the Holocaust*, chap. 2.

90. Judah Nadich was appointed to this post on August 24, 1945. See Kochavi, *Post-Holocaust Politics*, 93. Nadich was replaced as special adviser after three months by Judge Simon Rifkind.

91. Mankowitz, *Life between Memory and Hope*, 132. Jacob Olejski was interviewed by the psychologist and sociologist David Boder, who journeyed to Europe after the war and made voice recordings of his interviews with Holocaust survivors. The Olejski interview can be found on spools 54 and 209 of the Boder collection at Illinois Institute of Technology and the United States Holocaust Memorial Museum. A transcript of the Olejski interview, conducted in Paris at the Grand Hotel, August 20, 1946, can also be found on the Web site "Voices of the Holocaust" (http://voices.iit.edu) created by the Illinois Institute of Technology, where Boder was on faculty. In the interview, Olejski describes his work with ORT and the DPs, conditions in Landsberg, and his assessments of the nature of the DP population. See also Donald Niewyk, ed., *Fresh Wounds: Early Narratives of Holocaust Survival* (Chapel Hill: University of North Carolina Press, 1998). ORT was founded in Russia in 1880. The name was coined from the acronym of the Russian words *Obshestvo Remeslenofo zemledelcheskofo Truda* (Society for Trades and Agricultural Labor).

92. *Landsberger Lager Cajtung*, vol. 2, October 20, 1945, in YIVO, Jewish DP Periodicals Collection, Reel 1 (my emphasis).

93. The call was issued in Landsberg on October 22, 1945, and published in the *Landsberger Lager Cajtung*, vol. 3, on October 28, 1945, in YIVO, Jewish DP Periodicals Collection, Reel 1. The term *mentsz* (as spelled in the text) can be translated as "human being" or "man." While in the context the term seems to be gender neutral, the call to the youths is addressed to "Jugntleche—jinglech un mejdlech!" (young men and women), a clear address to both genders. Thus, the task of building Palestine was seen as equally incumbent on both young males and females.

94. *Landsberger Lager Cajtung,* vol. 2, October 20, 1945. Various courses were taught at the Folks University including ones on philosophy, biology, history, the history of the Jewish labor movement, the history of Zionism, and sociology. In the October 28, 1945, volume of the *Landsberger Lager Cajtung,* vol. 3, Olejski described the People's University as already having approximately two hundred students.

95. *Landsberger Lager Cajtung,* vol. 1, October 8, 1945, p. 3, YIVO, Jewish DP Periodicals, Reel 1. For a thorough analysis of Gringauz's ideology, see Mankowitz, *Life between Memory and Hope,* chap. 8. The verse "Nikmat dam jeled hakatan od lobarah hasatan" [Satan has not yet created a fitting revenge for the blood of a small child] is taken from the Haim Nachman Bialik poem "'Al ha-Shehitah," written in 1903.

96. From Jacob Olejski: "A few words to the Youth of the She'erit Hapletah," *LLC* no. 10, December 14, 1945.

97. First Conference of the UZO, October 23–24, 1945, Yad Vashem, MP 1, Folder 3.

98. While there are no detailed demographic statistics for October 1945, by February 1946 there were some 12,268 Jewish youths between the ages of fifteen and twenty-four in Bavaria (40.5 percent). This meant that the 1,200 cited by Cohen in October 1945, before the beginnings of infiltration by Polish Jews, constituted at least 10 percent of DP youths organized formally in kibbutzim, if not more. YIVO, MK 488, Leo Schwarz Papers, Roll 9, Folder 57, p. 580.

99. First Conference of the UZO, October 23–24, 1945, Yad Vashem, MP 1, Folder 3.

100. For the UZO conference, see Frankfurt am Main, October 24, 1945, Yad Vashem, MP 1, Folder 3. As D. Cohen reported on Landsberg at the end of October, "We have four kibbutzim with many activities and cultural life; only the members of the kibbutzim participate in the vocational schools."

101. Gad Beck was a member of a Zionist youth movement before the war who managed to survive the war in hiding, living underground in Berlin as both a Jew and a homosexual. See his memoirs, *An Underground Life: Memoirs of a Gay Jew in Nazi Berlin* (Madison: University of Wisconsin Press, 1999).

102. Yad Vashem, MP 1, Folder 3.

103. Gad Beck to Nathan Schwalb, November 15, 1945, Lavon Institute Labor Archives, III-37A-1, Folder 43a, pp. 36–37.

104. *Landsberger Lager Cajtung,* November 4, 1945, no. 4(8), YIVO, Jewish DP Periodicals, Roll 1.

105. Based on a letter from Schwalb to the Hakhsharah and Aliyah Departments, November 12, 1945, Avodah and Hehalutz Archive, Hativah 37aIII, Folder 5, 43a, p. 34.

106. Chaim Cohen to Jewish Agency, December 25, 1945, Central Zionist Archives, S25/5332; see in Schein, "Ma'arehet ha-hinukh," 170. Nocham responsibilities based on letter from Schwalb to hakhsharah and aliyah deptartments, November 12, 1945, Avodah and Hehalutz archive, Hativah 37aIII, Folder 5.

107. CZA, L58/637, Germany, correspondence with the Jewish Agency and other agencies in Germany, November 11, 1945: request from Akiba Lewinsky (Child and Youth Immigration Department, Jerusalem) to Gad Beck (Zionist Center, Hakhsharah and Aliyah Department, Munich).

108. YIVO, DP Germany, MK 483, Roll 1, Folder 2 or 3, pp. 313–14 (Yiddish in Hebrew letters), and Roll 4, 46, p. 969 (Latin).

109. Joseph Levine (JDC) to Mr. Eli Rock (field supervisor, JDC), October 20, 1945, Schwandorf, Germany, YIVO, MK 488, Leo Schwarz Papers, Roll 16, Folder 148, p. 1046. For more on Eli Rock, see his oral history interview at the United States Holocaust Memorial Museum Archives, RG-50.030*0386.

110. YIVO, MK 488, Leo Schwarz Papers, Roll 1, 11, p. 1254.

111. YIVO, MK 488, Leo Schwarz Papers, Roll 1, 11, p. 1255.

112. Ibid.

113. See letter from Rock to Rifkind, November 8, 1945, YIVO, MK 488, Leo Schwarz Papers, Roll, 9, p. 63.

114. This was the case, for example, with Kibbutz Tosia Altman (to be discussed in chapter 2) and as noted in Irving Heymont, *Among the Survivors of the Holocaust: The Landsberg DP Camp Letters of Major Irving Heymont* (Cincinnati: American Jewish Archives, 1982), 85. With the infiltration of Jews into the American zone, Major Heymont, the American commander of the Landsberg DP camp, became convinced that Landsberg "is a stop on this modern underground railroad."

115. Kochavi, *Post-Holocaust Politics*, 134.

116. Ibid.

117. YIVO, MK 488, Leo Schwarz Papers, Roll 1, 11, 1306, Report of JDC activities, Western Military District, August 1–October 15, 1945.

118. American Jewish Historical Society (AJHS), I-249, NJWB-Military Chaplaincy Records, Box 22, Folder 141.

119. Grobman, *Rekindling the Flame*, 91. Grobman notes that the farm was also opened as a result of assistance received from Anne Liepah of the JDC.

120. Heymont, letter 19, October 22, 1945, in *Among the Survivors of the Holocaust*, 65 (my emphasis).

121. Judah Nadich, *Eisenhower and the Jews* (New York: Twayne, 1953), 231. See also the description of Ben-Gurion's visit to Landsberg in the *Landsberger Lager Cajtung*, vol. 3, October 28, 1945, p. 1.

122. Nadich, *Eisenhower and the Jews*, 233.

123. Ibid.

124. Kochavi, *Post-Holocaust Politics*, 134.

125. See Meir Avizohar, "Bikur Ben-Gurion be-mahanot ha-'akurim ve-tefisato ha-leumit be-tom Milhemet ha-'Olam ha-Sheniah" [Ben-Gurion's Visit to the DP Camps and His National Outlook in the Aftermath of Word War II], in *Yahadut Mizrach Eiropah Bein Shoah Le-tekuma 1944–1948*, edited by Benjamin Pinkus, 260 (Sde Boker: Ben-Gurion University, 1987). See also as described in Kochavi, *Post-Holocaust Politics*, 94, and Nadich, *Eisenhower and the Jews*, 238. Much of this report is based on Ben-Gurion Archives, Ben-Gurion's report of his visit to the DP camps, diary entry of November 6, 1945, in Kochavi and Avizohar. As has been noted elsewhere, Ben-Gurion's diary entries were often written with the conscious knowledge that they would eventually be read by others for historical purposes. Still, his description of the visit to the DP camps is valuable for his perception of the DP population and their value in his diplomatic goals.

126. This idea, it was feared, would arouse both Jewish and German opposition. Judge Rifkind (Eisenhower's new special adviser) doubted that all Jews would want to be in one location. Rifkind also believed that Jews would have to live among Germans because there were certain tasks that Jews would refuse to do. (Avizohar, "Bikur Ben-Gurion," 261).

127. Heymont, letter 19, October 22, 1945, in *Among the Survivors of the Holocaust*, 66. It is clear than Ben-Gurion's attitude toward the Jewish survivors betrayed an instrumentalist view of them, on the one hand needing to tend to people who were not capable of caring for themselves and on the other hand maximizing the value of the Jewish survivors for the benefit of the Yishuv. In the same letter, Heymont noted a revealing comment by Ben-Gurion in his discussions with some of the Jewish DPs at the camp. "He [Ben-Gurion] could not understand why the people were reluctant to move after I explained the overcrowded conditions and our efforts to get them to move to Föhrenwald. We went on a tour of the camp, and I took him to the worst buildings first. On seeing the overcrowding, he asked some of the people why they do not want to move to Föhrenwald. After listening to their replies he commented to me, 'It is a long and hard struggle to overcome their psychology.'" Before his departure from Landsberg, Heymont reported that "When he left, he commented that he clearly understood our problems and remarked, 'In Palestine too we have comparable problems. A voyage on a boat does not transform people.'"

128. Nadich, *Eisenhower and the Jews*, 137.

129. YIVO, MK 488, Leo Schwarz Papers, Roll 16, pp. 1077–81. The JDC reported on efforts to acquire land for hakhsharot as early as October 5, 1945, but found difficulties due to lack of understanding from U.S. Army and military gov-

ernment officials. See also LS 16, 146, p. 231, JDC report on Schweikelburg, Benedictine Monastery (October 19, 1945) and LS 16, p. 232 (November 12, 1945), report on the Herzogsaegmuehle farm school for Hachsharah.

130. Mankowitz, *Life between Memory and Hope*, 146, based on report of G. H. Muentz in YIVO, MK 488, Leo Schwarz Papers, Roll 16, Folder 159, pp. 1108–21.

131. YIVO, MK 488, Leo Schwarz Papers, Roll 10, 65, pp. 7–15.

132. YIVO, MK 488, Leo Schwarz Papers, Roll 16, p. 1079, Munich, October 21, 1945.

133. YIVO, MK 488, Leo Schwarz Papers, Roll 16, p. 1080.

134. YIVO, MK 488, Leo Schwarz Papers, Roll 10, 65, p. 15.

135. YIVO, MK 488, Leo Schwarz Papers, Roll 16, p. 1094, date unclear (perhaps December 27, 1945).

136. In the early period following the end of the war in Germany, the U.S. military government was most concerned with de-cartellization, industrial disarmament, denazification, and democratization. By 1946, however, U.S. priorities had shifted to anticommunism and capitalist economic reconstruction. For a thorough treatment of this topic, see Rebecca L. Boehling, *A Question of Priorities: Democratic Reforms and Economic Recovery in Postwar Germany* (Providence, RI: Berghahn, 1996).

137. Heymont, *Among the Survivors*, 162, reported that Greifenberg was secured on November 17, 1945.

138. YIVO, MK 488, Leo Schwarz Papers, Roll 1, Folder 11, p. 1303, October 31, 1945, Saul S. Elgart, senior field representative, report of JDC activities, Western Military District, August 1–October 15, 1945.

139. *Landsberger Lager Cajtung*, no. 11, December 21, 1945, Baruch Cheta, 4, YIVO Jewish DP Periodicals, Reel 1-1.

140. Jim Tobias, *Der Kibbuz auf dem Streicher-Hof: Die vergessene Geschichte der judischen Kollektivfarmen, 1945–1948* (Nurnberg: Dahlingen und Fuchs, 1997), 41.

141. *Landsberger Lager Cajtung*, no. 11, December 21, 1945, Baruch Chita, 4, YIVO Jewish DP Periodicals, Reel 1-1.

142. M. J. Joslow (JDC), Educational Survey, Greifenberg, January 1946, YIVO, MK 483, DP Germany, Reel 107, File 1503.

143. YIVO, MK 488, Leo Schwarz Papers, LS 16, p. 1079, October 21, 1945.

144. YIVO, DP Germany, MK 483, Roll 1, Folder 2 or 3, pp. 313–14 (Yiddish in Hebrew letters), and Roll 4, 46, p. 969. Other statistics gathered by the JDC recorded 8 hakhsharot with 870 inhabitants at the end of April. The discrepancy is perhaps explained by differing definitions of what constituted a kibbutz and a hakhsharah. For the JDC survey of hakhsharot in the U.S. zone on January 27, 1946, see YIVO, LS 9, 57, p. 576.

145. *Nitzotz* no. 8(53), January 21, 1946, Haganah Archives, Ha'aplah Project, 123/Maccabi/148.

146. Ibid. A summary of the January 21, 1946, seminar in Greifenberg appeared in the newspaper and included the topics of the lectures delivered to the fifty-eight male and female participants.

147. *Nitzotz* no. 8(53), January 21, 1946, Haganah Archives, Ha'apalah Project, 123/Maccabi/148.

148. YIVO, Leo Schwarz Papers, Roll 8, p. 1032–37. Jacob Trobe of the JDC summarized the situation of the Jewish DPs in Germany at the end of 1945, highlighting overwhelming Zionist enthusiasm but continuing concerns over disillusionment, lack of food and clothing, and idleness that could lead to black market activity.

149. See YIVO, MK 488, Leo Schwarz Papers, Roll 8, pp. 1032–37.

Chapter 2

1. See the table in Yochanan Cohen, *Ovrim kol Gvul: HaBrichah, Polin 1945–1946* (Tel Aviv: Zmora-Bitan, 1995), 469n90.

2. See, for example, in Haganah Archives, Ha'apalah Project, 123/Maccabi .0014, pp. 66–72, and Central Zionist Archives, S32/220.

3. Cohen, *Ovrim kol Gvul*; Yitzhak Zuckerman, *Yetziat Polin: 'al ha-Berichah ve-'al Shikum ha-Tnu'ah ha-Halutzit* [Exodus from Poland: On the Bricha and the Reestablishment of the Pioneering Movement], (Israel: Bet Lochamei Ha-Getaot, 1988); Shlomo Kless, Kless, *Be-Derekh Lo Slula: Toldot ha-Berihah, 1944–1948* [On an Unpaved Path: The History of the Bricha, 1944–1948] (Giv'at Havivah: Moreshet, 1994); Efraim Dekel, *Be-Netivei Ha-Brichah* [On the Path of the Brichah] (Tel Aviv: Ma'arachot, 1959); Shalom (Stefan) Grajek, *Ha-Ma'avak 'Al Hemshekh Ha-Hayyim: Yehudei Polin, 1945–1949* [The Struggle to Continue Life: The Jews of Poland in the Years 1945–1949] (Tel Aviv: Am Oved, 1989). See also Yehuda Bauer, *Flight and Rescue: Bricha* (New York: Random House, 1970).

4. From the preface to the diary, Shlomo Shaltiel, ed., *HaYoman: Yomano shel Kibbutz HaShomer HaTzair Lochamei HaGetaot al Shem Tosia Altman*. Giv'at Haviva: Yad Ya'ari, 1997.

5. See most notably Israel Oppenheim, *The Struggle of Jewish Youth for Productivization: The Zionist Youth Movement in Poland* (Boulder, CO: East European Monographs, 1989).

6. For more on Lublin after liberation, see Lucjan Dobroszycki, *Survivors of the Holocaust in Poland: A Portrait Based on Jewish Community Records, 1944–1947* (Armonk, NY: Sharpe, 1994), 3–4. See also Bauer, *Flight and Rescue*, and David

Engel, *Ben Shikhrur Li-Verihah: Nitsolei ha-Shoah be-Polin veha-ma'avak 'al Han-hagatam, 1944–1946* [Between Liberation and Flight: Holocaust Survivors in Poland and the Struggle for Leadership, 1944–1947] (Tel Aviv: Am Oved, 1996).

7. M. Szildkrojt, "Ven Lublin iz Bafrayt Gevoren," in *Dos Bukh fun Lublin: Zikhroynes, gvies-eydes un materialn iber lebn, kamf un martirertum fun lubliner yidishn yishev,* 599–600 (Paris: Paris Committee for the Creation of a Monograph on the Jewish Community of Lublin, 1952). The Peretz-hoyz was a Jewish communal center that had been built in Lublin before the war. After the war it became an immediate shelter for Jewish survivors who gathered in Lublin.

8. It is difficult to estimate the total number of Polish Jews who survived the Holocaust. The CKZP, the first official body representing Polish Jewry, registered seventy thousand Jews on liberated Polish territory on June 5, 1945; see Natalia Aleksiun, "Where Was There a Future for Polish Jewry? Bundist and Zionist Polemics in Post-World War II Poland," in Jack Jacobs, ed., *Jewish Politics in Eastern Europe: The Bund at 100* (New York: New York University Press, 2001), 227. During 1946 a large wave of repatriates from the Soviet Union returned to Poland (perhaps 130,000 Jews), leading the CKZP to estimate a total of 240,000 Jews in Poland in mid-1946. The constant emigration of Jews out of Poland made this number considerably less, however, with 90,000 Jews remaining in Poland by the spring of 1947 according to Aleksiun; see also *American Jewish Year Book* (Philadelphia: American Jewish Committee, 1950).

9. "The Situation of the Jews in Liberated Poland," Report from Jerusalem, Jewish Agency, March 23, 1945, Ha'apalah Project, Haganah Archives (Gordonia/Maccabi Tzair Archives, 3/111). The document is a summary of reports from Lublin in January 1945.

10. Engel, *Ben Shikhrur Li-Verihah,* 203–4n221. Engel suggests that on the basis of various Jewish community and youth movement reports, we can estimate that there were eight thousand Jewish youths in Poland in November 1945.

11. Aleksiun, "Where Was There a Future for Polish Jewry?" 228.

12. Ibid.

13. See Engel, *Ben Shikhrur Li-Verihah,* 73.

14. Ibid. See also Lucjan Dobroszycki, "Restoring Jewish Life in Postwar Poland" (1974, YIVO, 9/73698); Hana Shlomi, "Hitargenut shel Sridei ha-Yehudim be-Polin le-Achar Milchemet Ha-Olam ha-Sheniyah, 1944–1950," in *Kiyum Va-Shever: Yehudei Polin Le-Doroteihem,* edited by Israel Bartal and Yisrael Gutman, 523–48 (Jerusalem: Merkaz Zalman Shazar, 1997), and Aleksiun, "Where Was There a Future for Polish Jewry?"

15. David Engel, "The Reconstruction of Jewish Communal Institutions in Postwar Poland: The Origins of the Central Committee of Polish Jews, 1944–1945."

East European Politics and Societies 10 (1996): 85–107. See also Dobroszycki, "Restoring Jewish Life in Postwar Poland," 4. The Sejm was the interwar Polish parliament.

16. During 1944–46, Zionists were the majority in the CKZP, "undoubtedly a true indication of the mood of the people in Poland at that time" (Dobroszycki, "Restoring Jewish Life in Postwar Poland," 5). By 1946 the CKZP consisted of thirteen Zionists (three Ichud, three Poalei Tsiyon Right, three Poalei Tsiyon Smol, one Hashomer Hatzair, two Hechalutz, one Jewish Fighting Organization), four Bundists, six communists, and two members from the Union of Jewish Partisans.

17. Aleksiun, "Where Was There a Future for Polish Jewry?" 229. Nonetheless, the Zionists themselves did not compose one unified camp.

18. Engel, *Ben Shikhrur Li-Verihah*, 72–73, 82–84; see also Nachum Bogner, *Be-hasdei Zarim: Hatzalat Yeladim be-Zehut Sheulah be-Polin* (Jerusalem: Yad Vashem, 2000), 229. Bogner suggests that the children's homes were more likely to emphasize Polish language and some degree of assimilation.

19. Bogner, *Be-hasdei Zarim*, 229. With the large waves of repatriation from the Soviet Union, by the end of 1946 another fifty-four dormitories for Jewish children were established, housing a total of thirty-eight hundred children.

20. Engel, *Ben Shikhrur Li-Verihah*, 81.

21. Ibid., 82; Aleksiun, "Where Was There a Future for Polish Jewry?" 231–32. According to Engel, these debates with the Bund and the Polish Workers' Party on the Jewish committees only served to legitimize the Zionist groups in the eyes of the Jewish public (Engel, *Ben Shikhrur Li-Verihah*, 103).

22. Bogner, *Be-hasdei Zarim*, 204. As Bogner describes, however, in late 1945 and 1946 there was still a tremendous number of Jewish children in the hands of Polish rescuers who refused to give them up with the conclusion of the war. Whenever possible, the CKZP and local Jewish committees sought to return of Jewish orphans to Jewish society. This generally entailed a financial transaction to convince Polish rescuers to return Jewish children. While the CKZP was frequently constrained by the need to function within the bounds of legality due to its precarious position vis-à-vis the Polish government, other groups, such as Zionist youth movements, enjoyed much greater flexibility in their efforts to redeem Jewish children.

23. Engel, *Ben Shikhrur Li-Verihah*, 66.

24. See Engel, *Ben Shikhrur Li-Verihah*, and Asher Cohen and Yehoyakim Cochavi, eds., *Zionist Youth Movements during the Shoah* (New York: Peter Lang), 1995.

25. Aharon Weiss, "Youth Movements in Poland during the German Occupation," in *Zionist Youth Movements during the Shoah*, edited by Asher Cohen and Yehoyakim Cochavi, 227–44 (New York: Peter Lang, 1995). These leaders who left include Moshe Kleinbaum (Sneh), Apolinary Hartglass and Moshe Kerner (General Zionists), Heinryk Erlich and Victor Alter (Bund), Anshel Reiss (Poalei Zion), Y. Lev

and Nathan Buxbaum (PZ Smol), Zerach Warhaftig and Avraham Weiss (Mizrachi), Yitzhak Meir Levin (Agudes Yisroel), and Menachem Begin (Betar).

26. Weiss, "Youth Movements in Poland during the German Occupation," 233.

27. Ibid. See also Rivka Perlis, "Tnu'ot ha-Noar ha-Halutziot be-Polin ha-kvusha bi-yedei ha-Natzim" (PhD dissertation, Hebrew University, 1982), 106–7; Weiss, "Youth Movements in Poland during the German Occupation," 235.

28. See also Weiss, "Jewish Leadership in Occupied Poland," *Yad Vashem Studies* 10 (1977): 335–65.

29. On the kibbutz of Dror, see Zivia Lubetkin, *Biyemei Kilayon U-Mered* (Tel Aviv: Ha-Kibbutz Ha-Meuhad, 1989), 49–52; other ghetto diaries also describe youth movement activities. See, for example, Hermann Kruk, *The Last Days of the Jerusalem of Lithuania: Chronicles from the Vilna Ghetto and the Camps, 1939–1944* (New York: Yale University Press, 2003). Yisrael Gutman also describes kibbutz activity in the ghettos; see his *The Jews of Warsaw, 1939–1943: Ghetto, Underground, Revolt* (Bloomington: Indiana University Press, 1982). Tikva Fatal-Knaani, *Zo Lo Otah Grodno: Kehilat Grodno ve-Svivatah be-Milhamah uve-Shoah, 1939–1943* (Jerusalem: Yad Vashem, 2001), 227–40, discusses the efforts of the youth movements in Grodno to maintain underground activities in a comparatively smaller ghetto.

30. Weiss, "Youth Movements in Poland during the German Occupation," 238.

31. From M. Neustadt and *Hashomer Hatzair* newspaper, YIVO Library, vol. 4, July 15, 1946, 11; also in Yitzhak Zuckerman, *Surplus of Memory: Chronicle of the Warsaw Ghetto Uprising* (Berkeley: University of California, 1993). For more on the role of women in resistance activities and as couriers between ghettos in occupied Poland, see Dalia Ofer and Lenore Weitzman, eds., *Women in the Holocaust* (New Haven, CT: Yale University Press, 1998).

32. See Yisrael Gutman, "The Youth Movement As an Alternative Leadership in Eastern Europe," in *Zionist Youth Movements during the Shoah*, edited by Asher Cohen and Yehoyakim Cochavi, 7–116 (New York: Peter Lang, 1995). For example, Zuckerman, Lubetkin, Kaplan, Breslaw, and Anilewicz in Warsaw; Abba Kovner in Vilna; and Chajke Grossman in Bialystok. It should be noted that wartime resistance was not the exclusive province of Zionist youth movements. Bundist and communist Jewish youths, including Abrasha (Abraham) Blum and Marek Edelman of the Bund in Warsaw, played an active role in resistance. Nonetheless, the Bund's attitude to resistance was somewhat equivocal. See Daniel Blatman, *Le-ma'an Heruteinu ve-Herutchem: Ha-Bund be-Polin, 1939–1949* (Jerusalem: Yad Vashem, 1996), 151–200.

33. Gutman, "The Youth Movement As an Alternative Leadership in Eastern Europe," 10–11. According to Dina Porat, "Zionist Pioneering Youth Movements

in Poland and the Attitude to Eretz Israel during the Holocaust," *Polin* 9 (1996): 195–211, during the war Zionist youth movements felt increasingly abandoned by their colleagues in Eretz Israel, with increasing feelings of bitterness toward their friends in Palestine.

34. Weiss, "Youth Movements in Poland during the German Occupation," 239, 240, and 242.

35. Gutman, "The Youth Movement As an Alternative Leadership in Eastern Europe," 15–16; Abba Kovner was among the first to divine the scope of the Nazi Final Solution and its extent beyond Vilna.

36. Ibid., 13.

37. Bauer, *Flight and Rescue*, 10–11.

38. Abba Kovner, "Reshita shel Ha-Bricha ke-tnuah Hamonit be-eduyotav shel Abba Kovner," *Yalkut Moreshet* 37 (1984): 7–31; 38 (1984): 133–46. See also Engel, *Ben Shikhrur Li-Verihah*, 66.

39. Bauer, *Flight and Rescue*, 24–26. These members included Yitzhak Zuckerman and Zivia Lubetkin, commanders in the Warsaw Ghetto Uprising who had recently returned from liberated Warsaw, as well as Abba Kovner, Eliezer Lidovsky, Mordechai Rosman, Shlomo Kless, Nisan Resnik, Stefan Grajek, and Pasha Rajchman.

40. Aryeh Levi Sarid, *Be-Mivchan he-Anut veha-Pdut: Ha-Tnuot Ha-Halutziot be-Polin Ba-Shoah ve-Achareha, 1939–1949* (Tel Aviv: Moreshet, 1997), 198–99; Engel, *Ben Shikhrur Li-Verihah*, 69; Bauer, *Flight and Rescue*, 25.

41. Kovner, "Reshita shel Ha-Bricha ke-tnuah Hamonit be-eduyotav shel Abba Kovner." See also Shalom Cholawski, "Partisans and Ghetto Fighters: An Active Element among *She'erit Hapletah*," in *She'erit Hapletah, 1944–1948: Rehabilitation and Political Struggle*, edited by Yisrael Gutman and Avital Saf (Jerusalem: Yad Vashem, 1990), 250.

42. See Zuckerman, *Yetziat Polin*, 18.

43. Letter of June 20, 1945, from Krakow to Romania, in Zuckerman, *Surplus of Memory*, 592–93; also in Zuckerman, *Yetziat Polin*, 86.

44. Engel, *Ben Shikhrur Li-Verihah*, 67.

45. Ibid., 69.

46. Zuckerman, *Surplus of Memory*, 588.

47. See Engel, *Ben Shikhrur Li-Verihah*, 77; see references in Cohen, *Ovrim kol Gvul*, 198; Grajek, *Ha-Ma'avak 'Al Hemshekh Ha-Hayyim*, 18; Zuckerman, *Yetziat Polin*, 44; Sarid, *Be-Mivchan he-Anut veha-Pdut*, 200, Bogner, *Be-hasdei Zarim*, 226. In some places the address is given as Poznanska #38.

48. As Zuckerman described the meeting in Łódź, there were 163 delegates, 100 guests, and delegates from parties, HeHalutz, and youth movements and from the five kibbutzim in Warsaw, Łódź, Krakow, Sosnowiec, and Bytom. Zuckerman, Let-

ter from Krakow to Bucharest, June 20, 1945, *Yetziat Polin*, 82–83; see also *Surplus of Memory*, 592–93.

49. Engel, *Ben Shikhrur Li-Verihah*, 71.

50. Ibid.

51. National Meeting of Gordoniah and Hitachdut in Poland, June 24, 1945, Haganah Archives, Ha'apalah Project, Gordoniah-Maccabbi Tzair Archives, Huldah, Temporary Symbol, 24.247, Meichal 11, Folder 3.

52. For more on Miriam Yechieli's experiences during the war, see her "Be-vatei keleh Sovyetim (1939–1940)," *Yalkut Moreshet* 26 (1978): 159–86.

53. Miriam Yechieli interview with the author, May 30, 2003. For a similar example, see Yaakov Schwartz, "Ba-Derech Le-Eretz Yisrael," *Yalkut Moreshet* 55 (1993): 233–55. A prewar member of a Hashomer Hatzair hakhsharah in Częstochowaa, Schwartz escaped to Vilna in 1939 and spent the latter half of the war in Tashkent. He returned to Lublin with Shlomo Kless, Mordechai Rosman, and Ben Meiri and worked preparing forged documents for Jews leaving Poland in the Bricha. He led a group of sixty children (aged seven to eleven) from Poland to Germany in 1946 and eventually reached Palestine.

54. Miriam Yechieli interview with the author, May 30, 2003.

55. An educational program for Hashomer Hatzair shlichim and madrichim in the kibbutzim of the movement identified the central characteristics of this "new human material." From Sarid, *Be-Mivchan he-Anut veha-Pdut*, 284–86 (my translation), Hashomer Hatzair Archive (1).2.31, proposal written by S. Weinberg.

56. *Yoman Kibbutz Lochamei HaGettaot al shem Tosia Altman* (hereafter *Yoman KLGTA*), 20 and 42.

57. Haim Shorrer interview with the author, May 29, 2003.

58. *Yoman KLGTA*, 194, and Monish Einhorn interview with author, June 7, 2003.

59. Monish Einhorn interview with the author, June 7, 2003.

60. Haim Shorrer interview with the author, May 29, 2003, and Monish Einhorn interview with the author, June 7, 2003.

61. Miriam Yechieli interview with the author, May 30, 2003.

62. *Yoman KLGTA*, 185.

63. Ibid., 198–201.

64. Bogner, *Be-hasdei Zarim*, 230. Engel, *Ben Shikhrur Li-Verihah*, 120, notes that although the repatriation agreement between Poland and the Soviet Union was signed on July 6, 1945, the first official transport of repatriates did not arrive until February 8, 1946.

65. Zuckerman, *Surplus of Memory*, 610. For more on the details of repatriation see Hana Shlomi, "The Reception and Settlement of Jewish Repatriants from the

Soviet Union in Lower Silesia, 1946," *Gal-Ed* 17 (2000): 85–104; see also Engel, *Ben Shikhrur Li-Verihah*, 120–24. As Engel details, the delay in repatriating most Polish Jewish citizens from the Soviet Union until 1946 meant that by the time most Jews began to arrive in Silesia, the area had already been populated by non-Jewish repatriates, making the absorption of Jewish repatriates a more difficult process for the CKZP due to housing and work shortages. The Zionist groups were able to take advantage of this situation for their own benefit.

66. *Yoman KLGTA*, 196–98.

67. Ibid. 190–91.

68. Ibid., 203.

69. Ibid., 184.

70. A later survey of the kibbutz noted the wartime experience of the members of Kibbutz Tosia Altman as follows: "in the time of the occupation, 40 percent lived in concentration camps, 20 percent in bunkers and in the forests, 30 percent in Russia and Romania and 10 percent on Aryan papers and in the partisans." Kibbutz Tosia Altman report to Hashomer Hatzair leadership, Haganah Archives, Ha'apalah Project, 123/HaShomer Hatzair/410, pp. 314–17 (at Giv'at Chaviva, file 8.13.2), correspondence with Kibbutzei Hakhsharah.

71. In addition to those kibbutzim composed entirely of youths, the Bricha also included groups composed of family units and groups organized by former partisans and soldiers.

72. Most likely from *Sefer Ha-Shomrim: Antologiyah le-Yovel ha-XX shel ha-Shomer ha-Tzair, 1913–1933* [The Book of the Shomrim: An Anthology for the Twentieth Anniversary of Hashomer Hatzair, 1913–1933] (Warsaw, 1934). The book includes stories on the beginnings of the movement, profiles of founding members and leaders, songs, poetry, descriptions of major conferences, and lessons in movement ideology.

73. *Yoman KLGTA*, 43. The League for Labor Palestine was the umbrella organization linking Poalei Zion to Dror and Hashomer Hatzair in the organization of the Bricha movement.

74. Inka Weisbort, *Yoman KLGTA*, 198–201.

75. The Sosnowiec group elected a mazkirut as well. See *Yoman KLGTA*, 22.

76. Ibid., 44–45.

77. Haim Shorrer interview with the author, May 29, 2003.

78. *Yoman KLGTA*, 48.

79. At the kibbutz asefa on September 13, 1945, the kibbutz expelled the "lazy" Yakov HaSandlar; see *Yoman KLGTA*, 29.

80. Ibid., 24–27 (Sosnowiec) and 48 (Bytom).

81. The role of the JDC in supporting the work of the Zionist youth movements deserves separate extensive treatment. See the discussions in Zuckerman, *Surplus of Memory*, 574, 576, 587, 612; Yosef Litvak, "Trumato shel Irgun Ha-Joint le-shikumah shel She'erit Ha-Pletah be-Polin, 1944–49," in *Yahadut Mizrach Eiropah ben Shoah le-Tekumah, 1944–1948*, edited by Benajmin Pinkus, 339–40 (Sdeh Boker: Ben-Gurion University, 1987); Engel, *Ben Shikhrur Li-Verihah*; and Cohen, *Ovrim kol Gvul*. As Zuckerman describes, he drew on his wartime experiences with Guzhick of the JDC in the Warsaw underground to secure postwar funding for his movement from the JDC.

82. *Yoman KLGTA*, 50.

83. Ibid., 26.

84. Sarah Erlich oversaw the laundry operation, which at times would last the entire night (*Yoman KLGTA*, 25). Likewise, in Bytom the laundry operation was a nighttime affair, but members made sure to launder clothes with a minimum of soap, "because there is no money and we must save" (*Yoman KLGTA*, 47).

85. *Yoman KLGTA*, 26.

86. Ibid., 27.

87. Monish Einhorn interview with the author, June 7, 2003.

88. Inka Weisbort, *Yoman KLGTA*, 201.

89. Many of the Hashomer Hatzair guidelines were based on the scouting movement of Lord Baden-Powell in England. Among these was the creation of a "Ten Commandments" of behavior for members of Hashomer Hatzair in 1919. These guidelines instructed the shomer to be an individual of truth, a pioneer to his nation, and a lover of nature, filled with energy and spiritual and physical fulfill-ment. The tenth commandment—"The shomer is pure in his thoughts, speech, and actions"—included a prohibition on smoking, drinking alcohol, and sexual activity. See Zvi Lamm, *Shitat Ha-Hinkukh shel Ha-Shomer Ha-Tzair* (Jerusalem: Magnes, 1998), 78.

90. Monish Einhorn interview with the author, June 7, 2003.

91. Ibid. A number of pogroms against Jews did occur in Poland after the war, including one in Krakow in August 1945 and, most notably, the bloody pogrom in Kielce in July 1946.

92. *Yoman KLGTA*, 31–32 (Sosnowiec) and 50–51 (Bytom).

93. Ibid., 22–23. This was in accord with what Zuckerman described as the effort to educate the Jewish youths in the joint kibbutzim in the general outlines of kibbutz life. See the description of seminars in the June 20, 1945, letter from Krakow to Bucharest in Zuckerman, *Yetziat Polin*, 87.

94. *Yoman KLGTA*, 23.

95. Under pressure from Meir Ya'ari and the leadership of Hashomer Hatzair in the Yishuv (despite her reservations to the contrary), Chaika Grossman split off from her wartime comrades in Dror at the first postwar Zionist conference in London.

96. *Yoman KLGTA*, 33.

97. Ibid., 35. Yosef Gar traveled with a Dror kibbutz from Krakow disguised as Greeks. For a "humorous" misunderstanding which arose from this masquerade, see *In geloyf fun horeveh heymen* (New York: S.N., 1952), 91–92.

98. Table from Cohen, *Ovrim kol Gvul*, 469. Summary of HaBricha from Poland according to movements July 1945–46 (Bricha Archive, Efal, Hativah Z. Netzer, Box 3, Folder 4). According to Cohen's calculations, approximately 40,000 young adults and children traveled without parents (either because they were orphaned or sent ahead) within the framework of kibbutzim and children's homes. Of those who traveled in families or as individuals (71,041), perhaps 20 percent could have fallen into the category of "youth" under the age of twenty-five desired by the pioneering kibbutzim.

99. Engel, *Ben Shikhrur Li-Verihah*, 79.

100. For a sample of psychological studies of Holocaust survivors, see Robert Jay Lifton, "The Concept of the Survivor," in Joel E. Dimsdale, ed., *Survivors, Victims, and Perpetrators* (New York: Hemisphere Publishing Company, 1980), 113–26. In the same volume, see Leo Ettinger, "The Concentration Syndrome and its Late Sequelae," 127–62, and Dimsdale, "The Coping Behavior of Nazi Concentration Camp Survivors," 163–74. According to the *Diagnostic and Statistical Manual of Mental Disorders*, 4th ed. (Washington, DC: American Psychiatric Association, 1994), 424, "the essential feature of Posttraumatic Stress Disorder is the development of characteristic symptoms following exposure to an extreme traumatic event that involves actual or threatened death or serious injury, or other threat to one's physical integrity; or witnessing an event that involves death, injury, or a threat to the physical integrity of another person; or learning about unexpected or violent death, serious harm, or threat of death or injury experienced by a family member of other close associate. Response to the event must involve intense fear, helplessness, or horror . . . [and] the characteristic symptoms resulting from the exposure to the extreme trauma include persistent reexperiencing of the traumatic event, persistent avoidance of stimuli associated with the trauma and numbing of general responsiveness, and persistent symptoms of increased arousal (anxiety, increased arousal, insomnia, nightmares, hypervigilance, exaggerated startle response, irritability or outbursts of anger, and difficulty concentrating." For a recent overview of research on the subject, see Jonathan Davidson and Edna Foa, eds., *Posttraumatic Stress Disorder: DSM-IV and Beyond* (Washington, DC: American Psychiatric Press, 1993).

101. Engel, *Ben Shikhrur Li-Verihah*, 203n221: members of kibbutzim. Based on various sources, Engel concludes that there were more than 1,500 youths in the kibbutzim of the pioneering movements. From this we can conclude that the number of youths on Hehalutz kibbutzim increased by 500 percent between June and November 1945; this is also taking into account the likelihood that hundreds of youths probably left Poland on Bricha routes in the months preceding November 1945. Between November 1945 and January 1946 there was a decline in the population of Hehalutz kibbutzim, thanks to the work of the Bricha; in January 1946 the number of youths in Hehalutz kibbutzim was listed as 1,028 (Merkaz HeHalutz to "Dear Friends," January 13, 1946, CZA-S6/2085). Such numbers can be questioned based on other sources (Cohen, *Ovrim kol Gvul*, 463–65); nonetheless, it is possible to say that in the second half of 1945 there was a large increase in the number of kibbutz members. Engel concludes that overall, there were 8,000 Jewish youths in Poland in November 1945. Therefore, in the spring of 1945 the kibbutzim of the youth movements constituted 7.5 percent of the Jewish youth population, and by the fall this total had reached 17 percent.

102. Other sources also testify to the expansion in number and membership of the Zionist youth movement kibbutzim in postwar Poland. For a detailed list of youth movement kibbutzim, locations, and membership during 1945–46, see Yochanan Cohen, *Ovrim kol Gvul*, appendix 5. Cohen's numbers indicate that in the year between the summers of 1945 and 1946, the number of kibbutzim in the movements surveyed (Ichud Noar Zioni, Gordoniah, Hashomer Hatzair, Dror, and Mizrachi) increased by almost ten times (1,000 percent). (Depending on which figures are used, Gordoniah's membership increased from 120 members in early 1946 to either 2,000 in the summer or up to 4,000 by late 1946, with 4,000 already having departed with the Bricha.) While membership numbers are incomplete (and even more unreliable with Bricha groups departing every few weeks), these numbers also suggest an exponential increase in membership over the year.

103. Engel, *Ben Shikhrur Li-Verihah*, 93.

104. From Hana Shlomi, "Toldot HaIchud," in *Asufat mehkarim le-Toldot She'erit ha-Pletah ha-Yehudit be-Polin, 1944–1950*, edited by Hana Shlomi (Tel Aviv: Tel Aviv University, 2001), 197; see also Cohen, *Ovrim kol Gvul*, appendix 5.

105. See Engel, *Ben Shikhrur Li-Verihah*, 94, and Bauer, *Flight and Rescue*, 120, for descriptions of interrelations; see also Yochanan Cohen, *Ovrim kol Gvul*, 154. The Revisionists operated their own separate organization, although they maintained contact and cooperated with the Bricha organization.

106. Likewise, Left Poalei Zion continued to suffer in terms of representation on the local committees (Sztokfisz letter in Engel, *Ben Shikhrur Li-Verihah*, 95). This

sense of underrepresentation impelled the leadership of Left Poalei Zion to organize its own kibbutzim as well in the fall of 1945 under the banner of its ideological patriarch, Ber Borochov (Engel, *Ben Shikhrur Li-Verihah*, 95); see also Joel Roizman, *Ha-Noar Ha-Borochovi Ve-Dror: Noar Borochov Be-Polin Achrei Ha-Shoah* (Efal: Yad Tabenkin, 1999).

107. Engel, *Ben Shikhrur Li-Verihah*, 96.

108. In Zuckerman, *Yetziat Polin*, 21, speech in London at Zionist Congress, August 5, 1945.

109. See Anita Shapira, "The Yishuv's Encounter with the Survivors of the Holocaust," in Yisrael Gutman and Avital Saf, eds., *She'erit Hapletah, 1944–1948: Rehabilitation and Political Struggle*, 80–106 (Jerusalem: Yad Vashem, 1990).

110. See, for example, the quotation in Sarid (*Be-Mivchan he-Anut veha-Pdut*, 197) of Chavka Folman (Dror activist) describing the youths as "1000 kids, 1000 complexes."

111. Letter of Zilberfarb to leadership, March 23, 1946, SZ Archive (1)38.2, in Sarid, *Be-Mivchan he-Anut veha-Pdut*, 284. In the words of Zilberfarb: "One needs a great deal of strength of spirit in order to create from this material a new type of man . . . it will take quite a few days and months effort for them to be like us . . . we are working and endeavoring to serve as an example and a symbol in our private lives and behavior."

112. *Hashomer Hatzair* in Bratislava, November 17–19, 1945, Organization of Hashomer Hatzair (Moreshet Archive, Giv'at Chaviva, D.1.5320).

113. Ibid.

Chapter 3

1. See report of Susan Pettiss (child infiltree officer, UNRRA), "Report on Jewish Infiltree Children," November 4, 1946, YIVO, Leo Schwarz Papers, MK 488, Folder 371. Pettiss noted the importance of maintaining the kibbutz structure for children (under the age of eighteen) arriving in Germany from Poland in order to maintain "some emotional security." For more on Pettiss, see her memoir *After the Shooting Stopped: The Story of an UNRRA Welfare Worker in Germany, 1945–1947* (Victoria, BC: Trafford, 2004).

2. See Arieh Kochavi, *Post-Holocaust Politics: Britain, the United States, and Jewish Refugees, 1945–1948* (Chapel Hill: University of North Carolina Press, 2001), 103.

3. See the description in *Nocham* newspaper, June 28, 1946, vol. 2, YIVO, DP Periodicals.

4. *Landsberger Lager Cajtung,* November 4, 1945, no. 4(8), YIVO, DP Periodicals, Roll 1. The figure of twelve hundred comes from D. Cohen's estimate at the
October 23–24, 1945, conference of the United Zionist Organization in Frankfurt.
Gad Beck cites higher figures of five thousand members for Bavaria and Austria
at the end of November 1945; correspondence of Gad Beck to Nathan Schwalb,
November 15, 1945, Lavon Institute Labor Archives, III-37A-1, Folder 43a,
pp. 36–37.

5. Table from Yochanan Cohen, *Ovrim kol Gvul: Ha-Brichah, Polin 1945–1946*
(Tel Aviv: Zemorah-Bitan, 1995), 469. Summary of HaBricha from Poland accord-
ing to movements during July 1945–46 (Bricha Archive, Efal, Hativah Z. Netzer,
Box 3, Folder 4).

6. Departure routes of the Bricha also led to the American zones of Austria and
Italy as well as other destinations in western and southeastern Europe. See Yehuda
Bauer, *Flight and Rescue: Bricha* (New York: Random House, 1970), and David
Engel, *Ben Shikhrur Li-Verihah: Nitsolei ha-Shoah be-Polin veha-ma'avak 'al Han-
hagatam, 1944–1946* [Between Liberation and Flight: Holocaust Survivors in Poland
and the Struggle for Leadership, 1944–1947] (Tel Aviv: Am Oved, 1996). Accord-
ing to calculations made by the JDC at the end of 1946, the population distribution
for Germany and Austria was as follows: Germany 179,622 (U.S. zone 142,084;
Berlin 14,564; Bremen 885; French zone 2,089; British zone 20,000). The Jewish
population for Austria as of December 31, 1946, was 35,555. G. H. Muentz, JDC
Statistical Office, to Dr. Leo Schwarz, JDC zone director, YIVO, MK 488, Leo
Schwarz Papers, Roll 9, Folder 56, p. 525.

7. *Landsberger Lager Cajtung,* November 4, 1945, no. 4(8), YIVO, DP Periodicals, Roll 1. In November 1945, Nocham estimated its membership at 150 in
Landsberg. For the U.S. zone as a whole, the movement membership was estimated
at 1,200. See note 4, this chapter. By the end of 1945, Gad Beck estimated that there
were 5,000 members in the movement; it is unclear whether this count included
members of pioneering groups affiliated with other movements as well. Meanwhile,
Hashomer Hatzair stated in Bratislava that as of November, it had approximately
700 members in Bavaria (Bratislava, November 17–19, 1945, Moreshet Archive,
Giv'at Chaviva, D.1.5320). Dror counted a growth from 200–300 members in the
fall of 1945 to "1300 members in kibbutzim by January 1946, the majority of whom
arrived in groups from Poland." See CZA, S32/141, "Our Movement in the Entire
World," a report on Dror activities in Europe, 5–6. According to Yehoyakim
Cochavi, *Shoresh le-'Akurim: Tnu' ot ha-No'ar be-Mahanot ha-'Akurim be-Germanyah,
1945–1949* (Giv'at Havivah: Yad Ya'ari, 1999), 70n7, there were 1,500 members in
Nocham, 630 in Hashomer Haztair, and 600 in Dror at the end of 1945. This is
based on Haim Avni to the mazkirut of Kibbutz HaMeuchad, Munich, December

28, 1945, Ha'apalah Project, Avigur Archive, 44.29 [temporary signature]. For a survey of kibbutzim in Germany by 1947, see YIVO, LS 16, 159, 1108–21; Report of G. H. Muentz (JDC administrative assistant), Kibbutzim Survey, printed May 20, 1947. Ze'ev Mankowitz, *Life between Memory and Hope: The Survivors of the Holocaust in Occupied Germany* (Cambridge: Cambridge University Press, 2002), 272, writes that 9,500 DPs left Germany over the course of 1946, the vast majority of them being members of kibbutzim; this number must therefore be added to the 16,000 counted by Muentz in 1947.

8. For more on Betar, see the partisan but informative work by Haim Lazar, *Betar Be-She'erit Ha-Pletah: 1945–1948* (Israel: Jabotinsky Institute, 1997). The decision of Ichud not to participate in Nocham was made official at the April 1946 conference of the movement in Germany. See Ichud HaNoar HaZioni Conference of the movement in Germany at Erding, 9–10.4.46; Decisions of the conference, April 15, 1946, Central Zionist Archives, S32/403. Ichud Noar Zioni decided to withdraw from Nocham after hearing of poor treatment of its olim upon arrival in Palestine who were divided between kibbutzim rather than being allowed to remain in one group. See also the discussion in Ada Schein, "Ma'arehet ha-hinukh be-mahanot ha-'akurim ha-yehudiyim be-Germanyah ube-Austryah, 1945–1951" (PhD dissertation, Hebrew University, 2001), 172–74. In Mankowitz, *Life between Memory and Hope*, see chap. 7, "The Politics of Education." Cochavi dicusses the issue at length throughout *Shoresh le-'Akurim*. He suggests that Jungbor was opposed to participation in what it termed the "bourgeois" Histadrut.

9. See in Haganah Archives, Ha'apalah Project (HAHP), 123/Maccabi/0014, pp. 66–72, and Central Zionist Archives, S32/220.

10. Bratislava, November 17–19, 1945 (Moreshet Archive, Giv'at Chaviva, D.1.5320). Decisions of Hashomer Hatzair in Bratislava.

11. *Yoman KLGTA*, 69.

12. The above-mentioned kibbutz groups were named after individuals who participated in the Jewish resistance during the war. Mordechai Anielewicz (b. 1919) was the commander of the Warsaw Ghetto Uprising. He led the Hashomer Hatzair underground movement and helped to reorganize the Zydowska Organizacja Bojowa (ZOB, Jewish Fighting Organization) following the mass deportation during the summer of 1942. Anielewicz commanded the Jewish uprising that began on April 19, 1943. He was killed, along with the main body of the ZOB, in the bunker on 18 Mila Street on May 8, 1943. Tosia Altman (b. 1918, d. ca. May 24, 1943) was one of several Hashomer Hatzair activists who managed to return to Warsaw in 1939 after escaping to Vilna with the outbreak of the war. She spent much of the war traveling between ghettos in the Generalgouvernement to assist in organizing Hashomer Hatzair branches. During the Warsaw Ghetto Uprising, she was in the

main bunker on Mila 18 but managed to escape and crawl through the sewers to the Aryan side of Warsaw. She was killed several weeks later, around May 24, 1943, following a fire in the ZOB's safe house on November 11 Street in the Praga. (See *Hashomer Hatzair* movement newspaper, vol. 4, July 15, 1946.) Aryeh Vilner (b. 1917) was one of the founders of the ZOB in the Warsaw ghetto. Vilner was among those who escaped to Vilna in September 1939, but he returned to Warsaw in June 1941 following the German conquest of Vilna. Vilner established contact with the Polish underground (Armia Krajowa, or Home Army) and was active in securing arms for the ZOB. He was arrested by the Germans on March 6, 1943, during a search of his apartment on the Aryan side of Warsaw and was sent to a nearby concentration camp. Vilner was rescued from the camp and participated in the Warsaw Ghetto Uprising. He was killed in the ZOB command bunker on May 8, 1943. Yosef Kaplan (b. 1913) was one of the founders of the ZOB. He led the underground Hashomer Hatzair movement and was active in the publication and distribution of underground newspapers. He was captured preparing forged documents for a group of underground fighters on September 3, 1942, and killed. Zvi Brandes (b. September 3, 1917, d. August 7, 1943) organized the efforts of the ZOB in the Zaglembie region. Chaviva Reik (b. 1914) was born in Slovakia and immigrated to Palestine in 1939 as a member of Hashomer Hatzair. She volunteered to join the parachutist unit and was dropped over Slovakia on September 21, 1944, where she organized Jewish partisan groups to assist in the Slovak national uprising. She was captured and executed on November 20, 1944, at Kremnica.

13. Information on the following kibbutz groups is available at the Hashomer Hatzair archives and in the Ha'apalah Project, Haganah Archives (123/Hashomer Hatzair/410): (1) Kibbutz Mordechai Anielewicz, (2) Kibbutz Chaviva Reik bei Pocking, (3) Kibbutz Tosia Altman, (4) Kibbutz Aryeh Vilner, (5) Kibbutz Yosef Kaplan, (6) Kibbutz Ma'apilim al shem Zvi Brandes in Feldafing, (7) Kibbutz al shem Fareinigte Partizaner Organizatye in Vilna (FPO), (8) Kibbutz BaDerech, (9) Kibbutz LaMered, (10) Kibbutz BaMa'avak, (11) Kibbutz LeShichrur, (12) Kibbutz Vatikim in Herzog (July 1946), (13) Kibbutz Vatikim in Schlifing (older kibbutz with families), and (14) Kibbutz Bachazit (older kibbutz with couples and babies). There was apparently another kibbutz named after Shmuel Breslaw, but correspondence between it and the central leadership is not available.

14. Aryeh Levi Sarid, *Be-Mivchan he-Anut veha-Pdut: Ha-Tnuot Ha-Halutziot be-Polin Ba-Shoah ve-Achareha, 1939–1949* (Tel Aviv: Moreshet, 1997), 272.

15. See Nachum Bogner, *Be-hasdei Zarim: Hatzalat Yeladim be-Zehut Sheulah be-Polin* (Jerusalem: Yad Vashem, 2000).

16. For a description of one such children's home in Germany (the children's home in Blankanesee), see Yitzhak Tadmor, ed., *Duvdevanim 'al ha-Elbeh: Sipur Bet*

ha-yeladim be-Blankenezeh, 1946–1948 (Giv'at Havivah: Yad Ya'ari, 1996). Reumah
Weizmann, wife of Ezer Weizmann who later became the president of Israel, was a
nurse working in the home.

17. HAHP, 123/Hashomer Hatzair/410, pp. 158–62.

18. Ibid., 341–42.

19. Ibid., 71.

20. "Reshimat Vatikim in Schlifing," HAHP, 123/Hashomer Hatzair/410,
pp. 24–25.

21. Schein, "Ma'arehet ha-hinukh," 13 and chap. 4. See also publications of these
movements in YIVO, DP Periodicals Collection, *Dos Judische Wort* (Central Organ
of Agudes Israel in Germany, Reel 23-2).

22. Kibbutz Fareinigte Partisaner Organisatsye report to leadership, July 30,
1946, Haganah Archives, Ha'apalah Project (HAHP), 123/HaShomer Hatzair/
410, pp. 113–16.

23. See, for example, the report from Kibbutz Yosef Kaplan to the leadership,
March 16, 1946, HAHP, 123/HaShomer Hatzair/410, pp. 175–77 (written in
Hebrew).

24. Miriam Yechieli interview with the author, May 30, 2003.

25. *Yoman KLGTA*, 36–40 and 52–54.

26. See numerous sources; an emissary named "Sima" would later (April 26,
1946) describe Landsberg as a city full of kibbutzim. "One can find all shades of the
rainbow . . . when I walked in the evening I felt like I was in a Jewish city in Poland."
HAHP, 123/LOHM/65k, p. 12.

27. *Yoman KLGTA*, 56.

28. *Nitzotz*, no. 8(53), 21.1.1946, Haganah Archives, Ha'aplah Project, 123/
Maccabi/148.

29. *Yoman KLGTA*, 56.

30. Ibid., 58.

31. This period of time corresponded very closely to the resignation of Dr. Leo
Srole as senior member of the UNRRA team stationed in Landsberg. In his resignation letter, Srole charged that the camp was so overcrowded that there was "an
imminent danger of typhus and other epidemics that would mean the death of hundreds." See YIVO, Leo Schwarz, Roll 10, Folder 68, p. 318: Leo Srole, statement
upon resignation from UNRRA directorship. Soon thereafter the Leipheim camp
was opened to lessen overcrowding in Landsberg.

32. *Yoman KLGTA*, 58.

33. Ibid., 60.

34. Ibid., 66.

35. Ibid.

36. Miriam Yechieli Interview with the author, May 30, 2003. The trial was her idea, but she suggests that it was Monish's performance that made it successful. See *Yoman KLGTA*, 62.

37. Ibid., 63.

38. Ibid.

39. Ibid., 64.

40. Ibid., from Monish description of the trial.

41. Monish Einhorn interview with the author, June 7, 2003.

42. Noted in Monish Einhorn interview with the author, June 7, 2003, and *Yoman KLGTA*, 64.

43. *Yoman KLGTA*, 73. The Leipheim camp, not far from Munich, was opened in December 1945; the number of residents on December 31, 1945, was 1,196. See Angelika Konigseder and Juliane Wetzel, *Waiting for Hope: Jewish Displaced Persons in Post-WWII Germany* (Evanston, IL: Northwestern University Press, 2001), 234. The December 21, 1945, volume of the *Landsberger Lager Cajtung* (vol. 11) also announced the opening of the new Jewish camp in Leipheim, which Shmuel Gringauz declared "more beautiful and better than Landsberg."

44. *Yoman KLGTA*, 74–75.

45. See in Sarid, *Be-Mivchan he-Anut veha-Pdut*, 284–86 (my translation), from Hashomer Hatzair Archive (1).2.31.

46. Likewise, when Kibbutz Tosia Altman reached Leipheim, it was unacceptable for them to share a building with another Dror kibbutz; see *Yoman KLGTA*, 75.

47. Ibid., 69.

48. Letter from Hashomer Hatzair leadership to Kibbutz Mordechai Anielewicz and Kibbutz Yosef Kaplan, March 14, 1946, HAHP, 123/Hashomer Hatzair/410, p. 172. See also the report of Kibbutz Yosef Kaplan in Jordenbad, May 20, 1946, Haganah Archives, Ha'apalah Project (HAHP), 123/HaShomer Hatzair/410, p. 188.

49. HAHP, 123/Hashomer Hatzair/410, p. 172.

50. See, for example, Haganah Archives, Ha'apalah Project (HAHP), 123/HaShomer Hatzair/410, p. 312.

51. Kibbutz Yosef Kaplan report to leadership, March 16, 1946, HAHP, 123/HaShomer Hatzair/410, pp. 175–77 (written in Hebrew, with a few errors).

52. Kibbutz Yosef Kaplan report to leadership, March 16, 1946, HAHP, 123/HaShomer Hatzair/410, p. 175.

53. As noted by the Dror emissary Liuba Leck, "a large segment of the members of the kibbutzim do not work, because there is almost no work to be had within the DP camps." Liuba Leck to world headquarters of Dror-Hechalutz Hatzair, Bavaria, Feburary 1946, CZA, S32/141, "Leket Michtavim #4."

54. *Yoman KLGTA*, 61.

55. See memoranda from J. H. Whiting (UNRRA zone director) to the commanding general (Truscott), U.S. 3rd Army (March 5, 1946), YIVO, Leo Schwarz Papers, Roll 10, Folder 66, p. 150.

56. HAHP, 123/HaShomer Hatzair/410, pp. 22–23.

57. Information on Chaviva Reik at Eschwege, no date (1946), HAHP, 123/HaShomer Hatzair/410, pp. 34–41. With the turn to focus on pioneering and the building of kibbutzim in Israel, Hashomer Hatzair shifted to a coeducational model that emphasized equality between the sexes. Nonetheless, it is clear that in the division of labor, traditional work roles were assigned. See Zvi Lamm, *Shitat Ha-Hinkukh shel Ha-Shomer Ha-Tzair* (Jerusalem: Magnes, 1998), 128.

58. *Yoman KLGTA*, 78–80.

59. Major Irving Heymont, *Among the Survivors of the Holocaust: The Landsberg DP Camp Letters of Major Irving Heymont, United States Army* (Cincinnati: American Jewish Archives, 1982), 95, noted that "cigarettes, to say the least, are scarce and highly prized in Germany today—in fact, they represent hard currency." The report of Kibbutz Mordechai Anielewicz, April 27–May 13, 1946, HAHP, 123/HaShomer Hatzair/410, p. 6, detailed the budget: "the treasury contains 1083 marks and *80 packs of cigarettes (!)*."

60. *Yoman KLGTA*, 80–81.

61. Report of Kibbutz Aryeh Vilner, March 16, 1946, HAHP, 123/Hashomer Hatzair/410, pp. 341–42. See also Kibbutz FPO report, pp. 113–16, and Kibbutz Yosef Kaplan report, p. 176.

62. *Yoman KLGTA*, 82.

63. See ibid., 78, for descriptions of eating with the rest of the DPs in Leipheim.

64. Kibbutz Zvi Brandes to central leadership, January 1946, HAHP, 123/Hashomer Hatzair, p. 276.

65. Kibbutz Tosia Altman in Leipheim report to central leadership, HAHP, 123/HaShomer Hatzair/410, pp. 303–4.

66. Miriam Warburg, "Children and Youth Aliyah," October 26, 1945, Yad Vashem Archives, Hativah 037, Folder 32.

67. See the letter to the Jewish Agency from Haim Hoffman detailing health problems (TB, heart problems, poor diet, etc.) among the DPs, June 7, 1946, HAHP, 123/Maccabi/0013, 2.

68. See the letter from the leadership to Kibbutz Yosef Kaplan, HAHP, 123/HaShomer Hatzair/410, p. 199.

69. Letter from Kibbutz in Gabersee, HAHP, 123/HaShomer Hatzair/410, p. 74.

70. Report from Eschwege (probably Kibbutz LeShichrur), December 8, 1946, HAHP, 123/HaShomer Hatzair/410, pp. 234–36.

71. Report from Kibbutz FPO in Holtzhausen to leadership, July 18, 1946, HAHP, 123/HaShomer Hatzair/410, p. 111.

72. Report from Kibbutz Tosia Altman to central leadership (July/August 1946), HAHP, 123/HaShomer Hatzair/410, p. 296.

73. Natan to Hashomer Hatzair central leadership, November 27, 1946, HAHP, 123/HaShomer Hatzair/410, pp. 129–31.

74. Kibbutz FPO report to central leadership, December 23, 1946, HAHP, 123/HaShomer Hatzair/410, pp. 127–28.

75. Letter from central leadership to group in Ansbach, August 6, 1946, HAHP, 123/Hashomer Hatzair/410, p. 270.

76. From Sarid, *Be-Mivchan he-Anut veha-Pdut*, 284–86 (my translation), Hashomer Hatzair Archive, Giv'at Havivah (1).2.31.

77. Kibbutz Yosef Kaplan report to central leadership, March 16, 1946, HAHP, 123/HaShomer Hatzair/410, pp. 175–77.

78. *Yoman KLGTA*, 69–71. For more on the involvement of the emissaries in educational work, see Irit Keynan, *Lo Nirga Ha-Ra'av: Nitzulei Ha-Shoah ve-Shlichei Eretz Yisrael: Germanyah, 1945–1948* (Tel Aviv: Am Oved, 1996), 141–46. Shushan and Schwartz also conducted week-long seminars in Föhrenwald, Jordenbad, and in Hansbach with another emissary named Tuviah.

79. "The Seminar Action," *Hashomer Hatzair* newspaper, March 1946, YIVO Library, vol. 1, p. 28.

80. Kibbutz Yosef Kaplan (in Jordenbad) report to central leadership, May 11, 1946, HAHP, 123/Hashomer Hatzair/410, pp. 186–88.

81. Kibbutz Yosef Kaplan (in Jordenbad) report to central leadership (in Polish), July 3, 1946, HAHP, 123/HaShomer Hatzair/410, p. 206.

82. Central leadership letter to Kibbutz Yosef Kaplan, July 7, 1946, HAHP, 123/HaShomer Hatzair/410, p. 208.

83. This first comment was from the Kibbutz Yosef Kaplan report on March 16, 1946, HAHP, 123/HaShomer Hatzair/410, p. 175. In May, the kibbutz continued to note that members could only use the pamphlets sent to them by the leadership in Polish "because the majority of our members despite their participation and strong desire are not fluent in Yiddish." See report, HAHP, 123/HaShomer Hatzair/410, pp. 186–88.

84. *Yoman KLGTA*, 82–83. See Keynan, *Lo Nirga Ha-Ra'av*, 141–45. Schein's dissertation "Ma'arehet ha-hinukh" on educational networks in the DP camps provides the most thorough treatment.

85. *Yoman KLGTA*, 83.

86. Ibid.

87. Ibid.

88. Kibbutz Tosia Altman in Eschwege report to central leadership (no date, probably April 1946), HAHP, 123/HaShomer Hatzair/410, pp. 319–22; Kibbutz Yosef Kaplan report in Jordenbad to leadership, May 20, 1946, p. 188. For more on the movement's attitude to Jewish religion, see M. Zilbertal, "Ha-Hinukh Ha-Shomeri: Kovetz Hinukhi shel Hashomer Hatzair, 1913–1938" ["Shomer Education: An Educational Volume of Hashomer Hatzair, 1913–1938"], in Zvi Lamm, *Shitat Ha-Hinkukh shel Ha-Shomer Ha-Tzair* (Jerusalem: Magnes, 1998), 70.

89. *Yoman KLGTA*, 67–68.

90. Miriam Warburg letter, "Children and Youth Aliyah," November 30, 1945, Yad Vashem Archives, Hativah 037, Folder 32.

91. Ibid.

92. Kibbutz Yosef Kaplan report to leadership, March 16, 1946, HAHP, 123/HaShomer Hatzair/410, p. 176. See also *Yoman KLGTA*, 88. For the involvement of kibbutzim in theater life, see L. Kalisher, "The Kibbutzim in Föhrenwald," *Föhrenwalder Almanach: Bamidbar*, September 1947, YIVO, Jewish DP Periodicals Collection, Reel 4-7. In the article, Kalisher gave a brief history of the theater scene in the Föhrenwald camp, which included three theater groups—Bamidbar, Ma'apilim, and Bar Kochba—composed of kibbutz members. See also Yakov Biber, *Risen from the Ashes: A Story of the Jewish Displaced Persons in the Aftermath of World War II; Being a Sequel to Survivors* (San Francisco: Borgo, 1990).

93. Kibbutz Yosef Kaplan report, HAHP, 123/HaShomer Hatzair/410, p. 176.

94. *Yoman KLGTA*, 92.

95. See also Nocham educational materials, Osef-Homer, 1946 (Munich), YIVO call #15/5268.

96. *Yoman KLGTA*, 92.

97. *BaMidbar*, March 20, 1946, no. 4(6), 7, YIVO, Jewish DP Periodicals Collection, Reel 15-11.

98. Report of Kibbutz Yosef Kaplan in Jordenbad, May 20, 1946, HAHP, 123/HaShomer Hatzair/410, see p. 188. The emissary D. Etshtein reported attending the 1st Passover seder at the new hakhsharah near Föhrenwald with 600 participants, D. Etshtein letter, April 20, 1946, HAHP, 123/Maccabi/0013, 24.13, Box 20, Folder 5, reports of emissaries, 1946, p. 42. Some youth movements also created *haggadot* in honor of Passover for the first seder since liberation. Similarly, the *BaMidbar* newspaper in Föhrenwald noted the celebration of Passover at the Hochland kibbutz hakhsharah. YIVO, DP Periodicals Collection, Reel 15-11, May 7, 1946, 6(8), pp. 6–7. For more on this holiday, see chapter 5 in this volume.

99. See in *Yoman KLGTA*, 100–101; Kibbutz Tosia Altman report (no date, probably April 1946), HAHP, 123/HaShomer Hatzair/410, p. 321.

100. Kibbutz Yosef Kaplan report, May 11, 1946, HAHP, 123/HaShomer Hatzair/410, pp. 186–88.

101. Kibbutz Yosef Kaplan report, July 10, 1946, HAHP, 123/HaShomer Hatzair/410, pp. 212–21 (in Jordenbad).

102. Ibid.

103. See, for example, "Iggeret," Holzhausen, Kibbutz Dror al shem Hannah Senesh, YIVO DP Periodicals Collection, Reel 32-1.

104. Letter from leadership to Kibbutz Mordechai Anielewicz and Yosef Kaplan, March 14, 1946, 123/HaShomer Hatzair/410, p. 172. Other movements also published movement newspapers for distribution to the kibbutzim. Nocham followed the publication of *Nitzotz* with the beginning of the publication of *Nocham* in June 1946. Dror also published a movement newspaper and circulars for distribution. See YIVO, DP Periodicals Collection, Reel 29-1, "Deror Germaniyah." These circulars included "Lapid," "He-haluts," and a special circular dedicated to Yom Tel-Hai.

105. See letter from the Hashomer Hatzair leadership to Kibbutz Yosef Kaplan, March 1946, HAHP, 123/Hashomer Hatzair/410, p. 172.

106. HAHP, 123/HaShomer Hatzair/410, p. 208.

107. Zelig Shushan (emissary from Palestine), "The meeting with the members in the Diaspora," in *Hashomer Hatzair*, vol. 1, March 1946, p. 8.

108. Rosman in *Hashomer Hatzair*, vol. 1, March 1946, 21.

109. Hazan in *Hashomer Hatzair*, vol. 1, 16.

110. *Hashomer Hatzair*, vol. 2, April 1946, YIVO Library.

111. "Zog nit Keyn Mol" (Never Say), also known as "Song of the United Partisans' Organization," attributed to Hirsh Glik.

112. The youth movements also distributed circulars with educational materials. For Dror, see YIVO, DP Periodicals Collection, Reels 29-1 and 30-1. For Nocham, see Reel 30-2 and YIVO Library, Nocham educational materials, Osef-Homer, 1946 (Munich), 15/5268.

113. *Hashomer Hatzair* newspaper, vol. 2, April 1946.

114. Ibid. See also in *Yoman KLGTA*, 100.

115. For Nocham seminar, see *Nitzotz* 53, no. 8 (January 21, 1946), HAHP, 123/Maccabi/148. Dror seminars were held in February 1946 for five weeks and a second seminar in August for six weeks: subjects included Zionism, the geography of Palestine, socialism, and Hebrew. See in *Dror* movement newspaper, vol. 1, no. 5, September 1946. See Lazar, *Betar Be-She'erit Ha-Pletah*, 115–30, for descriptions of that movement's activities in Germany, including postwar conferences in April, June, and November 1946.

116. Monish Einhorn interview with the author, June 7, 2003.

117. For Inka and Fani, see *Yoman KLGTA*, 100–101; Kibbutz Aryeh Vilner report to leadership, March 16, 1946, HAHP, 123/HaShomer Hatzair/410, pp. 341–42.

118. Informational bulletin of Kibbutz Yosef Kaplan in Jordenbad, *Hedim Ba-Kibbutz* no. 3, July 10, 1946, HAHP, 123/HaShomer Hatzair/410, pp. 212–21.

119. Kibbutz Yosef Kaplan report to leadership, May 11, 1946, HAHP, 123/ HaShomer Hatzair/410, pp. 186–88.

120. Report on Kibbutz al shem Fareinigte Partizaner Organizatye (FPO, United Partisans' Organization) in Holzhausen, July 2, 1946, HAHP, 123/HaShomer Hatzair/410, pp. 109–20.

121. Keynan, *Lo Nirga Ha-Ra'av*, 141–45, mentions the difficulties that the educational networks in the DP camps had with securing teachers with adequate training, not to mention obtaining sufficient educational materials. Very few teachers had adequate prewar training; others were graduates of gymnasia or had perhaps attended an interwar Jewish (usually Tarbut) school in Poland.

122. Haim Shorrer interview with the author, May 29, 2003.

123. Kibbutz Yosef Kaplan (in Jordenbad) report to leadership, May 11, 1946, HAHP, 123/HaShomer Hatzair/410, pp. 186–88.

124. Memorandum from Charles Passman, JDC, Munich, to Central Committee of Liberated Jews, December 10, 1947. YIVO, Leo Schwarz Papers, Roll 10, pp. 876–90. According to existing JDC regulations, members of kibbutzim and hakhsharot were considered as workers and received rations according to these categories. Cigarettes were part of the workers' rations.

125. Kibbutz Ma'apilim al shem Zvi Brandes in Feldafing report and budget, May 25, 1946, HAHP, 123/HaShomer Hatzair/410, p. 273. See also Kibbutz FPO budget, November 11, 1946, HAHP, 123/HaShomer Hatzair/410, p. 125. See also the letter from Monish Einhorn, HAHP, 123/HaShomer Hatzair/410, p. 300. Report of Kibbutz Mordechai Anielewicz, HAHP, 123/HaShomer Hatzair/ 410, p. 6, budget for April 27–May 13, 1946.

126. *Yoman KLGTA*, 90.

127. Ibid., 67.

128. Ibid., 68.

129. Ibid., 84.

130. Ibid.

131. Ibid., 93–94.

132. Generally, such spaces were allocated for those leaving on Aliyah Bet, the movement of illegal immigration from Europe to Palestine. The prospects for legal immigration from the American zone were slim. During 1945–48, fewer than 1,000

aliyah permits were given to Jewish DPs in the U.S. zone; Aviva Halamish, *The Exodus Affair: Holocaust Survivors and the Struggle for Palestine* (Syracuse: Syracuse University Press, 1998), 5. Under the White Paper of 1939, British authorities in Palestine granted a quota of 1,500 aliyah certificates a month for new immigrants. Approximately 350 certificates were allocated to residents of the British zone of Germany, and an additional 300–400 were granted to relatives of Jews already residing in Palestine. The remainder were deducted from the number of illegal immigrants who reached the shores of Palestine with Aliyah Bet. Between 1945 and the spring of 1947, fewer than 10,000 Jews from the U.S. zone of Germany managed to reach Palestine through this method. After August 1946 the British began relocating illegal immigrants to the island of Cyprus rather than granting them gradual entry into Palestine in order to discourage illegal immigration. Following August 1946, 750 certificates from the monthly quota were allocated to Jewish DPs in Cyprus.

133. Letter from Hashomer Hatzair central leadership to Kibbutz Yosef Kaplan, April 12, 1946, HAHP, 123/HaShomer Hatzair/410, p. 184. This seems to have coincided with the period of waiting for the publication of the AACI recommendations. At the time, a total of twelve hundred members of Zionist youth movements were allocated spaces for aliyah. See Mankowitz, *Life between Memory and Hope*, 271. The kibbutzim were also allocated spaces from the Aliyat Hanoar, the aliyah dedicated to the youngest segment of the DPs. For more on the youth aliyah, see Shlomo Bar-Gil, "Ha-shikum veha-klitah ha-hinuchit shel yeladim ve-na'arim me-She'erit ha-Pletah be-Eiropah 'al yedei 'Aliyat Ha-No'ar," *Yalkut Moreshet* 64 (November 1997): 7–27, and Bar-Gil, "Batei Yeladim 'al Admat Eiropah," *Yalkut Moreshet* 65 (April 1998): 61–80. See also discussion in Schein, "Ma'arehet ha-hinukh," 207.

134. HAHP, 123/HaShomer Hatzair/410, p. 184.

135. Kibbutz Tosia Altman report (probably August 1946), HAHP, 123/HaShomer Hatzair/410, p. 296.

136. Kibbutz Tosia Altman report, May 1946, HAHP, 123/HaShomer Hatzair/410, pp. 314–17.

137. See USNA, RG 43 AACI BOX 12, March 1946: "The position of the Jews in Europe."

138. "Visit of the sub-committee to the American zone of Austria," Vienna, February 25, 1946, USNA, RG 43 AACI Box 12, 4–5.

139. Richard H. S. Crossman, *Palestine Mission: A Personal Record* (London: H. Hamilton, 1947), 75.

140. "Report of the Anglo-American Committee of Inquiry," Lausanne, April 20, 1946, YIVO Library.

Chapter 4

1. *Yoman KLGTA*, 91.

2. Ibid., 101.

3. Ibid., 91.

4. Ibid.

5. First Conference of United Zionist Organization, October 1945, Yad Vashem, MP 1, Folder 3.

6. Agricultural Division report, December 31, 1946, YIVO, DPG, MK 483, Roll 1, Folder 2 or 3, pp. 313–14 (Yiddish in Hebrew letters), and Roll 4, 46, p. 969 (Latin).

7. Israel Oppenheim, *The Struggle of Jewish Youth for Productivization: The Zionist Youth Movement in Poland* (Boulder, CO: East European Monographs, 1989), v. See also David Zayit, *Ha-Utopiah Ha-Shomerit: Ha-Shomer Ha-Tzair be-Polin, 1921–1931* (Giv'at Havivah: Hashomer Hatzair, 2002), especially chap. 12, "Hakhsharah ve-aliyah, 1924–1928."

8. A. D. Gordon, "People and Labor," in *The Zionist Idea: A Historical Analysis and Reader*, edited by Arthur Hertzberg (New York: Atheneum, 1971), 372.

9. Oppenheim, *The Struggle of Jewish Youth for Productivization*, vn1. See also Aharon Efrat, *Derekh shomrim be-hagshama: Hakhsharah ve-'aliyah shel ha-Shomer ha-Tsa'ir be-Polin uve-Galitsyah ben shete milhamot'olam* (Giv'at Havivah: Hashomer Hatzair, 1991), and Israel Oppenheim, "Hehalutz in Eastern Europe between the Two World Wars," in *Zionist Youth Movements during the Shoah*, edited by Asher Cohen and Yehoyakim Cochavi, 33–117 (New York: Peter Lang, 1995).

10. See the statistics relating to the growth and composition of the Hehalutz movement in Oppenheim, *The Struggle of Jewish Youth for Productivization*, 173–74.

11. Aharon Weiss, "Youth Movements in Poland during the German Occupation," in *Zionist Youth Movements during the Shoah*, edited by Asher Cohen and Yehoyakim Cochavi (New York: Peter Lang, 1995), 236. See also Rivka Perlis, "Tnu'ot ha-Noar ha-Haluziot be-Polin ha-kvusha bi-yedei ha-Natzim" (PhD dissertation, Hebrew University, 1982).

12. See the description in Aharon Brandes, *Ketz ha-Yehudim be-ma'arav Polin* (Merhavia: Hashomer Hatzair, 1945), and Weiss, "Youth Movements in Poland during the German Occupation," 236.

13. See, for example, Aryeh Levi Sarid, *Be-Mivchan he-Anut veha-Pdut: Ha-Tnuot Ha-Halutziot be-Polin Ba-Shoah ve-Achareha, 1939–1949* (Tel Aviv: Moreshet, 1997), 197, where Chavka Folman (Dror activist) is quoted as describing the youths as "1000 kids, 1000 complexes."

14. See the educational program for Hashomer Hatzair activists working with kibbutzim written by Shaike Weinberg, described in chapter 2.

15. *Nitzotz*, no. 10(55), February 25, 1946, 2, HAHP, 123/Maccabi/148.

16. Ibid., 8.

17. From the *Hashomer Hatzair* newspaper, vol. 2, April 1946, editor S. Luski, 53, "In the Movement."

18. Ichud Hanoar Hazioni movement conference resolutions, Erding, April 9–10, 1946, CZA, S32/403. The movement objected to what it saw as Nocham's effort to co-opt the independence, resources, and aliyah certificates of other movements in Germany. At the conference, Ichud also resolved to establish a new kibbutz named after the fallen hero Abba Berdichev, who, along with Chaviva Reik, had parachuted behind enemy lines into wartime Europe.

19. See, for example, *Histadrut Ha-Olamit shel Dror*, report following Dror all-European conference in Germany, March 1, 1946, 5–6, CZA, S32/141. For more on Betar, see Haim Lazar, *Betar Be-She'erit Ha-Pletah: 1945–1948* (Israel: Jabotinsky Institute, 1997), 134–36. Betar counted two training farms among its hakhsharah *plugot* (groups), including those at Walheim with forty-five chanichim and Darfon with forty-seven.

20. See, for example, the JDC report on efforts to acquire land for hakhsharot, October 1945, YIVO, MK 488, Leo Schwarz Papers, Roll 16, p. 1081.

21. J. Whiting, report on Jewish DPs in the U.S. zone, January 19, 1946, YIVO, MK 488, Leo Schwarz Papers, Roll 10, Folder 65, pp. 7–15.

22. Memorandum from J. H. Whiting (UNRRA zone director) to the commanding general, U.S. 3rd Army (March 5, 1946), YIVO, MK 488, Leo Schwarz Papers, Roll 10, Folder 66, p. 150.

23. Ibid.

24. Haim Hoffman (Yachil), "Ha-Mishlechet Ha-Eretz Yisraelit Le-She'erit Ha-Pletah," Part 1, *Yalkut Moreshet* 30 (1980): 19. The "political instruction" listed by Hoffman has been the subject of debate regarding the origins of DP Zionist enthusiasm before the AACI. As noted above, members of the AACI were aware of this effort by Yishuv emissaries and still concluded that the majority of DPs desired settlement in Palestine.

25. Hoffman, "Ha-Mishlechet Ha-Eretz Yisraelit Le-She'erit Ha-Pletah," Part 1, 21. The Jewish Agency team arranged its assignments with the UNRRA. See assignments of shlichim as listed in *Nitzotz*, no. 8(53), January 1946, 8.

26. Irit Keynan, *Lo Nirga Ha-Ra'av: Nitzulei Ha-Shoah ve-Shlichei Eretz Yisrael: Germanyah, 1945–1948* (Tel Aviv: Am Oved, 1996), 123.

27. Ibid., based on Hoffman, *Yoman HaMishlechet shel Ha-Sochnut be-Germanyah*, CZA, S25/5231.

28. JDC list of UNRRA team members assigned to various farms, YIVO, MK 488, LS 13, 114, p. 1159. In some cases, multiple farms were covered by one representative.

29. Hoffman, "Ha-Mishlechet Ha-Eretz Yisraelit Le-She'erit Ha-Pletah," Part 1, 28.

30. Liuba Leck to Dror-Hehalutz world headquarters in Tel Aviv, Bavaria, February 1946, CZA, S32/141, Leket Michtavim, no. 4, 2 (my emphasis).

31. Hoffman, "Ha-Mishlechet Ha-Eretz Yisraelit Le-She'erit Ha-Pletah," Part 1, 29.

32. Report from Shmuel Zamri (Jewish Agency agricultural adviser) to the JDC on farms in District III, April 15, 1946, YIVO, MK 488, LS Roll 1, Folder 10, pp. 1129–31.

33. Letter from Shmuel Zamri to the JDC in Munich, April 1946, YIVO, MK 488, LS Roll 13, Folder 114, pp. 1153–54. In the letter Zamri estimated that of the nineteen farms operating in the zone at that point in time, some sixty horses and one hundred cows costing three hundred thousand reichsmarks would be required immediately. In addition, another one hundred thousand reichsmarks would be required for securing agricultural machinery for these farms. For more on JDC support for farms, see the report of May–June 1946, YIVO, MK 488, LS 2, 20, 931.

34. Report of the Agricultural Department of the Central Committee, December 31, 1946, YIVO, MK 483, Roll 1, Folder 2 or 3, pp. 313–14 (Yiddish in Hebrew letters), and Roll 4, 46, p. 969 (Latin). It seems that Central Committee surveys tended to be more accurate in measuring the timing of farm creation, but for purposes of consistency with the recording of population growth, the JDC numbers will be used here.

35. *Nocham,* June 7, 1946 (8th of Sivan [third month of the ecclesiastical year in the Jewish calendar], Tashav), p. 1, YIVO DP Periodicals Collection. According to the calculations of the Central Committee, Nocham had established seventeen hakhsharot at the end of 1946.

36. JDC, Statistical Office, Munich, Jewish Population as of January 31, 1947, in the U.S. zone by age and sex, YIVO, MK 488, LS 9, 57, p. 733. Total U.S. zone population: 139,037 investigated (96.8 percent of total 143,633).

37. *Yoman KLGTA,* 96.

38. Ibid.

39. Ibid.

40. Cited, for example, in my interviews with Miriam Yechieli, May 30, 2003; Monish Einhorn, June 7, 2003; and Shmuel Leitner, May 29, 2003.

41. *Yoman KLGTA,* 96.

42. The Gevelber report counts eighty hectares of land at Eschwege. Report of Avraham Gevelber to Jewish Agency regarding kibbutzim, 10.4.47, Munich, CZA, S6/1911. See hakhsharah appendix.

43. *Yoman KLGTA*, 96.

44. Report from Shmuel Zamri (Jewish Agency agricultural adviser) to the JDC on farms in District III, April 15, 1946, YIVO, MK 488, LS Roll 1, Folder 10, pp. 1129–31.

45. Ibid.

46. *Yoman KLGTA*, 99.

47. *Hashomer Hatzair*, vol. 2, April 1946 (S. Luski, ed.), YIVO Library.

48. Hoffman, "Ha-Mishlechet Ha-Eretz Yisraelit Le-She'erit Ha-Pletah," Part 1, 24.

49. Mojse, "Pejsach in Hochland," *BaMidbar: Wochncajtung fun di bafrajte Jidn*, May 7, 1946, 6(8), YIVO DP Periodicals, Reel 15-11.

50. Ibid., 7.

51. Ibid.

52. Leo Schwarz, *The Redeemers: A Saga of the Years 1945–1952* (New York: Farrar, Straus and Young, 1953), 97.

53. Ibid., 97–98.

54. *Nitzotz*, no. 10(55), February 25, 1946, 2, HAHP, 123/Maccabi/148.

55. Ibid. Summary description of the Nocham conference held at Kibbutz Nili during February 17–19, 1946.

56. Other Hashomer Hatzair kibbutzim on farms similarly described receiving many guests from the U.S. Army and the UNRRA to their hakhsharot. See, for example, the report from Kibbutz Fareinigte Partisaner Organisatsye, HAHP, 123/Hashomer Hatzair/410, p. 110.

57. Report of Avraham Gevelber (Munich) to Jewish Agency regarding kibbutzim, April 10, 1947, CZA, S6/1911. See hakhsharah appendix.

58. Report of Kibbutz Chaviva Reik and Leshichrur in Eschwege to Hashomer Hatzair leadership, February 22, 1947, HAHP, 123/HaShomer Hatzair/410, pp. 85–86, and Aharon Kanonitz report from Eschwege, HAHP, 123/HaShomer Hatzair/410, pp. 103–6.

59. *Yoman KLGTA*, 98.

60. Ibid.

61. Judith Tydor Baumel, *Kibbutz Buchenwald: Survivors and Pioneers* (New Brunswick, NJ: Rutgers University Press, 1997), 54.

62. *Yoman KLGTA*, 102.

63. Ibid., 103.

64. Ibid.

65. This was also the case at Hochland. Kibbutz Hannah Senesh, a Dror kibbutz, noted that it was able to have its own separate dining room on the farm. *Dror,* vol. 8, December 1946, 22, Jewish DP Periodicals, Reel 4-6.

66. Miriam Yechieli interview with the author, May 30, 2003.

67. Report of G. H. Muentz (JDC administrative assistant), Kibbutzim Survey, May 20, 1947, YIVO, MK 488, Leo Schwarz Papers, Roll 16, Folder 159, pp. 1108–21. Muentz estimated that 20 percent of farms relied on German assistance. It is quite possible that this number was actually higher.

68. See Memo from Lt. Col. J. D. Cone to Whiting, March 1946, YIVO, MK 488, LS 16, p. 250.

69. See, for example, Carolyn Woods Eisenberg, *Drawing the Line: The American Decision to Divide Germany, 1944–1949* (New York: Cambridge University Press, 1996), 234, on concerns in the spring of 1946 over a decline in the German food supply that forced American authorities to cut calorie rations and the bread supply to the German population.

70. "Sphere of Activity of the Central Committee of Liberated Jews in the American Occupied Zone of Germany," July 11, 1946, YIVO, MK 488, LS Roll 11, Folder 124, pp. 4–5.

71. YIVO, MK 483, DPG Roll 5, Folder 50, pp. 632–33, no date (but probably the spring of 1946).

72. YIVO, MK 483, DPG Roll 4, Folder 46, p. 969.

73. *Landwirtschaftlecher Wegwajzer,* vol. 1, May 1946, YIVO, DP Periodicals Collection, Reel 11-3.

74. Ibid. Sienicki also suggested that short-term agricultural courses on chicken, cattle, rabbit, fish, and beekeeping be created.

75. *Landwirtschaftlecher Wegwajzer,* no. 10, November 1947, "A Year—the Agricultural Department of the ZK."

76. Info on Kibbutz Chaviva Reik at Eschwege (1946), *seder avodah* in the kibbutz in Eschwege (written by the work coordinator, Shaike), HAHP, 123/Hashomer Hatzair/410, pp. 34–41.

77. Monish Einhorn reported that they acquired cows and milking operation as a result of their sale of gasoline on the black market; interview with the author, June 7, 2003.

78. *Yoman KLGTA,* 105. It is unclear whether the members did not like the work or that it simply became too much for them to handle. Either way, they were forced to engage a professional German shepherd to conduct the work with the nearly two hundred sheep.

79. Ibid., 106, "Meshek haChazirim." The kibbutz provided the pigs with left-over food from the kitchen. Eventually the number of pigs reached forty-two.

80. Ibid.

81. Ibid. The kibbutz also reported eating yogurt for dinner.

82. Ibid. The farm also had a stable for horses (*urvah*); the horses were first used for plowing until the farm received a tractor for the work. The first horses belonged to the German agronomist.

83. See Gevelber report on kibbutzim to Jewish Agency, April 10, 1947, CZA, S6/1911.

84. *Yoman KLGTA*, 116.

85. Eliyahu Raziel interview with the author, May 30, 2003.

86. *Yoman KLGTA*, 118. According to the diary entry, turnips took up 6 hectares and potatoes 8.5 hectares.

87. Ibid.

88. *Yoman KLGTA*, 118.

89. "The Hakhsharah Work," *Nocham*, June 28, 1946, YIVO DP Periodicals Collections.

90. Ibid.

91. Schwarz, *The Redeemers*, 99–100.

92. *Dror*, vol. 8, December 1946, 22, YIVO, Jewish DP Periodicals, Reel 4-6.

93. See Gevelber appendix on farms with average size calculated.

94. Report of G. H. Muentz (JDC administrative assistant), Kibbutzim Survey, May 20, 1947, YIVO, MK 488, Leo Schwarz Papers, Reel 16, Folder 159, pp. 1108–21.

95. Ibid. From Muentz report: "55.7 percent of total land (468 hectares) used for sowing (corn, clover, hemp/flax, potatoes & greens, garden, fruit cultures); 40.3 percent used for meadows, woods and ponds; 4 percent unploughed soil" (from Central Committee Agricultural Department figures).

96. Kibbutz Tosia Altman report to leadership, April 1946, HAHP, 123/Hashomer Hatzair/410, p. 321.

97. Ibid., 321.

98. Kibbutz Tosia Altman report to leadership, HAHP, 123/Hashomer Hatzair/410, pp. 314–17.

99. Ibid.

100. Kibbutz Fareinigte Partisaner Organisatsye in Holzhausen (by Marburg) report to leadership, July 2, 1946, HAHP, 123/Hashomer Hatzair/410, pp. 109–20.

101. Kibbutz Tosia Altman survey for leadership, HAHP, 123/Hashomer Hatzair/410, pp. 319–22.

102. Kibbutz Tosia Altman survey in Eschwege, May 26, 1946, HAHP, 123/Hashomer Hatzair/410, p. 351.

103. The Kibbutz named after the Fareinigte Partisaner Organisatsye in Holzhausen, July 1946, also adapted to the new schedule. Report to leadership, July 2, 1946, HAHP, 123/Hashomer Hatzair/410, pp. 109–20.

104. Kibbutz Tosia Altman report, HAHP, 123/Hashomer Hatzair/410, pp. 319–22 (no date, although this is probably before the report described on p. 351). See also *Yoman KLGTA*, 110.

105. *Yoman KLGTA*, 108.

106. Kibbutz Tosia Altman report, HAHP, 123/Hashomer Hatzair/410, p. 351.

107. Likewise, the celebration of the first year after liberation was held on the farm for the whole Eschwege DP camp. *Yoman KLGTA*, 101.

108. Ibid., 108–9.

109. *Nocham*, June 7, 1946, YIVO, DP Periodicals Collection.

110. Ibid.

111. Kibbutz Hannah Senesh at Hochland also reported engaging in intensive cultural work, with daily Hebrew education and a dramatic circle preparing plays and performances. See as described in *Dror*, vol. 8, December 1946, 22, YIVO Jewish DP Periodicals Collection.

112. *Nocham*, June 7, 1946, YIVO, Jewish DP Periodicals Collection.

113. Ibid., 15, description of June 5, 1946, Nocham regional meeting in Teublitz.

114. See *Nocham*, July 19, 1946 (20 Tamuz, Tashav), p. 3, YIVO, Jewish DP Periodicals Collection.

115. *Hashomer Hatzair*, vol. 5, August 1, 1946, YIVO Library. See 14–15, pictures of kibbutzim at work in Holtzhausen and Hochland.

116. *Dror* newspaper, vols. 5, 8, 9, 10, YIVO, Jewish DP Periodicals Collection.

117. *Yoman KLGTA*, 120, Regional Kinus in Eschwege.

118. Ibid., 115.

119. Ibid., 103.

120. *Nocham* newspaper, June 1946, "A half year Nili," 8, YIVO, Jewish DP Periodicals Collection. The meaning of the German names is unclear.

121. Schwarz, *The Redeemers*, 100.

122. *Nocham* newspaper, June 7, 1946, YIVO, Jewish DP Periodicals Collection (my emphasis).

Chapter 5

1. See, for example, Leonard Dinnerstein, *America and the Survivors of the Holocaust* (New York: Columbia University Press, 1982), and Malcolm Proudfoot,

European Refugees, 1939–1952: A Study in Forced Population Movement (Evanston, IL: Northwestern University Press, 1956). Immigration to the United States was still unrealistic with the prewar and wartime restrictive immigration policy still in effect.

2. Emmanuel Sivan, *Dor Tashakh: Mitos, Diyukan ve-Zikaron* [The 1948 Generation: Myth, Profile and Memory] (Israel: Ministry of Defense, 1991). He calculates that twenty-two thousand soldiers were enlisted from outside of Israel, both through conscription (Giyus Hutz La'aretz, or Gachal) and volunteers (Mitnadvei Hutz La'aretz, or Machal). A total of seventy-eight hundred DPs from Germany joined in the fighting, the majority arriving in Israel after May 1948.

3. *Hashomer Hatzair,* YIVO Library.

4. Letter from Kibbutz Gat to members in Germany, *Hashomer Hatzair,* vol. 10, December 20, 1946. Even so, the members who had reached Palestine let their colleagues know that "the work and life here are very hard."

5. See letter from Hashomer Hatzair central leadership to Kibbutz Yosef Kaplan, April 12, 1946, HAHP, 123/HaShomer Hatzair/410, p. 184, footnote 145 in chap. 3.

6. Most of this correspondence is contained in HAHP, 123/Hashomer Hatzair/410, correspondence between Hashomer Hatzair central leadership and kibbutzim. See, for example, Chaviva Reik, Zvi Brandes, Kibbutz Ma'apilim, Mordechai Anielewicz, etc., as discussed in chapter 4.

7. See Judith Tydor Baumel, *Kibbutz Buchenwald: Survivors and Pioneers* (New Brunswick, NJ: Rutgers University Press, 1997), for the difficulties of Kibbutz Buchenwald in settling in Israel. Hanna Yablonka, *Survivors of the Holocaust: Israel after the War* (New York: New York University Press, 1999), 123–25 and 129, also notes the settlement patterns of survivors in Israel. Sivan, *Dor Tashakh,* 84, notes that psychological studies of Giyus Hutz La'aretz soldiers in Israel revealed difficulties of integration. For a fictional perspective on the difficult integration of Holocaust survivors into Israeli society and their participation in the 1948 war, see Yehudit Hendel, *Anashim Acherim Hem* (Merhavia: Sifriat Poalim, 1950).

8. Kibbutz Tosia Altman to Hashomer Hatzair leadership, late summer 1946, HAHP, 123/Hashomer Hatzair/410, correspondence with Kibbutzei Hakhsharah, p. 296.

9. *Yoman KLGTA,* 110, 119.

10. See ibid., 111, for a list of those selected.

11. It seems that this HIAS representative was unaware of any desire on the part of the kibbutz members to actually journey to Palestine, although in many cases aid agencies were aware of the Mossad l'Aliyah Bet's efforts to facilitate illegal immigration to Palestine. For more on this relationship, particularly with regard to the JDC,

see Idith Zertal, *From Catastrophe to Power: Holocaust Survivors and the Emergence of Israel* (Berkeley: University of California Press, 1998), chap. 6.

12. *Yoman KLGTA*, 112. It is unclear whether any pressure was placed on members not to leave the kibbutz, although the diary does mention that members who left were replaced.

13. The members on the farm celebrated the first birthday of the kibbutz on August 24, 1946. This was a foreign tradition to many in the kibbutz but one that reinforced their collective rebirth into a new family following the war. The kibbutz also selected ten representatives to participate in the movement conference in Föhrenwald on September 12, 1946, where members were excited to meet Meir Ya'ari, head of Hashomer Hatzair in the Yishuv (*Yoman KLGTA*, 115).

14. Ibid., 123.

15. Ibid., 122, "Ha-Kongress Ha-Tzioni Ha-Kaf Bet" (The 22nd Zionist Congress), December 1946. The congress took place in Basel, Switzerland, and a group from the kibbutz attended (December 10, 1946). Participants were particularly impressed by Chaim Weizmann, the closing speaker, who "looked like a prophet."

16. *Yoman KLGTA*, 120.

17. For example, Kibbutz Mordechai Anielewicz received financial assistance from Kibbutz Chaviva Reik in the sum of eleven thousand marks in order to help them prepare for aliyah. Report of Kibbutz Chaviva Reik and Le-shichrur, February 22, 1947, HAHP, 123/Hashomer Hatzair/410, pp. 85–86. It would seem that the money the kibbutz groups could provide to other groups came from a number of sources most likely related to some form of trade on the black market.

18. *Yoman KLGTA*, 123.

19. Ibid., 123–24.

20. Ibid., 124–25, "Hochland—January 7–January 17."

21. Chronology of Kibbutz Tosia Altman from January 1947 until March 1948, *Yoman KLGTA*, 129–70: January 18, 1947, St. Valentina; January 22, 1947, Milan to Rome; January 24, 1947, UNRRA camp Cine-Citte; February 7, 1947, Monta Maria (Rome); March 17, 1947, leave Rome; March 22–30, 1947, board Ma'apilim ship *Moledet*, stopped by the British and not allowed to enter Palestine; April 1, 1947, arrive in Cyprus; May 1, 1947, arrive in camp no. 67; July 1947, protest of the whole camp in Cyprus on behalf of the *Exodus*; July 19, 1947, wedding of Yaffa and Zvi; July 23, 1947, hunger strike on behalf of boat *Knesset Israel* returned to Cyprus by British; August 5, 1947, Avramele is born to Dvorah and Moshe from the Belgian group; August 22, 1947, second anniversary of kibbutz; September 2, 1947, Miriam and Baruch leave Cyprus; September 12, 1947, party for the babies (Mordechai born August 22); September 15, 1947, Rosh Hashanah; November 25, 1947, Tzippora and Azriel make aliyah with their baby (Mordechai); December 20, 1947,

youth aliyah including the nine members from kibbutz; March 1948, the last group from Kibbutz Tosia Altman leaves Cyprus.

22. *Yoman KLGTA*, 123.

23. The change of Jewish population in the U.S. zone of Germany from January 1946 to December 31, 1946, JDC calculations, YIVO, MK 488, LS 9, 57, p. 713. The population rose from 39,902 to 145,735 (365 percent increase). See also appendix A in this volume.

24. Population report for the year 1946, Georg H. Muentz, JDC Statistical Office, Munich, to Leo W. Schwarz (JDC director, U.S. zone), YIVO, MK 488, LS 9, 57, p. 749. A total of 108,686 Jewish DPs entered the U.S. zone for 1946, with 6,504 able to emigrate. Summary: 158,000 Jews in the U.S. zone, 18,000–20,000 in the British zone, and 2,000 in the French zone.

25. Ibid.

26. Ibid. While the country of origin for the majority of the Jewish DP population continued to be Poland, by the end of 1946 there were more Jewish refugees arriving from Hungary and Romania.

27. YIVO, MK 488, LS Roll 9, Folder 57, p. 715.

28. Jewish population, U.S. zone Germany, November 30, 1946, JDC, YIVO, LS 9, 57, p. 682. See also appendix A in this volume.

29. Atina Grossmann, "Trauma, Memory, and Motherhood: Germans and Jewish Displaced Persons in Post-Nazi Germany, 1945–1948," *Archiv fur Sozialgeschichte* 38 (1998): 215–39.

30. Susan Pettiss (child infiltree officer, UNRRA), "Report on Jewish Infiltree Children," November 4, 1946, YIVO, Leo Schwarz Papers, MK 488, Folder 371.

31. Over the course of 1946 many more children arrived in the zone, affecting the UNRRA's efforts to accommodate them. See report on Jewish infiltree children, November 4, 1946, Susan Pettiss (child infiltree officer), UNRRA, LS, MK 488, Folder 371. She estimated a total of 76,924 individuals who infiltrated between June 15 and November 1, 1946. Of these, 13,878 were children, and 2,458 were unaccompanied children.

32. Survey of kibbutzim in Föhrenwald, February and April 1947, YIVO, DPG, MK 483, Roll 42, Folder 567, p. 1506, number and population on February 6, 1947. The kibbutzim surveyed at the time included a diverse representation of kibbutzim by movement, age, and families. The kibbutz of Poalei Agudat Israel, with 75 members, had 67 adults with an average age of twenty-four and 8 children under the age of eight. Kibbutz HaOwed counted 237 members, with a much higher proportion of older people and families, living in a number of different places. Hibbutz HaOwed of Poalei Zion Right had 46 members (out of 126) over age thirty-five, with the oldest aged sixty-three. On the other hand, the pioneering groups of Dror,

Hashomer Hatzair, and Nocham at Hochlandslager were closer in average age to twenty like the other pioneering kibbutzim in the U.S. zone.

33. According to Proudfoot, *European Refugees*, 360, table 36, the estimated immigration of Jews to countries other than Israel between 1946 and 1950 totaled 165,525, including Australia (4,745), Belgium (5,000), Brazil (4,837), Britain (1,000), Canada (19,697), France (8,000), the Netherlands (5,000), Sweden (7,200), the United States (105,000), and other Latin American countries (5,046). Other estimates indicate slightly different immigration numbers. For Australia during the period 1946–48, the total number of Jews to immigrate is estimated at almost 12,000 by the Australian Jewish Welfare Society. See H. L. Rubenstein, *The Jews in Australia: 1945 to Present* (Port Melbourne, Victoria: W. Heinemann, 1991); it is not clear how many of these were DPs. For other calculations, see Dinnerstein, *America and the Survivors of the Holocaust*; and Mark Wischnitzer, *To Dwell in Safety* (Philadelphia: Jewish Publication Society of America, 1948). According to JDC calculations, the emigration of Jews from the U.S. zone in Germany during 1946 totaled 6,871, with 4,057 sponsored by the JDC. Of these, 4,135 went to the United States (2,708 sponsored by the JDC), 793 went to Palestine (16 sponsored by the JDC), and 1,430 went to South and Central America (850 sponsored by the JDC). See YIVO, MK 488, Leo Schwarz Papers, Roll 9, Folder 56, p. 524.

34. See Ze'ev Mankowitz, *Life between Memory and Hope: The Survivors of the Holocaust in Occupied Germany* (Cambridge: Cambridge University Press, 2002), 272. Sivan, *Dor Tashakh*, 81, calculates that 21,500 immigrants managed to reach Israel in 1947; two-thirds of these were ma'apilim. Of the total 1947 arrivals, 36.2 percent were between the ages of eighteen and twenty-five; 62 percent of 1946–47 arrivals were between the ages of nineteen and twenty-five.

35. See Aviva Halamish, *The Exodus Affair: Holocaust Survivors and the Struggle for Palestine* (Syracuse: Syracuse University Press, 1998), 5–7.

36. Muentz population report for 1946 to Leo Schwarz, YIVO, MK 488, LS 9, 57, p. 757.

37. Arieh Kochavi, *Post-Holocaust Politics: Britain, the United States, and Jewish Refugees, 1945–1948* (Chapel Hill: University of North Carolina Press, 2001), 143–44. This came at the time that the International Refugee Organization prepared to take over operation of the DP camps from the UNRRA (July 1, 1947). The Bricha organization worked to overcome difficulties presented by this policy by moving Jewish refugees from more crowded areas (e.g., Vienna) to the American zone of occupation in Germany. The American occupation authorities' desire to reduce overcrowding in their zone led them to turn a blind eye to efforts to then remove Jews from the American zone of Germany for France and Italy. This, in turn, facilitated the illegal immigration operation of the Bricha and the Mossad l'Aliyah Bet.

38. Report of Avraham Gevelber to Jewish Agency regarding kibbutzim, April 10, 1947, Munich, CZA, S6/1911.

39. Ibid.

40. Georg Muentz survey of Kibbutz groups, May 20, 1947, YIVO, MK 488, LS 16, 159, 1108–21.

41. Letter from Dror in Germany to members in Cyprus, July 10, 1947, Munich, signed Yitzhak K. HAHP, Dror, 123/Lochem/0019, pp. 108–11. The letter detailed the difficulties faced in Germany including abandonments, preganacies, babies, illness, and lack of aliyah.

42. Gevelber report, CZA, S6/1911.

43. Nocham, March 1947 report (March 11, 1947), CZA, S32/205.

44. See report on Jewish infiltree children, November 4, 1946, Susan Pettiss (child infiltree officer), UNRRA, LS, MK 488, Folder 371.

45. Nocham, March 1947 report, CZA, S32/205.

46. Ibid.

47. Nocham movement survey, May 6, 1947, HAHP, 123/Lochem/0019. The July report of the movement also noted this change in focus away from hakhsharot. See HAHP (123/Maccabi/0014), Archion Gordoniah Maccabi HaTzair al shem Pinchas Lavon (Huldah), July 16, 1947, pp. 66–72 (titled "Between Hope and Disappointment").

48. Survey on the condition in Nocham for the months October 1947–January 1948, central leadership of Nocham in Germany, CZA, S32/204. See also the discussion on the Romanian residents of Kibbutz Buchenwald in 1947 in Judith Tydor Baumel, *Kibbutz Buchenwald: Survivors and Pioneers* (New Brunswick, NJ: Rutgers University Press, 1997), 126–27. There were few visits from shlichim, and interest in Zionist affairs was virtually nonexistent. The group belonged to a contingent of nineteen thousand Romanian Jews smuggled out by the Bricha from Romania. See also in Yehuda Bauer, *Out of the Ashes: The Impact of American Jews on Post-Holocaust European Jewry* (New York: Pergamon, 1989), 284.

49. Dror movement letter from Munich to the Hehalutz office in Tel Aviv, February 24, 1947, HAHP, 123/Lochem/0019, Lochamei HaGettaot Archive (temporary symbol, 44.19), pp. 90–91.

50. For a description of one children's home in Blankensee, see Yitzhak Tadmor, ed., *Duvdevanim 'al ha-Elbeh: Sipur Bet ha-yeladim be-Blankenezeh, 1946–1948* (Giv'at Havivah: Yad Ya'ari, 1996). Reuma Weizmann, wife of Ezer Weizmann who later became president of Israel, worked in this children's home.

51. See Ada Schein, "Ma'arehet ha-hinukh be-mahanot ha-'akurim ha-yehudiyim be-Germanyah ube-Austryah, 1945–1951" (PhD dissertation, Hebrew University, 2001), 181, and Nocham, Dror, and Hashomer Hatzair movement reports.

52. Dror movement letter, February 24, 1947, HAHP, 123/Lochem/0019, pp. 90–91.

53. Survey on the situation in the Nocham movement, May 6, 1947, Nocham central leadership, Munich, HAHP, 123/Lochem/0019, Nocham, pp. 101–11.

54. Hashomer Hatzair Be-Ha'apalah, February 1947, YIVO, MK 483, DP Germany, Roll 97, Folder 1374, pp. 159–549, 158.

55. Hashomer Hatzair Be-Ha'apalah, instructions from leadership regarding Lag Ba'Omer holiday (Holiday of the Jewish Youth), April 28, 1947, YIVO, MK 483, DP Germany, Roll 97, Folder 1374, p. 163. Schedule of the conference (May 7–8, 1947) in Furth bei Bensheim. See description in *Hashomer Hatzair* newspaper, May 1, 1947, vol. 6, no. 16, p. 16. On the intermediate days of Passover, April 8 and 9, the movement held its first half-nationwide movement conferences with five hundred members at Beiruth-Gemeine and the hakhsharah kibbutz Buchenwald in Geringshof.

56. *Hashomer Hatzair* newspaper, vol. 7, no. 17, June 1947, YIVO Library.

57. Letter from central leadership of Hashomer Hatzair to Kibbutz Chaviva Reik, June 10, 1947, HAHP, 123/Hashomer Hatzair/410, p. 93. A glance at the residence lists for individual kibbutzim also reflects the increasing numbers of members from Hungary joining kibbutzim. Hashomer Hatzair Be-Ha'apalah also worked to appeal to Hungarian and Romanian youths through the publication of a Hungarian-language newspaper in 1947. See *Hashomer Hatzair* movement newspaper, YIVO, Jewish DP Periodicals.

58. Schein, "Ma'arehet ha-hinukh," 185.

59. Hashomer Hatzair Be-Ha'apalah, "An Open Letter to Parents, Instructors, and Members," YIVO, MK 483, DP Germany, Roll 97, Folder 1374, p. 352.

60. Hashomer Hatzair Be-Ha'apalah, YIVO, MK 483, DP Germany, Roll 97, Folder 1374, p. 356. See also June 18, 1947, p. 292, list of the different summer camps and which kenim would be going where.

61. *Nocham* movement newspaper, May 20, 1947, no. 2 of 7, 1st of Sivan, Tashaz, 9, YIVO, Jewish DP Periodicals Collection.

62. Nocham, survey on the current situation in the Nocham movement, July 16, 1947, HAHP, 123/Maccabi/0014, Archion Gordoniah Maccabi HaTzair al shem Pinchas Lavon (Huldah), pp. 66–72.

63. Ibid. As was reported in the survey, madrichim training camps were held at Kibbutz Nili and in Bayrische-Gemeine, where members received "a real camp experience: with tents, forest life, scouting experience."

64. *Nocham* newspaper, July 8, 1947, nos. 3–4 of 8–9, 24, YIVO. The summer camps of Nocham were located near Feldafing, Kassel, at Schwarzbaren (near Frankfurt), and at Kibbutz Nili.

65. HAHP, 123/AZM/31, Central Zionist Archives (S86/343) 9.16 (31), p. 122.

66. See JDC operations in the U.S. zone of Germany, 1948, YIVO, LS, 108, Folder 1505, p. 86. The JDC publication presented the summer camps as part of an effort at "building up their health . . . and [providing] much-needed rest during the school vacation."

67. Dror-Hehalutz Hatzair in Germany, Structure and Statistics, September 19, 1947, HAHP, 123/Lochem/0019, Dror in DP camps, p. 122.

68. A letter from Dror in Germany to members in Cyprus, July 10, 1947, signed Yitzhak K., HAHP, Dror, 123/Lochem/0019, pp. 108–11.

69. See letter from Hashomer Hatzair central leadership to Kibbutz Le-shichrur, April 29, 1947, HAHP, 123/Hashomer Hatzair/410, pp. 247–52.

70. Survey on Nocham movement activity, July 16, 1947, HAHP, 123/ Maccabi/0014, Archion Gordoniah Maccabi HaTzair al shem Pinchas Lavon (Huldah), pp. 66–72 (my emphasis).

71. Ibid.

72. Kochavi, *Post-Holocaust Politics*, 264.

73. *Nocham* newspaper, May 20, 1947, no. 2 of 7, YIVO, Jewish DP Periodicals Collection.

74. *Nocham*, July 8, 1947, nos. 3–4 of 8–9, YIVO, Jewish DP Periodicals Collection.

75. Ibid. In the same volume, Dov Peltz (21–22) wrote about the activities of the Kovshei Ha-Yam (Conquerors of the Sea) maritime hakhsharah. Chaim Barlas had been the Jewish Agency representative in Istanbul during the war.

76. Nocham survey of movement activity, July 16, 1947, HAHP, 123/Maccabi/ 0014, pp. 66–72.

77. See Zertal, *From Catastrophe to Power*, 52–58; Halamish, *The Exodus Affair*; Kochavi, *Post-Holocaust Politics*, 266.

78. Halamish, *The Exodus Affair*, 13.

79. Nocham survey of movement activity, July 16, 1947, HAHP, 123/Maccabi/ 0014, pp. 66–72.

80. Zertal, *From Catastrophe to Power*, 67.

81. Ibid., 72.

82. Ibid., 83.

83. Ibid., 89 (my emphasis).

84. Inyanei Aliyah (Items related to Aliyah), August 10, 1947, CZA, S53/586. Aliyat Hanoar was a branch of the Zionist movement founded for the purpose of rescuing Jewish children and young people from hardship, persecution, or deprivation and giving them care and education in Palestine. The agency started its activities

in Germany at the end of 1932. For more on its activities in Germany in the 1930s, see the dissertation by Brian Amkraut, "Let Our Children Go: Youth Aliyah in Germany, 1932–1939" (PhD dissertation, New York University, 2000).

85. List of aliyat hanoar (youth aliyah) on the *Exodus*, February 23, 1948, Inyanei Aliyah (Items related to Aliyah), CZA, S53/586. The February 23, 1948, letter to members of the Directing Committee for Aliyah of Children and Youth discussed the number of youths eligible for youth aliyah on the *Exodus*, including 230 members in Hashomer Hatzair, 189 in Dror, 83 in Noar Zioni, 107 in Mizrachi, 28 in Poalei Agudat Yisrael, 7 in Pachach, and 50 in Betar.

86. Hashomer Hatzair Be-Ha'apalah, circular no. 10, August 27, 1947, YIVO, MK 483, DP Germany, Roll 97, Folder 1374, p. 173.

87. *Hashomer Hatzair* movement newspaper, no. 8 of 18, August 1947, YIVO Library.

88. *Nocham* movement newspaper, no. 6 of 11, November 14, 1947, YIVO, Jewish DP Periodicals Collection. See also *Hashomer Hatzair*, no. 10(20), October 1947.

89. *Hashomer Hatzair*, no. 10 of 20, October 1947, 3.

90. *Nocham* newspaper, October 1, 1947, no. 5 of 10, YIVO, Jewish DP Periodicals.

91. Ibid., 3. *Nocham* newspaper, October 1, 1947, no. 5 of 10.

92. Ibid., 9.

93. United Nations Special Committee on Palestine, Recommendations to the General Assembly, A/364, September 3, 1947.

Chapter 6

1. Haim Hoffman (Yachil), "Ha-Mishlechet Ha-Eretz Yisraelit Le-She'erit Ha-Pletah," Part 2, *Yalkut Moreshet* 31 (1981): 133–76, 159. The Revisionist Zionist movement, founded in 1925, never fully accepted the first partition of Palestine in 1921 and explicitly demanded a Jewish state on both sides of the Jordan River. See publications of the Irgun Tzva'i Leumi (Etzel, or National Military Organization), the Revisionist paramilitary organization in Germany, YIVO, MK 483, Reel 96, frame 654.

2. *Jidiscze Cajtung*, December 2, 1947, 1, YIVO, Jewish DP Periodicals, Reel 2-1.

3. Ibid., December 16, 1947, vol. 93 (161).

4. *Jidiscze Cajtung*, December 5, 1947. Levinthal, aged fifty-five at the time of his posting in Germany, served as a judge on the Court of Common Pleas in Philadelphia. He was also a judge on the World Court of the Zionist Congress. For a pro-

file of Levinthal, see *Weekend, the Magazine of Stars and Stripes*, December 6, 1947, vol. 2, no. 45.

5. *Jidiscze Cajtung*, December 9, 1947, p. 3.

6. *Jidiscze Cajtung*, December 19, 1947, vol. 94, no. 162.

7. For an extreme view of the giyus episode as a manipulation of the DPs, see Yosef Grodzinsky, *Homer Enoshi Tov: Yehudim mul Tsiyonim, 1945–1951* (Or Yehudah, Israel: Hed Artzi, 1998), 146–74. Grodzinsky singles out the giyus episode as one of the most striking examples of the Zionist effort to subjugate Jewish needs to Zionist ones.

8. Ya'acov Markovizky, *Gachelet Lochemet: Giyus Hutz la-Aretz be-Milchemet Ha-'atzmaut* [Fighting Ember: Gachal Forces in the War of Independence] (Israel: Ministry of Defense, 1995), 24.

9. Ibid. See also Yehuda Ben-David, *Ha-Haganah be-Eiropah* [The Haganah in Europe] (Israel: TAG, 1995), 208.

10. Markovizky, *Gachelet Lochemet*, 27.

11. Ben-David, *Ha-Haganah be-Eiropah*, 211.

12. Markovizky, *Gachelet Lochemet*, 32.

13. Ibid., based on second conference of Haganah in Europe.

14. Ibid., 33–34, for a list of officers and students who participated.

15. Ben-David, *Ha-Haganah be-Eiropah*, 221. Ben-David uses this number of 500, while Hanna Yablonka, *Survivors of the Holocaust: Israel after the War* (New York: New York University Press, 1999), asserts that at least 133 *mefakdim* were trained from the DPs.

16. "Curriculum of Haganah Schools," Haganah Archives, Hativah 80, Folder 1, *Pkudot Kevah*.

17. Shadmi testimony, Haganah Archives (63.45), 25 (my emphasis).

18. Markovizky, *Gachelet Lochemet*, 35, based on the Shadmi report.

19. Yablonka, *Survivors of the Holocaust*, 87.

20. Survey on the situation in *Nocham*, February 8, 1948, CZA, S32/204.

21. Ibid. (my emphasis).

22. "Minutes of a Meeting Held in the Office of the Jewish Adviser on Monday, March 15, 1948," recorded by Major Abraham S. Hyman, JAGD, YIVO, MK488, Leo Schwarz Papers, Reel 10, frame 1378. Also see the description in Yehuda Bauer, *Out of the Ashes: The Impact of American Jews on Post-Holocaust European Jewry* (New York: Pergamon, 1989), 262. See also Grodzinsky, *Homer Enoshi Tov*, 153–54.

23. "Minutes of a Meeting Held in the Office of the Jewish Adviser on Monday, March 15, 1948," recorded by Major Abraham S. Hyman, JAGD, YIVO, MK488, Leo Schwarz Papers, Reel 10, frame 1378.

24. Among those seated on the eighty-man committee selected at the congress were sixteen representatives from Poalei Zion Hitachdut, sixteen from the Revisionist Party, eight from Poalei Zion Right, eight General Zionists, eight members of Mizrachi, six from Poalei Zion Smol, six from Hashomer Hatzair, four from Pachach (the organization of ex-partisans and soldiers), and eight from Agudat Israel.

25. "Minutes of a Meeting Held in the Office of the Jewish Adviser on Monday, March 15, 1948," YIVO, LS, Reel 10, frame 1384.

26. "Exekutive Far Bitachon Le'Am U-Moledet" [Executive for Security for the People and the Homeland], circular no. 1, YIVO, DPG, MK 483, Reel 96, Folder 1354, p. 514, February 18, 1948. The parties signed on to the Executive included Poalei-Zion Smol, Poalei-Zion Hitachdut, the General Zionists, HaShomer HaTzair, Mizrachi, and Agudat Israel.

27. Yablonka, *Survivors of the Holocaust*, 90.

28. Conference of the Jewish Agency delegation in Paris, February 29, 1948, CZA, L58/703.

29. Jewish Agency (Munich) poster regarding Sherut Ha'am, YIVO, DPG, MK483, Reel 96, Folder 1355, p. 517, March 16, 1948.

30. YIVO, DPG, MK483, Reel 96, frame 544, date unknown.

31. "Proclamation of Magbit LeBitachon Ha'Am," *Jidisze Cajtung*, February 24, 1948, p. 2, YIVO, Jewish DP Periodicals (Reel 2-1).

32. *Jidiscze Cajtung*, March 2, 1948, p. 1.

33. *Jidiscze Cajtung*, March 2, 1948, p. 2: "Jewish Youth: Prepare Yourself for your duty to the People!" (signed by Nocham, Dror, Hashomer Hatzair, Bnei Akiwa, Hanoar Hatzioni, and Noar Borochow).

34. From the Hashomer Hatzair Be-Ha'apalah, Munich, to all of the party branches. February 21, 1948, YIVO, DP Germany, MK 483, Roll 97, Folder 1374, p. 305 (my emphasis).

35. From the Hashomer Hatzair Be-Ha'apalah, Munich, to all of the party branches, March 10, 1948, YIVO, DP Germany, MK 483, Roll 97, Folder 1374, p. 303.

36. Ibid., 194, March 15, 1948, circular no. 11.

37. Ibid., 201, April 8, 1948. See also p. 301, April 13, 1948, Munich.

38. YIVO, MK 483, Roll 97, Folder 1374, pp. 367–68. A poster published by Bnei Akiwa, Dror, HaNoar HaZioni, Hashomer Hatzair, Nocham, and Noar Borochow called on "YOUTH: FULFILL YOUR DUTY TO THE PEOPLE!"

39. Youth aliyah, February 24, 1948, circular no. 22, Dr. G. Landauer, CZA, L58/703.

40. CZA, L58/703, youth aliyah, February 24, 1948, circular no. 21, Dr. G. Landauer. There were also questions over what to do with youths between the ages of sixteen and seventeen who had not completed their youth aliyah hakhsharah. The basic decision taken was to modify the length of hakhsharah so they will be ready to go in March 1948. "All graduates of aliyat hanoar are required to fulfill giyus at the end of hakhsharah."

41. YIVO, DPG, MK483, Reel 24, frame 113.

42. Protocol from meeting with members of the Central Committee to discuss formation of giyus committee and magbit bitachon with Eife on March 19, 1948, YIVO, DPG, MK483, Reel 24, frame 628, and Reel 26, frame 1082. The committee included representatives from the camp committee, ORT, and youth movements and two representatives from the Haganah.

43. Protocol from meeting with Central Committee members, Eife, Feldafing, March 19, 1948, YIVO, DPG, MK483, Reel 24, frame 628.

44. Protocol of the 3rd Congress of the She'erit Hapletah at Bad-Reichenall, March 30–April 2, 1948, YIVO, DPG, MK 483, Reel 1, Folder 5, p. 552.

45. Ibid., 580.

46. Ibid., 639.

47. Ibid., 640. Exclusions from "social and political life" would include being barred from serving on camp committees, being placed on lists of those prohibited from making aliyah, and being publicly shamed through the publication of the names of shirkers in the DP camp press. See more on this later in this chapter.

48. Circular no. 31, Central Committee in Munich to Jewish Committee in Feldafing, April 11, 1948, YIVO, MK483, Reel 26, frame 1144 (Feldafing). See also, for example, Reel 7, frame 25, and Reel 5, frame 223, for circulars sent to Rochelle and Schwabenhausen.

49. "Executive for security for the people and the homeland," YIVO, MK483, Reel 96, Folder 1354, p. 512.

50. Yablonka, *Survivors of the Holocaust*, 97.

51. Hoffman, "Ha-Mishlechet Ha-Eretz Yisraelit Le-She'erit Ha-Pletah," Part 2, 159–61.

52. Ibid.

53. Survey on the condition of Nocham (in the months February, March, and April), Munich, May 9, 1948, HAHP, 123/LVOD/0028n, Archion HaAvodah veHehalutz, Machon Lavon 25.28 (50).

54. Ibid.

55. Letter to Hashmer Hatzair regarding giyus of ken (bozlow?), March 16, 1948, HAHP, 123/Hashomer Hatzair/407, p. 187.

56. Nocham survey on activity in the movement (for the months February, March, and April), May 5, 1948, Munich, HAHP, 123/LVOD/0028, pp. 135–36.

57. Avraham Zelig to Maccabi/Gordoniah, March 2, 1948, Agmatz, 1/128, quoted in Ada Schein, "Ma'arehet ha-hinukh be-mahanot ha-'akurim ha-yehudiyim be-Germanyah ube-Austryah, 1945–1951" (PhD dissertation, Hebrew University, 2000), 187. Schein also cites a letter from Eli Zisser to the effect that the movements applied social and economic pressure on those responsible for giyus and they were also the first to fulfill their quotas (HaAvodah Halutz archive, File 126 VII, Folder 44).

58. Nocham survey on activity in the movement (for the months February, March, and April), May 5, 1948, Munich, HAHP, 123/LVOD/0028, pp. 135–36.

59. Hoffman, "Ha-Mishlechet Ha-Eretz Yisraelit Le-She'erit Ha-Pletah," Part 2, 159–61.

60. Letter from the "Sanctions Committee of the Civil Committee for Mas Am Lochem," Stuttgart, December 21, 1948, YIVO, MK 483, Reel 1, frame 130.

61. Ben-David, *Ha-Haganah be-Eiropah*, 232.

62. Reports by the Bundist executive committee, as well as letters from Bund members to family and to *Undzer Shtime*, the Bund newspaper in Paris, would soon relate "Zionist terror" in the camps, directed against those who did not fulfill their giyus duty. See, for example, YIVO, Bund Archives, MG2-108, as well as reports in *Der Wecker*, the Bundist newspaper (e.g., May 1948, p. 11).

63. See for example, in the Rochelle DP camp, YIVO, MK 483, Reel 63, frame 734, April 18, 1948. For an example of JDC concern over abuse of rations by Central Committee of Liberated Jews, see the letter from Abraham Cohen (JDC director in Frankfurt) to representatives of the Central Committee, YIVO, MK 483, Reel 64, frame 1375, Frankfurt, November 11, 1948.

64. Course no. 10, Haganah archive, Box (hativah) 80, Folder 1.

65. Markovizky, *Gachelet Lochemet*, 64. Via the base in Marseilles (Aliyah Base 1), 7,467 immigrated to Israel, principally in the months March–July 1948 (6,203 men and 1,264 women of giyus age); 1,500 immigrated via Aliyah D (500 by plane); 2,646 immigrated via Aliyah Base 2 in Italy; 3,000 tried to immigrate on illegal ships with Aliyah Bet and were deported to Cyprus; 2,826 (including the Zionist youths of Bulgaria) immigrated from Yugoslavia on three boats; 4,300 were left for future immigration in camps in Europe in Marseilles, Italy, Poland, Czechoslovakia, Germany, Hungary, and Western Europe.

66. Emmanuel Sivan, *Dor Tashakh: Mitos, Diyukan ve-Zikaron* [The 1948 Generation: Myth, Profile and Memory] (Israel: Ministry of Defense, 1991), 76.

67. Monish Einhorn interview with the author, June 7, 2003.

68. Sivan, *Dor Tashakh*, 76.

69. Ibid. His source is M. Sikrun, *Giyus Koach Ha-adam be-Milkhemet Ha-Komemiyut* (ZHL archives).

70. Markovizky, *Gachelet Lochemet*, 118, also supports this conclusion. Before May 1948, Giyus Hutz La'aretz soldiers played a small role in the fighting; only 716 were conscripted before May 1948, 118.

71. Sivan, *Dor Tashakh*, 78.

Conclusion

1. *Landsberger Lager Cajtung*, no. 1, October 8, 1945, p. 3, YIVO, Jewish DP Periodicals, Reel 1. For a thorough analysis of Gringauz's ideology, see Ze'ev Mankowitz, *Life between Memory and Hope: The Survivors of the Holocaust in Occupied Germany* (Cambridge: Cambridge University Press, 2002), chap. 8.

2. Rogers Brubaker, *Citizenship and Nationhood in France and Germany* (Cambridge: Harvard University Press, 1992). Especially useful in this regard is the first chapter, which discusses the institution of citizenship as an introduction to the political theory of nation-state membership.

3. For literature on American policy in postwar Germany, see, for example, Richard L. Merritt, *Democracy Imposed: U.S. Occupation Policy and the German Public, 1945–1949* (New Haven, CT: Yale University Press, 1995); Lucius D. Clay, *Decision in Germany* (Garden City, NY: Doubleday, 1950); Michael J. Hogan, *The Marshall Plan: America, Britain, and the Reconstruction of Western Europe, 1947–1952* (New York: Cambridge University Press, 1987); Carolyn Eisenberg, *Drawing the Line: The American Decision to Divide Germany, 1944–1949* (New York: Cambridge University Press, 1996); Edward N. Peterson, *The American Occupation of Germany: Retreat to Victory* (Detroit: Wayne State University Press, 1977); and Harold Zink, *The United States in Germany, 1944–1955* (Princeton, NJ: Van Nostrand, 1957).

4. Yad Vashem Archives, Hativah 037, Folder 32, Miriam Warburg, "Children and Youth Aliyah," November 30, 1945.

5. See, for example, Aryeh Levi Sarid, *Be-Mivchan he-Anut veha-Pdut: Ha-Tnuot Ha-Halutziot be-PolinBa-Shoah ve-Achareha, 1939–1949* (Tel Aviv: Moreshet, 1997), and Yehoyakim Cochavi, *Shoresh le-'Akurim: Tnu' ot ha-No'ar be-Mahanot ha-'Akurim be-Germanyah, 1945–1949* (Giv'at Havivah: Yad Ya'ari, 1999).

6. Most works that have focused on survivors tend to study the validity of survivor testimony taken years after the event. See, most notably, the work of Lawrence Langer, *Holocaust Testimonies: The Ruins of Memory* (New Haven, CT: Yale University Press, 1991). Henry Greenspan has been one of the few to focus on survivor

testimony collected soon after liberation. See Henry Greenspan, "'An Immediate and Violent Impulse': Holocaust Survivor Testimony in the First Years after Liberation," in *Remembering for the Future: The Holocaust in an Age of Genocide*, Vol. 3, *Memory*, edited by John K. Roth and Elisabeth Maxwell, 108–16 (London: Palgrave Macmillan, 2001). Greenspan contradicts the idea that survivors tried to avoid thinking about "it" after the war and details the work of the Central Historical Commission in collecting testimonies. See also Laura Jockusch, "'Collect and Record! Help to Write the History of the Latest Destruction!' Jewish Historical Commissions in Europe, 1943–1953" (PhD dissertation, New York University, 2007); Jockusch, "A 'Folk Monument for Our Destruction and Heroism': Jewish Historical Commissions in Displaced Persons Camps in Germany, Austria, and Italy," in *"We Are Here": New Approaches to Jewish Displaced Persons in Postwar Germany*, edited by Avinoam J. Patt and Michael Berkowitz (Detroit: Wayne State University Press, forthcoming); Boaz Cohen, "Holocaust Research in Israel, 1945–1980: Trends, Characteristics, Developments" (PhD dissertation, Bar-Ilan Unversity, 2004); and Cohen, "The Children's Voice: Postwar Collection of Testimonies from Child Survivors of the Holocaust," *Holocaust and Genocide Studies* 21, no. 1 (2007): 73–95.

Glossary

Aliyah—Ascent. Jewish immigration to the Land of Israel.

Bricha—Flight. The movement to lead Holocaust survivors out of Europe to Palestine.

Chalutz(im)—Pioneer(s). Agricultural laborers in Palestine.

Chanich(im)—Student or trainee. A term used to refer to members of Zionist youth groups.

Eretz Israel—The Land of Israel.

Giyus—Conscription for military service.

Ha'apalah—Upward struggle. Clandestine immigration to Palestine.

Hakhsharah—Preparation. Agricultural training in preparation for aliyah.

Kibbutz(im)—The term used to refer to collective groups organized by Zionist youth movements in postwar Europe. Also used to refer to agricultural settlements in Palestine.

Madrich(ah)—Leader. Title applied to instructors in Zionist youth groups.

Oleh (olim)—Jewish immigrant(s) to Palestine.

Shaliach (shlichah [f.], shlichim [pl.])—Emissary. Representative from the Yishuv assigned to promote aliyah from the Diaspora.

She'erit Hapletah—Surviving Remnant. The term used to refer to the community of Jewish Holocaust survivors in Europe.

Yishuv—Settlement. The term used to refer to the Jewish community in Palestine.

Zionist Youth Movements

Dror (lit. "freedom")—Pioneering socialist youth movement founded in Poland in 1915 out of a wing of Tze'irei Zion that remained independent from Hashomer Hatzair; Dror and Gordoniah were affiliated with the United Kibbutz movement.

Gordoniah—Pioneering socialist, non-Marxist youth movement established in Poland in 1925 and named after A. D. Gordon, whose writings formed the ideological foundation of the Labor Zionist movement in Palestine.

HaNoar Hatzioni (lit. "the Zionist youth")—Formed in 1932, it constituted the youth movement of the nonsocialist General Zionists.

Hashomer Hatzair (lit. "the young guard")—Zionist socialist pioneering youth movement officially established in Vienna in 1916, first originated as part of Tze'irei Zion and Hashomer in Galicia. Ideologically, the movement combined an orientation to settlement in Eretz Israel with left-wing socialism and Marxism.

Hehalutz (The Pioneer) movement—An umbrella organization of Zionist youth movements that worked to train its members for aliyah to Palestine.

Nocham—As described in chapter 1, the Noar Chalutzi Meuchad (United Pioneering Youth) movement was formed by the United Zionist Organization in the American zone of Occupied Germany and was intended as a comprehensive Zionist pioneering youth movement for all Jewish youths in Bavaria.

Bibliography

Primary Sources—Unpublished Material

Archives

ISRAEL

Central Zionist Archives (CZA), Jerusalem

L58   Youth Aliyah Department, European Office

S6   Immigration Department

S32   Youth and Hehalutz Department

S53   Office of Eliezer Kaplan, Items related to Aliyah

S75   Youth Aliyah Department

S86   Emissaries Department

American Joint Distribution Committee Archives, Jerusalem
    Displaced Persons Camps in Germany

Haganah Archives, Tel Aviv
    Archives of the Haganah
    The Shaul Avigur Inter-University Project for the study of the Ha'apalah, Ha'a-
       palah Project (HAHP), collection housed at the Haganah Archives
    Central Zionist Archives, Jerusalem
       123/AZM/24—(CZA, S/86)
    Ghetto Fighters House Archives, Kibbutz Lochamei Ha-Getaot
       123/Lochem/65k
       123/Lochem/0019
    Hashomer Hatzair Archives, Giv'at Chavivah
       123/Hashomer Hatzair/407
       123/Hashomer Hatzair/408
       123/Hashomer Hatzair/409
       123/HaShomer Hatzair/410
       123/Hashomer Hatzair/412—*Yoman Kibbutz Lochamei HaGettaot al shem
       Tosia Altman*

Kibbutz Ha-Meuchad Archives
    123/KBO/250a
Labor and He-Halutz Archives, Lavon Institute
    123/LVOD/0028n
Maccabi-Gordoniah Archives, Huldah, named after Pinchas Lavon
    123/Maccabi/0012
    123/Maccabi/0013
    123/Maccabi/0014
    123/Maccabi/148
Mapai Archives, Beit Berl
    123/MPLG/105
Moreshet Archives
    123/MORSH/6
Kibbutz Gazit Archive
    Diary of Kibbutz Lochamei Ha-Gettaot al shem Tosia Altman
Kibbutz Ha-Meuchad Archive, Ef'al—Yad Tabenkin
    2: Folders of department outside Israel
    36: Information on Nocham
Yad Vashem Archives, Jerusalem
    M-1P, She'erit Hapletah Collection, Central Historical Commission
    M-1E—Testimonies
    VD/1–200, Video testimonies
Personal documents from DP camps in Germany

UNITED STATES
Center for Jewish History, New York
    YIVO
        Leo Schwarz Papers (MK 488)
        DP Germany (MK 483)
        Jewish DP Periodicals
        YIVO Library
    American Jewish Historical Society (AJHS)
        I-249, NJWB–Military Chaplaincy Records
    Leo Baeck Institute
United States Holocaust Memorial Museum, Washington, DC (USHMM)

Selected DP Newspapers from YIVO Jewish DP Periodicals Collection

Reel 1
  Landsberger Lager Cajtung (Landsberg)
  Jidisze Cajtung
Reel 4
  Dror
  BaMidbar: Wochncajtung fun di bafrajte Jidn (Föhrenwald)
Reel 6
  Dos Wort (Munich)
Reel 7
  Undzer Wort (Bamberg)
Reel 9
  Der yiddisher kemfer (Pachach)
Reel 10
  Nocham
Reel 11
  Landwirtschaftlecher Wegwajzer
Reel 12
  Ichud Olami
Reel 13
  ORT jedies fun der U.S. Zone
  Najwelt (Left Poalei Zion in Germany)
Reel 14
  Dos Fraje Wort (Feldafing)
Reel 22
  Unzer Welt (New Zionist Organization, Munich)
Reel 23
  Ojf der Wach (Hashomer Hatzair Be-Ha'apalah)
Reel 24
  A Heim (Leipheim)
  Fun Letstn Khurbn (Central Historical Commission, Munich)
Reel 26
  Najwelt (Borochov-jugnt)
Reel 29
  Deror Germaniyah (educational circulars)
Reel 30
  Igeret (Holzhausen, Kibbutz Dror)
  Hashomer Hatzair (educational circulars)

Interviews

Zelig Litwak, May 29, 2003
Shmuel Leitner, May 29, 2003
Eliyahu Raziel, May 29, 2003
Haim Shorrer, May 29, 2003
Miriam Yechieli, May 30, 2003
Monish Einhorn (Haran), June 7, 2003

Primary Sources—Published Material

American Jewish Year Book. Philadelphia: American Jewish Committee, 1950.
Beck, Gad. *An Underground Life: Memoirs of a Gay Jew in Nazi Berlin.* Madison: University of Wisconsin Press, 1999.
Biber, Yakov. *Risen from the Ashes: A Story of the Jewish Displaced Persons in the Aftermath of World War II; Being a Sequel to Survivors.* San Francisco: Borgo, 1990.
Clay, Lucius D. *Decision in Germany.* Garden City, NY: Doubleday, 1950.
Crossman, Richard H. S. *Palestine Mission: A Personal Record.* London: H. Hamilton, 1947.
"Declaration of the Establishment of Israel." In *Israel Yearbook and Almanac 1991/92,* edited by N. Greenwood, 298–99. Jerusalem: International Publication Service, 1992.
Dekel, Efraim. *Be-Netivei Ha-Brichah* [On the Path of the Bricha]. Tel Aviv: Ma'arachot, 1959.
Diagnostic and Statistical Manual of Mental Disorders. 4th ed. Washington, DC: American Psychiatric Association, 1994.
Dos Bukh fun Lublin: Zikhroynes, gvies-eydes un materialn iber lebn, kamf un martirertum fun lubliner yidishn yishev. Paris: Paris Committee for the Creation of a Monograph on the Jewish Community of Lublin, 1952.
Efros, Israel. *Heymloze Yidn: a bazukh in di Yidishe Lagern in Daytshland.* Buenos Aires: Tsentral Farband fun Poylishe Yidn in Argentine, 1947.
Engelshtern, Lazar. *Mit di vegn fun der Sheyres Ha-Pleyteh.* Israel: Igud Yotsei Vilna veha-sevivah be-Yisrael, 1976.
Gar, Yosef. *In geloyf fun horeveh heymen.* New York: S. N., 1952.
Grajek, Shalom (Stefan). *Ha-Ma'avak 'Al Hemshekh Ha-Hayyim: Yehudei Polin, 1945–1949* [The Struggle to Continue Life: The Jews of Poland in the Years 1945–1949]. Tel Aviv: Am Oved, 1989.
Harrison, Earl Grant. *The Plight of the Displaced Jews in Europe: A Report to President Truman.* New York: United Jewish Appeal for Refugees and the JDC, 1945.

Heymont, Irving. *Among the Survivors of the Holocaust: The Landsberg DP Camp Letters of Major Irving Heymont, United States Army.* Cincinnati: American Jewish Archives, 1982.

Hochberg-Marianska, Miriam. "Tipalti be-Yeladim Nitzulim." *Yediot Yad Vashem* 8–9 (1956): 12–13.

Hochberg-Marianska, Miriam, and Noe Gruss, eds. *The Children Accuse.* Portland, OR: Valentine Mitchell, 1996.

Hoffman (Yachil), Haim. "Ha-Mishlechet Ha-Eretz Yisraelit Le-She'erit Ha-Pletah." Part 1. *Yalkut Moreshet* 30 (1980): 7–40.

———. "Ha-Mishlechet Ha-Eretz Yisraelit Le-She'erit Ha-Pletah." Part 2. *Yalkut Moreshet* 31 (1981): 133–76, 159.

Hulme, Kathryn. *The Wild Place.* Boston: Little Brown, 1953.

Kleiman, Yehudit, and Nina Springer-Aharoni, eds. *The Anguish of Liberation: Testimonies from 1945.* Jerusalem: Yad Vashem, 1995.

Kovner, Abba. "Reshita shel Ha-Bricha ke-tnuah Hamonit be-eduyotav shel Abba Kovner." *Yalkut Moreshet* 37 (1984): 7–31; 38 (1984): 133–46.

Kruk, Hermann. *The Last Days of the Jerusalem of Lithuania: Chronicles from the Vilna Ghetto and the Camps, 1939–1944.* New York: Yale University Press, 2003.

Leitner, Shmuel. *Yamim Shkhorim, 1938–1945.* Israel: Kibbutz Dalia, 2001.

Lubetkin, Zivia. *Biyemei Kilayon U-Mered.* Tel Aviv: Ha-Kibbutz Ha-Meuhad, 1989.

Nadich, Judah. *Eisenhower and the Jews.* New York: Twayne, 1953.

Patt, Emmanuel. *Yidishe Kinder Tzurik Tzum Leben.* New York: Jewish Labor Committee, 1946.

Rabinovitz, Eliezer. *Be-Madei UNRRA im She'erit HaPletah, 1946–1948.* Tel Aviv: Moreshet, 1990.

"Report of the Anglo-American Committee of Enquiry regarding the Problems of European Jewry and Palestine." Lausanne, April 20, 1946, YIVO Library.

"Report of Proceedings of the 22nd Zionist Congress." Basel, Switzerland, December 9–24, 1946.

Rosensaft, Menachem Z., ed. *Life Reborn: Jewish Displaced Persons, 1945–1951, Conference Proceedings.* Washington, DC: United States Holocaust Memorial Museum, 2001.

Schwartz, Yaakov. "Ba-Derech Le-Eretz Yisrael." *Yalkut Moreshet* 55 (1993): 233–55.

Sefer Ha-Shomrim: Antologiyah le-Yovel ha-XX shel ha-Shomer ha-Tzair, 1913–1933 [The Book of the Shomrim: An Anthology for the Twentieth Anniversary of Hashomer Hatzair, 1913–1933]. Warsaw: Hotza'at Ha-Hanhageh Ha-Eliorah Le-Histradrut Ha-Shomer Hatzair, 1934.

Shalit, Levi. *Azoy zaynen mir geshtorbn.* Munich: Farband fur Litvishe Yidn in Daytshland, 1949.

Shaltiel, Shlomo, ed. *Ha Yoman: Yomano shel Kibbutz HaShomer HaTzair Lochamei HaGetaot al Shem Tosia Altman.* Giv'at Haviva: Yad Ya'ari, 1997.

Shner-Nishmit, Sara. *Ve'el Ha-menuchah Lo Bati.* Tel Aviv: Ha-Kibbutz Ha-Meuhad, 1985.

Stone, Isidor F. *Underground to Palestine.* New York: Boni & Gaer, 1946.

Szildkrojt, M. "Ven Lublin iz Bafrayt Gevoren." In *Dos Bukh fun Lublin: Zikhroynes, gvies-eydes un materialn iber lebn, kamf un martirertum fun lubliner yidishn yishev,* 599–600. Paris: Paris Committee for the Creation of a Monograph on the Jewish Community of Lublin, 1952.

Turkow, Jonas. *Nokh der Bafrayung: zikhroynes.* Buenos Aires: Tsentral-farband fun Poylishe Yidn in Argentine, 1959.

Wischnitzer, Mark. *To Dwell in Safety.* Philadelphia: Jewish Publication Society of America, 1948.

Ya'ari, Meir. *Nokh di martirer yorn: A rede tsu partizaner-oylim in Kibutz Evron.* Merhavyah: La-Herhageh Le-Eloreh Shel Hashomer Hatzair, 1945.

Yechieli, Miriam. "Be-vatei keleh Sovyetim (1939–1940)." *Yalkut Moreshet* 26 (November 1978): 159–86.

Secondary Sources

Abzug, Robert H. *Inside the Vicious Heart: Americans and the Liberation of Nazi Concentration Camps.* New York: Oxford University Press, 1985.

Aleksiun, Natalia. "Where Was There a Future for Polish Jewry? Bundist and Zionist Polemics in Post–World War II Poland." In *Jewish Politics in Eastern Europe: The Bund at 100,* edited by Jack Jacobs, 227–42. New York: New York University Press, 2001.

Amkraut, Brian. "Let Our Children Go: Youth Aliyah in Germany, 1932–1939." PhD dissertation, New York University, 2000.

Angress, Werner T. *Between Fear and Hope: Jewish Youth in the Third Reich.* New York: Columbia University Press, 1988.

Avizohar, Meir. "Bikur Ben-Gurion be-mahanot ha-'akurim ve-tefisato ha-leumit be-tom Milhemet ha-'Olam ha-Sheniah" [Ben-Gurion's Visit to the DP Camps and His National Outlook in the Aftermath of Word War II]. In *Yahadut Mizrach Eiropah Bein Shoah Le-tekuma 1944–1948,* edited by Benjamin Pinkus, 253–70. Sde Boker: Ben-Gurion University, 1987.

Bar-Gil, Shlomo. "Batei Yeladim 'al Admat Eiropah." *Yalkut Moreshet* 65 (April 1998): 61–80.

———. "Ha-shikum veha-klitah ha-hinuchit shel yeladim ve-na'arim me-She'erit ha-Pletah be-Eiropah 'al yedei 'Aliyat Ha-No'ar." *Yalkut Moreshet* 64 (November 1997): 7–27.

———. *Mehapsim bayit mots'im moledet: 'Aliyat Ha-No'ar be-hinukh uve-shikum She'erit ha-Pletah, 1945–1955.* Jerusalem: Yad Yitzhak ben Tzvi, 1999.

Bartal, Israel, and Yisrael Gutman, eds. *Kiyum ve-Shever: Yehudei Polin Le-Doroteihem.* Jerusalem: Merkaz Zalman Shazar, 1997.

Bartrop, Paul R. *Surviving the Camps: Unity in Adversity during the Holocaust.* Lanham, MD: University Press of America, 2000.

Bauer, Yehuda. *Flight and Rescue: Bricha.* New York: Random House, 1970.

———. "The Initial Organization of the Holocaust Survivors in Bavaria." *Yad Vashem Studies* 8 (1970): 127–57.

———. *Out of the Ashes: The Impact of American Jews on Post-Holocaust European Jewry.* New York: Pergamon, 1989.

Baumel, Judith Tydor. *Kibbutz Buchenwald: Survivors and Pioneers.* New Brunswick, NJ: Rutgers University Press, 1997.

———. "Kibbutz Buchenwald and Kibbutz Hafetz Hayyim: Two Experiments in the Rehabilitation of Jewish Survivors in Germany." *Holocaust and Genocide Studies* 9 (Fall 1995): 231–49.

———. "The Politics of Religious Rehabilitation in the DP Camps." *Simon Wiesenthal Center Annual* 6 (1990): 57–79.

Ben-David, Yehuda. *Ha-Haganah be-Eiropah* [The Haganah in Europe]. Israel: TAG, 1995.

Bernstein, Leon. "Emigrants and Khalutzim: Some Remarks on DP Psychology." *Jewish Frontier* 14 (June 1947): 10–13.

Blatman, Daniel. *Le-ma'an Heruteinu ve-Herutchem: Ha-Bund be-Polin, 1939–1949.* Jerusalem: Yad Vashem, 1996.

Bloch, Herbert A. "The Personality of Inmates of Concentration Camps." *American Journal of Sociology* 52 (1947): 335–41.

Bluhm, Hilde O. "How Did They Survive: Mechanisms of Defence in Nazi Concentration Camps." *American Journal of Psychotherapy* 2 (1948): 3–32.

Boehling, Rebecca L. *A Question of Priorities: Democratic Reforms and Economic Recovery in Postwar Germany.* Providence, RI: Berghahn, 1996.

Bogner, Nachum. *Be-hasdei Zarim: Hatzalat Yeladim be-Zehut Sheulah be-Polin.* Jerusalem: Yad Vashem, 2000.

Bornstein, Shmuel. *Geulat yeladim Yehudim mi-yede ha-notsrim be-Polin ahare ha-Shoah.* Kibbutz Lohamei ha-Getaot: Bet Lohamei Ha-Getaot, 1989.

Brandes, Aharon. *Ketz ha-Yehudim be-ma'arav Polin.* Merhavia: Hashomer Hatzair, 1945.

Brenner, Michael. *After the Holocaust: Rebuilding Jewish Lives in Postwar Germany.* Princeton, NJ: Princeton University Press, 1997.

Brubaker, Rogers. *Citizenship and Nationhood in France and Germany.* Cambridge: Harvard University Press, 1992.

Chodoff, Paul. "The German Concentration Camps As a Psychological Stress." *Archive of General Psychiatry* 22 (1970): 78–87.

Cholawski, Shalom. "Partisans and Ghetto Fighters: An Active Element among *She'erit Hapletah.*" In *She'erit Hapletah, 1944–1948: Rehabilitation and Political Struggle,* edited by Yisrael Gutman and Avital Saf, 249–57. Jerusalem: Yad Vashem, 1990.

Cochavi, Yehoyakim. *Shoresh le-'Akurim: Tnu' ot ha-No'ar be-Mahanot ha-'Akurim be-Germanyah, 1945–1949.* Giv'at Havivah: Yad Ya'ari, 1999.

Cochavi, Yehoyakim, and Asher Cohen, eds. *Zionist Youth Movements during the Shoah.* New York: Peter Lang, 1995.

Cohen, Boaz. "Holocaust Research in Israel, 1945–1980: Trends, Characteristics, Developments." PhD dissertation, Bar-Ilan University, 2004.

Cohen, Yochanan. *Ovrim kol Gvul: Ha-Brichah, Polin 1945–1946.* Tel Aviv: Zemorah-Bitan, 1995.

Cole, Michael, and Sheila Cole. *The Development of Children.* New York: Scientific American, 1993.

Davidson, Jonathan, and Edna Foa, eds. *Posttraumatic Stress Disorder: DSM-IV and Beyond.* Washington, DC: American Psychiatric Press, 1993.

Des Pres, Terence. *The Survivor: An Anatomy of Life in the Death Camps.* New York: Oxford University Press, 1976.

Dimsdale, Joel, ed. *Survivors, Victims, and Perpetrators: Essays on the Nazi Holocaust.* Washington, DC: Hemisphere, 1980.

Diner, Dan. "Elements in Becoming a Subject: Jewish DPs in Historical Context." *Jahrbuch zur Geschichte und Wirkung des Holocaust* (1997): 229–48.

Dinnerstein, Leonard. *America and the Survivors of the Holocaust.* New York: Columbia University Press, 1982.

Dobroszycki, Lucjan. "Restoring Jewish Life in Postwar Poland." YIVO, 9/73698, 1974.

———. *Survivors of the Holocaust in Poland: A Portrait Based on Jewish Community Records.* Armonk, NY: Sharpe, 1994.

Efrat, Aharon. *Derekh shomrim be-hagshama: Hakhsharah ve-'aliyah shel ha-Shomer ha-Tsa'ir be-Polin uve-Galitsyah ben shete milhamot'olam.* Giv'at Havivah: Hashomer Hatzair, 1991.

Eisenberg, Carolyn. *Drawing the Line: The American Decision to Divide Germany, 1944–1949.* New York: Cambridge University Press, 1996.

Eisenstadt, S. N. "Archetypical Patterns of Youth." In *Youth: Change and Challenge,* edited by Erik Erikson, 24–42. New York: Basic Books, 1963.

Engel, David. *Ben Shikhrur Li-Verihah: Nitsolei ha-Shoah be-Polin veha-ma'avak 'al Hanhagatam, 1944–1946* [Between Liberation and Flight: Holocaust

Survivors in Poland and the Struggle for Leadership, 1944–1947]. Tel Aviv: Am Oved, 1996.

———. "The Reconstruction of Jewish Communal Institutions in Postwar Poland: The Origins of the Central Committee of Polish Jews, 1944–1945." *East European Politics and Societies* 10 (1996): 85–107.

Erikson, Erik. *Identity: Youth and Crisis.* New York: Norton, 1968.

Ettinger, Leo. "Concentration Camp Survivors in the Post War World." *American Journal of Orthopsychiatry* 32, no. 67 (April 1962).

———. "The Concentration Camp Syndrome and Its Late Sequelae." In *Survivors, Victims, and Perpetrators: Essays on the Nazi Holocaust,* edited by Joel Dimsdale, 127–62. Washington, DC: Hemisphere, 1980.

Fatal-Knaani, Tikva. *Zo Lo Otah Grodno: Kehilat Grodno ve-Svivatah be-Milhamah uve-Shoah, 1939–1943.* Jerusalem: Yad Vashem, 2001.

Friedman, Paul. "Some Aspects of Concentration Camp Psychology." *American Journal of Psychiatry* 105 (1949): 601–5.

Friesel, Evyatar. "The Holocaust: Factor in the Birth of Israel?" In *Major Changes within the Jewish People in the Wake of the Holocaust,* edited by Yisrael Gutman, 519–52. Jerusalem: Yad Vashem, 1996.

Gelber, Yoav. "The Meeting between the Jewish Soldiers from Palestine Serving in the British Army and She'erit Hapletah." In *She'erit Hapletah, 1944–1948,* edited by Yisrael Gutman and Avital Saf, 60–80. Jerusalem: Yad Vashem, 1990.

———. *Toldot ha-Hitnadvut: Nosei ha-degel—shlichutam shel ha-mitnadvim la'am ha-yehudi.* Jerusalem: Yad Yitzchak ben Zvi, 1983.

Genizi, Haim. *Yo'ets u-Mekim: Ha-Yo'ets Le-Tsava ha-Amerikani vele-She'erit ha-Pletah.* Tel Aviv: Moreshet, 1992.

Gordon, A. D. "People and Labor." In *The Zionist Idea: A Historical Analysis and Reader,* edited by Arthur Hertzberg, 368–374. New York: Atheneum, 1971.

Gringauz, Samuel. "Jewish Destiny As the DPs See It: The Ideology of the Surviving Remnant." *Commentary* 4 (July–December 1947): 501–9.

———. "Our New German Policy and the DPs: Why Immediate Resettlement Is Imperative." *Commentary* 5 (January–June 1948): 508–14.

Grobman, Alexander. *Rekindling the Flame: American Jewish Chaplains and the Survivors of European Jewry, 1944–1948.* Detroit: Wayne State University Press, 1993.

Grodzinsky, Yosef. *Homer Enoshi Tov: Yehudim mul Tsiyonim, 1945–1951.* Or Yehudah, Israel: Hed Artzi, 1998.

Grossman, Kurt. *The Jewish DP Problem: Its Origin, Scope, and Liquidation.* New York: World Jewish Congress, 1951.

Grossmann, Atina. *Jews, Germans, and Allies: Close Encounters in Occupied Germany.* Princeton, NJ: Princeton University Press, 2007.

———. "Trauma, Memory, and Motherhood: Germans and Jewish Displaced Persons in Post-Nazi Germany, 1945–1948." *Archiv fur Sozialgeschichte* 38 (1998): 215–39.

———. "Victims, Villains, and Survivors: Gendered Perceptions and Self-Perceptions of Jewish Displaced Persons in Occupied Postwar Germany." *Journal of the History of Sexuality* 11 (January/April 2002): 291–318.

Gutman, Yisrael. *Ha-Yehudim be-Polin ahare Milhemet ha-'olam ha-sheniyah.* Jerusalem: Merkaz Zalman Shazar, 1985.

———. *The Jews of Warsaw, 1939–1943: Ghetto, Underground, Revolt.* Bloomington: Indiana University Press, 1982.

———, ed. *Major Changes within the Jewish People in the Wake of the Holocaust.* Jerusalem: Yad Vashem, 1996.

———. "The Youth Movement As an Alternative Leadership in Eastern Europe." In *Zionist Youth Movements during the Shoah,* edited by Asher Cohen and Yehoyakim Cochavi, 7–116. New York: Peter Lang, 1995.

Gutman, Yisrael, and Avital Saf, eds. *She'erit Hapletah, 1944–1948: Rehabilitation and Political Struggle.* Jerusalem: Yad Vashem, 1990.

———. "Yehudei Polin Me-Shihrur Le-Hagirah." In *Yahadut Mizrah Eiropah ben Shoah li-Tekumah, 1944–1948,* edited by Benjamin Pinkus, 113–24. Sdeh Boker, Israel: Ben-Gurion University, 1987.

Ha'apala: Me'asef Le-Toldot Ha-Hatzala, Ha-Bricha, ve-She'erit Ha-Pletah. Tel Aviv: Tel Aviv University, 1990.

Halamish, Aviva. *The Exodus Affair: Holocaust Survivors and the Struggle for Palestine.* Syracuse: Syracuse University Press, 1998.

Hendel, Yehudit. *Anashim Acherim Hem.* Merhavia: Sifriat Poalim, 1950.

Hogan, Michael J. *The Marshall Plan: America, Britain, and the Reconstruction of Western Europe, 1947–1952.* New York: Cambridge University Press, 1987.

Jacobs, Jack, ed. *Jewish Politics in Eastern Europe: The Bund at 100.* New York: New York University Press, 2001.

Kestenberg, Judith S., and Ira Brenner. *The Last Witness: The Child Survivor of the Holocaust.* Washington, DC: American Psychiatric Press, 1996.

Keynan, Irit. *Lo Nirga Ha-Ra'av: Nitzulei Ha-Shoah ve-Shlichei Eretz Yisrael: Germanyah, 1945–1948.* Tel Aviv: Am Oved, 1996.

Klein, H. "Holocaust Survivors in Kibbutzim: Readaptation Reintegration." *Israel Annals of Psychiatry and Related Disciplines* 10 (March 1972): 78–91.

Kless, Shlomo *Be-Derekh Lo Slula: Toldot ha-Berihah, 1944–1948* [On an Unpaved Path: The History of the Bricha, 1944–1948]. Giv'at Havivah: Moreshet, 1994.

Kochavi, Arieh. "Anglo-American Discord: Jewish Refugees and United Nations Relief and Rehabilitation Administration Policy, 1945–1947." *Diplomatic History* 14 (Fall 1990): 529–51.

———. *Post-Holocaust Politics: Britain, the United States, and Jewish Refugees, 1945–1948.* Chapel Hill: University of North Carolina Press, 2001.

Konigseder, Angela. *Flucht Nach Berlin: Judische Displaced Persons, 1945–1948.* Berlin: Metropol Verlag, 1998.

Konigseder, Angela, and Juliane Wetzel. *Lebensmut im Wartesaal: Die judischen DPs im Nachkriegsdeutschland.* Frankfurt Am Main: Fischer Taschenbuch Verlag, 1994.

———. *Waiting for Hope: Jewish Displaced Persons in Post-WWII Germany.* Evanston, IL: Northwestern University Press, 2001.

Kurisky, Leibl. "Ha-coordinacja Ha-tzionit le-geulat yeladim." *Gal-ed: On the History of the Jews in Poland* 5 (1985).

Lamm, Zvi. *Shitat Ha-Hinkukh shel Ha-Shomer Ha-Tzair.* Jerusalem: Magnes, 1998.

Lavsky, Hagit. *New Beginnings: Holocaust Survivors in Bergen-Belsen and the British Zone in Germany, 1945–1950.* Detroit: Wayne State University Press, 2002.

———. "She'erit Ha-Pletah ve-Hakamat Ha-Medinah: Hizdamnut asher Nutzlah." *Katedra* 55 (1990): 162–74.

Lazar, Haim. *Betar Be-She'erit Ha-Pletah: 1945–1948.* Israel: Jabotinsky Institute, 1997.

Lifton, Robert Jay. "The Concept of the Survivor." In *Survivors, Victims, and Perpetrators*, edited by Joel E. Dimsdale, 113–26. New York: Hemisphere, 1980.

Litvak, Yosef. "Trumato shel Irgun Ha-Joint le-shikumah shel She'erit Ha-Pletah be-Polin, 1944–49." In *Yahadut Mizrach Eiropah ben Shoah le-Tekumah, 1944–1948*, edited by Benajmin Pinkus, 334–88. Sdeh Boker: Ben-Gurion University, 1987.

Mankowitz, Ze'ev. "The Formation of She'erit Hapletah: November 1944–1945." *Yad Vashem Studies* 20 (1990): 337–70.

———. "Ideology and Politics in the She'erit Hapletah in the American Occupied Zone of Germany, 1945–1946." PhD dissertation, Hebrew University, 1987.

———. *Life between Memory and Hope: The Survivors of the Holocaust in Occupied Germany.* Cambridge: Cambridge University Press, 2002.

———. "Zionism and *She'erit Hapletah*." In *She'erit Hapletah, 1944–1948: Rehabilitation and Political Struggle*, edited by Yisrael Gutman and Avital Saf, 211–30. Jerusalem: Yad Vashem, 1990.

Markovizky, Ya'acov. *Gachelet Lochemet: Giyus Hutz la-Aretz be-Milchemet Ha-'atzmaut* [Fighting Ember: Gachal Forces in the War of Independence]. Israel: Ministry of Defense, 1995.

Mendelssohn, Ezra. *The Jews of East Central Europe between the World Wars*. Bloomington: Indiana University Press, 1983.

———. *On Modern Jewish Politics*. New York: Oxford University Press, 1993.

Merritt, Richard L. *Democracy Imposed: U.S. Occupation Policy and the German Public, 1945–1949*. New Haven, CT: Yale University Press, 1995.

Michman, Dan. *Holocaust Historiography: A Jewish Perspective*. Portland: Valentine Mitchell, 2003.

Myers, Margarete. "Jewish DP's: Reconstructing Individual and Community in the U.S. Zone of Occupied Germany." *Leo Baeck Institute Yearbook* 42 (1997): 303–24.

Naor, Mordechai, ed. *Tnu'ot Ha-No'ar, 1920–1960*. Jerusalem: Yad Yitzchak ben Zvi, 1989.

Nicosia, Francis R. "Jewish Farmers in Hitler's Germany: Zionist Occupational Retraining and Nazi 'Jewish Policy.'" *Holocaust and Genocide Studies* 19 (2005): 365–89.

Niewyk, Donald, ed. *Fresh Wounds: Early Narratives of Holocaust Survival*. Chapel Hill: University of North Carolina Press, 1998.

Ofer, Dalia. "The Dilemma of Rescue and Redemption: Mass Immigration to Israel in the First Year of Statehood." *YIVO Annual* 20 (1991): 185–210.

———. "From Survivors to New Immigrants: *She'erit Hapletah* and *Aliyah*." In *She'erit Hapletah, 1944–1948: Rehabilitation and Political Struggle*, edited by Yisrael Gutman and Avital Saf, 304–36. Jerusalem: Yad Vashem, 1990.

Ofer, Dalia, and Lenore Weitzman, eds. *Women in the Holocaust*. New Haven, CT: Yale University Press, 1998.

Oliner, Samuel P., and Pearl M. Oliner. *The Altruistic Personality: Rescuers of Jews in Nazi Europe*. New York: Free Press, 1988.

Oppenheim, Israel. "Hehalutz in Eastern Europe between the Two World Wars." In *Zionist Youth Movements during the Shoah*, edited by Asher Cohen and Yehoyakim Cochavi, 33–117. New York: Peter Lang, 1995.

———. *The Struggle of Jewish Youth for Productivization: The Zionist Youth Movement in Poland*. Boulder, CO: East European Monographs, 1989.

Papanek, Ernst. "Di Yiddishe Yugnt Nochn Churbn." *Yivo Bleter* 31–32 (1948): 193–207.

Peck, Abraham J. "'Our Eyes Have Seen Eternity': Remembrance and Identity of the She'erit Hapletah." *Modern Judaism* 17, no. 1 (1997): 57–74.

Pederson, Stefi. "Psycopathological Reaction to Extreme Social Displacements (Refugee Neuroses)." *Psychoanalytic Review* 36, no. 4 (October 1949): 344–54.

Perlis, Rivka. "Tnu'ot ha-Noar ha-Halutziot be-Polin ha-kvusha bi-yedei ha-Natzim." PhD dissertation, Hebrew University, 1982.

Peterson, Edward N. *The American Occupation of Germany: Retreat to Victory.* Detroit: Wayne State University Press, 1977.

Pinkus, Benjamin, ed. *Yahadut Mizrah Eiropah ben Shoah li-Tekumah, 1944–1948.* Sdeh Boker: Ben-Gurion University, 1987.

Pinson, Koppel S. "Jewish Life in Liberated Germany: A Study of the Jewish DPs." *Jewish Social Science* 9, no. 2 (April 1947): 101–26.

Porat, Dina. "Zionist Pioneering Youth Movements in Poland and the Attitude to Eretz Israel during the Holocaust." *Polin* 9 (1996): 195–211.

Proudfoot, Malcolm J. *European Refugees, 1939–1952: A Study in Forced Population Movement.* Evanston, IL: Northwestern University Press, 1956.

Pur, David. *El Ha-Hof Ha-Nichsaf: Masa 'im shemonim yetome Shoah le-Erets Yisra'el.* Kibbutz Dalia: Bet lohame ha-geta'ot, 2001.

Rinott, Chanoch. "Major Trends in Jewish Youth Movements in Germany." *Leo Baeck Institute Yearbook* 19 (1974): 77–96.

Roizman, Yoel. *Ha-Noar Ha-Borochovi Ve-Dror: Noar Borochov Be-Polin Achrei Ha-Shoah.* Efal: Yad Tabenkin, 1999.

Ronen, Avihu, and Yehoyakim Cochavi, eds. *Guf Shelishi Yahid: Biyografyot shel havre tenu'ot no'ar bi-tekufat ha-Shoah.* Giv'at Havivah: Moreshet, 1994.

Rubenstein, H. L. *The Jews in Australia: 1945 to Present.* Port Melbourne, Victoria: W. Heinemann, 1991.

Sachar, Abram. *The Redemption of the Unwanted: From the Liberation of the Death Camps to the Founding of Israel.* New York: St. Martin's, 1983.

Sarid, Aryeh Levi. *Be-Mivchan he-Anut veha-Pdut: Ha-Tnuot Ha-Halutziot be-PolinBa-Shoah ve-Achareha, 1939–1949.* Tel Aviv: Moreshet, 1997.

———. "Reshit ha-Hiarchut ha-Tnu'atit be-Kerev Yehudei Polin veha-Mishlechet ha-Eretz Yisraelit." In *Yahadut Mizrah Eiropah ben Shoah li-Tekumah, 1944–1948,* edited by Benjamin Pinkus, 274–333. Sdeh Boker: Ben-Gurion University, 1987.

Schein, Ada. "Ma'arehet ha-hinukh be-mahanot ha-'akurim ha-yehudiyim be-Germanyah ube-Austryah, 1945–1951." PhD dissertation, Hebrew University, 2001.

Schreiber, Ruth. "The New Organization of the Jewish Community in Germany, 1945–1952." PhD dissertation, Tel Aviv University, 1995.

Schwarz, Leo. *The Redeemers: A Saga of the Years 1945–1952.* New York: Farrar, Straus and Young, 1953.

———. *The Root and the Bough: The Epic of an Enduring People.* New York: Rinehart, 1949.

Segev, Tom. *The Seventh Million: The Israelis and the Holocaust.* New York: Hill and Wang, 1993.

Shapira, Anita. "The Yishuv's Encounter with the Survivors of the Holocaust." In *She'erit Hapletah, 1944–1948: Rehabilitation and Political Struggle,* edited by Yisrael Gutman and Avital Saf, 80–106. Jerusalem: Yad Vashem, 1990.

Shlomi, Hana. "Hitargenut shel Sridei ha-Yehudim be-Polin le-Achar Milchemet Ha-Olam ha-Sheniyah, 1944–1950." In *Kiyum Va-Shever: Yehudei Polin Le-Doroteihem,* edited by Israel Bartal and Yisrael Gutman, 523–48. Jerusalem: Merkaz Zalman Shazar, 1997.

———. "The Reception and Settlement of Jewish Repatriants from the Soviet Union in Lower Silesia, 1946." *Gal-Ed* 17 (2000): 85–104.

———. "Toldot HaIchud." In *Asufat mehkarim le-Toldot She'erit ha-Pletah ha-Yehudit be-Polin, 1944–1950,* edited by Hana Shlomi, 197. Tel Aviv: Tel Aviv University, 2001.

Sivan, Emmanuel. *Dor Tashakh: Mitos, Diyukan ve-Zikaron* [The 1948 Generation: Myth, Profile and Memory]. Israel: Ministry of Defense, 1991.

Smith, Marcus J. *The Harrowing of Hell: Dachau.* Albuquerque: University of New Mexico Press, 1972.

Solkoff, Norman. *Beginnings, Mass Murder, and Aftermath of the Holocaust: Where History and Psychology Intersect.* Lanham, MD: University Press of America, 2001.

Srole, Leo. "Why the DPs Can't Wait: Proposing an International Plan of Rescue." *Commentary* 3 (January–June 1947): 13–24.

Sterba, Editha. "Emotional Problems of Displaced Children." *Journal of Social Casework* 30 (1949): 175–81.

———. "Some Problems of Children and Adolescents Surviving from Concentration Camps." Detroit: Wayne State University Conference, 1964.

Tadmor, Yitzhak, ed. *Duvdevanim 'al ha-Elbeh: Sipur Bet ha-yeladim be-Blankenezeh, 1946–1948.* Giv'at Havivah: Yad Ya'ari, 1996.

Tobias, Jim G. *Der Kibbutz auf dem Streicher-Hof: die vergessene Geschichte der judischen Kollectivfarmen 1945–1948.* Nurnberg: Dahlinger und Fuchs, 1997.

———. *Vorubergehende Heimat im Land der Tater: Judische DP-Camps in Franken 1945–1949.* Nurnberg: Antogo, 2002.

Tsamriyon, Tsemach. *The Press of the Jewish Holocaust Survivors in Germany As an Expression of Their Problems* (Hebrew). Tel Aviv: Irgun She'erit HaPletah Mehe-Ezor HaBrit, Bi-Yisrael, 1970.

Tzahor, Zeev. "Holocaust Survivors As a Political Factor." *Middle Eastern Studies* 24, no. 4 (1988): 432–44.

Vulman, Dr. Leib. "Yidishe Kinder in Eyropah Noch Der Milkhome." *YIVO Bleter* 33 (1948): 84–94.

Webster, Ronald. "American Relief and Jews in Germany, 1945–1960: Diverging Perspectives." *Leo Baeck Institute Yearbook* 38 (1993) 293–321.

Weiss, Aharon. "Jewish Leadership in Occupied Poland." *Yad Vashem Studies* 10 (1977): 335–65.

———. "Youth Movements in Poland during the German Occupation." In *Zionist Youth Movements during the Shoah,* edited by Asher Cohen and Yehoyakim Cochavi, 227–44. New York: Peter Lang, 1995.

Weitz, Yechiam. "She'elat ha-Plitim ha-Yehudim ba-Mediniut ha-Tzionit." *Katedra* 55 (1990): 162–74.

Woodbridge, George. *UNRRA: The History of the United Nations Relief and Rehabilitation Administration.* New York: Columbia University Press, 1950.

Wyman, Mark. *DPs: Europe's Displaced Persons, 1945–1951.* Ithaca, NY: Cornell University Press, 1998.

Yablonka, Hanna. *Achim Zarim: Nitzulei ha-Shoah be-Medinat Yisrael, 1948–1952.* Jerusalem: Yad Yitzchak ben Tzvi, 1994.

———. *Survivors of the Holocaust: Israel after the War.* New York: New York University Press, 1999.

Zayit, David. *Ha-Utopiah Ha-Shomerit: Ha-Shomer Ha-Tzair be-Polin, 1921–1931.* Giv'at Havivah: Hashomer Hatzair, 2002.

Zelinger, Eliyahu Kuti. *Lamrot ha-kol: tenu'ot ha-no'ar ha-halutsiyot be-Germanyah ba-shanim 1933–1943* [Despite Everything: Pioneering Youth Movements in Germany in the Years 1933–43]. Giv'at Havivah: Yad Ya'ari, 1998.

Zertal, Idith. *From Catastrophe to Power: Holocaust Survivors and the Emergence of Israel.* Berkeley: University of California Press, 1998.

Zink, Harold. *The United States in Germany, 1944–1955.* Princeton, NJ: Van Nostrand, 1957.

Zuckerman, Yitzhak. *Surplus of Memory: Chronicle of the Warsaw Ghetto Uprising.* Berkeley: University of California, 1993.

———. *Yetziat Polin: 'al ha-Berichah ve-'al Shikum ha-Tnu'ah ha-Halutzit* [Exodus from Poland: On the Bricha and the Reestablishment of the Pioneering Movement]. Israel: Bet Lochamei Ha-Getaot, 1988.

Index

berurim. *See* selection process, aliyah
Betar, 45, 302n8; hakhsharah, 110,
    158, 159–60, 191, 313n19. *See also*
    Revisionist youth movements
Bialik, Haim Nachman, 138, 168
Bialystok, Poland, 72, 138
Biblical references, 233, 275n4
black market activity: cigarettes' value,
    127, 146–47, 306n59; discouraging,
    25, 36, 53, 54, 161, 162, 264; emi-
    gration as solution, 242; gasoline
    sales, 168, 182, 195, 316n77;
    speculation, 98, 127
Bnei Akiva: goals, Jewish state, 113;
    migration to Germany, 110; as
    movement, 80, 159–60, 217;
    prewar hakhsharah, 169
Boder, David, 285n91
Bolivia, 207
*The Book of the Shomrim (Sefer Ha-
    Shomrim)*, 89–91, 296n72, 297n89
Borochov Youth, 72, 110. *See also* Left
    Poalei Zion
Brandes, Zvi, 112, 303n12
Brenner, Yosef Haim, 138
Breslaw, Samuel, 75
Bricha movement, 3, 52, 54, 68–70,
    74; departure/travel organization,
    96, 98–101, 110, 115–16, 209,
    298n98, 301n6; *Exodus* Affair,
    228–33; families within, 202; finan-
    cial operations, 146; framework/
    organization, 76–79, 81, 100,
    296n73; German and U.S. zone
    infiltration, 107–10, 165, 213,
    287n114; growth, 98–101; moving
    defense forces, 242–43; non-
    European travel arrangement,
    207, 229

Britain. *See* Great Britain
Brit Ha-Irgunim Ha-Halutzi'im
    (Pioneering Groups Organization),
    217
British Mandate, 203
British zone, postwar Germany, 16, 41,
    111, 321n24. *See also* Bergen-Belsen
Bronstein, Haim, 86–87, 88
Bruk, Yehoshua, 208, 209
Buchberg by Toelz, 29–30
Buchenwald, 13–14, 15, 28. *See also*
    Kibbutz Buchenwald
Bundist party: aims, 16–17, 22, 28, 66,
    73; enlistment and, 253, 330n62;
    inception, 72–73; resistance activity,
    293n32; status, 74
Bytom, Poland kibbutz, 70, 80, 81;
    departure, 97–98; joining, 83–89,
    91, 103; Landsberg DP camp
    arrival, 109–11, 114, 117; Lands-
    berg DP camp life, 117–24; life,
    89–98. *See also* Hashomer Hatzair
    kibbutzim; Kibbutz Mordechai
    Anielewicz; Kibbutz Tosia Altman

camps, postwar DP: committees, 57,
    127; conditions, 18–21, 28; con-
    scription from, 237–53; daily
    activities, 114–15, 125–28; disease
    dangers, 19–20, 20, 29, 128–29,
    162, 304n31; kibbutzim difficulties,
    128–31, 216; later influxes/
    overcrowding, 54–56, 61, 107–8,
    109–10, 215–16; schools, 133,
    163; stays, duration, 241. *See also*
    Harrison Report
camps, recreational. *See* summer camps
castles, 169
casualties, 1948 War, 253–54, 255–57

Central Committee of Liberated Jews: Agricultural Department, 160–61, 177–81, 180, 182, 184, 263, 314n34; assistance, training farms, 109, 157, 160–61, 177, 178–81, 196; DP youths focus, 36–37, 39–40, 42–45, 178, 241–42, 252, 265; elections, 241–42, 328n24; Haganah support, 239–42, 247–50; inception, 20, 27, 36–37, 66; leadership, 37, 250, 268; Organization Department, 248–49; Partition Plan, 236; Productivization Department, 178–80; record-keeping, 7, 314n34; UZO approval, 43–44

Central Committee of Polish Jews (CKZP): children's aid, 73, 81, 292n22; first convention, 73; history, 292n16

central leadership, Hashomer Hatzair movement: farming assistance, 177; orders, aliyah, 206; reports, aliyah preparation, 149–50, 205, 221–22, 311n133; reports, death, 129; reports, education, 132–33; reports, emissaries', 130; reports, farm transition, 188, 189–91; reports, financial, 146–47; reports, general, 111, 113–15, 125–26; visits and speeches, 170

certificates, aliyah: American organization, 45, 108; political rejection, 41; shortages, 34–35, 283n75; small group distribution, 148, 150; totals granted, 152, 311n132

Chafetz Chaim. *See* Kibbutz Chafetz Chaim

chalutzim. *See* halutzim

Chanukah celebrations, 136–37, 148, 265

chaplains: burial duties, 17–18, 35; camp assistance, 21, 37; kibbutzim assistance, 25, 32, 35, 36; land acquisition assistance, 53, 156, 196

Charchas, Shlomo, 170

Chayenu (newspaper), 139

Cheta, Baruch, 63, 172–73, 195. *See also* Kibbutz Nili

children: aliyah chances, 212, 224, 229, 231, 311n133; childhood interrupted, 31, 82, 277n19; demographic details, 210–11, 321nn31–32; kibbutz structure, and stability, 108, 266, 300n1; movements' targeted focus, 219–25; redeeming and rescuing, 74, 81–82, 212, 325n84; specific kibbutzim, 112. *See also* children's homes; families

children's homes, 52, 73–74, 112, 210, 292n18; conscription/enlistment, 246, 251; Lindenfels (photos), 137, 141, 220; movements shift into, 219; traveling members, 298n98

cigarettes, black market sales, 127, 146–47, 306n59

Citizens Committee for Conscription for the Homeland, 244

citizenship, 263; military responsibilities, 243, 257–58, 264

CKZP. *See* Central Committee of Polish Jews (CKZP)

Clay, Lucius D., 215

cleaning. *See* housework, kibbutzim

clothing: camp/kibbutzim distribution, 91, 117, 126; kibbutzim laundry, 93, 297n84; needs, 19, 20, 39, 55

Cohen, Henry, 171

Cold War origins, 15

collaborators' postwar presence, 15, 17, 18, 20, 37

collectivism: complaints, 82, 121–23; kibbutzim makeup, and, 216; principles and demonstrations, 25, 32–33, 48, 50, 267; shift to, 91–92, 94–95, 120, 165

Colombia, 229

commitment, Zionist. *See* passion, Zionist

Committee of Pioneering Youth. *See* Va'adat Ha-No'ar Ha-Halutzi

Committees for Service to the Nation, 248

communist influence: postwar Polish politics, 28, 66, 72–73; resistance group activity, 293n32

Communist Polish Workers' Party, 100

concentration camps: former inmates' movement involvement, 7, 22–27, 40, 56, 62, 68–69, 296n70; liberation, 13–15, 17. *See also* specific camps

conferences: Central Committee of Liberated Jews, 37, 38–39; Central Committee of Polish Jews (CKZP), 73; first Zionist conference, 30–31; Föhrenwald movement conference, 320n13; Hashomer Hatzair Be-Ha'apalah, founding, 221; Hashomer Hatzair meeting, 111, 119; Hashomer Hatzair movement, first, 111–12, 124; Hashomer Hatzair movement, 171, 221–22; holidays and, 193–94, 221, 324n55; Ichud Hanoar Hazioni movement, 159; Jewish Council, first meeting,

161–62; Liberated Jewish Political Prisoners in Germany, founding, 35, 38–42; Łódź kibbutzim planning, 95, 294n48; Nocham movement, 207, 302n8; Nocham youth movement, Kibbutz Nili, 159, 193; Paris Giyus conference, 242–43; preparation, First Zionist conference, 45; Third Congress of the She'erit Hapletah, 247–49; twenty-second Zionist Congress, 139, 213; UZO, First Conference, 45, 49–52, 156–57, 285n88, 286n100; Zionist Conference: Basel, 207, 320n15; Zionist Conference: Landsberg, 44; Zionist Congress: London, 100

connections (proteksiah), 92, 118, 121

conscription, military, 202, 237–53, 257, 264, 319n2; committees, 245–47, 252; conferences, 242–43, 247–50; sample form, 244; shirking, 247–48, 251, 252, 253, 329n47; totals, 253, 255–56

cooking, kibbutzim, 92–93, 176

crops, 169, 181, 183–85, 186, 187

Crossman, Richard, 152

cultural enrichment activities, 32, 34, 40, 42, 63; camp establishment/formalization, 46–47; centers, 217; challenges in hakhsharot, 187–89, 217–18; kibbutzim descriptions, 131–47, 189–93; rehabilitative nature, 82; unrealized, 130; Zionist focus, 94, 109, 136–38, 263

Cyprus: diversion to, path to Palestine, 70, 209, 213, 226, 234, 311n132; relocation from, 236

Czech Jews, 17

U.S. zone of occupation. *See* American Zone, postwar Germany
UZO. *See* United Zionist Organization (UZO)

Va'adat Ha-No'ar Ha-Halutzi, 28–29
vegetables. *See* crops
veterans' kibbutzim, 112
Vilna, resistance/ghetto, 76, 77, 114, 138, 140, 142, 144
Vilner, Aryeh, 112, 303n12
vocational schools and training, 131, 216, 240, 242, 268; as formalized education, 48; Kibbutz Buchenwald, 25, 31; kibbutzim/hakhsharah as, 109, 186; Nocham, 51, 65; opening, camps, 43, 45–47, 126; ORT, 46, 178, 216, 240, 285n91; social opportunities, camps, 127; united Zionist source, 36, 44, 45
volunteering, military. *See* conscription, military

Wa'adot Liszrot Ha'am, 248
Warburg, Miriam, 129, 137–38, 265
War of Independence. *See* Israeli War of Independence, 1948
Warsaw: kibbutz proposals, 79–80; kibbutz relocation, 111, 126; returns to, 75, 76
Warsaw Ghetto Uprising, commemoration, 142, 144–45, 171
weaponry, camps/kibbutzim, 95, 238, 239
weddings, 35, 230
Weinberg, Shaike, 81, 103, 124, 131, 295n55
Weintraub, Yolek, 88
Weisbort, Inka, 85, 91, 94

White Paper (1939), 311n132
Whiting, Jack, 61, 107, 161–62, 177–78, 264
Wind, Baruch. *See* Yechieli, Baruch
Wind, Miriam. *See* Yechieli, Miriam
Winogrodzki, M., 1, 2, 29
Wolfratshausen, 61
women: German, 32, 33, 194; kibbutzim balance, 113, 129–30; military obligations, 243; work roles, 92–93, 127, 176–77, 181
work. *See* employment
World Jewish Congress (WJC), 18, 27
World War II: aftermath/legacy, 1–9, 234; Jewish service, 282n60; kibbutzim during occupation, 158; Poland, prelude to war, 75; refugee repatriation after, 263

Ya'ari, Meir, 140, 141, 194
Yaffa (Sosnowiec kibbutz member), 91, 119
Yalta Conference, 16
Yechieli, Baruch, 70, 81–83; experience, 91–92; group father, 93; kibbutz diary, 115; kibbutzim education, 133, 136; kibbutzim leadership, DP camp, 117–24, 127, 128; kibbutzim leadership, Poland, 96, 97; kibbutz migration, Germany, 108, 111, 114; photo, 83
Yechieli, Miriam, 70, 81–83, 84–85, 295n53; group mother, 93; hakhsharot leadership, 155–56, 175; kibbutz diary, 89, 115; kibbutzim education, 133, 138; kibbutzim leadership, DP camp, 116–24, 149; kibbutzim leadership, Poland, 95, 96–97; kibbutz migration, Ger-